KAYAK FISHING

Jon Shein

Keith,

Tight Lines!

All photographs by the author, except the following (numbers indicate pages):

John Merwin:	3 (photo)	Tony C.:	133 (lower)
Field & Stream:	3 (repro)	Polo Velez:	142 (middle)
Chris Mautino	6, 128, 158	Jim Sammons:	147, 177, 199 (lower)
Legacy Paddlesports:	14, 25, 28, 206, 207 (top)	Bruce Hitchcock:	167
Tim Geist:	26	Larry L.:	172
Mark Kenyon:	38	Creative Feathers:	173 (top)
Scott Owitz:	41 (top), 62	Allen Sansano:	199 (top)
Danny V:	37, 52, 132, 165 (all), 192	Jon Schwartz:	200 (top)
Joe Cambria:	191 (bottom)	Howard McKim:	200 (bottom)
Coastal Kayak Tours:	124	Josh Harvel:	196
Bob Quirk:	103, 168, 169, 185 (second)	Jim T.:	140 (top)
Troy Eastman:	106	Joe Warren:	153 (bottom)
Mike Angelo:	113	Mark Brassett:	191 (top)
Joe Vanasse:	121 (lower), 122 (top)	Greg Davey:	198
Taurus V.:	123	Bassyaks, Inc.:	207 (bottom)
Jim Dolan:	131		

ISBN: 0-9822787-0-5

Editing: Cathy Shein, Peter Shein
Design and Layout: Bill Donovan
Cover Design: Bill Donovan
Printed in China

Contents

Acknowledgements

This work owes its existence to a great many people. Some provided invaluable production assistance, while others helped more indirectly. I'd first like to thank my siblings, Cathy and Peter Shein, who did most of the editing. Bill Donovan created the layout of the book, and did the typesetting and cover design. Scott Owitz provided early editing and advice as well.

Indirect support came about all throughout my journey of becoming a kayak fisherman, and also through my associated business ventures. Each of the people listed here provided much-appreciated support along the way: Joe Cambria, Tim Surgent, Dennis Spike, John Barrell, Derrick Washington, Jeff Sanders, Tony Cox, and the thousands of people I've gotten to know through this fascinating sport of kayak fishing.

I'd also like to thank all those who provided photos for the book. These folks are listed on the copyright page.

Introduction

This book has been several years in the making. I began writing it in 2002 but then my kayak fishing business exploded. Selling kayaks and gear along with writing magazine articles kept me too busy to focus on the book. For me, and many others, kayak fishing is a passion and writing this book has been a labor of love that I am excited to share with you.

Since I first started writing this book 6 years ago, much has changed within the sport. I had to rewrite and update certain sections; the book had to evolve as the sport has. As the sport grows there will be more books than the few now available. I recently met some guys down in Florida who were visiting for a few days from Tennessee. One of them, Stan, had a kayak for over a year and loved the sport. A buddy of his was fishing with him and they were using kayaks they rented from *Everglades Kayak Fishing*, and the other two members of their party had never been in a kayak. We chatted, and in conversation it came up that I had founded *Kayakfishingstuff.com* (KFS). It turns out Stan reads the site regularly and I ended up talking kayak fishing with the guys for quite some time - kind of an impromptu seminar. Whenever I talk with people who are new to the sport, I realize how beneficial a detailed book about the sport would be.

Through KFS I met a lot of people, as I either directly or indirectly got them into kayak fishing. When I started the final push to complete the book I took a day off from writing to hit the Jersey shore. I ran into Pat ('Pat the Battleship' on KFS forums) and he asked where I'd been and what I'd been up to after the sale of KFS. I told him I was working on the book and was going to head to the Everglades for the winter and spring to finish it. He asked if the book was going to be an autobiography. Puzzled, I replied that it was going to cover all the aspects of kayak fishing that needed to be put into a book, but wouldn't necessarily be about me. Pat urged me to tell my story, which he characterized as interesting and unknown to most. I considered his suggestion and the first

chapter, which describes my perspective and background, developed.

The next chapter covers attributes of kayaks, what they are and how to best choose the features most important for one's needs. Beyond that, I cover the accessories that are an integral part of fishing from a kayak. While many people have rigged a few kayaks for themselves, it's quite different rigging them for thousands of people and shipping them around the globe. I've personally rigged hundreds and supervised thousands. While kayak fishing is still fishing, it does differ from boat or shore fishing and I discuss these differences along with tackle and techniques that apply to kayak fishing.

While I haven't fished everywhere from a kayak, I have fished quite an array of environments from the Caribbean to Alaska to Baja (the California peninsula which is part of Mexico) up to New England, in dozens of kayak models, in all kinds of weather. I've successfully fished many waters that were new to me at the time, and my approach will help you do the same, even if it's just down the road from where you live.

Since I began kayak fishing, I've been sharing the sport with others. Believe me, there is much to share! There is more to kayak fishing than hopping in a kayak and taking some fishing gear along. Sure, if you wish to hit your local pond you don't need much else on a warm summer day. However, the sport is diverse, as is my background within the sport, from both a leisure and professional perspective.

I've guided and run trips and have always done a wide variety of fishing, long before I discovered kayaks. I grew up fishing freshwater in New Jersey and graduated to the salt. I've hiked and backpacked to remote mountain lakes and streams and car-camp fished throughout the West. I had a 23-foot sportfisherman in San Diego where I pursued offshore species. When I wasn't fishing San Diego's offshore waters I was in the Sea of Cortez in Baja. I've roamed the East Coast and now I spend a lot of time in

Florida. I've fished many methods from ultralight to 130-pound gear. I'm comfortable with spin, conventional and fly gear and have taken the same approach to kayak fishing. Since I like diversity, I fish all environments from kayaks.

Along with selling lots of kayaks and gear through KFS, I've seen and experienced my share of problems and have learned how to both fix and prevent them. I've helped run tournaments and I've been a participant. While not a competitive fisherman, I recognize that competition is a part of the sport. Last, I've been involved in important aspects of the sport's development and I've got some ideas on where it's going.

As kayak fishing continues to grow and we see more books on the subject, I expect most are going to be written by really good kayak fishermen - guys who spend a lot of time on the water. Many books will be written by guides, likely with excellent information, but they'll be different than this book. I have guided and will continue to, but what I really bring to the party is how I have helped the sport grow.

I recognized early on that simply talking about the sport was only going to get it so far. Until the kayak industry recognized kayak fishing, separate from kayaking, we'd play second fiddle. I knew fishermen would love kayak fishing, but if they had to struggle to find appropriate gear, as the early practitioners did, the sport wouldn't attract enough participants to get the industry catering to our needs.

At times throughout this book, individuals are referenced by their "Internet name". Internet names are also called *screen names* and they are used in online discussion boards called *forums*. Screen names are to forums as CB handles are to truckers. Said differently, a screen name is an online handle.

Kayak fishing owes a great deal of its growth to the Internet, and it has become commonplace in kayak fishing circles to refer to folks by their screen name. In fact, there are some folks I only know by their screen name! Throughout this book, when people are referred to by their screen names, we'll surround those names with single quotes.

- JS

That's why I started outfitting and selling kayaks and gear, and it's why I've written this book. I moved a lot of gear and helped many fishermen get into the sport, having spoken with thousands of people along the way and outfitted hundreds of kayaks. I've fished from several dozen kayak models and have consulted with manufacturers. By wearing all the hats I've worn, I've gained a great deal of experience that I want to share with you. Up until now nobody has put it into a book. My goal is to cover the intricacies of kayak fishing from this perspective.

Throughout these pages, I'll discuss kayaks and gear in depth, and explain how to determine which gear is appropriate for one's needs. While different sections of the book can be read separately and used for reference, I highly recommend reading the chapters in sequence and in their entirety. Some of the content assumes the reader has already covered the material, and skipping around might leave one wondering to what I'm referring. I wrote the book to be read from start to finish to maximize understanding.

I am a lifelong fisherman who enjoys diversity and thrives on discovery. I am inclined to get good at something before proceeding to the next thing, and enjoy enlisting past experience to figure things out. There's always somewhere new I'd like to wet a line - new places to see, people to meet, and fish to catch. Let's turn the page and get started!

- Jon Shein

Chapter 1
My Story

My journey began as a frustrated surf fisherman on the New Jersey shore in the late 1990's. Much too often I'd be on the beach watching blitzes of bass, blues and false albacore beyond the range of my farthest casts. It can get pretty discouraging driving up and down the coastline looking for fish that have pushed up onto the beach while there are schools going nuts a half mile out. One day my buddy Chris and I were fishing the surf when we happened across a huge blitz in front of the wall in Monmouth Beach. The sky was thick with thousands of diving gulls. Hundreds of acres of fish were breaking the surface chasing the schooling bait. I had never witnessed such an expansive blitz. There was just one problem; they were several hundred yards off the beach and far beyond our reach.

We spent the rest of the day looking for fish within range and stopped by Monmouth Beach several times just to see if they had come any closer. At sunset we headed north for home. When I checked the reports online in the morning I learned that as the sun was setting, part of the school crashed the beach several miles to the south. Adding insult to injury, the fish averaged 15 to 30 pounds! For several weeks thereafter, lots of peanut bunker were piled up in nearby Raritan Bay, with hungry bass devouring them - and still out of reach. I was both frustrated and determined to find a solution to reaching those fish.

I had been fishing from a float tube in freshwater for about two decades and I wanted something similar for saltwater, but I knew the tube wasn't the answer. I came across an article on *Stripersurf.com* (SSC) about fishing from a kayak, and found it very intriguing. I had been in a kayak only once and found it to be very tipsy, but at that point I knew it had to be the answer. Being that I didn't know much about kayaks, let alone about fishing from them, I searched for books or magazine articles and came up empty, so I returned to the Internet.

The best information available back then was the forum of *Coastal Kayak Fishing* (CKF) and *Allen's*. I read every article and post I could find. The author of the article on SSC used a Sit-Inside Kayak (SIK), but

I determined through my research that a Sit-On-Top (SOT) model was the best choice for me. An associate of mine was a good friend with the owner of a kayak company, and he arranged for me to purchase a kayak on pro form, meaning getting the kayak at below the price the dealers pay for it. The company had one model I felt would work for fishing. When I got to the plant, the owner talked me into a more advanced model, feeling I'd outgrow the one I had chosen. It turned out the more advanced model wasn't a good choice for me (I'll elaborate in the chapter on choosing a kayak).

While loading my kayak to go fishing for the very first time, a gent stopped by. His name was Derrick. He asked me about the kayak and I told him I bought it to fish from. He was familiar with kayaks, having been involved in white water and other forms of paddling for years. He felt I wouldn't like the kayak for fishing and had a bunch of catalogs and brochures in his car. He started going through them and showed me a Cobra brochure and said I'd be better served by a few of their models. After a few forays on the water, I realized my kayak was not what I needed for fishing. My eyes were opened to how cool fishing from a kayak was going to be, but this wasn't the right 'yak. I put it up for sale and with Derrick's help got a Cobra Explorer, which served me well. It was light and had good surfaces for attaching accessories and was short enough to fish the smaller rivers near my home, while still performing reasonably well in the salt.

Early on it was pretty lonely on the eastern Internet forums. I was one of the first members of *StripersOnline.com* (SOL) and I wrote about my kayak fishing adventures. I also posted on SSC, CKF and a couple of other sites. Most of the online kayak fishing activity was in southern California, Texas and Florida. That first summer and fall I usually fished alone and on occasion I would hook up (no pun intended) with fishermen I met on the Coastal forums. Two of them, John and John, plus Dennis Spike, owner of CKF and known as 'Spike', provided me with most of the information that helped me get started.

I voraciously read every single post on kayak fishing I could find. 'John1' owned a kayak and surf shop in southern New Jersey. He was in the process of writing a detailed article about kayak fishing and sent me the draft. 'John 2', who posted as 'docjohn' on CKF, had been fishing from a kayak for a few years. I learned much fishing with him and he introduced me to another fisherman named, you guessed it, John. Too many Johns, don't you think? That's four, including me, although my name has no 'h' in it.

Early that summer I was fishing freshwater in my kayak and by mid-summer I had graduated to salt. I'll always remember that first day in the salt. It was a beautiful sunny day and I started fishing from a jetty at Monmouth Cove Marina in New Jersey, with my kayak still strapped on the roof of my vehicle. Blitzing blues erupted a couple of hundred yards off the beach and half a mile to the east. It was a classic situation, as the fish weren't reachable from shore.

No longer destined to watch and pray for the school to move in, I unloaded my kayak, set it up and wheeled it to the water. By the time I launched the fish were directly in front of me but still not within reach of shore-bound anglers. Several paddle strokes propelled me into the breaking fish. For the next couple of hours I floated in the heart of a massive school and had a fish on every cast. What a blast! I brought a fly rod along and set it up. I never even had to cast. I dangled the fly above the water and the voracious bluefish attacked it. I was in angler heaven.

As dusk approached I was starting to get chilled, so I paddled to shore, where some of the fishermen told me the most anyone had caught from the beach was three fish. I lost track of how many I landed but it was definitely well over 50. I now had a full-fledged case of kayak-fishing fever.

My next trip to the salt took me to an area of Raritan Bay a bit west of my previous location. There were bluefish milling about but I couldn't get any to hit. Then, to the west and behind me, I heard a sound reminiscent of a waterfall or rapids in a river. As I looked towards the noise I saw blitzing bluefish churning the water to froth. I couldn't believe how loud this school was. I paddled toward the school, which was actually heading towards me. I fired off a cast and immediately hooked up with a feisty blue. As I fought the fish, the school kept getting closer. They were leaping and porposing and at that point it occurred to me that I might want to get out of the way.

I refer to bluefish as hacksaws with fins because of their incredibly sharp teeth, which they use to maim and dismember their prey. They're dangerous and can hurt you; a large blue can easily remove a finger. The thought of several of them jumping into my kayak was making me nervous. I had never heard of blues leaping into boats, but a SOT kayak sits very low in the water. Only a few inches separated the top of my gunwale from the ravenous carnivores. I decided to see what would happen, but I was ready to quickly get out of Dodge should the need arise.

When the school and my kayak converged, thankfully they went under. It was incredible, as hundreds of fishes' backs hit the hull, taking over a minute for the school to pass. The constant thuds on the hull were a trip. In four decades of angling, I had never experienced anything like that.

There weren't many kayak fishermen in the New York metro area at that time, and the few practicioners met quickly via online exchanges. I recall 'Scott', 'Santiago 2', 'Porter', and 'Mullet Miller' as a few of the earliest members of the fraternity here. Through the forums we exchanged ideas and got together to fish.

I had decided to look for a used kayak the following spring so I could take friends or family along. I found a Cobra Explorer for sale on the CKF forums, and 'Joeykayak' was the seller. He lived along Long Island Sound in Westchester County, New York, and his Explorer was a bit short for fishing the salt exclusively, so he sold it to me. Joey used to post regularly on *Noreast.com* as, you guessed it, 'Joeykayak'. We became friends and whenever we fished in New York, boaters would come up and ask if I was

Next month: Rigging kayaks for fishing.

The May and June, 2002 issues of *Field and Stream* contained a two-part article featuring the author. This may have been the first in-depth treatment of kayak fishing to appear in a mainstream national publication.

'Joeykayak'. I'd say, "No, he's over there." When fishing in New Jersey waters they'd ask if I was 'JonS', which is how I've always posted on forums.

I did a lot of my online postings on SOL and suggested to the site owner, Tim, that he create a forum for kayak fishing. Tim agreed, on the condition that I would moderate it. I agreed and he set up the forum in the summer of 2000. That was the first forum dedicated to kayak fishing in the Northeast - well, sort of. I say that because CKF had an East Coast forum, but it wasn't nearly as user-friendly as the format used by SOL. It was lonely that first year on both the SOL and Eastern forums, but the SOL forums helped a great deal in the evolution of kayak fishing in the New York /metro area.

I met folks like me who were avid participants. It took about a year until the forums, and the sport, exploded in the area. There was a lot of interest. I remember about 30 of us who met on SOL got together in April of 2001 and did a trip to the Susky flats in Maryland. The area has the largest run of striped bass on the East Coast and they all have to pass where we were launching. It's strictly a catch and release fishery. Porter got out in the morning and landed a 30 pounder, but then the predicted cold front came through and by the time we got onto the water the fish had turned off. We covered a lot of ground and didn't catch anything. The next morning we awoke to a couple of inches of snow on the kayaks and a howling wind.

About this time John Merwin, a senior editor for *Field and Stream Magazine*, contacted me. He was going to do an article about kayak fishing and wanted to interview me and get some pictures, so we got together for a day in Sandy Hook, NJ. The following May and June the two-part article about kayak fishing was printed. I believe it was the first article in a mainstream national magazine about the sport.

That spring I purchased a used Scupper Classic so I could familiarize myself with another kayak. I didn't like it and sold it to a guy named Jack. He needed some rod holders and asked for suggestions. The problem back then was there wasn't a reliable source for accessories. Jack was actually belittled by one accessory source because the owner didn't approve of his kayak choice. Jack suggested that I, as someone who was sharing the sport, do something about it. At first I spoke with kayak shops and suggested they include kayak fishing into their businesses. Though I knew kayak fishing was going to explode and become

a very important part of the kayak world, I was basically ignored and laughed at. The sport needed an entity that not only dispensed information, but also reliably supplied gear. I never wanted to sell accessories and kayaks, but in order for the sport to grow, someone had to. I spoke with industry people for feedback and I remember what Jeff, from *Surf to Summit*, said to me.

"Take care of customer service and you'll own the market."

I started a business and took care of my customers. I treated folks like friends, not as a source of revenue. I always focused on satisfying their needs and not concerning myself with the money aspect, believing in Jeff's sage advice about taking care of people. What I created eventually evolved into *KayakFishingStuff.com*.

At first I worked with Derrick, as he had a sport shop in Bloomfield, NJ, working out of his shop that first summer and fall, meeting prospective customers and taking them fishing. I remember getting an email from a guy named Mark. We chatted a few times and then I told him it was time to get on the water. We met at a tackle shop and hit the salt. I put Mark in a Cobra Fish and Dive, which I used to affectionately call a "kayak with training wheels" because of its stability. Within five minutes after launching, Mark had his first fish from a kayak. It was a slot-sized striper and he was on his cell phone calling his buddies telling them they had to get a kayak. Mark became my first customer and a friend.

The Bloomfield location, which was a half-block from Newark, wasn't working and I wanted Derrick to move west so we could create something the sport desperately needed. Derrick wanted to stay put. I knew Joey ('Joeykayak') was looking for something else to do and I proposed he join me in expanding the business. He did. When it came to choosing a name for the business, my first choice was Kayakfishinggear.com but it had been taken just a week before. Then I came up with Kayakfishingstuff.com. It brought a smile to one's face and was easy to remember - the place with all the stuff for kayak fishing!

Joey set up and handled the website, helped with product research, ran trips, ordered inventory and took people fishing. I, too, ordered product, packed and shipped gear, took prospective clients fishing, wrote articles, taught technique, ran trips and outfitted kayaks. It was a lot of work. At this time I was operating the business from my house. I didn't have a garage so I had to do installations outdoors in nice weather and fish when it was lousy.

KFS grew rapidly and things started getting out of hand. I had 80-foot tractor trailers delivering kayaks to me in a residential area. Several times they tore the cable lines down. I remember one Saturday when customers at the house picked up eight kayaks. Right about then I received a warning notice from the zoning commission about running a business in a residential area. I explained that I was actively looking for a new place, so the commissioner gave me a short grace period. I soon found a place nearby and we set up a retail location. I remember Mark telling me if I started a retail store I'd miss lots of fishing time and not to do it. I understood, but it was a necessary evil to continue helping the sport evolve. I figured a few years and then I'd reevaluate.

A few years prior, Joey wanted to start a kayak-fishing tournament. I was against it because I was already much too busy and didn't have any time to devote to it. I knew it would be good, however, and Joey was persistent. He took on the majority of the planning and it's become a terrific, annual event due to his efforts and lots of volunteers. Since he was going to do it, I suggested Jamaica Bay, NY. Our shop was in New Jersey but J-Bay was an incredibly reliable fishery, the most reliable in the region in spring. Joey agreed.

We decided on the first Sunday in May and after the 7:00 a.m. launch we prepared for a demo day that ran from 9:00 a.m. until 1:00 p.m. with the contest ending at 2:00 p.m. We worked with Gateway Parks using the Floyd Bennett Field facility. The demo and launch were at the old seaplane launch. That first tournament was a great success! I pushed for it becoming the multi-day affair it now is.

One day I received an email from a guy named Scott, whose title was something like "Director of Sales and Marketing, New York, ESPN2 Outdoors". I decided to give him a call rather than returning the email. Turns out Scott had seen the full-page ad for the Ocean Kayak Prowler. People were fishing from kayaks and he thought it was exciting. He visited one of the largest kayak shops in the country to learn more and they didn't know much. He then turned to the Internet and found the KFS site. He told me he read the site about a month before contacting me.

We discussed the sport and I felt the time to get it on TV was nearing. It was a terrific conversation. Scott did some research and we spoke again. The industry wouldn't support a show. TV is all about advertising and the kayak companies weren't ready to fork over the money. Scott made the same mistake so many people make about this sport. It isn't a kayaking sport - it's a fishing sport - and the kayak is simply a piece of tackle. Kayak fishermen use the same gear as other fishermen. Sure we have some specialized equipment that's kayak fishing-specific, but the vast majority of our gear is the same used by shore and boat anglers.

As of this writing, a show about kayak fishing still doesn't exist but with Scott's help, ESPN2's *Bassmasters* did a show about the Jamaica Bay tournament. They got a lot of great footage, too much to air on the original show, and some segments were aired at other times.

I got a call from my buddy Chris one day, who had just seen one of those segments, an interview they did with me. It covered the sport in general and included a segment discussing types of kayaks. The crew was shocked at the quality fishing we had. On camera they had a participant landing a 12-pound weakfish. The day before, Ridler had one in the 15-

pound range! It wouldn't surprise me if a new world record comes soon.

At the fourth event, we had already sold the business and I didn't have any responsibilities. Joey is still the tournament organizer and I was able to go as one of the fellas. I had a blast camping out and spending time with the guys. How great it was to experience the event from the other perspective, a weekend party of like-minded people doing what they love.

The Annual Jamaica Bay Tournament is a wonderful event. Picture yourself fishing in the shadow of the Manhattan skyline catching a variety of species including blues, weakfish and striped bass. All proceeds go to charities and it's become one of the world's most successful kayak fishing events.

In my earliest forum posts, I discussed that I wanted better gear, both accessories and kayaks, and by selling a lot of this stuff I knew I could gain credibility and have some influence. Ken Daubert's book, *The Kayak Fishing Revolution*, identified what was occurring with kayak fishing. Professional guides saw the trend but the kayak industry had not yet caught on. If you wanted a kayak you went to a kayak shop, most likely staffed by people who didn't fish - not a great way to buy a product for a specific sport. When you want skiing, scuba or any specialty sport gear, you're best served by shopping at a specialty shop but, as I've mentioned, kayak fishing is not really a kayaking sport. Sure we use kayaks but it's fishing with the kayak as a piece of equipment. My challenge, along with others who were also pushing the sport, was to get the industry to wake up and smell the coffee.

As with most things, it's all about the Benjamins. Moving product makes money, so I moved a bunch of product. KFS grew very quickly. In a few years it went from a "backyard enterprise" to the largest kayak fishing business in the world. I would get regular visits from the kayak manufacturers. I remember when the crew from *Liquid Logic* came by. Woody, the owner, said he learned more about kayak fishing in an afternoon in the shop than his entire experience prior to the visit.

When we started selling Hobie kayaks we sold 11 the first year, 55 the second and well into the 300's the third, then sold the business in the fourth year. Kayak Fishing Stuff helped change how kayak companies thought about kayak fishing. It's funny how selling thousands of kayaks to fishermen, and having 10,000 online members, gets attention. Go figure!

Somewhere along the way I started writing articles for a few publications. The first was with a regional magazine entitled *New Jersey Angler*. I've been writing a monthly column 'Yaking About Fishing' for years. I usually talk about kayak fishing but I'm not restricted to the subject. I've been fishing for five decades and 'yak fishing isn't the only thing I've done or do. A few years back Tony, who was putting together a magazine he named *The Kayak Fisherman*, contacted me. He asked if I'd be the east coast editor and I've been writing for that publication ever since. I've also teamed up with Joey in producing the online magazine *kayakfishingmagazine.net*. I've authored several dozen online articles and spoken at dozens of seminars for fishing and outdoor groups.

Tom Gilmore, author of *False Albacore* and *Tuna on the Fly* is a member of the same fly club as me, the Coastal Flyrodders, in Wyckoff, NJ. He is one of its founders and heard I was writing a book. He shared with me from his readers' feedback that one of the aspects of his book they liked the most was the stories, so he included more of them in his second book. I had planned on using stories in conjunction with information when putting this book together. Tom's experience provided reinforcement for my incorporating many personal stories throughout this book. It has been my pleasure recreating them for you and I hope you enjoy them!

So now you know part of my journey in the kayakfishing world. This book has been a long time coming, as I originally started it several years ago. It's said that life is what happens while making plans. My intention was to have this book on the market much sooner but my business and other responsibilities kept me too busy to work on it for a few years. It has truly been a labor of love and I sincerely hope you find it helpful.

Chris from *Liquid Adventures* with a nice silver salmon taken in Resurrection Bay, Alaska.

Chapter 2
Choosing a Fishing Kayak

As the sport of kayak fishing has gotten more popular, manufacturers have begun taking notice and our choices continue to increase. Kayaking as a sport, profitability-wise, hit its peak around the year 2000. It experienced tremendous growth in the 1990's but had a finite market. Let's face it, there are only so many people who are going to get into anything, and that includes kayak fishing. However kayak fishing, while no longer an infant, is probably only in grade school.

After bird-watching, fishing is the largest outdoor activity practiced in this country. It is estimated that nearly one out of every seven people go fishing at least occasionally. I think that estimate is a bit optimistic, but it's easily tens of millions of people. That's a lot of potential kayak fishermen. It's hard to determine how many kayak-fishing participants there are, but I'd guestimate the current number to be between 100,000 and 200,000.

As mentioned in the introduction, Joey and I were typically recognized when fishing the local waters around New York City in the early days, Joey more so in New York and me in New Jersey. The fact that fishermen regularly motored over to us and asked if we were Jon and/or Joey is indicative of what a small world it was back then. This hasn't happened to either of us in years, as it's now fairly common to see kayak fishermen here in the Northeast and many places. I would expect at least a million people to eventually join the sport of kayak fishing; hopefully, this book will help you become one of them.

A while back, a publisher contacted me asking if I knew anyone who'd be interested in writing a book about kayak fishing. I told him I was working on one. He said he was looking for an intro to the sport, something in the neighborhood of 20,000 words. I told him 20,000 words would barely cover a chapter in helping prospective kayak fishermen determine which kayak to buy. I forwarded him a copy of my outline and this chapter, which contains approximately 17,000 words. His comment back to me was he hadn't realized how much there was to think about in selecting a kayak and felt I was on the right track.

While I will be discussing the characteristics that contribute to a good fishing kayak, I won't be recommending specific makes or models. The discussion will encompass many facets of design, weighing their pros and cons for our purposes. As with many consumer goods, there are several brands and models within a category that will meet an angler's needs. My purpose here is to better educate folks on defining which category is right for them.

Not all kayaks are created equal. For our purposes, we need to select a model to accentuate our primary goal of fishing. We're selecting a tool to get us to where the fish are and to allow us to fish effectively. Most fishermen have never been in a kayak. Their typical understanding is that a kayak is something that is long, thin and rolls over a lot. However, models used in fishing tend to be very different - usually shorter, wider and tremendously stable. This is very important to remember. In fact, learning to use a kayak as a fishing platform is akin to learning to ride a bike. What initially feels new and shaky eventually becomes second nature. After only a couple of hours in a kayak, most anglers begin to feel comfortable and start to understand the kayak's potential.

If you're perusing this book, chances are you've also started looking at kayaks. Long ones, short ones, wide ones, narrow ones, red ones, blue ones - there are a lot of them out there. For purposes of our discussion though, let's state that a kayak is a watercraft that can be propelled by its occupant a distance of at least one mile. If a vessel requires a motor, electric or gas, to cover a mile, then for our purposes it isn't a kayak. With these guidelines to define a kayak, we see there are essentially two types. Those you sit on, known as Sit-On-Top Kayaks (SOT) and those you sit in, referred to as Sit-Inside Kayaks (SIK or SINK). There are a lot of choices within each style; some are great for fishing, some are okay, while others make miserable choices.

SIKs are the traditional designs that most people envision. The occupant sits inside the kayak and usually covers the hole (cockpit) they are in with a skirt typically made of nylon or neoprene. The skirt grabs a lip around the cockpit and effectively seals the inside of the kayak from the outside world. If the cockpit opening is large, and a skirt not used, then this kayak is a fair-weather craft at best. Any water coming over the sides of the yak ends up inside where its physical removal is necessary with small hand pumps or sponges. SIK's dominate kayaking worldwide. Vast bodies of water have been traversed in them and they are used in general for touring, recreating, and whitewater environments.

SOT kayaks are the new breeds, the interloper on the tradition of kayaking. SOT's are essentially glorified surfboards; hollow tubes of polyethylene plastic with molded-in places to sit, store things, and keep things dry. They use a system of tubes called scuppers that run from the top of the yak to the bottom, which aid in draining any water that accumulates in the open cockpit. They are self-bailing, and no sponges or pumps are required.

Envision sitting in a kayak on a lake with someone pouring a bucket of water on your head in a SIK kayak with a skirt on. The water makes your upper body wet, but the skirt sheds all the water off the yak into the lake. If the skirt wasn't there or came loose, the water would be in the kayak. If someone pours a bucket of water on you in a SOT, you most certainly get wet, but the excess drains straight through the scuppers. When in very wet or rough surf conditions, having water quickly drain away from you, without you having to remove it, is a very good thing.

Each style has pros and cons that must be considered when choosing a kayak. It's all about compromise. What are your needs as a fisherman and what are the environments you are taking your kayak into? SOT's are newer on the market and geared more to recreational paddlers. Originally planned for warm water play and use at resorts, their popularity has gained an ever-increasing foothold as a tool for fishermen.

The majority of kayaks we are going to discuss are made of plastic, polyethylene mostly. While there are other materials used in making kayaks, I believe plastic is best for fishing models because it provides strength, resilience and tolerates abuse. We are fishermen looking for a tool to get us to the fish. We go places that will scrape, scratch and crush other types of materials. You want to focus on fishing, and not have to worry about what your kayak is brushing up against.

For those of you who care about technical stuff, the polyethylene kayaks start as grains of plastic loaded into a mold. The mold is put into an oven where computer controlled machinery turns and tilts it, getting the melting grains of plastic to spread out in just the right thickness. When cooled they are removed and hardware is then added (eyelets, handles, etc.).

Ar you confused yet? A bit dazed, perhaps? Don't be! All of us who fish from kayaks have been in this position. Take a deep breath and keep reading; you'll shortly be able to make a decision that will enable you to get out fishing, and to do so effectively. The thousands of anglers who regularly fish from kayaks did it and you will, too. There is a lot to consider when making this decision and in this chapter I've tried to cover everything. Though there is a lot here, utilizing this information will help you in deciding on a kayak that will suit most of your needs.

The majority of fishermen who purchase a kayak for fishing do so because they want to fish. Most fishermen, this author included, wouldn't purchase a kayak if it weren't for fishing. This is a very important concept, which the industry has only recently begun to understand. They recognize the huge market available and are designing models with the kayak fisherman in mind.

Most kayak sales are still to customers who only want to paddle for recreation. Fishermen are not recreational paddlers. For the most part we don't want to go sightseeing, or paddle because it's a great form of exercise, or any of the other reasons the general population buys a kayak. Fishermen look upon the kayak as a tool that will allow them to catch more fish.

Unfortunately here's what usually happens when you go to a kayak shop to buy a kayak for fishing. Enthusiasts and experts of a particular sport, whether they sell skis, motorcycles, bicycles, or whatever, staff most specialty shops. Usually the salesperson knows considerably more about the products and how they function than you do. This is rarely the case in kayak fishing. Unless the business specializes in it, or has an expert on the staff, you're probably not going to get proper advice and there is a chance you're about to be sold something inappropriate for your needs. Don't walk into a kayak shop, tell them you want to fish from a kayak and buy what the salesperson recommends. I want to make an extremely important point. Fishermen do something that nobody else in the sport of kayaking does from kayaks – THEY FISH!

Interview the salespeople; if they are fishermen you will know right away. If the salespeople don't even fish, there isn't any reason to be asking for their advice, as you know more about the sport than they do. For starters, you're a fisherman. If the salespeople do fish, talk fishing with them to get a sense for their level of experience. To some people, being a die-hard angler means going once or twice a year. You will find most salespeople are clueless, because they're either distance paddlers or whitewater enthusiasts who will pick up a rod on occasion.

My fly fishing club was doing a winter fishing event at one of the local outdoor stores that carries both fishing gear and kayaks. I participated to help promote the club. One of my customers heard I was going to be there and he posted this on a couple of regional forums. Several people showed, thinking I was a featured speaker. I ended up doing an impromptu talk about kayak fishing. Since I was a guest I used the kayaks the shop sold in my presentation and discussed the best ones available there. One of the employees came by and said they had fishing models. So, I asked him a series of questions. It turns out he was a kayaker who brought a rod and a handful of lures with him a few times a year. The kayaks he fished from weren't modified at all - not even a rod holder. This isn't advice I would want if I were about to plunk down hard-earned cash for a kayak.

If the salespeople aren't serious fishermen who fish from a kayak then they're really no help in making a selection. They will most likely point you towards a fishing model, which is a kayak with some installed rod holders. Sometimes they include an anchor. You'd be better off getting the same model in a non-angler version and have it customized, if it is an appropriate model for your needs. Also, some of these fishing models are wolves in sheep's clothing. It's getting better each year but still keep in mind that if the salesman doesn't use the kayak the way you plan

on fishing, you still can end up in the wrong kayak even by purchasing a fishing model.

As I began to tell you in the intro, my first kayak purchase is a great example of what not to do. By taking advice from someone who did not fish from a kayak, I bought the wrong one for my needs. Even though I had little experience fishing from a kayak, I knew the places I wanted to fish, the things I wanted to do and the potential benefits of fishing from one. My first kayak wasn't capable of handling this. It had very pronounced front and rear skegs that made it track extremely well and its narrow design made it fast. This is great for covering distances but the kayak wouldn't turn because of the skegs. The kayak required the occupant to place it into a lean in order to effectively turn. Being new to kayaking I wasn't going to do these advanced maneuvers. Also the kayak lacked accessible storage for gear, so leaning could result in loosing things that would be sitting precariously on deck. It was so difficult turning I found it easier to go backwards to repeat a drift rather than take the turn radius the kayak presented.

I did some more research and paddled several at an on-water demo, including the model I originally wanted. It was much better for my purpose than the model I was talked into buying. I tried a few others and my favorite was one from the company Derrick had recommended. I bought it and put mine up for sale. Several of the prospective buyers wanted the kayak for fishing. I told them they wouldn't like it and suggested they consider a different model. I sold the kayak to a guy who wanted to use it for what it did well. Most mistakes don't work out so well.

In retrospect, the odds were against me getting what I needed. I had purchased a kayak that wasn't a mainstream choice. Few fishermen were using this model for fishing, which is a good indicator as to its fishing prowess, or lack thereof. The advice I was given wasn't worth much to me, because the gentleman I purchased the kayak from didn't fish. Because he didn't know or understand the requirements of a fisherman, let alone my needs, he had no perspective to comment on the kayak's suitability for fishing. He knew about designs, but his perspective was that of a paddler, a kayaking enthusiast.

I want to reiterate the point that anyone who doesn't fish from a kayak can't understand what a kayak fisherman needs. Up until a couple of years ago most manufacturers didn't make a kayak specifically for fishing. Many took recreational models and added rod holders, then pronounced them fishing kayaks. My first kayak went through this evolution. The company added three rod holders, manufactured it in a drab color and called it a fishing kayak. They even got a fly-fishing magazine to declare the kayak as the magazine's top choice as a fly-fishing kayak. It still had the same poor fishing features but had become a top choice by the editors of a magazine. So, because of an effective marketing campaign, this kayak got sold to a bunch of fishermen.

I know someone who bought one of these kayaks. He had seen Joey fishing from a kayak, was excited and asked a lot of questions about the sport. He wanted to get into kayak fishing badly and decided to go to a kayak shop to check things out. Joey's advice was to look but not to buy anything. He recommended the guy talk to me before making a purchase, as I had just started a business selling kayaks and gear and only sold models that fished well. Unfortunately the gent didn't heed Joey's advice. He erroneously assumed that the salesperson at the shop knew more than he did. Wrong. He was shown a specialty fishing model that the editors claimed was the best kayak for fly-fishing and this poor guy bought it and spent a lot of money.

The first time he used the kayak a big striper ran perpendicular to the kayak and pulled him right into the water. Luckily Joey was fishing nearby and rescued him. He rarely fished from the kayak again, using it instead for accessing places to fish from shore or wade. He had a lot of trouble selling it even at a substantial loss, and eventually settled for a fraction of the purchase price. Unfortunately I've met several fishermen who bought mistakes and either lost a substantial amount of money or don't fish from their kayaks. That's a shame, because fishing from the right kayak is fantastic. It has given me and others so many incredible experiences.

When visiting a retailer to get a kayak, keep in mind many shops will recommend a short Sit-In Kayak (SIK) even though more fishermen prefer Sit-On-Top (SOT) designs. Most shops assume when you say you wish to fish from a kayak that you want to fish a small lake or pond. If that is your intention, a short yak will be fine. If you want to fish a large saltwater bay or paddle beyond the breakers into the ocean, you'll need a larger kayak. While the manufacturers have done a good job providing models for all types of environments, many salespeople don't adequately understand the needs of a kayak fisherman

and won't be able to properly advise you. Again, if they don't fish from a kayak, and don't talk intelligently about fishing from a kayak, don't listen to their recommendations! One of the outdoor shops near my home in New Jersey sells kayaks and fishing gear along with outdoor clothing, equipment for camping, hunting and the like. In the winter and early spring they do seminars and expositions. The manager of the fishing department asked if I'd be interested in joining the fly tying group. I did and as usual I ended up talking kayak fishing. One guy I was chatting with had come into the store sometime during the past year and wanted to buy a kayak for fishing. He was sold a small SIK. He took it down to Raritan Bay, which is a large saltwater bay, and went out fishing. The wind came up and he couldn't get back in. Luckily a long touring kayak came along and towed him to shore. The salesman never qualified what the customer wanted the kayak for. He erroneously assumed the customer wanted to fish local ponds and lakes and sold him a kayak he felt would be appropriate for such.

I did things very differently when I was selling kayaks. When someone called and told me they wanted a fishing kayak I asked them a bunch of questions. How they were built, how they fished, for what and where. I wanted to know how they planned on using it and what opportunities and future uses of the kayak might arise. I surprised most people, but I really was interested in giving them the best choices so they could determine which model was most appropriate. We talked fishing in general, too. I inquired about which species they had access to, methods, etc. I was interested because I was a fisherman but also because I wanted to help them make the right choice for their needs. Many times I put them in a less expensive kayak. Profit wasn't my motive, and because of this I got tons of referrals.

Before we discuss the merits and differences of each type of kayak, let's first discuss kayaks for fishing in general. What makes a kayak a good fishing kayak? Generally fishermen cite stability, storage, maneuverability, the ability to accessorize, and comfort. Next are the specifics of height, weight, where you'll fish and such. Each person has certain decision-making criteria that are going to point him or her towards particular models because of these characteristics.

In my experience, most fishermen who purchase a kayak for fishing have never been in one before. Like anything, we all come into the sport with preconceived notions of what kayak fishing is all about. Here's an analogy I like to use. As a newbie you're a lot like Dorothy, sitting in Kansas, in the movie the *Wizard of Oz*. You haven't any idea what Oz is like and trying to imagine it is impossible. The world that is about to open up to you fishing from a kayak is similar to landing in Oz. You're going to experience things you haven't thought of yet. So while considering the features you think you're going to want in your first kayak, keep in mind this will probably change.

I met my buddy Bill when he purchased a kayak from me. He is a great example of how first intentions can change quickly. Bill had his primary home in New Jersey and a weekend house up in the Catskill Mountains of New York. He wanted a small, light kayak to better access the fishing on the river near his mountain home. He purchased, with my recommendation, a small, light SOT that suited this use well. Upon reading about the great saltwater kayak fishing in western Long Island Sound, he decided to give it a try. He found catching striped bass and bluefish from a kayak a blast. Taking both spin and fly gear along with other accessories, he overloaded that small SOT. Turned out it was not a good choice for where Bill was now doing most of his fishing. He has since added a longer, more sea-worthy kayak, which

he uses most of the time. He planned on using a kayak mostly to fish small waters but things turned out differently. Bill now fishes saltwater 90% of the time in the second kayak. He keeps a smaller yak up in the mountains.

Fishermen like to catch fish and once a kayak becomes part of your angling gear it often changes your perspective. The reason many people get into kayak fishing here in the New York metro area is because they are frustrated surf fishermen. Surf fishing can be exasperating because more often than not the fish are beyond casting range, as I mentioned earlier in the introduction. Can there be anything more frustrating and annoying as watching a school of fish go nuts beyond your reach? All surf fishermen experience this on a regular basis. You know if you can only reach the fish you'd hook up. Then someone in a kayak comes along, paddles out, and has a blast catching fish while the landlocked fishermen watch. After getting a kayak to fish the open ocean, most of these fishermen discover the back bays and estuaries offer better fishing most of the time. In this environment the kayak becomes the best means to access the virtually untapped fishing, as there are many places that can't

Fishing the protected waters of Great Kills Harbor, NY isn't much different than fishing a lake. The difference is what you're going to catch. Here's Tony with a nice bluefish, one of a few hundred our group caught on a single May outing.

be reached or effectively fished otherwise.

Here's another scenario I see all the time. A fisherman wants to get into kayak fishing and is purchasing a kayak to fish lakes and ponds. He doesn't consider the salt because he feels it's too much to handle, not realizing that the protected bays and estuaries, for the most part, are very easy places to fish and not much different from fishing large lakes. So besides bass, trout and panfish he can be catching striped bass, weakfish, fluke, bluefish, redfish, tarpon, jacks and other saltwater species. I always suggest a prospective purchaser consider this, as he'll have everything he needs to access this great fishing. Oftentimes they'll end up like Bill and spend much more time fishing the salt than freshwater. Who can blame them? All summer long in the northeast you can catch bluefish that will put fish like bass and trout to shame in their fighting abilities. Also it's not unusual to catch 50 or more of these great fighting fish in an afternoon. It's the same in most locales that have both fresh and saltwater fishing. Instead of fish like the Northeast's bluefish and striped bass, it may be redfish, sea trout and snook.

The opposite happens, too. I regularly speak with fishermen who live far from saltwater and want a kayak for fishing the salt. Often they need to travel a few hours to access saltwater when they have lots of great fishing nearby. Many of them haven't fished freshwater in a long time. Usually it's because they're shore-bound and the fishing can be quite limiting from there. But Oz awaits and their fishing world is going to dramatically change.

I live about an hour from the nearest salt, and traffic on the roads can often double the driving time. While I love to fish the salt, sometimes it isn't practical. Like many of us I can usually get away for a few hours. To spend the time traveling, rather than fishing doesn't make sense. I really enjoy hitting the local rivers where I can catch lots of fish in a variety of species. The best part, as opposed to fishing lakes and ponds, is that I always have the rivers to myself. It's great to drive a few minutes and catch 50 or more fish in the time it would take me to drive to the salt and back. I advise inland fishermen to consider this.

Choose a model a bit shorter, while still getting a kayak that will handle the salt. As a general rule, this would be about a 12- to 13-foot kayak. This compromise will also handle small bodies of water like ponds and rivers. Inland kayak fishermen have great fishing to be discovered near their homes. Because it's close

they will end up fishing more than they initially anticipate. You can stretch your parameters a bit. You're about to get a very versatile craft that will fish more diversified environments better than any single vessel you've used before.

Kayak Considerations

So let's get down to it, so to speak. You want to get into this exciting sport. There are some absolutes you will need to consider in order to make a good purchase.

Your Build

The first factor to consider is you. What are your height, weight, inseam measurement and general condition? If you're a big person, there are certain kayaks you need to look at. If you're a small person, getting a kayak that's big and has a 600-pound capacity probably isn't your best choice. Some kayaks suit different body types better than others. Some have a generous seat area while others are narrow. Sometimes one particular attribute becomes the key feature in making a decision. For instance, if you have long legs then the amount of room in the cockpit of the kayak will be the principal feature for you. A few models accommodate long inseams well, but many don't.

Your Vehicle

If you have to transport your kayak to go fishing, as most of us do, what vehicle are you going to use? Most people keep the kayak at their home, so it's going to have to be transported to the water. If you're using the bed of a pickup truck, a heavier kayak isn't a problem. Some folks opt to get a trailer, which is even easier. With any other method you're going to have to load it onto the roof, so you have to be conscious of the weight, taking into account the height of your vehicle. This is especially important if you're not a big, strong person. Whatever you do is going to require some thought, because wrecking your back isn't any fun and will cut down on fishing time.

Storing the Kayak

Where are you going to be keeping it? Sometimes you have a limited amount of space in which to store the kayak. If you've only got room to keep a 12-foot kayak in your garage then it doesn't make any sense to purchase a 14 footer.

Places Where the Kayak Will Be Used

Where do you plan on using the kayak? Is it strictly going to be used in fresh water? If so where? Small, protected waters such as lakes, ponds, small rivers and creeks or large, open bodies of water? Do you plan on using it in saltwater? Do you expect to fish in the ocean and gain access by launching through the surf? How are you planning on getting the kayak to the water? Can you simply drive it to the water and launch or do you plan on going into more remote areas where you can't use a vehicle for the final leg?

Fishing Methods

What fishing methods do you like to use? Do you only use one type or a variety? Do you use artificials, bait or both? If you're going to use bait, do you want to use live baitfish or dead bait? If you're using live bait then do you need a bait tank? If you do, you will need a model that can accommodate both the space the bait tank needs and be able to displace the weight. Do you plan on anchoring? Do you fly fish? Do you want to stand up and sight fish? The type of gear you plan on taking along and the way you plan on fishing can be very important as well as what you plan on attaching to the kayak.

Keeping Fish or Catch and Release?

What type of fisherman are you? Are you strictly a catch and release fisherman? Do you like to take the occasional meal home or are you regularly taking fish home? The category you're in is important in choosing a kayak. If you're going to keep fish then where are you going to store them while you continue to fish? If it's hot outside the fish can spoil if you don't keep them cooled. A soft cooler either inside a hatch or in the tank well may be necessary. Some people use a stringer over the side. Depending upon where you are it might not be a great idea. I'll elaborate a bit later in the chapter.

Sit-On-Top Kayaks vs. Sit-In Kayaks

Now let's have the SIK/SOT debate. I'm going to discuss both types and provide information so you can make your own assessment as to which is the better choice for you.

Sit-In Kayaks (SIKs) are the traditional type of kayaks. When the layperson thinks about a kayak this is what comes to mind. They have an open cockpit where there is a seat. Depending upon the model,

your legs are either partially or completely covered. They offer more initial protection from the elements; however they are more exposed in rougher conditions and can fill with water if not used with a skirt. In adverse conditions they require one. A skirt is a covering that goes around you and the opening in the kayak that prevents water from entering. When a skirt is used you must undo it to access the items stored in the kayak.

Sit-On-Top (SOT) kayaks are the new breed of kayaks and were originally brought to market by Ocean Kayak. They are essentially highly modified surfboards and you sit on them rather than inside. They have what are known as scupper holes, which allow water to drain from the kayak compartment. So when water washes over the kayak it briefly floods the cockpit and then drains. This is especially beneficial in places where water is going to regularly wash over the deck and most advantageous in the surf.

Stability

Fishermen do things in a kayak that most people don't - they fish. Having a stable platform is very important, especially for the person who is inexperienced with kayaks. When kayakers discuss stability they talk about two types, initial and secondary. Initial stability is the side-to-side wobble you feel when you sit in a kayak. Secondary stability is when the kayak is nearing its point of flipping and how much forgiveness (the amount of warning the kayak gives you) it has before you flip. Some recreational kayaks used for fishing have tremendous initial stability but have a very abrupt secondary. When they reach their secondary limit you're literally dumped. Conversely there are kayaks that wobble like mad but are very forgiving when they come to the dump point. As kayak fishing grows and evolves I'm seeing better and better offerings from the companies. Some models that were the mainstays of fishermen a few years ago aren't nearly as popular because they lack the performance of the newer kayaks. Since you sit on or near the floor of a SIK they tend to be more stable. In SOT's you sit on the kayak and because of this you sit higher. This higher sitting position makes a SOT inherently less stable. If you have one of each (SIK and SOT) that are the same length and width, the SIK will almost always be more stable. SOT designers tend to make their kayaks wider to compensate for this. As with anything you get extremes and

different approaches. Some SOT models will use a lower sitting position, which allow their kayaks to be narrower. Other models use a higher sitting position and in so doing they need to make the kayak wider. Initial stability is more important to beginners and secondary stability is more important to seasoned kayakers. It makes sense. The beginner hasn't developed a sense of balance yet. It's a lot like learning how to ride a bicycle. When you start out it's new so you think about it. Many of us as children used training wheels in our initial bicycle rides. Once you become accustomed to balancing, however, it's done unconsciously and the training wheels come off. It becomes second nature and you don't think about it at all. Shorter, wider kayaks tend to be more stable, but there is a trade-off, which brings us to our next characteristic.

Speed

Generally, the longer and narrower a kayak, the faster it is. SIKs are usually faster, however there are also fast SOTs. There is a trade-off with our next characteristic. If a kayak is long it's not going to turn as easily as a shorter kayak. If the majority of your fishing is close to shore or in small, protected areas, then sacrificing maneuverability for speed probably isn't the way to go. If you're fishing a big reservoir, bay or sound, the ability to cover distance becomes much more important. The faster kayaks used for fishing are generally known as touring style kayaks.

Speed is only important if you need it; however it's very misunderstood. Most beginners gladly sacrifice speed for stability. What they fail to consider are the limiting factors involved in kayaking. A kayak is a non-motorized craft. The occupant is the engine so you can't think of it as a car or similar vehicle. A kayak has limitations as to how fast it can go. Part of this has to do with its design and the rest is dependent upon its power source - you. Some kayaks have a top speed of only a few miles per hour while others are much faster. There are also two types of speed - top speed and cruising speed. Top speed is how fast the kayak can travel when maximum effort is applied. It's similar to the top speed of your vehicle. It doesn't serve much of a purpose, as you can't drive that fast most of the time. Your body is the kayak's engine and you simply can't maintain that much output for very long.

Cruising speed is more important. It's the velocity at which you can comfortably propel the kayak. Your cruising speed will increase as your conditioning and technique improve. Then it will become a relative constant that is affected by other factors such as wind and current.

Here's a practical example of how this works. Let's say the place you plan on fishing is one mile from where you've launched your kayak. Kayak 'A' is shorter and wider and kayak 'B' is longer and narrower. Kayak 'A' cruises at 2.5 mph and 'B' at 4 mph. 'A' is going to take 24 minutes to cover the mile while 'B' is going to take 15 minutes. That's a difference of 9 minutes. Should the distance turn out to be 2 miles then its 18 minutes. This is a simple example and doesn't add other variables that will most likely exist like current, wind and waves/chop. All of these will affect the movement of the kayak over the water and its cruising speed. The less efficient hull of 'A' will be more greatly affected by these additional factors than the hull of 'B'. This means the actual difference it takes each kayak to cover the mile could be considerably greater than the 9 minutes. It would probably end up being double or more. The longer narrower kayak 'B' is going to handle these variables much better, as its hull was designed to handle more varied conditions. Perhaps more important than the time factor is the amount of energy expended traveling. You don't want to be too tired from paddling to enjoy the experience, or worse, lack the energy to get back to land.

On a trip we took in June 2004 to Cape Cod, three people decided to fish Barnstable Harbor one day. While on the water the wind increased out of the south to over 25 mph. This happened to be the direction they had to paddle in order to return to the launch point. All three kayaks were capable of a bit over 5mph; however two weren't efficient touring style hulls. They had wide flat bottoms and a hull configuration that lacked another feature called rocker. The design was best for calm water. The third kayak was a pedal-drive system. Even though the pedal craft wasn't faster it was a completely different design that is radically different from other kayaks but functions similarly to a more efficient touring-style hull. The two conventional kayaks could barely make any headway against the strong wind and seas.

There is an 8-inch difference in hull width between these kayaks. It's obvious which is faster.

They were only able to sustain about 1 mph while the other kayak could maintain close to its normal cruising speed. The pedal craft ended up towing the two kayaks back to the launch.

The two kayaks weren't designed to handle the conditions they encountered. The strong wind and waves kept pushing the kayaks backwards, so most of the energy expended wasn't being translated into forward progress. In fact, the less efficient a hull the more the variables of wind, current and waves will rob the craft of forward movement.

Speed is more than how fast a kayak can travel. It is a function of efficiency over the water. The propulsion is limited by your physical ability and the amount of energy you have. Both of these are finite. I have found many people who purchase a less efficient, slower kayak end up trading up to a more efficient one if they are fishing locales where the above variables exist. In practice, that turns out to be most places.

Maneuverability

Maneuverability is a feature that is hard to do without if you need it. It's a necessity when fishing small, tight places. Shorter kayaks do this better simply because they're small. I fish many places where a long kayak would be impossible to use. Both kayak types have models that do this well. Maneuverability is also relative. Its need isn't restricted to small creeks

and waters. In many saltwater environments I frequently find the need to maneuver as well. Fishing close to jetties and breakwaters, areas where there is a lot of rock, strong currents, estuaries, mangrove creeks and the like all require some maneuverability.

Weight

How much a kayak weighs can be important. This applies mostly to handling it out of the water - transportation and storage - but also during some in-water situations as will be discussed a little later.

Transportation

You need to be able to transport your kayak. Many of us who are fishermen drive SUV's or trucks with caps. You're going to have to be able to get the kayak on and off the vehicle. Perhaps you have determined the best choice for you is a long kayak because you live near a large open body of water. If you're of average strength and not a big person, it probably doesn't make sense to get a kayak in the upper weight range of this group. Kayaks of this type are going to weigh more because of their length. So if you've determined you're going to be best served by a touring kayak, you will want to look at the lightest members of this group that still fish well.

A friend of mine has MS and because of this he doesn't walk well. His number one criterion in choosing a SOT kayak is weight. He fishes from a Phoenix, which is made from a light plastic called Trylon. His kayak is 30% lighter than a similar poly kayak.

Fishing Logistics

The first thing you should do is determine where you're going to be using the kayak. I fish all kinds of environments from large bays and sounds and even the open ocean, but I regularly fish some very small waters, too. A small, shallow river is best fished with a small, light kayak. Not only will it handle the environment better, but I sometimes encounter obstacles requiring negotiation, like logs, log jams, deadfalls, rocks, waterfalls, fast water and shallows. There are going to be times when you need to carry or drag the kayak around, over or through places. A lighter kayak is not only easier to do this with but in some situations too heavy a kayak will make it impossible.

Just getting to the water in some places presents challenges where weight could be a factor. You may end up fishing where you can't simply drive up and launch. Again, weight or lack of it becomes important. There are many places where it is difficult or impossible to fish a heavier kayak and when in one of these situations the lighter the kayak the better.

Accessory Friendly

We as fishermen take a recreational kayak and make it a fishing vessel by adding accessories. Some fishermen just take a rod and a few flies or lures along and others like to take lots of gear. At the very least, adding a rod holder greatly increases the fishability of a kayak. Since a kayak cruises at trolling speed you should always have an offering in the water when paddling to your intended fishing area. Oftentimes trolling turns out to be the preferred method for catching fish.

Some kayaks accept accessories better than others. It's the addition of accessories that can often dramatically improve the fishing. Lots of flat surfaces are nice for mounting things. On some kayaks it's simple and you have many choices of where you can mount stuff. With some models you even get a lot of choices in the variety of what you can attach. Some kayaks require much more thought and limit what

you can and can't do.

How you're going to fish matters, too. If you plan on doing a lot of flats fishing with a fly rod, the ability to stand up is going to be significant. Some kayaks accept outriggers better than others. Also, standing up is more than putting outriggers on a kayak. You're going to need somewhere to put your feet. Some models have large flat areas, which make stand-up sight fishing practical, while others turn the endeavor into an undertaking better kept performed by gymnasts and acrobats.

Weight Capacity

Manufacturers list the carrying capacity of their kayaks. Unfortunately you can't always use the figure that is stated. I used to fish a model that has a listed weight capacity of 400 pounds. I weigh less than 200 pounds and in this particular model with a normal amount of gear, water washes over the center hatch! So even though the kayak has a rating of double my body weight, it is far from realistic. The true capacity of the kayak is more like 250 pounds.

Some models are accurate and some aren't. If you weigh less than 200 pounds, most models will be fine; however there are a few that won't work. Although rare, some models need a minimum amount of weight to function properly. For a couple of years one company's models needed at least 250 pounds to activate the sponsons. If the sponsons weren't in the water the kayak was very tippy and wobbled a lot.

If you weigh over 200 pounds the more cognizant you need to be of capacity. You have to factor in the gear you'll be taking along. This varies depending upon you and the type of fishing you do. It also makes a difference regionally. In some environments fishing with live bait is important and the need to have a live

bait system along is imperative to consistent fishing. If your quarry requires large baits like mackerel you're going to need a big bait tank to hold a few to several gallons of water. Water is approximately 8 pounds per gallon so you could end up with 50 pounds in water weight alone. The accessory weight could be 75 to 100 pounds, and the kayak needs to comfortably handle this when added to your body weight.

When considering the weights of gear you're going to bring along I recommend being conservative - in other words, figure high. This way you know you will be able to handle any contingencies that may arise. The last thing you want to do is get a kayak that doesn't have the capacity to handle you and your gear.

Seat Position

Bottom line, if you're uncomfortable nothing else is going to matter. With many SOT kayaks you have the option of which seat you're going to use, but some have integrated seats. SIKs come with a seat. The first thing of which you have to make certain is that you're going to be comfortable. If you're not comfy you're not going to enjoy yourself on the water. I will cover this more in the seat section.

However there is another attribute of the seat area - the design of the pocket and the angle. You're going to want a nice pocket that is curved to accept your bottom. I've found I need a nice angle for my legs. I like a deep pocket so my thighs are at least 25 degrees from the kayak. If my legs are too straight I

(opposite page) This OK Prowler is typical of SOT kayaks that fish well. It has many good places for mounting accessories. **(below)** A customer chose a layout I wouldn't have for this Cobra, but many of the kayak's great features - a large center hatch, an accessory-friendly center rib, and beveled edges - are nonetheless apparent.

find it bothers my sciatica and I get very uncomfortable. It doesn't take long either; usually within a half hour I simply can't tolerate being in the kayak anymore.

Storage

There are different types of storage to consider when talking about kayaks. There is initial, which is the storage you can access easily while seated and fishing from the kayak and then there is secondary, the storage you can't readily access. It requires some thought and movement on your part or a buddy to retrieve. Both depend upon the design of the kayak and the way in which you outfit it.

Some kayaks are very poorly laid out for fishing. My first kayak, discussed earlier, is a great example of this. As you'll recall, it received the editor's top choice as a kayak for fly fishing, so it had been endorsed as a kayak that was not only suitable for fishing but was being called the best. This particular model has miserable initial and secondary storage. There isn't anywhere to attach accessories and nowhere to put gear on deck.

While there is a lot of below-deck storage capacity, the manufacturer chose to use two 10-inch round hatches to gain access and they're not accessible while on the water. Even if you could access the hatches, they are too small to accommodate many of the things you'd want to put in them. Its shape and layout doesn't allow for attaching storage, either. This model existed long before the company decided to market it as a fishing kayak and there was absolutely no thought put into its design with the fisherman in mind, other than adding some rod holders, of course.

Storing Carts

For some fishermen there are times where you park and where the kayak will be launched can be quite a distance from each other. If you use a cart to cover this area, it may not be practical or wise to return the cart to the vehicle, as you would have to leave your kayak and gear unattended. I fish a lot off the sandy beaches of the New York metro area and do not leave my stuff unprotected.

When accessing the water from these areas I use the big tire cart from Wheeleez™. It requires a large area and hatch to store the big wheels of this cart and its wide frame. If my kayak couldn't handle storing it, I would need to walk back to the vehicle, therefore often leaving my kayak out of sight.

So here's the scenario: You just wheeled your kayak from the parking lot to the water. You have a fly and spin rod, fish finder, GPS, radio, lures, tools, etc. It is quite a bit of gear and the value of this gear is anywhere from a few hundred into the thousands of dollars. If you have to walk back to the vehicle to put the cart away you will have to leave the kayak unattended. If the water temp deems it, you could be wearing waders, dry top and such, and this is a lot of exercise in soft sand while clothed in this gear. On some of the beaches this could amount to five to ten minutes you'll be away from your kayak, much too long to leave expensive, easily removed gear unattended, increasing the chance items will be missing when you return. The ability to store the cart inside the kayak is a major plus.

There are also occasions where you may need to land the kayak farther from the launch point than you planned. Many times upon returning there might be a lot of fishermen with lines out in the surf and you need to avoid them. The weather may have changed and you may need to get to the nearest shore. Having your wheels along might save a lot of unnecessary trudging and worry.

Storing Fishing Rods and Gear

When fishing the ocean and launching or returning through the surf, it's a good idea to store whatever you can inside the hull. It's the best place to leave gear just in case things don't go well, so your gear is protected. Not all kayaks allow one to get in and out of hatches while on the water. Some designs prevent proper loading of rods even though the hatch opening is accessible and there is sufficient room inside the hull. If you're going to be spending much time in the surf zone, this is important.

Everyone is different and so are his or her needs. Some folks don't need much but a lot depends upon you and where you plan on going and what you plan on taking with you. If you're like me and use both spin and fly gear, then you're going to be carrying more stuff. Besides at least two rods, you're going to need to take accessories for both. Some items are universal and some aren't. A stripping basket is one such item that can be invaluable for some places you may access. If you're fishing a pond or body of water where you won't be venturing far, you don't need much gear, as it's easy to go back to the vehicle.

Conversely you may be out all day and have a major

commitment in travel to get to the fishing. This will require you to carry more gear, food, water, extra clothing (for changing conditions) and such. Because you're farther away from both your starting point and help, you will need to be more independent. You should err on the side of caution and take along items to cover unexpected events.

The first time I made an excursion to Nauset Inlet on Cape Cod, my three companions and I didn't know what to expect. Our plan was to launch well back in Town Cove and fish our way towards the inlet. The distance was a few miles and we were going to encounter a variety of environments and most likely variable weather conditions. We were using an outgoing tide to transport us to the inlet and when it reversed use the incoming to return. Utilizing the tide would save us a lot of energy. Cape Cod has big tides that average nine feet, so they were part of our planning. There is no reason to work harder than necessary.

Since we didn't know what to expect and were dedicating over 12 hours to the day (the tidal cycle) we wanted to be prepared. We brought fly rods, a couple of spin rods and a surf rod each. The surf rod wouldn't seem to be something that you would think of when going kayak fishing but kayaks are also great access vessels. The beaches of Nauset Inlet are famous for surf fishing and we didn't know what we would find when we got there. The surf and conditions in the inlet might have made it difficult or impossible to access the ocean. There could have been significant action taking place in the surf zone requiring long rods and big lures to score. We didn't want to go through all the effort of getting there and then not have been able to take advantage of any fishing opportunities.

Besides the rods, we carried flies and lures for the gear we had selected. Additionally we had extra clothing, a gallon of water each, food and tools. It was better to keep the majority of the gear in the hull, as we probably wouldn't need it. Having the storage capacity was nice.

We never needed the surf rods but the binoculars I brought along enabled me to spot fish working about ¾ of a mile to the northeast of the inlet. We ended up experiencing an epic day catching dozens of striped bass averaging 32 inches! It was fantastic fishing but we might not have even discovered it without the binoculars. It was such good fishing that we repeated the trip the following day.

When fishing unfamiliar places it's a smart idea to carry certain items that can be invaluable under rare circumstances. I always carry extra warm clothing and rain gear with me, even in the tropics. That's right, in the tropics, even in summer! The reason I do so is because I had an experience where Joey and I were trapped on an island in severe thunderstorms and got chilled. You'll read about it in the chapter about clothing.

There are fishermen who combine kayak fishing with camping. There's one gent I know who lives three hours from the Jersey shore. He launches his kayak Friday evening and returns Sunday night. He spends the entire weekend out in the sedge islands of a central New Jersey bay. Camping requires a considerable amount of gear and obviously lots of storage space. It's better to have too much storage than too little, and more gear than you will likely need. Better to have and not need than need and not have.

Besides the amount of storage a kayak has, there is also the ability to access it. Some models have lots of storage inside the hull but it's sometimes difficult to get to. As discussed above, some manufacturers insist on designing their kayaks using small hatch openings. Common sizes are 8 and 10 inches. These small hatches severely limit the gear that can be stored below deck. It eliminates rod storage that one would think is fundamental when you're discussing a kayak for fishing. Small hatch openings make it difficult to store tackle, lure boxes and bags, safety gear and clothing.

Standing in the kayak

Sometimes the ability to stand in the kayak is going to be significant. The shallower the water the more sight fishing comes into play. The first time I fished the Florida flats Joey was in a WS Ride while I was in a Tarpon 16. It's very easy to stand in the Ride and Joey spotted fish that I never saw. I recall he saw almost two-dozen bonnet head sharks and I didn't see one. When *Everglades Kayak Fishing* increased its fleet of kayaks, Chuck's top priority was the ability to safely and practically stand. I used the word practically because you can stand in a lot of kayaks but to propel, cast and land fish while standing and staying in the kayak takes more than just being able to stand. They need to allow all these to be done. Some models were designed with forethought to this need and it's obvious. Besides being stable they have a large flat area to place your feet. They don't need

Freedom Hawk is the king of the standup kayaks.

outriggers to enable you to stand and fish.

Now that we've covered important considerations, let's get back to SOTs and SIKs. Most people, when they first think of a purchasing a kayak, consider a SIK. SIKs have models that fish well and for many fishermen make a good choice. Let's talk about different places and ways of fishing with kayaks and look at the practical uses of each type.

Flats Fishing

One of the best things about a kayak is access to shallow flats. There are lots of these types of environments, especially on the Atlantic and Gulf coasts, and Caribbean Islands. Some flats are shallow and don't have much of a tidal differential. The farther north you go the more degree of difference. You may find yourself fishing a flat and you'd like to get out and wade fish. There are a few reasons why you may wish to do this.

1. You've been sitting for a while in the kayak and it's nice to get out walking and stretching. It's a good idea to take every opportunity you can to get out of the kayak. Your legs and back will thank you for it. It greatly prolongs the amount of time you can spend out fishing, as sitting in a kayak all day gets old and tiring.

2. There is a breeze and it's difficult to control the kayak in such conditions. Fishing is a hands-on sport and stabilizing and positioning your kayak will require the use of the paddle. It is challenging working the paddle and casting at the same time. Hopping out eliminates the need to constantly adjust the kayak.

3. By standing you're higher up. The higher you are on a flat the more you're going to see. This is a big advantage on the flats.

OK, you've decided to get out of the kayak. If the water depth is only a foot or so this doesn't present a challenge in either type of kayak. Now let's see how things change in a couple of feet of water with an incoming tide. There's a good chance when you decide to get back into the kayak it could be three feet deep and possibly more.

A popular flat up in Cape Cod, called Brewster Flats, has a significant tidal surge you can see. The water can rise a foot every 15 minutes! In a SOT you sit on rather than in the kayak so getting in and out is actually getting on and off. It's easy to do. Conversely in a SIK it's quite challenging and your chances of capsizing the kayak are much greater. I'm fairly athletic but I wouldn't want to be getting back into a SIK in 3 feet of water. Getting back onto a SOT is easy under the same circumstances. Now imagine that you're wearing waders, which raises the degree of difficulty.

I once received a call for advice from a guy who had just purchased a SIK and wanted to get some accessories to outfit it. Since he was new to the sport I wanted to get a feel for what he planned on doing with the kayak so I could better advise him on how to set it up. Turns out he wanted to use the kayak to get to flats in southern New Jersey bays. This would require getting out of the kayak on the flats far from shore. As usual I asked his height, weight and inseam along with his general agility and condition. He was a big man and from the information he provided I didn't think the kayak he had was going to work for him. I suggested he put on his waders and try getting in and out of the kayak while it sat on his lawn. He called me up realizing he didn't want to start mounting stuff on this kayak because it wouldn't work for his needs. He found a stable SOT at a great price and purchased it. The SIK was put up for sale.

Accessing the Ocean

If you plan on fishing the open ocean you're either going to have to do a beach launch or at times access via an inlet. Sometimes the surf is so calm that you'd think you were at a lake, however this is unusual. It's great when it happens but don't count on it. You need to anticipate and be prepared for waves. As you go out through the breakers a wave might break over the kayak. When a wave comes over the bow of a SOT the cockpit briefly fills with water and then it drains. It happens quickly and by the time you're beyond the surf the water that entered the cockpit has returned to the ocean. You retrieve whatever gear you've stashed below and you're ready to fish. Having the ability to store gear away from the elements below deck and being able to retrieve it while on the water is invaluable. Should a wave knock you off a SOT your gear is where you left it.

Conversely a SIK needs a skirt to go through even moderate surf. Otherwise should a wave come over the bow of the kayak it will fill with water and by design whatever water enters will remain. Once beyond the waves you would have to remove the water from the kayak. This would require pumping, bailing or sponging the water out. It would be impossible for the kayak not to fill with water if any waves broke over the kayak and they usually do.

That's the best-case scenario. Many SIK models don't have bulkheads; in other words all the gear is now exposed to the water and the surf. Any gear that was in the cockpit is now wet. In, or rather on, a SOT you simply fall off and go retrieve the kayak. It's prudent to use a skirt should you choose a SIK for going through the surf. In a SIK you are in the kayak and should you flip none of the consequences are good. Should you go through the surf and misjudge it, a wave could flip the kayak, perhaps throwing you out. If this happens the skirt will pull away from the kayak and go with you. At the very least you have a kayak full of water and in the worst scenario you're upside down and still in the yak with your gear bouncing around with you in the surf.

When a SIK flips the popular wisdom is to do an Es-

kimo roll. That's OK if you're in calm waters with a narrow kayak, but most SIK's used for fishing are often wider and they don't roll well even under ideal conditions, and the surf is as far from ideal as one can find.

Shallow Rivers

A kayak will take you into many environments that are difficult if not impossible to reach via any other means. A shallow river is just such a place. Sometimes you can paddle and at times you will need to drag the kayak up, around or through objects. These obstacles can be rapids, waterfalls, trees, logjams, and all sorts of things. Often you will find that you will be getting in and out of the kayak a lot. It's much easier to get off of a kayak than out of one. In some situations it will be like our flats scenario and you need to get on or off in a couple feet of water or more. The more you find yourself leaving the kayak, the more you will appreciate a SOT.

Keeping Fish

Some anglers consider taking home dinner part of fishing so if you like to take fish home then you need a place to keep your catch. If it's smaller fish this isn't a big deal but if the fish are big it is. In a SIK the storage is either in the cockpit, a fish bag or on a stringer. A stringer is OK in freshwater areas where you don't need to travel very far, but a stringer full of fish provides drag, which is no good if you need to

Scott taking a break as he watches Joey and Terry stalk bonefish on a Turks & Caicos flat.

cover distance.

In some places it can attract predators. When I used to fish from a float tube in Long Island, a stringer of bass led to several arguments with large snapping turtles. Even though I wasn't in danger, it was unsettling to be playing tug of war with a big turtle. I carried a club to help settle these arguments. In the south you have to be concerned with alligators and in the salt its sharks, or even seals in some places. It isn't a good idea to encounter these animals with their desired meal attached to you.

Many SOTs have an area called a tank well, originally intended for transporting scuba tanks on the kayak, and is a great place to keep fish. You can either place a cooler in it or put the fish there and cover them with a wet burlap sack. Another place to keep your catch is inside the kayak. A soft cooler is a great way to go, as it can conform to the space you have and with the addition of a few cool packs works extremely well inside the hull. Obviously the larger the hatch the easier it's going to be to put a cooler inside the kayak. Hatches vary greatly from kayak to kayak. Some are enormous while others are so small they are impractical. There are a few kayaks that have built-in fish storage. As the sport evolves, we're going to see more and more of these.

Comfort

A SIK is an enclosed vessel and because of this your freedom of movement is restricted. Your legs are stuck; you don't have much choice where you can put them. Since you sit on a SOT it's easy to change positions. You can sit sidesaddle and put your legs over the side. In hot weather the SIK can really heat up. With a SOT it's easy to dip one's feet in the water - fantastic on a hot day. SIKs come with a fixed seat. Some are very comfortable but some are awful. With few exceptions SOTs utilize after-market seats. These seats run the full gamut from basic to incredibly posh and comfortable. Some models even have pump-up lumbar supports.

Wetness

One thing I've always been asked by people looking for their first kayak is whether or not it's a dry ride. I interpret this to mean they're asking if they're going to be sitting in a pool of water. In a SIK generally not but that depends upon where it's being used. The first SIK I ever used was in Raritan Bay, New Jersey. I did not anticipate needing a skirt. It was a very warm day in May and I was looking forward to not having to wear waders and a top with the 80-degree temperatures. If I were paddling a SOT the cool water necessitated their use. There was a chop on the water and it kept coming over the sides of the kayak. It didn't take very long for me to be wet and cold. I had to paddle back to shore, change clothes, and put on protective gear.

Some SOTs have drainage in the seat area. It's generally provided two ways - scupper holes or drainage ridges. Scupper holes work much better and are a feature worth considering. It's going to depend upon the model and your weight. How much you displace the kayak will determine the water level. With some people the scupper holes won't drain the seat area because they end up below the water line. They will actually let water in and some owners plug the holes. Most of the time whether or not a kayak has seat drainage isn't important enough for me. Sure I'd prefer to have it but there are only limited circumstances when it matters. If the water's cold I'll be wearing protective clothing anyway. When it's hot out it can help cool me down. When it's in-between is when I'd prefer not to sit in water, but I can deal with it by what I wear.

Even though I didn't actually tell you which type of kayak you should be fishing from, the choice seems obvious to me. SOTs, based upon my experience, are superior fishing craft and they are what I recommend for most situations, especially for first-timers. SIKs are much more limited in their design. Many fishermen considering their first kayak look at and want a SIK. The comment I hear the most is they want to be protected from the elements. Kayak fishing is a water sport and one must always be prepared for immersion. If you don't prepare for being in the water at some time, then you're a potential disaster waiting to happen, seeing that accidents do happen and not being prepared could cost you your life.

In many environments using a kayak to access places is often more productive than fishing from the kayak. You will catch fish from either type of kayak. An analogy I like to use is fishing only surface lures or flies. By only fishing the surface you will catch fish sometimes, however by not being able to fish throughout the water column there are going to be days when you're not going to catch anything.

Sometimes the fish won't come to the surface. A SIK is like surface fishing. It's more limited. A SOT allows you to maximize your access to the environment. I prefer to have the most versatility in my kayak choice and a SOT affords it, which is why I usually recommend them. Ah, I did say usually. That's because there are situations where a SIK is a better choice. A long, sleek touring SIK is superior if you're covering extreme distances and your primary fishing won't be from the kayak but you're using it as transportation. Also in rivers with rapids in excess of class II, small whitewater SIKs are the kayaks of choice. However these are limited, specialized circumstances.

So which kayak should you get? As you can see there are a lot of variables, however it isn't rocket science, either. There are a few significant variables that all kayaks have. You need to make a decision between SIK and SOT. Next you need to consider length, width and hull configuration.

Length

So you've decided on a type. Let's look into the next variable - length. How long a kayak you need depends on where you'll be using it. The shorter the kayak, the better it's going to perform in small places.

If you fish small rivers, a small kayak works really well. Anything over 12 feet is simply too big for many places. Also, a smaller kayak is a better choice if you're going to cart it into a remote location. Wheeling a long kayak down a twisting trail is frustrating, as you'll constantly be hanging up as you try to maneuver around trees, rocks, roots and such. The longer the kayak the more it's going to weigh, all things equal, so besides dealing with more length you have the weight issue as well. There will also be places where you need to lift the kayak over things.

If you're going to fish a lot of environments then you're going to need to compromise on length. There are models that will do most things well and they tend to be in the 11- to 13-foot range. If the majority of your fishing will be in freshwater and in tighter places, but you will venture to the salt and bigger water occasionally, then consider the shorter end of the range. Conversely if the opposite is true, then go to the longer end of the spectrum. Keep in mind you will be compromising somewhere and only you can determine where it should be.

Width

Generally relates to stability and to a certain degree of comfort. Let's look at the latter first. If you're a big person then you're going to need a kayak that has sufficient space to accommodate your lower body. A wider kayak is going to have a broader seat pocket, giving one more room. My buddy, Derrick, is 6'5" and 340 pounds (reminds me of an NFL lineman) and I used to call him my big guy test pilot when I owned *Kayak Fishing Stuff*. There are some popular models of kayaks he tried which would become a semi-permanent part of his anatomy. When he got up the kayaks tended to stay with him and he had to pry himself out.

Generally the wider the kayak the more stable it is. There are models that are a yard or more wide. These models are incredibly stable and are virtually impossible to tip over. I've watched people at demo days literally stand on the edge and jump up and down trying to tip them. They end up falling off but don't flip the kayak.

Some SIKs are very narrow with some touring models being less than 2 feet wide. Their long and narrow stature makes them very fast and they have impressive ranges. I know some guys who launch on the mainland of Cape Cod and paddle to Martha's Vineyard to fish. You need a very efficient kayak and superior skill and conditioning levels to make that trip.

Hull design is another factor. There are models in the 30-inch width range that are equally as stable as kayaks a yard wide. They tend to have flat hulls that provide a lot of surface area and lack camber. Camber is the curve from bow to stern and generally the more a kayak has the higher the performance of the hull. I'm not going to get into kayak engineering here and if you'd like to learn more about it there is info on the topic available. The trade-off of a flat hull lacking camber is a lot of surface area. All the surface area, while providing stability, also provides drag. Drag is friction and the more there is the more it slows the kayak down. Generally these kayaks will do well in calmer waters. When the going gets rough their hull designs get significantly slower.

There are hull configurations that vary within each type. There are flat-bottomed kayaks that, as their name implies, have flat bottoms. Another style is what I call the winged kayaks. These kayaks have a center area that is lower than the rest of the kayak. The wings are called sponsons. They come in a few variations - rounded edges or sharper, more pronounced edges. It has been my experience that the sharper-edged kayaks tend to have a more abrupt transition to secondary stability than those with a rounded, more gradual edge.

Color

I have found the color of the kayak is unimportant to the fish. Choose a color based upon what you like or where you plan on fishing. Most anglers who fish wide-open areas, especially saltwater, tend to favor brightly colored kayaks. This makes sense, as a bright kayak is easier to see. In my non-scientific experiments I have found the most visible color is orange, followed by lime, and yellow. Red, generally considered a bright color, isn't, because when light levels get low it disappears quickly. Colors like white, although bright, are too easily mistaken for a wave or disturbance on the water. Most other colors don't show up well.

In freshwater many anglers prefer a stealthy color - one that blends into the environment. This is because for a variety of reasons they'd rather not stand out. Some of the more popular colors are camo (if available) and various shades of dark green and tan. If you're uncertain on color keep in mind that you can always make a dull, stealthy kayak more visible by adding bright accessories such as a flag, clothing, PFD and paddle blades, but you can't make a bright kayak dull.

Leg or Pedal-Driven Kayaks

I have been deliberate in not discussing brands or models in this chapter. I have been using pedal-drive kayaks for several years and since they offer increased fishing opportunities they get their own discussion. In my opinion they are in a separate class because of their inherent properties.

The first company to successfully design and market a pedal-drive is Hobie Cat Company. They call it the Mirage Drive™, which is a center-mounted, pedal-drive device that converts an easy pushing and pulling motion of the legs into forward progress. There are flippers that Hobie calls sails that move perpendicular to the kayak. The design and engineering is such that this produces a forward motion. If you were to insert the drive backwards in the kayak you'd go backwards (it isn't advised, as I had a customer who tried it going down a river and it was a disaster). The drive will only propel the kayak forward. For going backwards a paddle is necessary.

The drive inserts into a recess just forward of the seat position of the kayak. The space around the drive is open to the water and functions as the forward scupper holes. The tank well has traditional scupper holes and the seat has adjustable ones. A rudder operated with the hand accomplishes steering.

Like a thoroughbred racehorse, the Hobie gets up to full speed almost immediately, requiring only a couple of strokes. The drive provides tremendous torque and is similar in function to a tugboat. It has tremendous towing capability (refer to the speed section earlier in this chapter for an example). It makes sense, as it utilizes the largest muscles of the body - the thighs. The company started out with one model but has since added a bunch of models from the Sport (just over 9 feet) up to the 16-foot Adventure. Once your legs are conditioned to the exercise, you will have significantly more range than all except the most efficient paddle kayaks.

New to the group is the Ultimate™ Multi Propel, from Native Watercraft, debuting in the summer of 2008. While I have used mirage kayaks while fishing for years and have hundreds of days in them on the water, I have only spent about 15 minutes in the Ultimate Multi Propel. Both companies use the legs for propulsion but that's where the similarity ends.

The Ultimate Multi Propel uses a propeller that is driven by a bicycle crank. The circular motion is the same as that of a bicycle. There is significant gearing and it surprised me when I first started pedaling. It was very stiff but once inertia came into play it wasn't nearly so difficult. It's the same as hopping on a bicycle that's in too big a gear for starting out. As soon as you have a little speed it's easier. The difference here is most bicycles have gears and the Ultimate Multi Propel doesn't. To go faster you pedal faster and vice versa for going slower.

I found cruising easy because of the circular motion. However the gearing is too low to spin, which means you're not going to mistake this for a bicycle. You still gain momentum because it is a circular motion, as opposed to the mirage with its back and forth motion, but you will never feel like you're on a bicycle. A significant difference is the Ultimate Multi Propel goes backwards. Just spin the pedals in reverse and you'll stop quickly and reverse course. While it has a larger turning radius than the mirage, the addition of reverse makes maneuvering very easy and far superior. To accomplish close quarter maneuvers with a mirage kayak, you really need to pull up the rudder and use a paddle.

Native Ultimate Multi Propel

Besides different approaches in how to use leg power, the kayaks are completely different. All mirages are SOTs while the initial Natives are SIKs with the first SOT model, the Mariner, being released in the spring of 2009. Each has strengths and weaknesses. The Hobies can access any environment and if you are fishing big water where there are waves or you need to go out through the surf, they are the only choice. They will handle anything - big water, wind, waves as rough as you're willing to fish in. I've fished in 8-foot seas with 25mph winds and caught fish. The Natives are best in protected waters, backcountry lakes and deeper creeks, freshwater and the like, environments where you don't expect water to come over the sides.

Essentially the Ultimate Multi Propel is a hybrid canoe. It ditched the high bow and sides that catch wind and uses much better seating. There is a tunnel to facilitate stability and standing. Where it is going to shine are places where standing makes sense, or when you'll need to access gear easily, or want to have several rods rigged and out of the way of branches and roots that could grab them. The mangrove backcountry is one such environment.

The best thing about the leg drives is they make the kayak hands-free. Fishing is a hands-on sport. While cruising along you can be casting, talking on the cell phone or radio, scanning the water with binoculars for activity, changing lures, having a drink, eating, tying on a fly, all because your hands are free. It's very convenient. It isn't a perfect system though, and as with anything there are applications where it isn't the best craft. One of my favorite features of a kayak is how shallow they can perform. Most kayaks can operate in less than six inches of water. Both drives require about 16 inches to operate so if you plan on being in water less than that, you will need to use a paddle or pole. The Ultimate Multi Propel can't operate any shallower but the mirage can be feathered and will propel the kayak in shallower water, however it isn't very efficient and I only do so for short distances. If you fish shallows a lot these drive systems might not be practical for you unless you have expanses of deep water, too. If so, the greater efficiency of using your legs will be welcome.

While pedal drive kayaks cost more, they also function well as paddle kayaks in their own right. The longer Hobie models paddle wonderfully and the Natives have the same characteristics as their non-pedal drive siblings, being that they utilize the same hull design with a modification for the drive. If you're going to fish a place with weeds, they can become a nuisance by getting tangled up in the drive. Shallow rivers are another place where the drives wouldn't be a good choice. The kayaks can be used without the drive. The Hobie drive can be easily removed while the Native drive is mounted on a swing arm which allows it to be lifted out of the water.

Some of the Hobie models paddle poorly while some are excellent. I discovered this by accident one day when I was filming a TV show with the folks at *New Jersey Angler*. I provided the Hobies for the crew. I forgot one mirage drive so I did without and paddled. The Hobie Revolution paddled beautifully. The Natives are going to perform the same as their non-drive models.

The two most difficult things to deal with in a kayak are current and wind. If you're going to fish a spot in currents with a paddle yak then you get very little fishing in for the effort expended unless you anchor, and anchoring isn't always an option in some places. Bridges in a river are a perfect example. Fish like to hold behind the structure of the bridge. In a paddle craft you make a cast and the current sweeps you downstream. When you're in windy conditions and stop paddling, you'll be blown away from the area you're fishing. By pedaling you can hold yourself in position while you fish.

I spent a bunch of time in the Everglades in the 10,000 Islands, where there is a lot of current flow and in late winter, lots of wind. The pedal-drive allows me to hold my position in currents and wind and fish places I'd otherwise either have to anchor or not fish at all. Even when anchored I often can't effectively fish the spot. Again pedaling allows you to stay where you want while you fish.

Multiple Seat Kayaks

For our discussion these are kayaks that seat two or more people. Some are really singles that use rear-facing jump seats that will accommodate a child, while others have true multiple adult seating. A tandem refers to two people. There are also triples and quads.

Many beginners, when considering their first fishing kayak, ask about tandems. They want to be able to take along a friend or significant other. I'd always been of the opinion tandems were a poor choice for fishing and I had advised people to get a single kayak. As with any idea things evolve and I've since changed my opinion. There are applications where a tandem can be a superior choice. Here's how I came to this way of thinking.

A gentleman, Andrew, contacted me, as he wanted

Here's the author showing what hands free is all about as he pedals a Hobie Revolution in the wind. He's chatting on the cell phone and checking his handheld GPS in a comfortable recline.

four kayaks for a place he owned in the Caribbean and asked my advice on which kayaks he should get. They were going to be an asset for his rental, which would broaden the appeal of his property. Since this was not the usual scenario I encountered when recommending a kayak purchase, I gave it some additional thought before making a suggestion. His estate was on the Caribbean Sea and across the street was a sound. The kayaks would be handling multiple functions. They'd be used for fishing, snorkeling and general recreation so versatility was going to be important. I knew the primary sport fish was going to be bonefish, which means flats fishing. Even though I had never fished for bones I had read more than my share about them to understand what was going to be required. I needed to make a choice that would best accomodate the guests' parameters.

I decided on two single and two tandem kayaks. There are a lot of tandems on the market and not all tandems are created equal. Some have seating for two adults while others have three-position seating.

Sight fishing for bonefish from a tandem in Turks & Caicos. Terry's on the bow as Joey propels the kayak.

This means besides functioning as a traditional tandem - one person up front and another in the rear - there is also a middle seat position. Why is this important? When a tandem kayak is used as a single you need to be properly seated for it to perform well. Having a centered dedicated area that has been molded with a seat pocket makes it much more comfortable and enhances performance.

A few years back I used a model with this very setup as a single in Puerto Rico while chasing Tarpon. I became familiar with how important this attribute was in increasing the versatility of the kayak. Tandems are designed to support two people. They tend to be wide and stable, which would make them good for snorkeling and diving and great for taking kids out who might move around a bunch. Because they are wider they are also going to be slower. By being comfortable it's going to be easier to use and maximize the performance.

Four of us ended up taking a trip to the Caribbean to visit Andrew's property - myself, Joey, Scott and Terry. After all, someone had to un-wrap the kayaks and make sure everything worked properly. A tough job, but my companions and I were up to the task. While the plane was preparing to land, it flew over an area of flats that looked fantastic. Before leaving on the trip I had spent a lot of time looking over satellite images of the islands and had seen a road that went to the area we had just flown over. So, our first morning we did some reconnaissance.

We were able to drive to the area and found a great place to access those flats. The next day Joey and Terry decided to go out with a guide on a flats boat on the other end of the island. Scott and I hit the area we had scouted. It was very windy so we weren't sure if we could find fish, but it would be a learning experience. I did spook a few fish, which I'm fairly certain had to be bones.

The next day all four of us decided to fish this area. We could only transport two kayaks on the rental van. We had two singles and two tandems, so it had to be tandems to accommodate all four of us. The previous day we had already established in the backyard of the house that one person could stand up and sight-fish in the front of the kayak while the other paddled while sitting. We were eager to put it to use.

Sight fishing is where the tandem has a distinct advantage over a single kayak. While the person in the rear propels the kayak, the front person can stand. A standing angler has a tremendous benefit over a

seated person. It is so much easier to spot fish. Almost immediately Joey and Terry, who were in the other kayak, yelled that they spotted some tailing bones near shore. This was very encouraging, as they were only a short distance from the launch in an area we didn't consider prime. Scott and I headed directly to an area we felt was an excellent spot for getting fish. Within minutes of getting there I spotted, hooked and landed my first bonefish, a scrappy 4.5 pounder. All four of us fished from the kayaks using this technique in addition to walking the flats as we stalked tailing bones. We caught fish and had a great time and if it weren't for the tandems it would not have been nearly as productive.

Bonefish are not the only flats species where this tandem technique will be effective. In the northeast there are striped bass and bluefish that invade the flats each spring. As one moves south redfish, snook, tarpon, jacks, barracuda and bones. From Cape Cod south all the way to Honduras there are flats.

The model we used in the Caribbean was a great choice for that circumstance but other situations might lend themselves better to different tandems, depending on one's specific needs. One of the shortcomings of the model we used in the Caribbean was its lack of storage. It's not a very large kayak, with most of the deck space dedicated to passenger use. It has the ability to accommodate a few 6-inch hatches but they are not going to provide much storage. For the Caribbean it wasn't important but for other situations there will be a need for more room.

The model we used has a bigger sibling that is a foot longer and has greater weight capacity. It will allow two paddlers to spread out a bit more and also has provisions for installing larger hatches. It will accept two 8-inch rounds and a larger oval, sufficiently big enough to fit items like multi-piece rods, dry bags, soft coolers and the like. The kayak, like its smaller sibling, is a rock of stability. Scott and I overtaxed the kayak we used in the Caribbean, as our combined bodyweight was over 450 pounds. As a result water pushed up through the scupper holes, creating a wet ride. Not a big deal in the Caribbean with warm water in sheltered, shallow areas, but not what I want in other places. The bigger sibling would have alleviated the water situation.

There are also triple and quad kayaks. What is nice about a triple, when used by two people, is the added length helps spread the fishermen apart. Also there is a ton of storage, both on top and below deck. Large rectangular hatches give access to the interior storage. You could take a lot of gear along and could even island hop and camp out. Being a triple, you could take a third person along.

Kayaks with rear-facing jump seats are great for taking children out on the water. They are limited in the amount of legroom; you're going to play footsies because both of your legs will occupy the same area. Several years ago I started taking my cousin Joshua fishing with me and I used this style of kayak. It worked well until he got to be 8 years old, at which point it wasn't comfortable for either of us. Besides playing footsies, all that weight so far forward significantly decreases the performance of the kayak. Something nice about this style of kayak is that it is a single-person kayak and they tend to perform better than tandems when used solo. The negative is they don't accommodate two adults comfortably.

I had a customer who ordered a kayak of this style and he was a small guy. I brought up how large and cumbersome the kayak was and he told me he wanted to be able to take his two children along. The model he had chosen has the rear facing jump seat option on the front hatch and the tank well is set up to accommodate a seat, with enough room for a small adult. The kayak was a great choice for his needs.

So consider tandems. If it is going to be your primary kayak for all situations, then look to a smaller model that will be easier to handle alone both loading and on the water. If it is going to join a fleet then you can get more precise and choose a model that will fit a specific need.

Hybrids

There are different interpretations of what a fishing kayak is or should be. As the world of kayak fishing continues to grow, manufacturers will strive to produce innovative designs to capture market share. Hybrids are an example of this; some combining features of a SIK and SOT while others veer heavily towards one. They are not really SOTs or SIKs, but something different, while others are essentially altered canoes. The Native Ultimate hull, mentioned above, shares many features with canoes. Some hybrids have double hulls just like SOTs, but they lack scupper holes. With them you get below-deck storage, but should water enter the cockpit it needs to be removed by the user. It all comes down to what your needs are.

Try Before You Buy

I often read and hear the advice given to try out or demo as many kayaks as you can before making a selection. It has been my experience this isn't nearly as important as many think, especially for first-time users. The majority of fishermen who get into the sport have never paddled a kayak before. My buddy Ken said it best: "Beginners trying out kayaks is akin to someone who doesn't have a driver's license going out and test-driving cars." There isn't any point of reference.

When I owned KFS I helped a lot of people get into kayak fishing. My observation is many beginners, after attending a demo day, usually bought the most stable kayak they tried. Many of these folks had the kayak up for sale after using it only a few times and bought a narrower and faster model. As I discussed earlier in this chapter, the learning curve is very fast. I also found that some people got too confused to make a choice.

Another scenario is that while kayak fishing has hot beds of activity where the ability to try out a lot of models is realistic, many areas are far removed; you may have to travel hundreds of miles to demo a couple of yaks. If you do your homework and go with a choice that will handle you and what you want to do with it, you will be fine.

If you need a truck you don't buy a two-seater sports car. It's the same with kayaks. Determine what you need and choose among a class of kayaks. Get a model used by other people built similarly to you with similar needs and you can't go wrong.

The Native Ultimate is a hybrid that is essentially an evolved canoe.

Used Kayaks

If you're still confused, a used kayak may be a great option available in many parts of the country. Wherever kayak fishing is popular there are going to be second-hand kayaks that have been used by fishermen, and there are many reasons they are for sale.

The most common reasons are buying the wrong kayak for one's intended use, the kayak never gets used, or the owner wants to get a newer model. Whatever the reason, you can save a bunch of money and get a kayak ready to fish. Only as a participant are you truly going to understand kayak fishing, whether or not it's for you, and whether or not the kayak you are using suits your needs. If the sport isn't for you or you determine you need a different model, the price you paid for the kayak is essentially what you will get when you sell it.

Another great reason to buy used is you may be able to purchase more than one kayak. I personally own several kayaks. I fish a lot of different environments all over the continent. If I only owned one kayak for everywhere I fished I'd be compromising many situations. Having more than one kayak allows me to fish lots of places and take other people along.

Should you decide to buy used, still adhere to the advice I've given earlier in this chapter. Determine your needs and go with a kayak with a fishing pedigree for what you want to do in the places you plan to use it. Obviously a mistake isn't nearly as critical with a used kayak. While plastic kayaks are tough, they are not indestructible, so look over the kayak for cracks. With SOTs the most common possible problems are the scupper holes. If the kayak is going to leak, it's usually there. Fortunately it can be repaired. I have a Tarpon 100 that a shipping company put a hole through with a forklift. I was able to repair it and have been using it for several years now.

Integrated Sail Systems

After you get a kayak you're going to find that wind can be both an ally and an enemy. Wind at your back makes traveling across water easier but fighting it can be tough. If you think you would like to sail, for fun or as a means of accessing fishing, then it's an attribute you need to consider when making a decision on which kayak to buy. This is especially important if you truly want to sail. By this I mean in all directions. There are add-on systems and modifications you can make to accommodate sailing. It just depends upon how seriously you want to take it.

At present Hobie Cat is the only major kayak company making kayaks that fish well and integrate a sail and other sailing accessories within the design. I'm going to cover sailing, with regards to kayak fishing, later in the book; so if sailing is something you're interested in, I suggest also reading that section.

Not sure if sailing is important? Do your research. the fact is that very few kayak fishermen sail. One percent is probably a generous figure. However, I think it's going to increase as sailing gains more exposure. Using the wind as an ally makes sense.

Conclusion

I know I presented you with a lot of information, but please don't be paralyzed with indecision. The biggest mistake you can make is not getting into the sport. There are lots of kayaks out there and each year we have more choices; however the majority of anglers are using fewer than two dozen models. So if you get an appropriate kayak within that group you really can't go wrong.

When one asks kayak fishermen the most important piece of advice they can give, the most common answer is simply that they wish they had gotten involved in the sport sooner. Is it your turn to join us?

Demo Day at the first annual Jamaica Bay Tournament, Brooklyn, NY.

Josh prepares to release a nice Matlacha, Florida redfish.

Chapter 3
Gear and Accessories

Kayak fishing, like most sports, has gear and accessories that are essential, some that are very useful, and those that are either esoteric or highly specialized. The indispensable items I consider essential. In order to fish from a kayak you are obviously going to need a kayak, a paddle, a fishing outfit and, even though others might not consider it to be essential, a seat. Then there is gear that is important, but not absolutely essential. Items like proper clothing and rod holders fall into this category. Finally, there is the esoteric, luxury or specialty gear that is nice to have, but certainly not something most anglers need or will even own, or are only used for specialized fishing or circumstances.

Paddles

A paddle is the first accessory you need after you get a kayak. It is the most common means of propelling one across the water. We fishermen, for the most part, are not paddlers. We use a kayak as a fishing tool and it's our reason for being out on the water. We generally don't paddle for dozens of miles or need a very large blade for surf or whitewater. There are exceptions, but our needs are generally simple.

The one attribute we really need is durability. We do things with paddles that recreational kayakers don't, so it's more important to get a paddle that can take some abuse. If you only use your paddle on open waters, any will do. However if you're going to be in places where you will push off rocks, paddle across shallow rocky areas, use it to pole along or push off of trees or docks, then durability is a must. The lighter the paddle the less fatiguing it will be, so if you have a touring style kayak and plan on many miles, consider weight. You can always have more than one paddle to cover contingencies.

Paddles consist of two parts, the shaft and the blade. Design and materials vary with both. We'll discuss shafts first.

Paddle Shafts

Paddles come with three basic types of shaft materials. The shaft is the area on which you put your hands. The material can be aluminum, wood, fiberglass or composites. Aluminum is the least expensive and is very commonly used by anglers. It's durable and does a good job. It is less forgiving on the body and more fatiguing. Since it's a metal it conducts temperature, and in temperatures less than 50 degrees you might need to wear gloves or put a sleeve on the shaft for insulation. Some aluminum paddles come with sleeves. Wood has a nice feel to it, is a very forgiving material and doesn't conduct cold. Fiberglass, graphite and Kevlar are composites. Shafts made from these materials have a very nice feel and they don't conduct temperature. Generally, they cost at least twice as much as aluminum shafts.

Fiberglass is the least expensive of the composites. I started off with a paddle in this group as recommended by Spike. Graphite paddles are the nicest. They tend to weigh the least and feel the best. They also cost the most. Low end for a composite is going to be over $75 and the sky's the limit.

Paddle shafts are available in one-piece or multipiece versions, with two-piece being the most common, and my personal favorite. They only cost a bit more than single shaft models, and they're well worth it. In some situations a one-piece is a hassle. When rolling a kayak on a cart into a remote lake, the paddle will stick out and catch trees, brush and assorted obstacles that will try your patience, whereas a two-piece can easily be stored in the cockpit or inside a hatch. There are also multipiece shafts with four being the ones I regularly see. Most are inexpensive paddles to be kept inside the kayak in case they are needed. You might have either lost or broken your paddle and having a spare could come in handy.

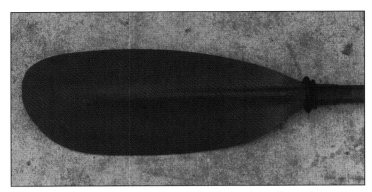

The typical recreational paddle blade is the size and style the author recommends.

However, at least one company that I know of makes a high end multi that's all graphite. It's terrific for travel. Shafts are also available either straight or bent. Both are as the names imply. Bent shafts are great because they are more ergonomic. They are easier on the connective tissue of the body, as the position they put you in reduces the stress placed upon the paddler. They are available in either aluminum or composite.

Blades

Blades come in a variety of materials and styles. The less expensive paddles have plastic blades. They do a good job and can handle lots of abuse. The negative is that plastic has flexibility that reduces its power generation. Better paddles have composite blades. Many are strong and durable with less flex and better power transmission. Materials used are fiberglass, carbon or a combination of all materials. Carbon is the lightest and significantly reduces the swing weight of the paddle. It makes the paddle less fatiguing. Wooden shaft paddles usually have wood blades.

Another consideration is paddle shape and volume. Some paddles used by fishermen have massive symmetric blades. This means that the blade is the same no matter which way you hold the paddle. A bigger blade is better for shorter paddling where you may encounter situations where you need more power - such as when you need to move the kayak quickly in short bursts. The surf is the best example of this. You don't want to dawdle in the waves. This is especially important coming in, as the waves are moving faster than you can. So, the more speed you can generate the better. Asymmetric blades have a top and a bottom, and are more efficient. For the majority of

anglers a large touring blade is the best choice. It has a good combination of power and efficiency.

Length

This is measured from tip to tip and is done so in centimeters. There are 2.54 centimeters per inch. So 10 centimeters is just over 4 inches. The length to choose varies and is determined by a few factors - the width of the kayak, the reach of the paddler and personal preference. The most popular lengths are between 220 and 240. If you are buying a very wide kayak a 240 works better. If you're tall you will also prefer a longer paddle, as you're farther from the water and the shorter the paddle the sharper the angle. A paddle a bit too long isn't a problem, but one that is too short is. If it's too short you will keep whacking your knuckles on the gunwales of the kayak.

Where you sit in a kayak is obviously going to affect this too, as a high seat position puts you farther from the water. If you're in tight areas all the time then a shorter paddle would be beneficial, as it will be easier to fit through places. It has been my experience that a 230-centimeter paddle is the best choice for most people and kayak models. It's hard to go wrong with this size.

Blade Position

Paddles function best when put in a feathered configuration. Feathering means the blades are not on the same plane. This translates into your needing to rotate the paddle to properly get purchase in the water by the blade. At first it's awkward and most beginners don't like it. They don't want to paddle this way, however if you spend your first day doing it this way you won't want to paddle any other way. It's a more efficient stroke so it's going to be less fatiguing. You generate more power and as your blade is being moved forward it parallels the water, cutting through the air without creating resistance.

Conversely if the blade isn't feathered, every time you push the paddle forward you are actually slightly reducing the forward movement of the kayak. The paddle blade works as a small sail and over time the negative effects accumulate into a significant loss of distance and you end up using more energy to travel less distance.

Most paddles will have three positions into which you can put the blades. They are: neutral, feathered left and feathered right. The right and left depend upon your dominant side and which hand will rotate and which will remain on the paddle. Often one side of the shaft is flattened. This is deliberate as it gives the dominant hand a better grip.

Drip Cups

These are small circular disks at the end of the paddle shaft. Their function is to stop water dripping from the paddle blades down to your hands. They work and are highly recommended. Water constantly dripping on your hands is annoying and it can be cold.

Canoe Paddle

A canoe paddle is a single paddle designed for use with a canoe; however they have a place in kayak fishing. If you do a lot of fishing where you have to paddle small creeks and rivers, often the conventional two-bladed kayak paddle will be too long and you will get hung up. Over the years, I've found that in mangrove tunnels I easily spend half my time using a half paddle. You can take apart a two-piece paddle but a canoe paddle is more comfortable if you're going to use it a lot. I picked up a telescoping canoe paddle that doesn't take up much room and it's especially nice to have when I need to maneuver in a tight place with a Mirage kayak. The telescoping feature allows me to size its length to what I need.

So which paddle should you get? I recommend the best one you can afford. As with anything there is a point of diminishing returns. I like a carbon paddle that is as light as possible, within reason. I say within reason because, like with most things, the absolute best is very expensive. The difference between a $200 and $500 paddle isn't a lot (other than money) and as fishermen we're probably not going to notice much if any difference. Kayak fishing is an accessory-intensive sport and the difference can be better spent on other gear. Most serious kayak fishermen who have been at it a while eventually get a carbon fiber paddle. If you're going to fish from a kayak a lot, you might as well buy one from the start.

I've deliberately not discussed paddle strokes or technique. There exists a multitude of sources on

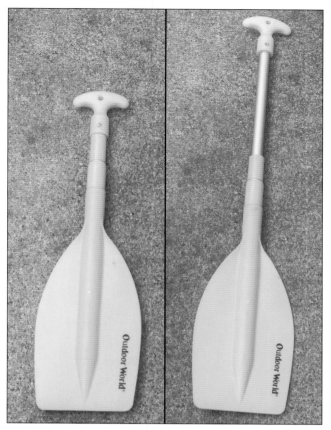

A collapsible canoe paddle is very handy. Used fully extended it's great as a paddle. Closed it works well with Hobie mirage kayaks to back up and maneuver.

how to paddle. You can pick up a book, video or do a search on the Internet and find a lot of information.

Seats and Cushions

As mentioned, even though not absolutely essential, a seat is nonetheless very important. Seats provide support and comfort. Most SIKs have an integrated seat while most SOTs don't. There are a few exceptions. At first the WS Tarpons were alone with offering an integrated seat, but now there are several manufacturers who have included them in their designs. There are the Manta Rays, Heritage Redfish and Natives, to name those I'm familiar with. All three of these come out of the same facility. Hobie Mirages require a specialized seat available only from Hobie. Even though the mirage seat comes out and attaches easily, you can't buy a mirage kayak without a seat and you wouldn't want to. The mirage seat has a pair of pegs on the bottom that are integral to the function of the system. Without the pegs the seat would slide and using one's legs for propulsion would not work.

My first kayak came with a back band and the company marketed their kayaks with them. It took years until they finally started offering a comfortable seat. The seat that comes with one major company's kayaks isn't much of a seat. I teasingly call it a butt bucket. I believe they decided to offer a seat because one of their top competitors had an integrated seat and this leveled the playing field from a marketing perspective.

I found myself stuck using one for an entire week while in the Turks and Caicos Islands. It wasn't much better than not having a seat at all, as it provided little support. It was comparable to a back band, which I find awful. One thing you have to consider is that fishermen use kayaks differently than many others in the sport of kayaking. When paddling a kayak, most aficionados will lean slightly forward, so they are not pressed against a seat back. Since they are going to paddle most of the time, it's not nearly as noticeable. While fishing we spend a great deal of time not propelling the kayak, but fishing instead. We use seats more like a car seat or one in our homes. We spend a lot of time leaning against them and we need support.

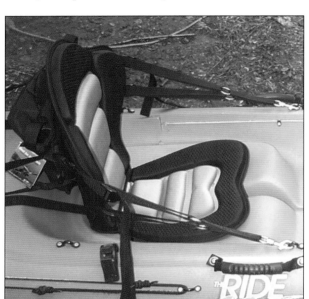

This GTS seat was a vast improvement over the stock seat of this rental WS Ride. It made the long days on the water in Alaska much more comfortable.

I cannot overemphasize the importance of a good seat. Oftentimes seats will determine how long you can stay out on the water. They run the gambit from butt buckets to models with built-in lumbar supports. Like anything, you get what you pay for. Which seat is best for you is a matter of personal choice. There are factors like your height, weight and age. Let's face it, kids and younger anglers can use almost anything but the older and heavier you are the more support you will want. If you're of average height or tall, you will most likely find a high back the best. Shorter folks might find a tall seat doesn't work for them.

You're going to spend a lot of time sitting in a kayak

so get the best you can afford. One of the top seats on the market is the GTS from Surf to Summit. I've had one since they came out and when using a paddle kayak it's my choice. There is a knockoff of the GTS, and for the money it is excellent, but I've found that after using the seat for a while it broke down in the small of the back area. The same thing happened with my previous STS regular seat. It actually buckled, creating a crease, and didn't provide the support I wanted anymore. So while the GTS costs substantially more I don't believe it will ever break down like the knockoff or any other model. Again, a quality product will last.

The new Hobie Mirage seat has a built-in lumbar support and I love it. Before the company produced the new seat I was having a rough time getting comfortable in the Hobies. I tried installing the pegs in several seats including the GTS, but none of them worked for me in the Hobies. The wraparound feature interfered with the pedaling motion and I would get irritated in the oblique area of my torso.

Some seats have built-in rod holders or units that detach containing holders. I call these fishing seats. My first seat was of this genre and I highly recommend them. By possessing one you can fish a new kayak before doing any customizing. Besides providing rod storage, they allow you to troll. I used mine several days before I decided where I wanted to mount permanent rod holders.

These are also great to bring along while traveling, as rental kayaks often have inferior seats and no rod holders. On a trip to Puerto Rico several years back, Joey and I brought our fishing seats. Besides a place to store and troll rods, the seats also had pouches for storing lures. The Ocean Kayak Malibu Twos available at one of the resorts came without any hatches or back bands. As expected, these rental kayaks weren't in the best of shape. Having our own seats was great. They provided great support, the ability to troll and the rear pouch gave us a place for loose gear we didn't want free on the deck of the kayak.

Seats consist of a few basic parts. There is the actual seat that consists of the back and the bottom. The back provides the support and the bottom provides comfort. Most bottoms aren't generally comfortable, but lately manufacturers have tackled this with built-in butt pads. Very early on I started using a cushion. At first I used an air pillow. It's amazing what a $7 accessory can do for comfort. I've since graduated to a more sophisticated unit that utilizes both foam and air. There are also pads with gel in them. I highly recommend using a cushion. I won't go out on the water without one, whether close to home or when traveling. Some come with Velcro kits and I recommend using them so the cushion doesn't blow away or get misplaced.

Seats attach to the kayak via straps. Most have two that connect forward of the seating area. They are attached to the upper part of the seat back. In the rear is a pair of straps that usually connects to deck loops on each side of the kayak. The straps have adjustments, which allow you to position it in a particular spot on the kayak and to change the angle of the seat back. While fishing, most anglers will want the seat more angled. While in motion you will want it more vertical which facilitates better paddling. Most use brass clips for attachment but Ocean Kayak used to use plastic connectors and if you have one of these models you need a seat that has the plastic on it. I used to remove them and install brass or use an adapter kit so I could use the same seat for both kayaks. On some kayaks I removed the plastic and installed deck loops.

Fishing from a kayak, while active, is much more passive than kayaking. Your ability to spend a lot of time on the water is directly related to how comfortable you are. Some folks can sit in anything, others can't. Make sure the seat you're planning on using works for you and if necessary go to a shop and sit in a bunch of them. If the shop has demo models, then see if they will lend or rent you seats so you can try them.

Clothing

What you wear can vary from inconsequential to something that will save your life. You need to realize kayak fishing is a sport that can put you in places and circumstances where outside assistance might be unavailable. You could be on your own and it's best to always think this way. Always prepare for the unexpected. The old adage, "plan for the worst and hope for the best", should be your guide. Have you noticed that weather seems to be more volatile these days? On one recent June day the Weather Channel had a story of 8-plus inches of rain in Roscoe, New York and 3-inch diameter hail in Minnesota. The hail was so deep that from a distance it looked like snow. The report on the Roscoe rain is it happened very quickly and most people had no warning. The forecast was for scattered thunderstorms, which is very common in many places in June. In warm climates, or in the summer, it's usually more important to protect oneself from the sun, than worry about anything else; however stuff happens.

We use clothing for comfort and protection and dress for the expected temperatures. However, kayak fishing isn't only practiced on warm summer days when the water temperature is near 80 degrees. In our regular activities when one decides what to wear for the day, you consider what the anticipated weather and air temperature are going to be. That's because people are land animals and that's where we spend our time. This is where the mistake is made. Kayak fishing is a water sport and because of this you need to dress for the water temperature, not the air. Should something go wrong and you end up in the water not properly prepared, it can be life threatening.

Cold Water Wear

In some parts of the country water temperatures vary significantly with the seasons. What one chooses to wear can be vitally important. In the Northeast I've heard so many times from folks considering entering the sport that they are going to wait until spring to get their first kayak to take advantage of the warmth. The air may be getting warmer but the water will be at its coldest. Spring officially starts in late March and the water temperatures will be near seasonal lows. In northern parts of the U.S. the water doesn't warm sufficiently to not require protective gear until July! In March, water temps around the New York City area are going to be in the 40s. After a long winter anglers are ready to hit the water and catch some fish. There is some great fishing available but you cannot go early season kayak fishing without being properly attired. Don't let warm, sunny days lull you into a false sense of security. The coldest water of the year is at hand and if you're unprepared it could end up being the last thing you ever do. More so than any other season, you need to recognize springtime's water temps. The water is so cold, if you should end up in it, you will only have seconds before your muscles won't respond. You must strongly err on the side of caution. I have a saying, "If in doubt, don't". It's a long season so don't be in a hurry. Pick your days wisely. This isn't the time of year to be launching through the surf and fishing the ocean unless you know what you're doing and are properly attired. Avoid areas with strong currents. If you are new to the sport be especially cautious. The back bays and estuaries are the place to be in the salt and in the fresh avoid places with current. Even though you take every precaution you must be dressed for immersion. Simply put, you have to be prepared to end up in the water. Your survival might depend upon it. If you are sufficiently concerned, I have made my point, because this must be taken seriously. Cold water is life threatening and to ignore this is asking for disaster.

Instead, you may consider waiting until things warm up and become a bit safer. There are many who

do just that; however there is some great fishing available for the properly prepared. I'm not going to tell you how to dress. I'll cover the topic and provide you with information so you can make a decision that's best for you.

When dealing with cold to cool water temps, the best and safest thing to wear would be a one-piece, breathable, waterproof dry suit. This is the closest thing to the ideal setup for cold water kayaking. You'll be sealed from the neck down. Until recently a dry suit cost as much as a kayak but there are now manufacturers who offer suits for under $500. If you're going to do a lot of cold weather fishing a dry suit is the best outer layer you can wear and deserves serious consideration. It does exactly what you want an outer layer to do - keep you dry. Other great features are that it's easier to put on and take off than a dry top and models are available with a relief zipper. I don't know about you, but when I'm active I drink fluids and in cold weather nature calls. The relief zipper is a fantastic feature and well worth the additional dollars for me.

Each of us has to weigh the merits of each article of clothing we put on and

This retail display shows a great selection of cold weather wear perfectly suited for kayak anglers.

acknowledge that this is a risk sport. Many of us tackle this important subject by wearing a system of clothing that consists of underlying insulating layers and an outer garment(s) that keeps us dry. Some people wear wetsuits as a first layer and then wear outer layers that I'll describe a bit later.

Should you decide to go the wetsuit route I recommend that you get one that allows for good movement. I would think suits made for surfing will do nicely. The reason I used the word "think" is that I don't use wetsuits and don't consider them the best choice for my needs. In some regions their use is more widespread. They are a remnant piece of gear from other sports, mainly surfing and windsurfing, and do not apply well to the needs of the kayak fisherman.

One reason is in the clue derived from the name itself, as the operative word in wetsuits is "wet". To function properly they're designed to trap a layer of water between you and the suit. Your body heats this layer of water providing additional insulation. The problem, besides being wet, is the water seeps out and you have to replenish it. That's fine if you're surfing, because you're constantly getting in and out of the water, but with kayak fishing there isn't any reason to get wet in the first place. Unlike sports where you will spend a lot of time immersed in the water, like surfing, wind surfing, snorkeling and diving, kayak fishing is usually done dry, or close to it. I don't like getting wet so I don't use a wet suit. I like dry systems for the most part until the water is warm enough to forego protective wear. You're always going to be better off being dry as opposed to being wet.

I suggest you consider items that are versatile. This way you have options and can adjust to what nature brings forth. Weather can change quickly any time of year, but especially early in the season. I will detail what I've worn for many years and it's worked for many others as well. We'll work from the skin outward.

You want a layer next to the skin that is comfortable and can wick away moisture while also providing insulation and freedom of movement. Kayak fishing is a form of exercise and you will sweat. Moisture, if it's allowed to accumulate next to the skin, could cause you to become chilled when you stop and fish. Depending upon the temps, that chilling could lead to more severe things such as hypothermia.

There are many fabrics to consider but by far the

Dry Suits are great for comfort and are the best thing to wear for tough conditions, such as the author's recent trip to Alaska.

best base layer I have found is micro fleece. Many companies make it and I've mostly used a product called Mysterioso™. It's a high tech clothing system that is simply amazing. Everyone I know who uses it feels the same way. For this application I wear it like long underwear. It can also be used as a light wetsuit, as it insulates when wet. I find when my base layer of Mysterioso isn't enough; some fleece or a Mysterioso short sleeve over it is just the ticket. Check out flea markets or warehouse stores for fleece, as you can get both bottoms and tops at great prices.

I feel very strongly that the outer layer needs to be waterproof and breathable. It also needs to keep water from getting in should you end up dumping. You don't want to get wet. As stated above, the best thing you can wear is a one-piece dry suit and if you're going to be spending a lot of time fishing when the water is cold, it should get serious consideration.

I actually prefer what is referred to as a semi-dry suit. The semi-dry designation is because the neck is neoprene rather than latex rubber. The neoprene when submerged might let some water into the suit whereas latex won't. I don't plan on diving in the suit and I find the latex uncomfortable. Also if I'm wearing a PFD, which I always will in such situations, then my head can't end up under water. Another feature I like about the semi-dry is its light weight. The fabric is thinner so I can stay comfortable in warmer temperatures by controlling my under layers. The lightness of the semi-dry is welcome because air temps often surpass those of the water. It's very common to have 50-degree water with air that's in the 70s.

After a dry suit the next best setup is essentially a two-piece dry system. I use this system a lot; it provides a very high level of protection and a great degree of versatility. My primary objective is to stay out of the water and keep dry. Should I happen to end up in the water, I want to get out as soon as possible and continue to remain dry. Kayak fishing is still a relatively minor sport and a great deal of its participation is in warm or temperate environments where this discussion isn't necessary. As it grows in popularity there is going to be more participation in colder climes. Eventually the sport will have its own specific clothing. Until that day comes we must borrow from similar sports.

The closest sport to kayak fishing is whitewater kayaking. It has clothing designed for extreme environments and dealing with cold water, including total immersion. Whitewater kayaking is more extreme and much more dangerous than what kayak fishermen do and they've been doing it longer than we have. In whitewater there are tops made specifically for the sport. Participants are often upside down with their upper torso fully immersed and the system keeps them dry.

These tops are called dry tops. They are essentially the top half of a dry suit and designed to prevent water from entering both the person and the kayak. They consist of wrist, neck and waist closures that keep water out. These closures consist of latex, neoprene or both and often Velcro is used as the outer, secondary closure. The waist is a two-part system consisting of an inner sleeve and then an outer closure system. The best ones have an elastic and Velcro pull system that cinch the outer layer over the skirt of the kayak. The tops keep water out of the kayaks and do a terrific job. A kayak full of water could be disastrous for a whitewater paddler.

Dry tops are designed for SIKs to be used in conjunction with a skirt. Most people who fish are using SOTs for fishing. A skirt is a non-functional accessory with a SOT, however for those anglers who are using SIKs, it's an important feature for ocean and fishing rivers of class II or higher. So using a dry top with a SIK is obvious, as it was designed for just this purpose. For the angler who uses a SOT we can use the technology to our advantage in a system. There are a few different pant options one can employ with these dry tops. There are specific waterproof/breathable pants made for whitewater kayaking with ter-

rific ankle and waist closures. For the feet you can use waterproof socks and kayak boots. Instead of kayak pants I use breathable waist-high waders. That's right, I did say waders. I've been using waders for years in conjunction with dry tops.

There is a lot of misunderstanding within the kayaking community with respect to the use of waders. One thing I often hear is that waders full of water will pull you to the bottom. This just isn't true. A few years back ESPN2 did a piece on waders. They had a gent hop in the water with all types of waders. He floated even with the waders full of water. More recently, Jim Sammons did the same experiment in a pool. He came up with the same results and in a recent discussion with Jim he shared with me that he really likes waders and staying dry and wished he'd been using them a lot sooner.

The reason you don't sink if the waders do fill with water is the specific gravity of water, whether inside or outside the waders, has exactly the same properties. The laws of physics don't miraculously change because the water is inside rather than outside the waders. What waders full of water will do is make it challenging to get back into the kayak.

So, our goal remains to keep the water out. Remember earlier I said I like to stay dry. That's why I would not wear waders without a proper top and you shouldn't either. To do so is at the very least asking to get wet and it can be disastrous. So, *please don't wear waders in a kayak without a proper top that will keep water out!* A wading jacket, commonly used in

A two-part waist wader system utilizes a whitewater dry top. **(left)** The inner sleeve is tucked in and the belt of the waist-high wader is secured. **(right)** The dry top is then secured over top of the belt.

fishing, is not a proper top. It lacks proper waist and neck closures.

There are a couple of reasons why waders are so popular in the Northeast. The majority of people joining the sport are surf fishermen. They already own and are familiar with waders. There is a lot of shallow water and kayaks are often used as access vessels. They are a means of transport to places where the angler gets out of the kayak and fishes on foot while wading. Wading is a very effective technique. Wading in cold water is better if you stay dry and nothing wades better than waders; after all that's what they were designed to do. The second reason is Joey and me. While not the first kayak fishermen in the New York metro area, we were the first to post regularly about our excursions - Joey on *Noreast* and me on *Stripersonline*. We met early on and I turned Joey onto the wader/dry top attire. Between the two of us we introduced a lot of people to the sport who adopted the two-piece system and they in turn introduced others. It was a cascading effect, much more so than in other regions where there were a lot of people sharing the sport.

Waders come in both chest and waist-high versions. As the names imply, chest-high waders come up to the chest and waist-highs fit like pants. Chest-highs dominate the wader world, which makes sense since they offer more versatility while wading, as they allow the user to wade deeper. Waist highs are much harder to find. Waders come either with stocking feet or built-in boots. For kayak fishing I prefer the stocking foot but if I'm doing a lot of fishing in the surf, the boot feet are better. The stocking feet allow the use of a lot of different shoes/boots and depending upon the situation I can use anything from oversized sneakers to a variety of sophisticated boots and sandals. Some even have interchangeable soles that can be switched from felt, carbide spikes or regular soles. No matter which boot is used over the stocking foot, debris can enter the boot. I don't find this a problem except when dealing with sandy areas such as the surf or places with a lot of current or tidal flow, where the boots have a tendency to collect sand. I still prefer stocking foot waders because I have lots of choices in boots. The boots are smaller than the boot foot, which in some kayaks becomes important, as room can be limited.

Even though chest-high waders are much more common I prefer waist-highs for kayak fishing. The ones I wear have built-in neoprene socks and a belted waist. The inner sleeve of the dry top gets tucked into the pants, just like I'd tuck a shirt into a pair of jeans. Next the outer closure system goes over the waist.

Another option is to use chest-high breathable waders. They're not quite as good as waist-highs mentioned above because they only offer a single seal mechanism for the waist, however many fishermen already own a set. I know fishermen who use them the same way as the waist-highs by changing their approach. They remove the shoulder straps and roll the waders down to the waist and tuck in the top. It works just like the waist-high system and since most anglers already own a set of chest-highs, why not use what you already have? The first two bottoms provide the security of a double system. Stocking foot waders are preferred for this, as the boots are then a separate item providing a snugger fit. Depending on the environment I plan on fishing, I can then choose from a few different pairs of kayak and flats boots.

You can use chest waders without rolling them down, as you will get good protection using them with a top. Keep in mind that you won't be able to tuck the inner sleeve into the chest-highs unless you roll them down. When using a dry top with chest-highs I use a wading belt over the inner sleeve above where the closure system of the outer sleeve is secured. This provides a good seal.

Earlier I said to use a proper top with waders. In some situations I use a splash top instead of a dry top. A splash top, also referred to as a semi-dry top, is the next level of top below a full-fledged dry top. The ones I like have good waist and wrist seals, similar to the better dry tops, but not nearly as good a neck seal. That's OK when used with a personal flotation device (PFD) because again it will keep your head above water. I've used chest-highs for years with splash tops in moderate weather and conditions. I tested them in the water and for the time that I've spent in the water they've kept me dry. However, I don't recommend a splash top for cold water. They should only be used when conditions are near where you can go without a protective outer layer. In the Northeast, that's usually May to early June. Up north at Cape Cod that would be what I would wear in the summer. A splash top is often used over wetsuits in places where wetsuits are common.

There are some additional items that you either should or must have along. Always wear a PFD.

There are some incredibly comfortable units on the market so there are no excuses not to wear one at all times. They are designed to float you head up, so should you wind up in the water your head will remain above it. This also helps prevent any water entering through the neck.

Speaking of heads, we lose the majority of our heat through them. There are many options for keeping one's head warm in chilly conditions. The best headwear on the market is the Aquaskinz™. This is a very serious unit. At the very least you should have a hat made from a material that will keep your head warm when wet - fleece or wool.

Also have a pair or two of gloves along. There are many manufacturers of good gloves. Many years ago, 'docjohn' recommended a pair of Stearns neoprene and I've still got them. I also like Sealskinz, and the pair of Warmers I have. If it's warm enough that you don't need them, keep a set handy just in case.

It's a good idea to carry a dry bag with spare undergarments. This way if you're a bit chilled you can add a layer or have somewhere dry to put stuff you need to take off. Now you should have a better idea of how to outfit yourself for cold water.

Warm Weather Wear

Though I am repeating myself, I cannot overemphasize that weather is fickle. It's best to be prepared regardless of the season. Cold-water temps are the most life-threatening element but are not the only threats. There are other scenarios that can either make you uncomfortable or much worse. It's a good idea to be prepared for rain, which can be a relief; a nuisance or it can be much more.

Most kayaks have plenty of storage so it's easy to bring along additional gear just in case. I learned this lesson one July in Florida when I exhibited the early stages of hypothermia. You read that correctly, I was in early hypothermia in Florida in July. Joey and I were fishing the Gulf Coast of Florida and the temps were in the 90s. We got caught in some very strong thunderstorms while out on the water and we didn't want to risk paddling back to the mainland until they let up. Being struck by lightning would have put a real damper on the trip. We ended up taking refuge on an island in the jungle, wearing t-shirts and shorts. We got soaked. The down drafting of the storms really cooled things off; we were losing body heat quickly and were so cold our teeth started chattering.

Then I had an idea to use our PFDs as vests. They helped slow down our heat loss but we were losing core temperature and it couldn't continue much longer without more serious consequences. We took advantage of a small break in the weather and made a mad dash back to the mainland. Just as we got back the weather got even worse and didn't break for several hours. I don't want to think about if I had to spend another four or five hours on that island. Now, no matter where I am I take along a layer of insulating clothing and a packable waterproof breathable jacket and pants. The above scenario won't happen again.

Another mistake I made on the Florida excursion, besides not having warm back-ups, was wearing clothing made out of cotton, which doesn't insulate when wet or dry quickly. Cotton is a lousy material when it gets wet. I still wear cotton t-shirts when it's warm but I bring along better fabrics in case conditions change. My shorts are usually a fast dry material. Thunderstorms can have a tremendous cooling effect, and as I discussed earlier, it seems that weather has become more bizarre and unpredictable in recent years. One can easily be caught miles and hours from help and there isn't any substitute for being prepared. I keep the additional clothing below deck in a dry bag. Always take it along with your safety gear in the kayak.

Sun exposure can lead to melanomas and dermatologists recommend covering up as much as possible. Most guides in tropical areas wear flats wear. They consist of fast drying materials of long pants and long sleeved shirts. The pants are usually convertible to shorts via zippers on the legs. The shirts have straps, so should you decide to roll the sleeves up, they will stay put. The shirts are also vented to help with cooling. The other benefit of long pants and sleeves is should you encounter bugs there is much less exposed skin for them to bite.

In Between

Sometimes it's too warm for cold weather wear but not warm enough for my normal hot weather clothing. I've tried a bunch of stuff and combinations and find myself wearing wetsuit or Mysterioso shorts and a fast dry top. Sometimes I'll wear a semi-dry top over the shirt. Although I prefer being dry, I find this works very well.

There is a lot of diversity in what's being worn. I've

spoken with anglers who wear paddling pants and tops. Each region has different climactic conditions and kayak fishermen in those areas tackle them differently. It's best to get on the Internet and ask on the forums within that region as to what's being worn.

Footwear

Kayak fishing takes place in lots of environments. When launching from a sandy beach and fishing the ocean, nothing more than bare feet is required. Conversely, wading flats with oyster bars present will destroy your feet if not properly protected, hence the need for some serious footwear. If it's rocky, and they're wet and slippery, traction might be the most important feature I want, either boots with spikes or an add-on system like Korker™ sandals.

When wearing boots over wader booties, I find I have to go up one to two sizes. The exception is wader-specific boots, which are designed and sized for wearing over booties. I have several pieces of footwear I use: Crocs, sandals, heavy sandals with closed toes, rugged water shoes, kayak and flats boots and wading boots. All have their place in my arsenal. When I first started fishing the Everglades I wore heavy dive booties, and destroyed them in short order. Then I tried a pair of Crocs but sharp oyster shells go right through them. Next I used the heavy, closed-toe sandals that are best exemplified by the offerings from Keen. However, every now and then I'd get stabbed in the heel. Some of these injuries were enough to keep me off the water for a couple of days. I finally settled on wearing wader boots when I intend to do a lot of wading. They fully protect my feet so I can wade and not worry about injury. If I don't plan on getting out but might, I wear rugged water shoes.

Again, it all comes down to what you need. Sitting in a kayak doesn't require much but if or when using it to access other environments, then think about what you're going to do and wear something appropriate. If unsure, bring a second pair along, just in case. I do this a lot in the Everglades. I'll wear my

(left) Just a few of the shoes the author utilizes for kayak fishing. (above) A broad-brimmed hat is the right choice for bright sun and the tropics.

closed-toe sandals but have the wader boots in the front hatch.

I remember one time fishing western Long Island Sound when we hopped off onto one of the many islets. I climbed to the top of one and when I decided to hop back into the yak, I slipped and slid down the entire face. I was lucky to land on a small sand beach. Now I bring a set of Korkers along if I'm fishing an area like that.

Headwear

Hats offer great protection from the sun. I usually wear some type of ball cap but if the sun is very intense I'll opt for a broad-brimmed one. Besides protection from the sun in warmer weather they also provide protection from insects.

Bug Wear

Insects can be either a nuisance or so bad that they will prevent you from fishing. Usually repellent is the answer but one of the most annoying bugs, the no-see-um, laughs at everything I've tried. The answer is a bug shirt or jacket. They're designed to completely seal you in so the bugs can't get at you. My favorite is the Original Bug Shirt. It folds up into its pouch and completely covers you from the waist up, excluding the hands. I used mine for fishing at night in the Everglades. I would fish the Barron River for snook, tarpon and jacks. I was able to wear my glasses underneath and still see well enough to fish. It enabled me to handle fishing when I wouldn't have been on the water otherwise. When the no-see-ums are out it's my salvation.

There is also bug wear with built-in repellent. They work great for mosquitoes and there are hats, kerchiefs, shirts and pants available. The ones with the built-in repellent are usually good for 25 or more washings. Technology keeps getting better and I'm sure this will increase. There are also shirts and jackets that you treat with repellent.

Rod Holders

To fish from a kayak, you're going to need a rod. Although you can effectively fish from a kayak without rod holders, they make fishing so much easier and make the kayak more versatile. Rod holders are the single most important accessories that will turn a kayak from a recreational vessel into a dedicated fishing craft. Because of this they are the first items that really make a big difference in how you're going to fish.

Rod holders serve two basic functions. They store the rods you take with you and they allow you to troll. Both are important functions. Some fishermen only use one rod and the ability to bring multiple rods isn't important, however most serious kayak fishermen tend to bring two or more outfits with them. I've seen as many as half a dozen on one kayak. However you do so, it's best to keep extra rods securely out of the way while you're fishing.

Oftentimes the place where you launch the kayak isn't close to where you plan on fishing. You may be covering some distance and it's a smart idea to troll while traveling to your intended destination. If you don't troll, you're wasting water, as there might be fish you could have caught. The kayak's speed is always perfect for trolling. No matter what the water depth, the stealth of a kayak makes trolling an effective technique. Even in shallow water, dragging a lure, live bait or fly behind the kayak is deadly. There are many times when you will discover more effective water while on your way to where you intended to fish. Also some techniques are much more effective when you troll.

A rod holder's function is to hold a rod, just like its name suggests. There are three types of fishing rods: conventional, spin and fly. Some holders are specific to each type of outfit. Generally a unit that will hold a spin rod will also hold a conventional outfit. Fly rods usually need a specific unit, especially ones that don't have a fighting butt (smaller freshwater models).

There are a few types of rod holders. The first type I used was incorporated as part of the seat. These seats are called fishing seats for that reason. Next there are permanent holders that are either molded into or installed in the kayak. They can be removed but will leave large holes, which are difficult to fix. These permanent holders are the same styles found on the gunwales of boats. They are flush to the kayak, hence the name, flush-mounted rod holders. The last types are units, which are attached to the kayak on the surface and can be detached. Let's look at each type more closely.

Fishing Seats

A fishing seat is nice to have for a lot of reasons but its ability to transport a couple of rods is especially valuable. If you purchase a kayak with a fishing seat you can immediately effectively fish from the kayak, and this includes trolling. What's nice is they give you time to determine where you'd like to install permanent and/or detachable holders.

Another feature I really like is if you should travel to a resort that has kayaks, you can bring the seat along. This will enable you to fish from the resort kayak much more effectively since it's highly unlikely the resort kayak will have rod holders. A few major seat manufacturers have one or more fishing seats to choose from.

The holders in the seat will hold all three styles of rods and you can troll both spin and conventional rods from them. I don't recommend trolling a fly rod from one unless the rod has a very long butt. Once you've made a decision on which regular holders you're going to mount, the seat holders are great for pliers, lip grippers and other tools when not holding rods.

Flush Mounts

These come in two styles, angled or straight. The angled is by far the most popular. They are mostly available as an aftermarket product and require installation, but some kayaks come with them molded into the kayak. Most of the flush mounts you find in kayaks are angled and are behind the seat. A couple of models have places to accommodate them up front. Behind the seat they're great for trolling or bringing along an extra rod or two. Up front they are only going to be used for trolling or storing a rod while unhooking a fish.

Straight flush mounts are used much less frequently. They are great when used on kayaks that have a beveled edge along the side up front. In this application they are placed forward of your farthest reach with the paddle. They work very well for trolling when placed here, as you can always see your rod tip to determine if your offering is working properly or has picked up any weed.

Flush mounts require a large hole for installation, so it's important that they are installed in the correct spot. They have to be considered a permanent part of the kayak, since you're not going to remove them. Many companies make angled flush mounts while fewer make the straight type. For use in a kayak, I'd stick to those made of plastic. Metal would be overkill and they're much heavier. The only real difference that I've seen between manufacturers is the size of the flange. That's the part that sits on the kayak and where the fasteners attach it. This only becomes important if you have a curved or limited amount of surface where you can place the holder. The more limited your space, the smaller the flange should be. Cobra has the smallest flange of any holder.

(top) Fishing seats hold two rods and are a good solution. (bottom) Straight flush mount rod holders work very well with a beveled edge.

Detachable

This group consists of the remaining rod holders. There are quite a number of units in this group represented by several manufacturers. We'll discuss each style. As the title of this section states these holders detach from the kayak. They come in a variety of configurations, are very popular and my preferred type of holder for most applications. Some of the manufacturers are Attwood, Berkley, RAM, Roberts, Scotty and Titelock. RAM and Scotty dominate the kayak fishing world. Some companies only have one style and some have a few. They all work similarly and I'm most familiar with RAM and Scotty. All detachable holders keep the rods farther away from the water than a flush mount. This is a nice feature, as it reduces the exposure on the reels.

Attwood, Berkley, Roberts and Scotty (RAM has both two- and three-plane units) operate in two planes, having a vertical and horizontal adjustment.

(above) A retail display showing several types of detachable rod holders and some of the available accessories. (right) The Ram 117, which the author refers to as the "Ram Rod", holds many types of outfits and is extremely versatile.

They consist of a base that is attached to the kayak and an upper part where the rod is held. This upper part is removable and interchangeable within a manufacturer and sometimes even from one brand to another. This is a nice feature. My two favorite Scotty's are the Powerlock for spin and conventional outfits and the fly rod holder when you bring a long wand along.

For transporting a rod the Powerlock works great for any type of rod. It has a ring that literally locks the rod into the kayak. I always have one on my port rear to transport and hold a spare rod. I never have to worry about the rod when it's in this holder because of the locking feature. Scotty has several base styles and extenders available for these units. They range from the standard mount that is raised a bit to flush bases (circular and rectangular) among others with an assortment of extenders.

There are extended tube types that are as the name implies. Both Titelock and RAM make them. I've been using the RAM ball mount units for years. They consist of a ball that is mounted to the kayak and the rod holder tube is attached to the ball. The standard base has a round bottom, but various sized rectangular bases are also available. They all have the same diameter mounting ball and are thus interchangeable amongst all the RAM rod holders. The rod holder attaches via a cam that you tighten. These units have a long tube in which the butt end of the rod is placed. They're very easy to use. They don't have a locking

mechanism to hold the rod so it's advisable to tether the rod, especially if you are where there is a chance of tipping.

My favorite is the RAM-Rod fishing rod holder system. It's a three-part system constructed of brushed aluminum and plastic. Its base, like the tube, is a ball and is attached to the kayak. There is an arm connecting the ball of the base to a ball that's on the business end of the holder. The rod is placed in this third part and is secured with an attached clip. The middle section has a tightening handle you turn.

There are two features that I really like about the RAM-Rod, the first being it will hold conventional, spin and fighting butt style fly rods and allow you to effectively troll all three. Also, due to the dual balls on each end it has an infinite range of adjustment. Whereas all the other units function in the X- and Y-axis, this unit functions in X, Y and Z. This allows the user a myriad of positions and angles and will work with practically any kayak. RAM has recently introduced an assortment of plastic rod holders selling for far less than their brushed aluminum models.

Miscellaneous Rod Holders

There are lots of other rod holders that are used in varying ways. There are plastic tube types or home-made PVC styles. They are commonly used for storage but can be used for trolling, too. I-Fly makes a unit for fly rods and it's a nice way to store fly rods. There are also commercially made PVC holders mounted on a rack. These are often attached to milk crates and tackle boxes for carrying extra rods. Also straight PVC can be attached to both and used for storage and trolling. Lots of fishermen set up a crate as a temporary or permanent means of carrying rods and trolling.

PVC can be used to extend factory rod holders and I use them with Hobie flushes. The Hobie factories flushes aren't deep enough at only six inches to adequately hold a rod. If you use them without modification or tethering your rod, there is a very good chance you will lose it. However, if you take a foot-long piece of PVC and put it in the hole, you will have a very effective rod holder. On the Outback model you can cut out the factory pre-mold and replace it with an aftermarket angled flush mount. The additional three inches of depth cures the problem. The other Hobie fishing models won't accept the aftermarket flush mount, though. Hobie in response to this deficiency now has a tube-style rod holder designed specifically to work in the holder and solves the problem. They call it the Hobie Rod Holder Extender.

Simple as they may seem, leashes are important, if not necessary items for the kayak angler.

An Effective Rod Holder System

Different rod holders work better for different uses. I've found I like certain holders for specific tasks. I tend to set up my own kayaks with a RAM up front. Its versatility allows me to use conventional, spin or a fly rod, depending upon which holder I use. I can troll all but a non-fighting butt fly rod. If the kayak will allow the installation of a flush mount up front I'll put one on each side, but most models won't support this installation without a lot of customization

so I don't bother. I will have an angled flush mount behind the seat on either side. I don't often put rods in them but they're good to have. The one on my starboard side usually has a lip gripper in it. On my port rear you will always find a Scotty Powerlock, the reason being it will transport any type of rod and reel combo. It holds them securely with no chance of loss. When a rod is behind me I don't want to worry about losing it. On my port rear I'll also have at least one RAM ball for a tube. This is to carry a spare rod. I usually like to keep all my spare rods on the port so they don't interfere with casting, as I'm right handed.

Leashes

A leash is a means of keeping an item attached to the kayak. There's a common saying in kayak fishing, "leash it or lose it". Simply put, any item that isn't attached to the kayak, you risk losing. If an item floats it isn't nearly as important, especially if it's large. A large floating object that gets away from you most likely won't get lost, but it can be inconvenient. However, any item that is dropped and sinks often becomes Neptune's property, even in shallow water. I once had a client lose a rod in less than 2 feet of water. We looked for some time and never found it. Everyone was shocked that an outfit could disappear under such a circumstance. There was current, but it was a sand bottom that we could clearly see. Using a leash is a good habit to have.

Paddle Leashes

These are relatively simple items and as the name implies they attach to the paddle and then to the kayak. If you don't have a leash, your paddle can easily get away from you. Should you lose a paddle, the proverbial saying, "up a creek without a paddle", will resonate true. A paddle is your motor and to be without one means paddling with your hands. Having your paddle get away from you has the potential to be

An **alternative** to using a leash on a rod is to do what my buddy Bob does. He uses foam rod floats. That way if he drops a rod in the water it'll float!

a major problem if you're in current or wind. A paddle leash is such an inexpensive item; there isn't any excuse or reason not to have one.

A paddle leash can be as simple as a section of cord, although I prefer a leash that has been designed for the task. Simple leashes start at just a few dollars and some shops include them with kayak packages. There are essentially two types of paddle leashes. One style utilizes a bungee/shock cord and the other is coiled like a telephone cord. Attachment to the paddle is usually via Velcro and the other end has some sort of clip fastening it to the kayak.

The bungee leash is the style most often used by fishermen because it won't interfere with lines, especially fly lines. If you use the long wand this style makes a better choice. The coiled style is commonly called a telephone leash and is more convenient to use because it retracts. It won't interfere with spin or conventional gear, so if you don't fly fish they are highly recommended. Often beginners use a rope but I don't recommend this. When you really need a leash you may need to have some elasticity in the system. Sometimes in dumping a kayak you can create a windmill effect. These forces can turn the paddle into a dangerous object flying through the air. Serious injury can occur. Both the bungee and telephone leashes have elasticity that absorbs the shock and thus defuses the energy and potential problems.

Rod Leashes

Not tethering a rod can be asking for trouble, especially when new to the sport or trying a new environment. You could drop your rod or flip the kayak. I know enough guys who have lost some pretty expensive outfits. A $1,000 fly set-up is not the kind of gift one would enjoy giving to Poseidon. Even veterans lose rods, so use the ounce of prevention a leash provides. Again just like paddle leashes, you can make your own or buy one. Factory units are usually straps or telephone cord. Attachment to the rod is usually via Velcro but other methods work. I like rod leashes with a quick release feature so it is easy to separate the rod when needed. I don't like to cast with a leash attached, especially fly rods, but it's a good idea to use one while trolling from the rod holder in a fishing seat.

I like to attach a brass or plastic snap to the end of leashes. This allows you to quickly attach them to the kayak and remove them just as fast.

Tethers are leashes used for accessories. Accessories vary greatly and so can tethers. In most instances the construction isn't important. It just needs to keep the kayak and the accessory connected to each other. With some items a retractable, high tech gizmo is very convenient. One model I like comes from Gear Keepers. These are designed for diving and constructed of stainless steel cable and plastic and come in a wide array of styles. They're really nice to use on items like pliers, radios, cell phones and the like - items that you want to keep out of the way except when you use them. For some applications a simple cord is all you need. I use cord for items like lip grippers and pliers.

Paddle Holders and Keepers

Paddle holders are exactly that. They hold the paddle on the kayak. Many kayak fishermen, myself included, put their paddle across their laps while fishing. This is fine but there are times when you need the paddle completely out of the way. One situation would be when you're doing a lot of casting, especially with a fly rod, and having the paddle securely out of the way is beneficial. With the paddle stowed you're free to do whatever you want and not be concerned where the paddle is. When landing a fish it's often better to have the paddle secured, especially if the removal of the hooks is a bit complicated.

There are several ways to stow the paddle against the kayak. I saw my first bungee paddle keeper on Porter's Necky Dolphin and thought it was great. Much more user-friendly than the rubber paddle clips I was using at the time, Porter's consisted of a bungee attached to the kayak at two points and a hook. When the bungee is placed over the hook it forms a very broad triangle that holds the paddle against the kayak. When Wilderness Systems released the Tarpon 120, they incorporated bungee keepers into the design.

Many models now come with a bungee paddle keeper system. The bungee-style clips are my favorite. If your kayak has them you're all set and if it doesn't they're easy and inexpensive to add - less than $10 in parts (see the Outfitting chapter). Some people don't want to drill holes in their kayak. There are companies that make paddle keeper systems that attach to deck loops. Surf to Summit's is the one I'm familiar with.

Your other option is paddle clips. There are two styles - plastic ones that I call the Deluxe Paddle Holder, and rubber units. The Deluxe are spring-loaded, plastic clips and are very easy to use. They lock the paddle in place and can also hold a rod or two. They work great, but you have to be careful with them because they stand away from the kayak and can be knocked off with a moderate blow. Because of this I never put them on any of my kayaks. I prefer the rubber clips. There are a few styles but my favorite is a unit designed as a rod holder for party boats. If you're from the west coast you know

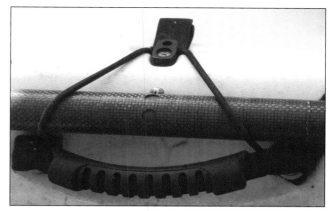

The Tarpon 120 had one of the earliest paddle keepers.

these as cattle boats. They work very well for holding paddles on kayaks and are terrific for keeping a lip gripper handy. The rubber clips are indestructible, which is nice. You don't have to be concerned with how you load or store your kayak, as you can't break them.

Anchoring Devices and Accessories

Anchors do for kayaks what they do for other vessels - hold them in a position. However, that's not always what an angler fishing from a kayak needs. Kayak fishing is diverse; anchors and their variations can serve a lot of different functions. Anchors and their associated devices help us position our kayaks so we can catch more fish. Kayaks are light so it doesn't take much to hold one or for environmental factors to move them. A lot depends on where you plan on anchoring. Some anglers use a ¼ to ½-gallon plastic bottle filled with sand or gravel. This will work for many situations. I use anchors with kayaks in different ways and I discuss this in detail later in the Techniques chapter. Here I'll introduce the equipment.

Anchors
Almost anything can be used as an anchor. For many situations a rock or brick will do. However they aren't very kayak friendly and we have to be able to bring them along conveniently. Also since they're not used often it's best if they're easy to

A few anchors. On the left is a 3-pound folding style. In the center is a 1.5-pound opened. On the right is a 5-pound bar type.

store. I have two basic styles of anchor in my collection of gear - a simple bar-style that weighs five pounds and a grappling, four pronged folding one which weighs 3 pounds. Another style to consider is a mushroom anchor. If you spend a lot of time fishing rocky streams and rivers a small boat mushroom anchor is worth having.

Anchor Trolley

This is a name that's used to describe a trolley or pulley system on the kayak that's used to move the anchor line. It's essentially a glorified clothesline. What it does is allow you to move the anchor from the cockpit to the point of the yak where you wish to position it. Most often you want the anchor out the stern, but not always (more on this in Techniques). It's also used to set up a drift sock.

A simple anchor trolley is used to move either an anchor, stakeout pole, or as in this instance a drift sock to the rear of the kayak.

Buoys

An anchor buoy is handy to have. It can be incorporated in the anchor line. You can then attach the kayak to the anchor line on a quick release. This allows you to quickly unhook from the anchor to fight a big fish. The buoy gives a visual of where your anchor is when it's time to retrieve it. A plastic bottle also works especially small, brightly colored detergent bottles. You can also buy brightly colored buoys or floats. I've seen sections of pool noodles used. Anything that floats and can be seen will do.

Stakeout Pole

This is an item that I never used while fishing my home waters in the NY Metro area but discovered while fishing Florida. It's a tremendous tool whenever fishing shallow water. From Texas on up the eastern seaboard, there's an abundance of inside shallow water fishing generally referred to as flats fishing; however it isn't all flats. What these waters have in common is they're shallow. A stakeout pole is merely a pole that gets jammed into the bottom and by some means is connected to the kayak. Most anglers who use SOT kayaks run the pole down through a scupper hole. Another way of using it

when in a kayak without scuppers or a kayak where the scuppers aren't convenient is to hook it to an anchor trolley. There are fancy manufactured poles or you can make your own. My first was an old ski pole with the basket and handle removed. Golf shafts with the club removed work fine. Sometimes a longer pole is needed. I picked up a piece of aluminum conduit from Home Depot and made my own. I cut the one end to a point and attached some cord for hooking to the trolley. It works great.

Drift Sock

I refer to this item as a drift sock but it's also commonly called a sea anchor. What it does is slow down a vessel in wind. It's basically a parachute. Instead of filling with air to slow down an object, it uses water. As the wind pushes the kayak, the sock digs into the water and slows it. I have a section of bungee on the end of mine. It provides a bit of shock absorption to cushion wave action. I attach it to the anchor trolley and toggle it to the stern of the kayak.

Hatches

Kayaks are vessels and just like boats most of the storage is below deck. Hatches give access to the interior of the kayak. There are several types of hatches and different manufacturers have varying ways in which they offer them. It all depends upon the manufacturer and model you choose. You're either going to have no choice, some choice or a lot of choice. Hatches are either integral to the design and come with the kayak or there is space specifically designed for their addition.

The Ocean Kayak Scuppers were one of the first kayaks used in mass by fishermen and they came with the front hatch as part of the kayak. Cobra was another early popular kayak company used by fishermen. They offered the opposite concept - Cobras could be purchased absent of any hatches or in several combinations.

My first Cobra was an Explorer. I purchased it with a 10-inch center hatch with a bucket and I really liked that hatch. The bucket was great for keeping a variety of gear and lifted out, providing interior access.

I rigged an internal pulley system (see installation section of book) that allowed me to clip all sorts of accessories to it and they were easy to retrieve. I could have added a 10-inch round or a small rectangular hatch up front but opted for an 'A' hatch, which opened up a cavernous area in the bow that allowed me to take a lot of gear along. I could store rods inside the kayak, which wasn't possible in either my first kayak or the Explorer without the hatch. The 'A' hatch wasn't accessible while on the water, as the hatch had several 'T' latches and I couldn't safely reach the forward 'T's. Whenever I got out of the kayak, I could get gear from it, so it didn't present too much of an issue except while in the ocean. When fishing the ocean with a buddy, I'd enlist his help in retrieving rods.

I also started fishing a Cobra Tourer soon after that, and in addition to sharing the bow and center hatches of the Explorer, it had a space behind the tank well for another 10-inch round. Why would you want to access a bow hatch? Rod storage is the most common reason. A large hatch you can access while on the water gives you the ability to leave your rods fully rigged and out of harm's way should you dump while launching or returning through the surf.

The first kayak I owned that allowed me to store fully rigged rods and retrieve them unassisted was a Tarpon 16. The 16 was the predecessor to the 160, the main difference being the 16 had the same large hatch in the rear as it had up front instead of the 160's tank well. It was great for storing rods and items I didn't need much, but the 16 didn't provide storage for readily accessible gear. There was only a small hatch in the center cockpit. I would have to sit sidesaddle and open the rear hatch and retrieve my lure boxes and other such items. I started keeping my gear in a Plano 1612 so I only had one item to retrieve. I later rigged a milk crate on a bungee system and placed it over the rear hatch. It was more important for me to have this type of primary storage than the secondary below deck for all my fishing, except while fishing the ocean alone. The 16 had ample storage in the front hatch and I became adept at shimmying up the cockpit and utilizing it. It wasn't hard but not everyone was willing to perform such maneuvers while fishing. When the 160 hit the market I switched kayaks.

I'm a big fan of large center hatches, because they are always accessible. The larger the hatch the more and varied the gear you can store through them. They do present design problems, however, especially in the faster, touring-style kayak hulls, but they're really nice. In many designs hatches larger than a 10-inch round aren't practical. Some manufacturers could have used or designed their kayaks to use substantially larger hatches in the cockpit, but didn't. Practically any kayak could have a 10-inch round center hatch. Once you've used a kayak with a hatch of this size it's hard to do without. I've owned Tarpons with anemic 4 and 5-inch hatches, which aren't very useful from a storage standpoint. Ocean Kayak revamped the center hatch and went to a long, narrow hatch in the Trident series of kayaks. This design is great for rod storage and retrieval, and was

The author came up with this simple hatch keeper system that prevented the loss of gaspachi hatches on WS Tarpons.

very well received on the original Trident. Because of this they expanded the line to add two shorter siblings.

That brings me to the other thing I like about hatches. Besides storage, they give access to the interior for doing installations. Whenever possible, I want to through-bolt anything I attach to the kayak. The more and larger the hatches the better the chance I can reach inside to where I need. For me, a 5-inch hatch is the smallest size that still allows my arm to fit inside without getting stuck.

Types of Hatches

The first type I call strap-ons. There is a raised lip that's molded into the kayak hull and the hatch consists of a lid that straps over the opening. Most use a couple of straps but variations exist. Gaskets in combination with pressure are used to hold it down and provide a seal. These hatches are large and many companies use them, especially in the bow. Ocean Kayak and Hobie are the two I'm most familiar with.

My favorite front hatch is the one originally introduced by Hobie on the Quest. Hobie added a hinge so the lid stays attached to the kayak. The hinge is on the forward part of the hatch and a couple of bungee cords are used to hold down the other side. They hook in the front of the cockpit. At KFS we affectionately called it a toilet bowl hatch, as it reminded us of one.

A similar style hatch was incorporated in the Hobie Revolution. The great thing about these hatches is how easy they are to access while on the water. I remember fishing one day with my buddy Dave. He had just added a Revolution to his fleet and hadn't realized how easy it was getting into the front hatch. Dave also owned a Hobie Adventure and it wasn't possible to reach the front hatch from the cockpit area. I pulled my cooler with my lunch from the hatch while on the water. Dave was surprised and commented that he didn't know that could be done.

Gaspachi or Tupperware-type hatches function just like the lid on a Tupperware container—they provide a watertight seal. These are the hatches found on the Tarpons, Liquid Logic Mantas, Heritage Redfish, etc. While they work great, the lids have been known to come off in transport while on the vehicle. I lost one on a Tarpon 120 while heading to a get-together in western Long Island Sound one morning. It was the wee hours and the hatch came off while on Interstate 80. Fortunately, I heard it

come off, so I turned around at the next exit and retraced my path. I found the lid, but recognized that if I lost one, others could too. From that experience, I started using a bungee cord in a system and made it available to customers. We called it a hatch-keeper system. I recommended it to all Tarpon purchasers and many went with this option. It was cheap insurance, as the system was very inexpensive. I remember one customer who lost two lids from his 140 before he finally added the keeper. Lids cost a lot more than the keeper. While some kayaks come with the Tupperware already installed and leave you no choice, Ocean Kayak is representative of companies that have it available as an option. The place where the Gaspachi goes is raised and the center is cut out to function as a hatch. Models such as the Ocean Kayak Malibu, Zest and Scramblers have this option.

The third major group consists of the plastic hatches, which come in several configurations. The screw-in lid types are by far my least favorite. That's because if there is any sand around it will get into the threads. Even without sand, kayaks are flexible and the lids bind up easily, making it difficult to tighten or loosen them. Also in this group are hinged or latch hatches. My first kayak had these in the form of the Viking 10-inch rounds. It's the same style of hatch that my Explorer had in the center cockpit. These hatches have one or more 'T' handles that you turn 90 degrees to open the hatch. The lid isn't attached and you have to understand this, because anything that isn't attached can be lost. The 'A', large square and rectangular hatches all use 'T's.

Some hatches have solved the potential loss by adding a hinge. The first large hinged hatch I remember is the one used on the Emotion Fisherman. It had a hinge on one side and on the handle side there were two dials (instead of T's). By turning the dial 90 degrees you either opened or closed the hatch. The hinge was plastic and the lid could be removed if desired.

When KFS started selling Hobie Kayaks, I decided to live with an Outback for a while. This was when only the Sport and Outback existed in the Mirage fishing line. It was the second generation Outback and came with a 10-inch round in the rear and a four-inch screw type access hatch under the seat. I liked the hands-free fishing but the interior access was pitiful. Customers were telling me that they felt like the Beverly Hillbillies because they had to lash all their gear to the top of the kayak since there was so little accessible interior. I found a rectangular hinged hatch that would fit in the center where the tackle tray strapped in. I put it in my demo and it worked great. It significantly increased the below-deck storage. However, I couldn't recommend it to folks over 225 pounds. That's because a person of this weight with gear would have the water line from the center well too close to the hatch and this would almost guarantee water would enter the kayak. Also it only solved half of the available storage issue. I kept eyeing the huge bow area and considered altering it to allow me to mount an 'A' hatch there. I could have done it with a welding gun, but it wouldn't have been a practical solution - too cost prohibitive due to the amount of labor required to make it available to customers. Also it would have been a substantial alteration and I doubt if Hobie would then warranty the hull.

Meanwhile, I had sent pictures off to Hobie with the rectangular center hatch installed to make sure they would warranty the hull with the center hatch, before I offered it as an option to customers. Hobie got in touch, told me the hull would still be under warranty, and asked where I was getting the hatches. The person I spoke with told me they were considering a redesign of the Outback and incorporating a 10-inch center hatch. I was all for it and while I had the Hobie person on the phone I suggested a change to the front and at least make it flat so installers could put a hatch up there. Better yet, Hobie should include a hatch. The following year the third generation Outback had the large center hatch and a bow hatch. It went from anemic storage to outstanding in one fell swoop. Hobie has since improved the center hatch. They put a hinge on it and added a cam in the closure mechanism. The cam creates downward force and the addition of an 'O' ring provides a watertight seal.

As I stated earlier, sometimes you don't have any choice because the kayak comes with hatches. There are models where you have some choice, while others leave all the decisions up to you. The first group is easy since there isn't any decision to make. Many models come with a bow hatch and it's your choice whether or not to add a center hatch. Generally I'd answer yes but in some models I wouldn't. After living with the Prowler 15 for a while, a kayak whose hull I loved, I started recommending to customers not to get the center hatch. Since the 15 lacked drain

ridges in the foot wells, water tended to collect and eventually it would flood over the hatch. The screw-in hatch didn't seal well and at 6 inches didn't offer much access. I felt folks would be better off without it. Models from Cobra and Malibu Kayaks give the owner total decision regarding hatches, as the hulls are available without any preinstalled. This way you can customize them to your specific needs. Also since hatches add significantly to the cost of a kayak, you can add them based upon need and/or finances, whichever apply. In some models the price difference between a bare kayak and one with a full compliment of hatches can be considerable.

Generally, the smaller the kayak the fewer and smaller the hatches it is going to have. However, this does vary quite a lot. Malibu Kayaks' Mini X has a lot of hatch availability for such a diminutive kayak. Usually small kayaks are used in smaller bodies of water and the ability to carry gear isn't as important. My Tarpon 100 has an 8-inch Gaspachi up front and a five-inch behind the seat. The larger the kayak volume the more interior space is available. When the Emotion Fishermen first came out I loaded one with gear just to see how much stuff I could get in there. I had much more stuff than I'd ever take on the water, even while camping. For fun I piled all the gear alongside the kayak and posted the picture. Larger and longer kayaks are going to have more capacity to store gear and in order to access the storage you are going to need hatches.

Lastly, some kayaks can accept hatches that weren't originally conceived by the manufacturer. At KFS we did a lot of modification. I was always tinkering. The first modification in hatches I ever made was replacing the 4-inch center in a Tarpon 120 with a 5-inch. It wouldn't seem like much but it allowed better access for installations. Next was the series 2 Hobie Outback I discussed earlier in this section. Another kayak that got slighted at the factory was the Redfish 14. It came with a 10-inch Tupperware hatch up front. There was lots of room for something much larger but the company didn't offer anything, so I put an 'A' hatch in it. It took a bit of work, as the recessed drainage area had to be filled in. At first I used sealant, but settled on filling the area with welding material. The effort was worth it, as it functioned wonderfully. It made for a terrific amount of storage that enabled the kayak to hold the largest of carts and other gear. We offered it as an option and many customers ordered it.

(above) The Fish Grip is terrific for toothy species like bluefish. (left) An assortment of Lip Grippers. The three in the middle have built in scales.

Lip Grippers

Lip grippers are tools used to securely grab a fish by the jaw. Most often this is to remove a hook. They're especially great for handling toothy fish. In the Northeast they are terrific for species like bluefish, which I call living hacksaws with fins. A large blue is a dangerous animal. Removing one of your fingers is well within their ability. They are also a species that sees as well out of the water as in, so they will attack with this weapon if given the opportunity. Every region has its toothy species and it's easier to secure the fish with a gripper. I use a gripper during hook removal on many fish because it allows me do so without having to touch them. This is better for the fish as it won't remove the protective slime that the fish needs to fight infection. When it comes time to free the fish, the gripper has a release mechanism.

There are several units on the market. All do the job and work similarly. Most units have a set of jaws

As I said, with some kayaks you're not going to have any choice at all. Should you decide to purchase kayaks like a Tarpon or Manta Ray, the hatches are part of the kayak design and the decision has been made for you. Then there are kayaks that come with the large bow hatch and leave the rest to you. Lastly there are models that are available without any hatches at all and you've got a lot of options. It's your kayak and you need to decide.

that open when a mechanism is pulled. Others are more like a plastic vice grip. They range from simple units costing under $20 to others over $200. The more expensive ones are lifetime tools that include a scale. The built-in scales available with the units range from 15 to 60 pounds. For kayak fishing it isn't very convenient to weigh fish once they get longer than a couple of feet. Lifting a heavy object too far up can make you very unbalanced, causing the kayak to flip. I remember 'Jim T' used to weigh fairly large striped bass, but this is when he owned a Fish 'n Dive, which is an incredibly stable kayak. I weighed a large bluefish one day while Terry snapped a picture of it. After he emailed me the photo I saw that part of the fish was still in the water.

If you keep your catch then you can weigh them when you reach shore. Also there are other circumstances like fishing from shore or a boat where you would have the opportunity to use the scale. The better units all have a scale. Since I have a scale I do use it, especially for freshwater fish. The most well known unit is the Boga™. It's been around for many years and is a terrific tool. Similar to the Boga, but not nearly as well known is the Lipper™ Tool. I love this unit. It's high quality, like the Boga, but has a neat feature that no other gripper has. When you open the jaws they will stay open until you push a button that releases the jaws. It took me a day to get used to but I find it easy to use with thrashing fish. My favorite grip tool is called the Fish Grip. It's essentially a plastic vice grip and works the same. It costs less than $15 and works great. Once a fish is on it they do not get off.

I like to keep lip grippers on a tether. Remember the adage, "leash it or lose it". It's also nice for when you want a picture of a fish. Rarely when you catch a fish you want a picture of is someone available and ready to take a picture at that moment. Often a buddy is quite a distance away and might not even have a camera. With the fish on the gripper, attached to the kayak via a tether, you can paddle over to another kayak. The fish swims along and

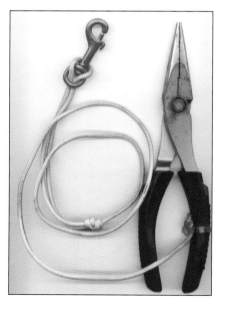

These $20 titanium coated pliers have worked well for years. The tether has a knot on the end and is secured with a cable tie.

below the kayak. It reminds me of a well-behaved dog on a leash. The fish even revives in the process. I find the fish are very frisky after their 'walk' and release well. Since the spring of 2007 I've been using a self-portrait camera system. If I didn't have the fish tethered on a leash I wouldn't be able to use it.

With respect to tether materials, many will work. All-purpose Paracord is what I use. A telephone rod leash works well, too. With either of these I like to use a small brass clip to attach the unit to the kayak or seat for easy on/off. The clip is great for when I wade. It's simple to bring the gripper along as I transfer it from the kayak to a belt, jacket clip, etc.

I keep my gripper handy and usually put it in a flush mount rod holder behind me. I like to land fish on the starboard side. If there isn't a flush mount available I'll use something else to secure it. It might be a bungee over the gripper. If the kayak has a pair of bungee paddle keepers I like to keep the paddle on the opposite side so the starboard one is free for the gripper. You can dedicate a spot if you wish and secure it with either a rubber paddle clip or a bungee. Even though a lip gripper isn't a necessary tool you won't find me on the water without one.

Pliers

Pliers are essential tools that are hard to do without when fishing from a kayak. They perform a few functions and which pair you choose will depend upon how you plan on using them. Their primary purpose is in removing hooks from fish. They provide greater leverage than using your hand and with toothy fishes they're mandatory so you won't get hurt.

Prices vary from a few dollars to hundreds. The cheap ones are made of steel and are going to rust. I suggest at the minimum getting stainless steel. Better yet is titanium coated stainless steel. Another material is aluminum. They are more money but won't rust. Totally rust-free are plastic pliers, which are made by X Tools, which work well. You're limited in that plastic will only grip so well. For many applications they are fine, and they float! The cutters on them are excellent, as well.

A good sonar unit will help you catch fish. These marks are bass holding near the bottom in 13 feet of water.

They also have some hybrid designs which incorporate stainless inserts in the jaws.

When I fish small freshwater rivers I rarely need more than a 6-inch pair unless there are pike and pickerel in the watershed. Then something longer is necessary. When I fish for bluefish I like a pair of 11-inch stainless steel. They're the longest I've found that are stainless. I did find some at a flea market that were 16 inches long but they seized up pretty quickly from saltwater and didn't respond well to lubricants.

I've been using two pairs of pliers for most of my kayak fishing for years. They are a stainless steel, titanium coated set of eight-inch and an aluminum pair. The aluminum sells for approximately four times the $20 price of the stainless steel titanium. They both function the same but the aluminum ones have a nice feature. The cutting blades, used often for cutting braided lines, are replaceable. It's nice to have this ability because in time that's what goes on all pliers. However there is an inexpensive solution - use something else for cutting line. I keep some braid

scissors in my shirt pocket for just this purpose. They go for about $5 and the $50 you save can be used on other things. Kayak fishing can get gear intensive so when you have a choice between two things that essentially do the same job and the price difference is substantial, I'd opt for the less expensive solution. You can use some of the money you save for our next item - lubricants.

Lubricants

I have found that most pliers are going to rust especially if you fish saltwater environments. If you wash and dry your tools after each use then you will prevent rust, however I don't often do this, so my pliers end up binding. I use lubricant to loosen them up. I've even been known to use lubricants when they're not bound up. Doing so helps prevent seizing, but even a seized pair will come back. There are lots of lubricants. I've been using Corrosion X and Reel X. I'll soak pliers a day or two and they will usually come back to full function.

The aluminum pliers won't rust, however salt build-up will bind them. I can soak them in water or a special salt stripping solution to dissolve the salt or use a lubricant. I tend to use lubricant.

Whichever set of pliers you get, make sure you put them on a leash. I like to keep mine alongside the starboard side of my kayak by my thigh. That way they're handy and available when I need them.

Electronics

You don't need electronic devices to go kayak fishing but they are nice to have. They do help me catch more fish and add a degree of safety. I refer to electronics as accessories that run on electricity; fish finders, GPS units, radios, cell phones and lights. Lights are an essential item that can't be considered an option if you're going to be on the water in low light or at night. They are on the Coast Guard list of required items. You will need them to see and be seen. Lights will be covered in depth in their own section. All the other electronic devices are not necessary, but certainly enhance the experience.

Fish Finders

A fish finder is the first item that comes to mind when considering an electronic accessory. Most display in black and white, but color models are also available for considerably more money. No other piece of equipment will help you as much in expanding your fishing opportunities. Units have become very reasonably priced. They provide valuable information that will help you find more fish and fish-holding structure. Fish finders vary but all work the same. They are mini sonar units. There is a main unit I call the brain that houses the screen and controls. It transmits information from the transducer to a display screen. The transducer is the part that sends the sonar signal through the water and receives the return echo. The time it takes for the signal to return is measured and the information is shown on the screen. You will receive information corresponding to depth as well as bottom configuration. Some units allow you to interpret the bottom composition and as you continue to use the unit you will become more proficient at deciphering the results.

There are simple units that work fine. It really comes down to what you want from them. Generally the more you spend the more features and resolution the unit will have. Fish are identified as arches or little fishes. Many units will vary the size of the fishes so you can tell the difference between small fish and ones you want to catch. The small ones are often bait. Arches are more sophisticated and the better units use them. They are the actual signal the unit sees and the information provided is easier to decipher. Resolution is measured in pixels and usually given in two numbers, which are the number of pixels across the horizontal and vertical planes. The least expensive units have the fewest pixels and some are less than 100. As you spend more the pixels increase.

Another very important feature to consider is a waterproof unit. With the exposure the fish finder is going to have kayak fishing, it really doesn't make sense not to get one that can be immersed. Even though you don't plan on the fish finder being in the water, at some point it probably will happen, especially if you do surf launches. Knowing that the unit can take it gives you one less thing to worry about. There are enough waterproof models whereby there isn't any reason not to own one.

The first time I realized the value of a fish finder was a day I spent fishing with a buddy at the Shrewsbury Rocks in New Jersey. I was fishing with 'docjohn' and there were stripers busting on the surface. I paddled around chasing these schools of fish

and I managed to land three. When John and I got near each other later I found out he had landed five fish for every one of mine. He had been using a fish finder and marking the fish on the bottom. All he had to do was drop a jig down to the fish and voila! That was enough for me and I've been using a fish finder ever since.

A fish finder won't catch the fish for you but they offer helpful information that assists you in several ways. Even when you're paddling a kayak quickly it moves very slowly, allowing the fish finder to do its job. Besides marking fish they mark schools of bait. They show the depth of the water and identify structure. Many also read the water temperature. While heading to your intended destination you will discover fish and structure you didn't know were there. This happens a lot. You'll be cruising to a place where you plan on fishing and pass over a school of fish. If they're active, an offering dropped in their midst usually produces action. Without the fish finder you wouldn't have any idea the fish are there. Anything different in an area will attract fish. Sunken islands, shoals, points, bars, debris and such are features you will find. These areas can then be marked either by triangulation or with a GPS.

One day the fishing at my local reservoir was slow so I decided to explore the bottom. I'd done this in the past on other bodies of water and found interesting fish attracting structure. This particular reservoir consisted of three parts - the lower section, the part I was in and the largest section, which held the least structure. Because of this it was fished less.

As I moved along the edge of the shoreline in approximately 15 feet of water, I noticed the bottom begin to slowly rise. I followed the outside edge of this rise, which led me into the middle of the basin. Eventually I found a rectangular area that rises to an average of 12 feet and all around it drops to over 20 feet. One small part came to within 8 feet of the surface. I'm fairly certain it's an old house that overlooks what was once a meadow. It's a great spot that holds bass and I wouldn't have found it without a fish finder.

Another thing I like about them is that they are kind of like watching TV. It gives you something to do while paddling about and you can actually watch your line, lure and fish in real time on the finder. Units have become so sensitive that your line shows up. You can even watch fish move off the bottom and take your offering.

GPS

Most people are familiar with GPS for their cars, but haven't considered having one for their kayak. The sophistication of some of these units is astounding and increasing all the time. For the uninitiated, GPS stands for Global Positioning System and that's precisely what it does. A GPS receives signals from satellites orbiting the earth. The satellites are the senders and the GPS is the receiver. The unit shows your location by utilizing several satellites and triangulating the received signals.

Basic units show your position on a blank screen. There will be an arrow illustrating your direction of travel, a track (more on this later) and your speed. The simple units function like an electronic compass and are too limiting for my purposes. A few years back, while on a trip to the Turks and Caicos Islands, I decided to explore the sound across the street from where we were staying. It was a mile wide by 4 miles long, and on the other end was a narrow peninsula separating the sound from a bay system we had been fishing. Terry and Joey drove around to the bay and I wanted to coordinate with them and catch a ride back. This would save me from paddling against the prevailing afternoon winds, which would have been a chore in my rudderless kayak. I didn't have Caribbean software in my hand held GPS so it functioned like a basic unit and wasn't a lot of help. Luckily I had studied charts and satellites of the area before my departure from the States and I had a very good feel for the terrain. I found the take-out point easily and caught a ride back with the guys.

The feature I lacked was mapping. Mapping is just what the name implies; there's a map in the unit. Models are so modestly priced there isn't a reason not to have this feature. I also recommend getting a marine version. The unit's software will have navigation information such as buoys, markers, lighthouses and other landmarks. Also a marine model is going to be waterproof and in everything you choose for kayak fishing you should opt for the most water-resistant. My favorite GPS's have software chips that enhance the units. They give greater detail and more information. I have five chips for my two units. I have the Navionics chip, which covers the marine waters of the U.S. It's like having a chart for all the coastal waters of the country. The other four are the full set of freshwater chips. These are divided into four regions. So far I've only used the Northeast. The chips contain the most popular fishing lakes and give detail on each body of water represented. It's great to go to a new place and have detailed topography of the water. I've used the freshwater chips a few times and find them invaluable. I especially like having charts when fishing somewhere for the first time. They show me structure and other places that look interesting. Two places I've used them are Lake Champlain, a huge lake, reminiscent of an inland sea that borders New York and Vermont, and the St. Lawrence Seaway, also in New York.

I have two units that share the same chips. One is a portable hand-held and the other is a combo. If you only plan on using your GPS for the kayak, then consider a combo, which combines a GPS with a fish finder. Combos offer great value, too, as there are models starting in the $200 range. Obviously, the more you pay the more features you will get. My color hand-held is fantastic but its well over $100 more than a baseline-mapping combo. Not only will the baseline combo tell you the information you're going to need for navigating and fishing but it has a fish finder in it as well! A combo unit doesn't give you the flexibility of a portable but if you don't need it why pay for it?

When using a fish finder you will find interesting underwater structure you will want to revisit at a later time. Most GPS units allow you to mark the spot and store it in memory. This is called a waypoint. You can rename the spot at a later time and in the future head directly to it. At times I'll mark fish in a specific position where the surrounding area is barren. It may be structure that has attracted them or they might be suspended. Since I paddled over them their position is along my track. I can zoom in and easily retrace my track to where I had marked the fish.

I have a couple of spots in western Long Island Sound that sit above the surface at low tide. During pre-dawn summer hours one can usually see tailing bass. This necessitates getting out to the spot in the dark. Without a GPS you could spend a lot of energy searching and not get there early enough to intercept cooperative fish. With the spot marked in the GPS all I have to do is launch with enough time to reach the location while conditions are favorable.

Interpreting the readout is simple. There will be an arrow that shows your direction of movement and a trail indicating your path. This trail is the track and it's the path you've taken. Not only do you see your position on the map in relation to other objects, but you'll also see your direction of travel and where you were. This is invaluable when you're on the water. Without a GPS it's easy to be mistaken regarding positioning, especially when you have factors such as wind and current. The GPS will assist you in knowing how current and wind are affecting the kayak, thus aiding your decision-making. You may have the wind at your back and wouldn't realize how much it was moving the kayak if it weren't for the GPS. You're eventually going to have to travel against it (unless you're doing a shuttle trip) and the GPS will tell you how well you are doing. You might determine that you have to expend too much energy over too great a distance for it to be worthwhile. If it turns out the wind is so strong you can barely make progress, you will probably want to reconsider your plans.

In addition to showing you where you are and the direction you're heading, it will show you the speed at which you are traveling. Sometimes knowing your speed is only a curiosity, but at other times it's significant. One such situation is trolling. Fish are sometimes finicky and a specific pace is required to elicit a strike. Some lures work best at a specific speed and knowing your speed will allow you to adjust your paddling to make the best presentation. Also, if you need to be somewhere at a certain time and know the distance, you can calculate the rate of speed needed to get there.

When fishing at night the GPS is great. It's easy to get disoriented at night but the unit will direct you to your chosen spot. One night Mark, Walt and I decided to fish around Strong Island in Pleasant Bay, Cape Cod. When we launched the kayaks it was still light out and we could clearly see where we were heading. I had only been to the island once and wasn't overly familiar with it. As night came we worked our way around. I've always had a very good sense of direction that has rarely failed me. When it came time to head back in I was fairly certain where we were but as a precaution I turned on the night light of my GPS. Oops, I had my bearings wrong! I turned on my stern light so Mark and Walt could follow me in. If I had followed my instincts it would have added over a mile of paddling and landed us far from our launch site. With the GPS guiding us we safely and efficiently returned to our vehicles.

I get a lot of inquiries about using a fish finder on a kayak. Hardly ever am I asked about a GPS. Like a fish finder, it's rare for me not to have a GPS along.

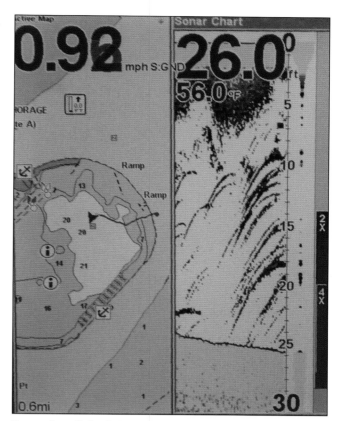

The combo unit view to the left is the GPS chart of Great Kills Harbor, NY and to the right is the fish finder view of big bluefish feeding on bunker.

As previously mentioned, I enjoy exploration and often fish alone in places I've never fished before. For investigating new places, a GPS is invaluable.

Besides aiding in navigation and providing lots of useful information, there is another great feature to having a GPS along. When the fishing is slow and you're trolling along, it gives you something else to occupy your time while waiting for a hit. Add a unit to your kayak. You won't regret it.

Electronic and Accessory Mounts

If you're going to install a fish finder or GPS you're usually going to need some type of mount. There are applications where the base of the unit can be attached directly to the kayak, but I found it was usually better to have a separate detachable mount. There are commercial units and if you search the various kayak fishing websites you will see quite an array of homemade set-ups. RAM dominates the market but there are others. Scotty and Johnny Ray are two additional companies whose mounts I've seen used on kayaks with good results. As with rod

(above) A 2-inch aluminum bar on a Ram mount allows for a variety of electronics and rod holders to be attached. **(right)** Clockwise from top left: headlamp, LED stern or PFD light, waterproof flashlight for around neck and a red cap light.

holders, the RAM is the most versatile as it uses the same ball system as the RAM rod. They make base plates for most units and there are also universal ones. The more versatile a mount the more places you can install one.

There is also a group of mounts that have bars or you can attach your own. They allow you to have multiple accessories on the bar. These can be rod holders, electronic mounts, and cup holders, whatever you like. I've seen some very creative stuff. I made one from a length of 2- inch by ¼-inch aluminum bar purchased at Home Depot and cut it to the size I wanted. Aluminum is easy to drill and I bolted the bar directly to my kayak via stainless steel nuts, bolts and washers. It's then a simple task to mark and drill the holes for whatever you'd like to attach.

Lights

Lights allow us to see in the dark and to be seen by others. If you're going to kayak fish at night you will need lights that serve both functions. Also, some regulations require you to carry a light. It doesn't have to be on but must be in the kayak. It only has to be a flashlight but you must have one with you.

Running Lights

The title says it all. You want to be seen on the water. That's the reason to have lights on a kayak at night, referred to as running lights. All motorized boats and non-motorized boats over a certain length are required to have lights. Many boats have a set of running lights which consist of a white light in the stern and a red and green light on the bow. Some kayakers set up running lights on their kayaks. This can either be a permanent, hard-wired system or self-contained units. It depends on your needs and how often you plan on using the lights.

I don't use the running light method of three lights and I consider it a potential cause of trouble. You could be mistaken for a boat on the water that can cause confusion as to who has the right of way. Imagine a boat approaching and the pilot thinks you're a small motorboat and he has the right of way. The boat would expect you to yield to him. The boat might be on top of you before realizing you were a kayak and not a boat, obviously a dangerous situation. I prefer using only the stern light. A single, bright white light often signifies a stationary object on the water or a non-powered vessel. That's what I'd like an approaching boat to consider me. When the boat approaches and sees the light, it will exercise caution until knowing the nature of what I am. Slowing down and determining what I am is exactly what I want an oncoming boat to do. I've been using a great LED unit for a few years that fits my needs beautifully. It's waterproof and runs on three AA batteries. The light is very bright and will run for 150 hours on the batteries! My friend Bill attached his to a rear safety flag. That puts the light over four feet off the water. It's the way I have mine attached now and is the best method I've seen yet.

PFD Light

This is a 360-degree, waterproof light that is visible for miles. They attach to the PFD (personal flotation device or life vest). In the event you and the kayak get separated at night, you have a means to be seen. Most models run on a couple of AA batteries.

Headlamp and Cap Lamps

These are lights that you wear on your head or cap. They're very popular, as they allow the free use of both hands. This is important when rigging, getting a hook out of a fish, etc. These units vary in the features they offer. Some are merely a flashlight that straps to a headband and others have multiple brightness settings, multiple colors and even flasher modes. A headlamp with these features can be used as a running light in places where you don't expect much boat traffic. If doing so, keep in mind that you're not going to be seen at 360 degrees, as it's a mono-directional light. Should a boat approach, face it so the light can be seen. The cap lamps are smaller and generally more comfortable to wear. They slip over the bill of a ball cap.

Flashlights

It's a good idea to always have a small, waterproof flashlight along. I keep one on a string so I can wear it around my neck. An alternative is to keep it somewhere handy such as in a PFD pocket. This way you've got another light as a back-up. Having back-ups is important, as you don't want to be out on the water without light.

Night Light

These lights have a colored lens - most are red or green. The importance of the color is twofold; it doesn't affect your night vision as it doesn't dilate your pupil, and secondly fish don't know you're using it. It's very beneficial while night fishing to rig lines connect lures, remove fish, without having to first experience a moment of blindness. My favorite ones are the cap lamp style.

When fishing in a kayak I always have at least one light along, even if I don't plan on fishing at night. Stuff happens and it's best to be prepared. When I do plan on fishing at night I have a few lights along. I have my bright LED stern light, a headlamp, a night light, a PFD light and a small waterproof light on a cord around my neck. This way, I'm prepared in the event that I have a failure of one or more lights. I use rechargeable batteries and I always bring along extras.

Cell Phones

You're not going to buy a cell phone because you have a kayak. You most likely already own one so why not take it along? You can store it in a dry bag or box as an emergency aid should you need to call for help. Besides having a phone along in case of an emergency, they're great for their primary purpose of calling others. Oftentimes when I'm out fishing I'll be part of a group and we may be spread out over a large area. FRS radios have quite limited ranges and cell phones fill the void. When on a trip with a group we often have guys fishing a few locales and we communicate via phones to see what each other is doing.

In June of 2004 while on a trip to the Cape we were way up inside a bay when Mark got a call from Jim. He had spotted a couple of schools of stripers out on the ocean. Jim was approximately 15 miles away scouting the beaches with his truck. Past experience told me that we should abandon the bay and get to the beaches. Almost 2 hours later, at the first beach with good access, we spotted a school of fish, launched the kayaks and got into some of the best fishing you can imagine. I personally caught a dozen stripers between then and sunset, with an average size of over 36 inches. The smallest I landed was 32 and the largest 44 inches. It was extraordinary fishing and wouldn't have happened without that cell phone call from Jim.

When using a cell phone on the kayak you need to protect it. You can put it in a protective case such as a watertight box or bag, or in a specially designed cell phone bag. I prefer the cell phone bags, as they allow me to talk while on the water without worrying about damaging the phone. There are a bunch of bags designed specifically for this. While the phone is fully protected you can speak through the bag. Put the phone in the bag, put the bag on a tether, and you're set.

Radios

There are two types of radios that are important to kayak fishermen. They are the VHF and FRS radios. As opposed to a cell phone that offers one-on-one communication, the radios allow everyone on the same frequency to be part of the communication.

The FRS is basically a limited range walkie-talkie, though they are getting better each year. What's nice is they are inexpensive and work well when distances are close but too far to yell. If you find yourself in this situation try an FRS.

VHF is a marine radio. I used to consider one a luxury but now I take one with me most of the time I'm out in the salt. They have a lot more range than an FRS and there are lots of places where you can't get cell phone reception. The VHF fills the void. They also have a weather band so you can get current weather forecasts. Even though many handheld VHF's are waterproof, I keep mine in a dry bag that allows me to use it without taking it out of the bag. I had a unit on a trip to Baja a couple of years back and it stopped working after getting wet even though it was labeled waterproof.

VHF **(left)** and FRS **(right)** are both extremely useful radios for kayak fishermen.

Rudders

A rudder is a device used to steer a kayak. It's an accessory I get a lot of questions about. Most people want to know if they're necessary. Rudders aren't necessary but they make a kayak more productive. The first item I add to a kayak is a rod holder, as it will do more for the fishing ability than any other accessory. The next is a rudder. Rudders aren't essential gear but if a rudder is available with a kayak I want one, and I wouldn't even think of owning a kayak over 14 feet without one. I spent two years fishing a Cobra Tourer without a rudder and then I added one. The difference was night and day. It's akin to power steering in your car. There was a time when cars didn't have power steering or it was an option. Nobody gets a car without it now and I don't even know if you can. The rudder changes how you

can use the kayak. I know a lot of folks who have added a rudder and everyone feels the same way. They won't own a fishing kayak without one. Rudders are very popular in the northeast but not as common in the rest of the country. Only you can determine if a rudder is for you. It's like all luxuries. My favorite analogy that best relates the rudder as an accessory is if you've ever owned a vehicle without air conditioning. I have and I would never buy one without air again. That's a rudder. Here are some of the things you can expect from one.

Steering

This is obvious. A rudder is used to steer the kayak. The longer the kayak the more important it is. The use of a rudder significantly shortens the turn radius, an important consideration when fishing tight quarters. When paddling in wind a rudder is very beneficial. There is a phenomenon called wind cocking, which is when the wind blows at an angle to the direction you want to travel. If the wind is blowing it's most likely going to come from an angle. Rarely will it be directly behind or in front of you. The longer the kayak the more surface area is presented to the wind. The more perpendicular the wind the more it will affect the kayak. It affects you when paddling, as you will have to compensate by making more paddle strokes on the leeward side of the kayak.

Let's use an example to better show the effects of wind cocking. The direction you wish to travel is 12 o'clock. The wind is 15 mph and it's coming at you from 2 o'clock. This makes the right side of the kayak the windward side (the side from which the wind is coming). It wants to push you towards the port (left). To compensate you will have to take more paddle strokes on the port side. The ratio might be 5 to 10 strokes port to one stroke starboard. People are bipedal. We have two arms and two legs. Paddling is a lot like walking. You do it one leg at a time, one foot in front of the other. Have you ever tried walking by taking one step with your right leg and five with your left? It's hard to do and very awkward. Taking five strokes port and one starboard, while not as difficult as walking that way, is a pain. It's much easier to get into a rhythm by alternating strokes. A rudder eliminates the need to make more strokes on one side. You simply paddle normally and steer with the rudder which is operated with your feet. Most models have rudder slides attached to a cable which turns the rudder. Others have a toe pilot system, also attached via a cable, which is similar to a gas pedal. In either case, you push left to turn left and push right to turn right.

The second day of my first trip to Cape Cod I was fishing Pleasant Bay. Doug, Jim, Joey and I launched out of a sheltered cove and paddled towards Strong Island. Doug and I were paddling Tarpon 16's with rudders, Joey had a Scupper Pro TW, and Jim a Fish 'n Dive. Neither Joey nor Jim had a rudder. As we got out of the cove the wind was at our backs, making the paddle out to the island an easy one. The fishing was lousy so after about an hour we decided to head back and try somewhere else. The wind was now in our face and had gotten stronger. The paddle back would not be fun. Doug and I got back to the launch first with Joey being about 10 minutes behind us. Jim was at least 10 minutes behind Joey. Joey couldn't help but notice how much more efficient my and Doug's paddling was, as we simply pointed our kayaks where we wanted to go without having to constantly make adjustments. It was the last time either Joey or Jim had a rudderless kayak.

Maneuvering

A rudder will help a kayak maneuver in tight places. Again it's like power steering. If you don't remember or if you're too young, parallel parking without power steering is difficult. When things get tight it's a nice feature to have. In some environments maneuverability is not really needed. If you fish open ocean there is nowhere to maneuver, however many places do have terrain where it can be invaluable.

In the Northeast we often experience excellent fishing amongst moored boats. Adult bunker, (an important prey species), seem to love such places. Where there is prey you will find predators. Having the ability to move easily in these tight quarters can be priceless. There are also lots of rocks in this region and again it can get tight. Small estuaries, rivers, and mangrove channels are all also places where a rudder is a great feature to have on your kayak.

Fish Fighting

Another way a rudder becomes handy is fighting fish. Without a rudder the kayak will tend to follow the fish. There are situations where you don't want the kayak to follow the fish. Consider the following: You've just hooked a large fish and it decides to head in a direction you don't want it to. There might be a rip, dock, rocks, any manner of places you and your kayak would rather not be. You can brace against the yak and lean to influence its path. This will affect the kayak somewhat but a rudder is a much more effective alternative. Bringing the kayak perpendicular to the fish greatly increases resistance and influences the fish to change direction.

Several years back I hooked a nice striped bass along the sod banks just below the confluence of Nauset Marshes and Town Cove out on Cape Cod. The tide was going out and the fish took advantage of the current and headed towards the ocean. There was a broad bend loaded with lobster pots and their attached buoys. Guess where the bass headed? That's right, straight for the pots. Had Mrs. Striper reached them she would certainly have tangled my line and gotten free.

Adjacent to the channel was a flat. I turned the rudder, forcing the kayak sideways. The kayak headed onto the flat. The additional resistance the fish felt was not to its liking. I have found that many species of fish will swim away from such resistance. Stripers are one of them. The fish being an aquatic creature couldn't climb the sod bank so it headed out onto the flat. Once on the flat I threw out an anchor, hopped out of the kayak, and fought the fish while standing in less than two feet of water. The battle ended with my landing a nice 36-inch bass. The rudder is also effective at repositioning the kayak while fighting a fish in other circumstances. As a hooked fish goes on a run, especially behind you, you can maneuver to keep your rod angle ideal for both effectiveness and comfort.

Drifting

Fishing is a sport that requires the use of your hands. Having a rudder allows you to eliminate the need to adjust your drift using the paddle. You may be casting towards shore, a weed line, drop off, or any manner of structure where you want to maintain a certain distance. You feather the rudder and precisely control your drift. This is really nice when fly-fishing because you can consistently cast the same distance. You control the amount of line you're going to throw by how much you strip off the reel. Sometimes you need to drop the fly very close to structure. It can be the shore, an undercut bank, a rip line, weed edge, under the mangroves, etc., and with a rudder you can easily maintain the distance you're drifting from that object.

The crate in this Tarpon 16 functioned as a tank well.

The first time I fished the Everglades was in a rudderless kayak. I was fishing close to mangroves and had to constantly grab my paddle to adjust my drift. Also, some species of fish love to run into the mangroves once hooked. With a rudder I can veer away without having to interrupt fighting the fish.

A rudder is a great accessory to have but don't keep it in the water all the time, because it produces drag which will slow you down a bit. Do use a rudder when it makes sense to do so, but like any accessory learn how to use it to maximize its benefits.

Storage

Earlier I discussed storage in "Choosing a Kayak". That was the storage inherent within the design of the kayak. When you decide upon a kayak your storage will be semi finite. By this I mean it is what it is. On a typical SOT you will have a tank well and hatches. The hatches access the interior of the kayak. That's not the kind of storage I'm discussing here. I'll be discussing how to stow and protect your gear while maintaining access to the most needed items. Some items simply can't get wet, as they will get ruined. Saltwater is especially destructive.

Crates

Many anglers set up a milk crate shortly after getting their first kayak. I started using one early on and it was especially nice when I started fishing from the Tarpon 16, which didn't have a tank well in the rear. Instead it had a large hatch, which was the same as the bow hatch. It was nice for storing rods and gear for surf launches but when I was fishing in more sheltered areas it was inconvenient to have to open the hatch to get to gear. So I rigged a crate over the hatch, using bungee and deck loops. It worked great.

Crates serve a variety of functions. A crate will store tackle and lure boxes. By attaching rod holders it will provide a means of trolling and storing rods. If you decide to use the rod holders on the crate for trolling then make sure you secure it to the kayak. Large fish have been known to rip the entire crate, with all its contents, from the kayak. Crates come in two basic types - square and rectangular. Choose a crate based upon your needs and the space available. When I started kayak fishing I used a rectangular crate. It was especially nice on my Tarpon 16. I could attach and remove it in seconds and it allowed me to have quick access to gear that would otherwise have been stored inside the hatch.

There are companies selling very versatile crate systems. While they cost more than homemade versions, they come loaded with many useful features.

Large Storage Boxes

There are a lot of boxes I use for storage with my kayaks. There is a series of larger tackle style boxes that are very useful - plastic versions of what are referred to as Ammo Boxes. These boxes are top loading and have an "O" ring seal around the lid. They are not waterproof but are water-resistant and float. Gear inside them tends to stay dry. The sizes vary and some are huge. As a group they're great for bringing gear along. With one of these boxes placed behind you in the tank well, gear is very easy to access. They provide convenient storage.

Some kayaks, like the Ocean Kayak Prowler series, have an area molded in specifically for such boxes. The Prowlers have a two-compartment tank well and the front compartment was designed to accommodate Plano's 1612 and 1412 boxes. The 1612 is a great size and will hold a fair amount of gear. The 1412 is the smallest and then there is the big brother of the group, the 1812. Another company, Sportsman's has a series of boxes that work very well. One model has a great flip top where you can store a lot of items that you can get at very quickly. A very nice feature for things you use a lot. Besides functioning well for storing gear I use these boxes another way. When placed behind the seat in a kayak that has outriggers attached, they make a great spot to sit while paddling. This puts you at least a foot higher than when you're sitting in the seat. The added altitude is great for spotting fish, especially on the flats. These boxes are highly versatile and you won't find me without them. I find setting one up with each type of fishing I do to be very beneficial. That way I'm not sorting through gear when grabbing my stuff for a day's fishing. I've got one for freshwater and a few for saltwater setup with the appropriate gear for the different types of fishing I do. Most of the gear will be different so it makes sense. It helps keep things organized and simple. These boxes are also great for when you travel by plane to kayak fish.

Dry Containers

These containers keep anything placed within them perfectly dry. This is important, as kayak fishing is a water sport. Water gets everywhere and many items we bring along are intolerant of being wet, especially from saltwater. They consist of two types - boxes and bags.

Boxes

There are a series of boxes that are truly waterproof. They're superbly made and will keep anything totally dry. The boxes range in size from small models suitable for keys and possibly a wallet up to whatever you wish to carry. They're used on scientific expeditions and will protect the most expensive and fragile gear. These are not cheap but after you ruin a camera or cell phone, they are a bargain. I use boxes mostly for cameras and have never had a problem. They're also great for wallets, keys, cell phones, whatever you wish to take along that you want to have with you but absolutely can't get wet. If you feel you need to have your laptop (I can't imagine why) along then you can. These boxes come in two styles. One style is an open box with its entire interior being hollow. Sometimes the box is padded. The other type is filled with foam. The foam is perforated into sections and easy to remove. This

Storage boxes can be used to hold many items. (above) Clockwise from bottom right: Plano 1412, 1612, 1812 and Sportsman. (left) Some boxes have topside easy access trays. Plano 1812 on left and Sportsman on right.

allows you to customize the interior to accommodate the shape of the object or objects you wish to store inside. It's great for cameras, which aren't very tolerant of being jostled about. Otter and Pelican are the two major manufacturers. The boxes are waterproof to 100-foot depths. Another great feature is they float. When I use the Otter boxes for cameras this is especially nice, as I will often paddle up to a buddy to have a picture taken and chuck the camera to him. The camera cocooned in padding is protected from jarring should it

(above) Dry boxes with padded inserts are the best method for protecting delicate gear like cameras. (right) Dry bags come in a wide array of sizes and styles. These are the basic styles for multiple storage options.

tether so you can keep the item attached to the kayak.

I like to keep my phone and radio in a bag tethered to the back of my seat. This way they're protected and handy when needed. It's easy for me to receive phone calls while out fishing. The larger bags are used for storing all manner of things. I use them for safety gear, clothing, rain suits, food, etc. There are bags large enough for sleeping bags and tents. I have one bag that is filled with items I consider essential. It's great as I just grab it and throw it inside the hull when I'm heading out.

Storage for Lures, Flies and Terminal Tackle

You're going to need to take gear to put on the end of your line. Some of the storage is a matter of convenience and some is needed to protect items from the elements. I use a variety of cases to accomplish this.

Any type of lure box will do if you put it in one of the large boxes discussed earlier or, if you want it to be waterproof, a dry bag. You can store quite a bit of tackle in the boxes. There are also so-called waterproof boxes. I consider them highly water resistant. They have an 'O' ring seal and work better than a box without a seal, but I've found they will let water in

be dropped. And, if it happens to end up in the water, it floats. I like bright colors just in case the box ends up in the drink, so it will be easy to spot and track. Definitely include some of these boxes in your gear, as they're invaluable.

Bags

Dry bags are a must item as far as I'm concerned. They provide versatile storage that will allow you to bring many important items along. They range from small bags suitable for cell phones and radios up to large types for storing tons of gear. The small electronics bags are great because they allow you to protect items like cameras, phones and radios while using them. That's right; you can still use the item even though it's in the bag. There are even cases for flip cell phones. You either talk or take pictures right through the bag, never exposing the device to the elements. As with the boxes, the air trapped inside floats the bag. Most of the smaller bags come with a

if submerged. However, if you don't dunk them they will keep their contents dry. What's nice about them is they don't need to be placed in another box. Sizes vary from small boxes suitable for hooks and terminal tackle to gargantuan ones that will even hold reels. Waterproof boxes are perfect for putting in a milk crate or keeping in the cockpit with you. Some kayaks have bungee set-ups specifically for holding a box. I prefer waterproof boxes for my lures even if they're going to be in another box. This gives me more flexibility and for me that's always a key because circumstances often change and I might find myself needing waterproof properties for another use. One of my favorite ways to carry plugs is with a surf tray. These are the inserts from a surf-fishing bag. The style I like consists of two rows of five rectangular tubes all glued together. Each tube will store a plug or two in an easy to access upright position. The tubes are great for holding metals too and can hold several per tube. All you have to do is flip the lid of a box like a Plano 1612 and you have 30 or more lures you can get to without pulling anything else out of the box. I find it very convenient.

There is another type of lure carrier that works well for flies, plastic lures and terminal tackle. They have pages in which some are removable. One type groups six pages together and attaches to the wallet via Velcro. Others are set up like a loose-leaf notebook that attach via rings with individual pages. The loose-leaf type is fine if you use them for freshwater but I find saltwater quickly ruins all the metal parts of the carrier. I prefer the style that uses Velcro, as there isn't any metal to corrode. They come in a variety of sizes and hold a myriad of different items. The smaller ones are great for hooks, hooks on leaders, leaders and terminal tackle. The medium and larger sizes are great for flies and plastic lures without hooks or one hook at most. The Velcro type is especially nice for flies, as the sections can be removed. They are available in an array of sizes and the combinations of pages and wallets are quite varied. You can mix and match creating quite an assortment. This way you can purchase extra inserts and have groups of different flies or lures, taking what you feel you're going to need for the day's fishing.

Mesh Bags

I use mesh bags all the time and I'm surprised when I don't see others doing so. They're great for all sorts of gear. My favorite use is for soft plastic lures, as most of them come in resealable plastic bags. I find this is the best way to store them and if they don't have a bag a zip lock is all I need. They're already waterproof, so I keep them in mesh bags. Mesh bags are available in many sizes and colors. They are common at stores that sell camping gear. Mesh bags are a must have in my storage arsenal.

Factory Options

As kayak fishing evolves we are continuing to see more specialized gear. This is great because these storage options were designed specifically for your kayak. Hobie has an innovative set of inserts for its eight-inch hatches. They have lids like a Tupperware

and removable inserts allowing you to customize the interior. I find them very useful. I've got one set up for each type of fishing I do and I keep my most commonly used items in them. The latest fishing kayak from Ocean Kayak has an insert that fits in the center hatch of the kayak. Companies are molding specific storage features right into the kayak. Many Hobie kayaks have trays built into the gunnels for putting things and their kayaks have side pockets with nets to keep whatever you place in them put. The Liquid Logic Mantas have trays in the cockpit. If you're a minimalist, keep it simple but don't scrimp to save a buck. Your gear is valuable and being able to bring it along and protect it is important. Get a variety of the storage items I've discussed and you'll be set.

Cameras

Kayak fishing is so much fun and it's great to get some pictures while on the water. Water and most electronics don't do well together, however. Kayak

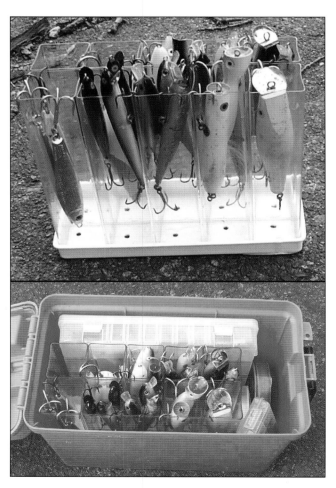

(above right) A Canyon insert is great for carrying plugs and various size lures. **(below right)** Here it is inside a Plano 1612 box.

fishing, as you know, is a water sport. Even worse, saltwater destroys things without them even getting wet. Moist salt air is very corrosive and will eat equipment. Delicate electronics are very vulnerable. I've been taking pictures ever since I got into the sport and have learned some things along the way. You have a few options on how best to tackle taking pictures from the kayak.

In this modern age I no longer use film cameras. I finally developed the roll that had been in my SLR film camera for several years and it was bad. I had taken some great pictures that are lost forever. If I had gotten the slides I'd then have to transfer the ones I liked to digital. That's why I don't use conventional cameras anymore. Too much hassle. It's a digital age and modern cameras can accommodate any photographic requirements. My first camera was a 1.2-megapixel Sony. My second was a bulky 2-megapixel waterproof and shockproof model. It served me well, but at only 2 megapixels it wasn't enough for magazine work. When Jim Freeda interviewed me and wrote an article for *Fly Fishing Salt Waters* they wanted some pictures. All I had were low resolution images. The picture I submitted couldn't be printed larger than 1/6 page. If I had higher resolution images to supply I could have had a two-page spread. That's quite a difference.

I currently have three cameras that I use regularly. The first of the group was my third digital camera purchase. It's a 5-megapixel Kodak Easy Share. I've had this one for a few years. It takes great shots and I especially like that it has a viewfinder. Many digitals lack this feature and only provide an LED screen. Using the screen in bright sunlight is guesswork and I find it very hard to get the shot I'm after.

My second camera is an Olympus SW. The SW stands for shock and waterproof. The model I have is waterproof to 10 feet and it's 7.1 megapixels. It doesn't have a viewfinder but I bought it to use mostly on a bow-mounted apparatus, which lets me take pictures of myself (see below). Used this way the viewfinder isn't necessary, however if it had one I'd use the camera for other applications.

My third camera is the newest in my stable. It's a Canon Rebel Xti digital SLR. It's 10 megapixels and loaded with features. I've got a macro zoom lens on it that covers most of what I want to do while on the water. I've got a 4-gig memory chip and at the highest resolution I can store 288 pictures. That sounds like a lot, but when shooting at three frames a second, memory goes fast. The camera gives me much more creative control over my pictures than any camera I've previously used from a kayak.

Besides being able to use multiple lenses and having total control over my pictures, the biggest feature I wanted was the fast shutter. One of the things I've had difficulty compensating for in digital photography was the delay from when you pressed the shutter button to when the camera actually took the picture. Taking action shots of fish jumping was almost impossible. I had to anticipate action, taking lots of pictures to try to get a good shot. Conversely the Xti takes three pictures a second and there isn't any shutter delay; so freezing action is much easier.

It's not the only feature I wanted. I love the control over shots I have. I can control shutter speed and depth of field, anything my old film SLRs did. I'm often on the water with all three cameras. The Olympus is part of my self-portrait system. The Kodak gets used in inclement weather when I'm not willing

(top) When closed, boxes are waterproof to 100-foot depths. **(bottom)** The foam padding allows you to custom fit the inside to the gear being stored.

to use the Canon; however I prefer to use the Canon whenever I can.

Not everyone is taking pictures for books and magazines as I am, so you're not going to take three cameras along. The obvious first consideration in making a choice is a waterproof model. However, if you already have a camera, why not take it? If it isn't waterproof, and most models aren't, then you need to protect it. Protection can take two forms essentially. Protect the camera while shooting and while stored.

Whatever you decide, don't use a zip top bag. Take it from someone who ruined his first digital this way. Zip top plastic bags are great for sandwiches, not for expensive and easily ruined electronics.

There are inexpensive camera bags for simple digitals up to sophisticated SLR styles that by design allow you to shoot through the bag. I've found them a good option for basic point and shoot cameras but I couldn't stand the $200 one I tried with my Rebel.

The other option, and the one I've used for years, is a waterproof storage container. I use boxes that protect the camera from water and shock when not in use. Dry bags will keep them dry, too, but they don't protect the camera from being knocked around. Also when the camera is in one of the boxes they float. That's important too. Often when I'm out fishing my companion doesn't have a camera; I can toss him mine so he can take a shot. When a camera is in a watertight, shockproof case that floats, the only bad thing that can happen is if you hit the person in the head when you toss the box.

My Kodak EasyShare is the camera I've had the longest. I keep it in a padded Otter Box. Besides the camera I keep the lense cover and a spare set of batteries in the box. I keep the lens cover unattached so I can open the box, turn on the camera and be ready to shoot. Practically all the pictures I've submitted for my articles in the *New Jersey Angler* and online were taken with this camera. Some limitations are that I can't shoot in all conditions, as the camera would be destroyed. The other limitation is the shutter delay.

My Rebel is also stored in an Otter case. I can always bring along the Canon even though there are conditions where I won't take it out to shoot. I leave it in the tank well if I might use it. If conditions determine I probably won't use it, then I put it in the front hatch.

The waterproof digitals don't need any protection other than a leash because should you drop it in the water they don't float. There are a number of brands and models. The two most popular are the Olympus SW series and the Pentax Optio. Both are similar with 7.1 mega pixels, and each lacks a viewfinder. In bright sunshine you end up guessing whether or not you're taking a picture of your subject. That's why I keep the Kodak in the stable.

Self Portrait Camera System

I do a great deal of fishing from kayaks. A hundred days on the water is a conservative figure. While in Florida I average four to five days a week. One of the greatest challenges has been getting pictures of me holding fish to show others this great sport. I often fish alone and getting a decent shot had been nearly impossible. The only things I'd been able to do were either put fish across my lap or hold them at arms length for the shot. My arms are only so long and a fish has to be fairly small to fit in the frame. There isn't much perspective without me in the picture.

While attending the third annual Jamaica Bay Kayak Fishing Tournament and Jamboree, I saw the answer. One of the participants, Carl, had rigged a system using PVC, wood and assorted stuff. I didn't care for the construction, but the concept was great. Carl had gotten the idea from somewhere on the Internet. The system consists of the camera being mounted on a stand that can pivot from the cockpit of the kayak to the bow. Used with a waterproof camera and the delay shutter mode, Carl was able to take self-portraits while holding fish.

The apparatus is basically a 'Z' with one end holding the camera and the other end having a pivoting base. Carl had his mounted on a Hobie Adventure, which has a mast hole in the front of the cockpit. The hole is perfect for inserting the base of the apparatus. For kayaks that lack this hole a Scotty base will work just fine. Here's how I built my system.

The first item I needed was a waterproof and shockproof camera. Waterproofing is obvious, as the camera has to sit on the bow of the kayak and will be subjected to getting wet. The camera needs to be shockproof because you have to toss it back from the cockpit and when it lands on the bow it's going to bounce. There are two cameras I considered - the Olympus SW and Pentax Optio. I decided on the Olympus for two reasons. It's the model Carl was using and it worked for him, and second I found more reviews on it.

The parts I used are a ¾-inch PVC pipe, aluminum one-inch square tube, one-inch by 1/8-inch aluminum bar, three SS bolts with nylon nut and two washers per bolt, some tape, a ¼-inch by ¼-inch by 20 SS bolt, some cord and a piece of foam. You're going to need to drill some holes and cut the square tubing. I used a Dremel but snips should work. This isn't rocket science. It just needs to function properly. I got the aluminum from Home Depot. I had some scrap PVC lying around and I keep lots of stainless hardware for rigging kayaks.

First I made the bracket by bending a 14-inch piece of the one-inch aluminum bar into a Z. The bars come in four-foot lengths and it's easier to make the bends first and then cut off the excess. On one end I drilled one 9/32-inch hole and on the other end I drilled two 3/16-inch holes. The camera attaches to the Z via the single hole. The tripod hole of cameras is ¼-inch by 20. A ¼-inch by ¼-inch by 20 SS bolt works perfectly.

On the middle section, near the camera hole side I drilled a hole for attaching the tether. The diameter of the hole depends upon the size cord you use. A knot on the end of the cord is all that's needed to secure it. Using the two 3/16-inch holes as pilots I drilled two holes thru the square aluminum. I used a 28-inch section. On one end I bolted the Z to the box and on the other end I made a pivot hinge. I used a Dremel to remove two of the sides so I could insert the ¾-inch PVC. The PVC is 12 inches and I put it inside the two remaining pieces of the box and drilled a hole through the sides. I bolted this together.

One thing you'll find is you need to bevel the top of the PVC so the hinge can pivot 180 degrees. If you don't do this it will hang up. Where the PVC enters the mast hole of the Hobie I wrapped some electrical tape. This was necessary to make it snug. Otherwise the PVC spins in the hole. If you're setting this up for a kayak without a mast hole then you will need to step up the diameter of the PVC to whatever base you decide to use. Again I'd use some tape so it won't spin or in the case of the Scotty base a pushpin would work. Where the base of the Z makes contact with the bow of the kayak attach a piece of foam. I used Goop on the foam. That's it. It's pretty simple.

The first thing you need to do is attach the camera using the ¼-inch bolt. Run the cord through the strap and snake it along somewhere in the kayak. In a pedal drive I wrap it around my rod holders. In a conventional kayak, lay it in the cockpit.

When I catch a fish whose mug shot I want, I put the fish on my lip gripper. The gripper is tethered to the kayak so I drop the fish in the water. I grab the tether that's attached to the camera and pull the camera to me. The Olympus has 25 modes. Most are for taking photos but a few are video so you can also take a movie of you and the fish.

I've experimented with a bunch of the picture modes. For most daylight situations I've settled on the portrait setting. It's important to position the kayak so the sun isn't directly behind you. On sunny days it's best to have it facing you. I turn the camera on and hit the delay shutter function, which delays the shutter 14 seconds. I hit the shutter button and toss the camera back to the bow while controlling it with the cord. The camera will invariably bounce a bit. That's why it's a shockproof model and the foam is on the contact point.

I have a spot where the camera needs to sit so I position with the tether to this spot. I have the camera zoom set at its widest so even if the alignment is off I will be in the picture. I shoot at the highest resolution and if need be I can crop it later. As soon as the camera is in position I grab the lip gripper, pulling the fish out of the water and positioning it for the picture. The fish has been in the water a while recuperating so expect it to be frisky. I usually take a couple of shots. In order to take another picture you have to repeat the process. It works very well and after a while you get very good at it. That's it - a great solution to a once difficult problem.

This is but one idea, and there are surely many ways to accomplish the same thing. Use your imagination or check out the various forums. 'Danny' did a side picture system that works great.

Video

Photos are great but video is better. The problem is it's difficult to film our sport. The majority of what's available has been taken with a cameraman on a boat. Jim Sammons stays on the mother-ship and takes a video of his trips and presents them to his clients. Most of us don't usually go fishing with a boat along. The folks from the *New Jersey Angler Magazine* also have a television program called the *New Jersey Angler Video Magazine*. Co-hosts Bill Donovan and Darren Dorris wanted to do an episode featuring kayak fishing, and contacted me for some help.

We decided to film on a lake, and we didn't have a boat available. We couldn't have launched one there even if we could get one. That meant we had to film from a kayak. Their camera crew were hesitant to do it, as they were afraid of ruining equipment. Luckily, one of the guys working for me at KFS at the time also shot video and was very comfortable in kayaks. So I hooked the two parties up and we went ahead and planned the show.

Another problem filming is maneuvering in a kayak to take a shot. You've got to have your hands on the camera, which makes it difficult to maneuver the kayak. We solved this by putting Bill (the cameraman) in a Hobie Sport with outriggers. It worked great. But again you're not usually going to have an experienced cameraman along.

When Bassmasters filmed the Jamaica Bay Tournament, one of the participants had a friend with a boat at a nearby marina and arranged for Joey and the film crew to go with its Captain. Ken Daubert mounted a camera on the rear of his kayak and ruined a few cameras making his kayak fishing DVD series. The *Fishing Magicians* have a show that is aired on The Discovery Channel Canada. When they filmed the show in the Everglades we did a segment in the backcountry, as a cold front had moved through and Charles felt it was going to be a slow day out front. We put the cameraman in the front of a tandem kayak and I paddled and maneuvered him about.

For those of us without a boat or film crew along, the easiest solution is one of the digital still cameras that also take video. Both my Kodak and Olympus will shoot video, albeit I wouldn't want to take a lot of footage with them. They are fine for Internet posting and to show friends and family.

The next step up is a small handheld. There is quite a range available now, ranging from conventional handhelds to waterproof models. I've got a small Sony handycam that isn't waterproof; however I bought it specifically to use with a helmet camera system. The system is completely waterproof and can be used for a variety of sports. It consists of a box that houses the actual camera and batteries. The remote lens is waterproof and is usually worn on the

(above) Here's a jack taken with the author's self-portrait system. **(left)** Here's how he used to take photographs of fish when alone in the kayak; by holding them at arm's length. The perspective and quality afforded by the self portait system is apparent.

helmet. This type of setup isn't practical in a kayak, since every time you turn your head the view changes. Besides, who wants to wear a helmet on their head while fishing? I mounted mine on a RAM mount attached to a PVC pole. The pole is placed in a RAM tube and it sits near the back of the kayak so that it shoots over my shoulder.

There are specific features the camera has to have in order to accept this system. They need to have A/V and LANC ports for the system to work. If you have any questions if your camera is compatible, the manufacturer of the helmet cam will have a chart on their site or you can email or call them and ask. That's what I did before I made a purchase. They were very helpful. The system I'm using set me back about a grand.

Specialized Accessories

There are accessories that are highly specialized and used for isolated or obscure applications. Most fishermen aren't ever going to use them but they are great when needed. Some items will be covered under broader subjects. A kelp anchor is one example. I included it in the anchor section because that's what it is, however only west coast anglers who want to secure themselves to the kelp would have a need for one. Accessories that don't have a logical home will be here.

Outriggers

Wherever sight fishing is practiced the question always comes up. Can I stand up? Gymnasts do amazing things on a four-inch beam and the things some people do on a high wire are amazing. However, these are gifted athletes and kayak fishermen run the full gambit. The addition of outriggers allows most fishermen to stand.

Early on we had the desire to stand up after visiting Cape Cod for the first time. The Monomoy Flats are famous for their sight fishing and elevating oneself another three feet is huge. I ordered in the available commercial units but we didn't like them much for use with kayaks. They were designed for canoes and didn't adapt well. Joey had an epiphany at the Somerset Fly Fishing Show one year. Why not use Ram tubes and extend them out with PVC? On the ends we could put some type of float. Doug came up with the floats - two lobster buoys glued together. It worked well. The system was removable and adjustable, which was important, as we only needed them for specific situations. All that remained on the kayak was a Ram ball on each side when they weren't needed. The negative aspect was they were bulky and hard to store. So we only took them along when fishing places where we expected to sight fish. However, kayak fishing is diverse and while the

The author's waterproof helmet cam is mounted on a pole, and is visible in this photo over his left shoulder.

intention may be for one type of fishing, another may present itself.

Hobie came up with a great solution; Sidekicks, the best outrigger system I've seen. They consist of five sections. Only the main cross bar that is attached to the kayak is permanent. It has three holes, just like a paddle, and functions the same. The arms click in and on the end of them is where the floats attach. The floats are inflatable and fill completely with only five to six breaths. The three holes allow you to have the floats well above the water, just above or pressing down. Because the floats are inflatable they can be stored below deck, along with the arms where they take up very little room and are available should the need arise. Otherwise the only item that is obvious is the cross bar attached to the kayak.

There are a lot of places where site fishing is beneficial. By adding outriggers you can expand the use of your kayak into this exciting aspect of kayak fishing. While outriggers will allow you to stand in many kayaks, the issue becomes whether or not there is a good place to put your feet.

The first kayaks on which we placed outriggers were Prowler 15's. While it worked well from a stability aspect, there wasn't anywhere to comfortably place our feet. So the P15 would not be a great choice if you were going to spend much time fishing places where standing is important. Large tackle boxes behind the seat did allow us to sit on them and still paddle about. This increased our seat height by one foot and the additional elevation helped us spot more fish than sitting in the seat did. While not offering as a good a view as standing, it did allow more efficient paddling compared to propelling the yak while fully upright.

Motors

I have to admit I wasn't sure whether or not to address motorizing kayaks or not. It's not what fishing from kayaks is really about. However, there are people doing it and commercial units are available, mostly electrics. Why put a motor on a kayak? Fishermen do so to increase their range. The motor takes physical requirements of propelling the kayak out of the discussion. Only the loading and unloading of the kayak remains physical. Because kayaks are relatively small and light a motor greatly maximizes range, speed and effectiveness. Also kayaks are very stealthy by nature, as are electric motors. By combining the two it becomes the stealthiest motorized

Ram tube, lobster buoy outriggers developed by Joey and Doug.

system available.

There are essentially a couple of ways to approach motorizing a kayak. You can add some type of bracket that allows you to attach the motor similarly as you would on a small boat. The other is by integrating the motor into a system in the kayak. Brackets are an easy solution and are much more widely used. Cobra and Malibu Kayaks have an accessory mount for adding a motor. It places the motor behind the seat on the side of the kayak. It works. I've seen homemade brackets that place the motor on the stern and an extension handle is used to work the controls. Both work but aren't nearly as user-friendly as an integrated system.

For a few years I've seen integrated creations on the Internet from handy individuals. These installations required significant modifications, usually to the trolling motor. While not the same they each share similar attributes. The control portion of the motor is removed from the shaft/propeller and mounted in the cockpit of the kayak. The shaft is shortened significantly and replaces the rudder. It is then connected to the rudder controls, which provides steering and up/down of the propeller and shaft. Where one places the controls depends on the kayak model. Steering is no different than it was with the rudder. Push on the left and the kayak goes left and vice-versa. A 12-volt, deep cycle battery provides power and there is quite an array of choices. Variables will depend upon kayak model and the weight capacity of the kayak. Battery weights will run from 20 pounds to over 70 depending upon the model chosen.

There is a company called Bassyaks that offers a

couple of additional options. They provide already assembled kits with instructions for several popular models. I know individuals who have used the system and love it. It takes only a few hours to do the installation. Also available from Bassyaks are complete kayaks with the system already installed. That's obviously the easiest, and it's what I did. I had Bassyaks install a system in an Ocean Kayak Trindent 13.

As I type this, Ocean Kayak is getting ready to release a fully integrated system called the Torque. I got to check out the prototype and it's great. I've been waiting for them to do something because their parent company, Johnson Outdoors, owns both Ocean Kayak and Minn Kota. Minn Kota already sells a unit to an Australian company, Viking Kayaks, so incorporating them into their kayak line should be an easy step.

A German company just came out with a system specifically designed for kayaks. The company is called Torqueedo and the entire unit, including the battery, only weighs 15 pounds. That's because they're using a state of the art, lithium magnesium battery. I see electric kayaks for fishing becoming a big part of the sport once the manufacturers offer ready-to-go models. I decided to set one up and one of the ways I'll use it is when taking pictures and filming.

Native offers the Volt, which I mentioned in the chapter, "Choosing a Kayak". There is a commercially produced kayak with a gas motor. It's called the Mokai and it uses a 5hp Honda motor to drive a jet. It was developed for reaching spots in shallow rivers in remote areas. Because of the jet drive it needs very little water in which to operate. I got to test drive one several years ago and found it to be very noisy, though I recognized it did have its place. However, I don't really consider it a kayak, as it can't be paddled very far. It's a highly specialized motorboat and the company markets it as such. I mention it because questions come up about it often.

Keep in mind when you put a motor on a kayak you become a motorized vessel. You're required to register it in all 50 states. I met several anglers who have put motors on their kayaks and most of them have not registered them. The authorities will fine you, as ignorance of the law isn't an excuse. Also as a motorized vessel you're subject to the rules as such. You're no longer a kayak in the eyes of the law or the rules on the water.

Bait systems

In some fisheries and environments having the ability to take live bait along in the kayak can be critical to success. I much prefer fishing with artificials but there are places where bait is the choice. While I rarely found it necessary to have live baitfish along in the northeast, I wouldn't want to fish places like the East Cape of Baja without it. In southern California bait tanks are a regular part of the accessories many anglers take along. There you can actually paddle up to bait receivers and purchase bait. During my few years in San Diego and Baja the only time we used artificials was when trolling for offshore pelagic species. Otherwise it was always bait that we either purchased or procured ourselves.

In the beginning anglers would rig systems using 5-gallon buckets, coolers, etc., and then Jim Sammons started making a system. It has evolved into his consulting with Shimano on the system they presently market. Hobie has one designed specifically for use in their kayaks. I got to test the early version and found it great. Malibu Kayaks has an integrated system as well. The few times I do use a system is while freshwater fishing. Usually I'm taking shiners along and a manufacturer's system like Frabill is all I need.

There are two ways to provide oxygen to baitfish in the tank: via bubbles or water exchange. Bubbles are the simplest and best for smaller fishes like shiners, while water exchange is the way to go for saltwater and larger baits. Bubbles supply oxygen by pumping air into the water. The water isn't replenished unless you decide to physically change it. The commercial units like Frabill are usually insulated, as the water will warm up in the sun. Fish are temperature sensitive and you don't want to cook them. Power is generally supplied by a couple of D batteries.

Some species of baitfish are really dumb. Herring for example must have a circular container as they swim in circles. It does make a difference. One day my friend Bill and I fished Spruce Run Reservoir in New Jersey for hybrid striped bass. Live herring is the bait of choice. I had two Frabills - one was round and the other rectangular. All the herring in the rectangular died while all those in the circular did great. The herring in the rectangular container kept crashing into the corners and literally bludgeoned themselves to death.

Water exchange is exactly as the name implies.

The water is constantly being changed from the source. Because of this it has ample oxygen and the temperature tends to stay the same as the body of water you're fishing. A pump is used to pull water from the source. The intake for the pump is a hose and it's either run over the side of the kayak or through a scupper hole. The water is pumped into the tank and there is an outflow. Since water is constantly coming in, there needs to be

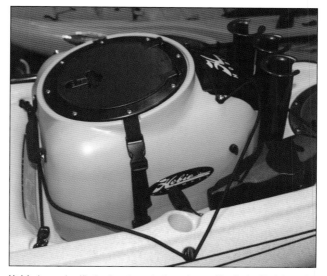

Hobie has a terrific bait system designed specifically for their kayaks.

an outflow so the excess water can escape, otherwise it will overflow into the kayak. There isn't any need to pump this water. The outflow is placed relatively high in the tank and gravity does the rest. Again it's either placed over the side or through a scupper hole.

The above-mentioned systems usually have the unit in the tank well of the kayak. When accessing them they require turning around, usually sitting sidesaddle to get your bait. While not a big deal, there is a more convenient means of procurement. There are bladder tanks that are designed to utilize the center hatch. They're very easy to use since all you need to do is open the hatch and grab bait - very convenient. The systems available are kayak model-specific as the inside shapes of the models vary. The bladder, when filled with water, fills the void. This gives it structure as the kayak provides support.

With either method, tank well or bladder, you're giving up storage space. It depends upon the use and need. If most of your fishing is going to require live bait, a bladder is a neat idea. A tank well system provides more versatility, as it's not a permanently installed system so you only bring it along when you plan on using it.

Spider Wand

This is an interesting accessory that was recommended to me by a few guides in the Everglades. In the backcountry there are mangrove thickets surrounding the creeks and they create tunnels. Throughout these passages, and especially at the

openings, there will be tons of spider webs. Basically whoever is breaking trail, the first person through, is going to encounter spider webs and along with the webs come the spiders - lots of them. Your choice is to knock the webs down with your paddle, but you really can't deal with the webs and paddle at the same time. The solution is a wand, unless you like spiders and webs all over you.

When in the Everglades during the cooler months, I spend a lot of time going through the tunnels and I find a wand invaluable. A spider wand is nothing more than a pole of some type on the front of the kayak. It is mounted vertically and catches the spider webs before your face does. It's simple but very effective. Mine is a fiberglass flagpole that's been trimmed to just above head height. Any additional height is only going to catch more webs and you'll have more spiders coming along for a ride, so keep the wand height no more than a couple of inches higher than your head. Also many branches have been trimmed to allow passage underneath and the wand, if too tall, will catch them.

Gimbal

Here's another really esoteric accessory that most anglers are never going to need. It is a gimbal that gets mounted to the kayak and allows you greater leverage when fighting large fish. Having a rod butt dig into your abdomen dur-

A gimbal is a nifty piece of equipment that helps anglers leverage large fish.

ing a long fight will leave you bruised. A gimbal eliminates this problem. You want to mount it just in front of your seat in the center of the kayak. If you have a center hatch the lid is a good spot.

Safety

Kayak fishing is a water sport, as I've mentioned several times thus far, and people are land creatures, so to participate in the sport we need to do so in/on an environment that isn't our natural element. People have been going to sea and dying there for millennium. We are visitors to the liquid world and it deserves serious respect. The first consideration is dressing for the environment. Clothing has already been addressed in its own section of this book. There are two types of gear I'll be discussing: what's required and what's important.

While kayak fishing, you may find yourself isolated and far from help. It doesn't take long to get into trouble should things go badly, so you need to be as independent as possible. A kayak's propulsion is limited to the physical ability and capabilities of the paddler. I've been on many outings where I've been several hours from where I disembarked. As you know well by now, I do a great deal of my kayak fishing alone and often nobody knows where I am. Should I have a problem, I've got a potentially dangerous situation. My excursions often find me miles from any source of help. I consider myself on my own, accompanied only by my adventurous nature and desire to explore new places and experiences. Being that help isn't necessarily going to be readily available, I prepare accordingly.

A kayak is a vessel and in our bureaucratic world we live with a lot of regulations. Just as we have rules on how to drive on roads with our vehicles, there are rules for vessels, regulated by the Coast Guard. There are items that

This **inflatable vest** from Stearns is the author's favorite PFD for warm weather fishing.

must be present with the kayak when you're on the water. This isn't a bad thing, because it forces paddlers to be better prepared. Aside from what is required per the regulations, there are some that I consider necessary. It's up to you to determine what you should bring along.

Essential and Required Equipment

PFD (Personal Floatation Device): This is the modern term for a life vest. It's the first item that you need to consider and Coast Guard regulations require that one be on board your kayak at all times. They come in different classifications. I recommend getting one designed for kayaking as they will provide greater freedom of movement and make both paddling and casting easier. They come in two basic styles - permanent and inflatable.

The permanent type is the most common and comes in various styles. They are akin to a vest and are bulky. There are units designed specifically for kayaking, offering ease of arm movement for paddling and are the best for fishing. Some have pockets for stowing gear. Units for SOT kayaks have mesh incorporated into the lower back area so they won't interfere with seat backs. This makes them more comfortable than units with full backs. Some styles have a thin lower back area to provide cushioning but aren't thick enough to cause discomfort.

Several manufacturers have combined the PFD with a fishing vest to make a fishing PFD. These are nice, as they offer storage for lures, flies, tools and the like. They are especially nice for wade fishing because you can hop out of the kayak and already have your gear with you. In some situations you might find you will be getting in and out of the kayak repeatedly and having the vest will make it much easier.

Inflatables obviously inflate, using a CO2 cartridge for the source of gas. When triggered, the CO2 that is under pressure in a small cylinder fills up a bladder in the PFD. Inflation is either automatic, designed to inflate when hitting the water, or you manually pull a mechanism that causes it to fill up. These PFD's are popular in hot climates as they are small, comfortable and don't provide insulation. The downside is when not inflated they provide zero flotation. Should the unit fail it could be dangerous and potentially fatal. I tend to use them in environments where it is highly unlikely I could get into trouble.

Which one should you use? I own and use both. When fishing flats, calm freshwater and such in warm weather, I prefer the inflatable. When it's cold I like the full vest, as it has insulating properties and the additional layer helps keep me warm. Also in rougher environments, regardless of the temperature, I wear this style.

An example would be while launching through the surf zone. Waves have a lot of power and should something go wrong there is potential for the kayak to hit me on the head and stun me, possibly rendering me unconscious. In either event should my inflatable vest not automatically inflate, and I don't have the wherewithal to pull the manual cord, I could drown. There aren't enough margins for error. Should something happen, I want to make sure that I'm floating face up in the water, and the permanent vest does just that.

Noise-Making Device: This is another required safety item. Most paddlers carry a whistle. Some of the better PFD's even have one that comes attached to them. You should always have a whistle because it's low tech and always works. An air horn is great when you really need to be heard from far away. However, it is a mechanical device and could fail you.

Signal Mirror: Another required item that allows you to communicate over long distances. Again it's low tech and will work as long as there is light to reflect. Keep it in your PFD so you will always have it available. You can improvise with any mirror. An old CD works fine but won't fit in a pocket as well as a mirror designed for the application.

Light: If you're going to be out at night a light is required. Even in the daytime I have one along, as you never know when you may need one. I usually have at least a couple on board. Lights are covered in their own section of this book.

Non-Essential Equipment

The following is a list of items that aren't required by law but you should consider taking along. Many, if not all, of these can be kept in a single dry bag stored inside a hatch.

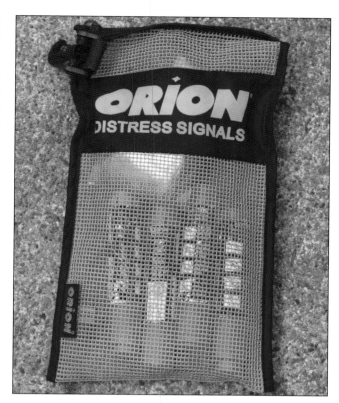

Mini flares might save your life. The author also carries a space blanket in the mesh pouch.

Flares: I must admit that I kayak fished for years and never carried flares. Now I do. They're a terrific item to signal from far away, especially at night, as a flare is going to be seen for many miles. I've read and heard numerous stories where a flare has been the reason a distressed paddler or boater was saved. They don't take up much room and should be stored inside the kayak. Always have them along.

Water: We must have water to survive. It's essential to life. We can go a long time without food, but not water. I usually bring it along with me on any trip. The reason I say usually is sometimes when I fish freshwater I'll bring along a filter and procure my water from the lake, river or stream. However, filters will only work for freshwater sources, not brackish or salt. When fishing salt I bring a couple of bottles— one to keep handy and the other to store below deck. The excursion and time of year determines how much I bring. The minimum will be a quart but most often I'll have a pint with another quart or a half-gallon back up. The farther my destination and the more isolated, the more water I bring.

If you've never gotten low on water and started

dehydrating, I can tell you from a personal encounter it isn't something you want to experience. When I lived in Reno I used to go mountain biking a lot. I would plan excursions with friends I had met through a ski club. There was an area just to the west of Reno, called the Virginia foothills. The mountains had an elevation of approximately 6,000 to 7,000 feet. I had told everyone to bring a minimum of a half-gallon of water and as much as a gallon, to be safe. One member of the group, Steve, only brought a pint and I wound up giving him about half of mine.

The place where we were biking was a long valley with small mountains. We were doing a loop of the terrain and on the return we had a slight up slope. It was only a few degrees of elevation but the kicker was we had a headwind of over 20mph with air temps in the mid 90s. The wind sucked the water from our bodies and I found myself very thirsty with a few miles of ride remaining. Within a half-mile of our vehicles I hit the wall and could no longer turn the pedals on my bike. I had to get off and walk the rest of the way. If I had known this was going to happen I wouldn't have shared my water. In retrospect, once Steve hit the wall, I should have had him stay where he was and I would have used my SUV to get him. Now I always check with my companions on any excursion to make sure they are carrying sufficient water.

How you transport it isn't really important; just make sure you bring it. It's better to have too much than not enough. Some paddlers use bladder systems like those used for bicycling. I prefer a few lexan bottles. In a kayak, the weight and volume is irrelevant.

Food: You can get by without food for a few days, however it's a good idea to bring along some high-energy nutrition just in case you get stranded for a while. Inclement weather might force you to spend time somewhere remote where you can't be rescued or found. Energy bars or drinks (either powdered or already mixed) don't take up a lot of room and are very welcome should you have to hunker down for any period of time. Other high caloric foods like nuts and trail mix are great too.

Rain Gear/Clothing: Always bring along an additional layer that will insulate when wet. (Refer to story in the clothing section.) You can get cold even in the middle of the summer. Packable waterproof/breathable rain gear takes up very little room.

Space Blanket: This is an inexpensive item that takes up little room and would be invaluable should you end up stranded on land.

Radio: A VHS radio can save your life. Should you get in trouble it's the item that will get you help the fastest. Also, though rare, there are times when boaters/jet skis can be a nuisance or dangerous. Having the ability to call the authorities when the act is occurring is best. It will probably discourage escalation of the situation.

Joey, 'Joev', Doug and I were fishing City Island, NY one day for monster bluefish when we ran into just such a situation. The blues were feeding on bunker in the boat moorings. The four of us and approximately a dozen boats were snagging and live lining bunker and having a great time catching the fish.

I was fighting a fish when all of a sudden a commercial boat came right at me trolling wire. I had to put the rod in the holder and get out of the way, as he wasn't yielding to me. After he passed me he ran over 'Joev''s line causing him to lose the fish he was fighting. We started a heated discussion with this jerk and then Joey and Doug joined in. The captain of the boat started threatening us with the boat. One of the people on the boats that were fishing with us called Harbor Patrol and they showed up pronto. Unfortunately these idiots trolling wire through the bunker schools had dispersed them and killed the fishing, so we called it a day. HP was still writing the boat up for many apparent violations. Since this incident a radio has been part of my regular gear.

Cell Phone: Like a radio, it's a means of communication and in many locations can be invaluable.

GPS: A GPS is a very useful tool in kayak fishing and it also provides safety. Knowing where you are is important. Sometimes knowing the speed of current and wind is vital information that can be important in assuring a safe trip.

Compass: Even if you have a GPS, a compass is good to have along and know how to use.

First Aid Kit: Injuries do happen and a kit could significantly prevent an injury from getting worse.

Flag: If you're going to fish areas where you're either

on open water or places with a lot of boat traffic, this is essential. Charter boat captains contacted KFS and expressed that they were having difficultly seeing kayaks while out on the ocean, being that kayaks sat so low to the water they disappeared behind the swells. Color helped but it wasn't enough. Even though a non-motorized vessel has the right of way, kayaks are hard to see, and if a boat can't see the kayak it can't avoid it. We then started offering a 4-foot, bright orange flag.

One day 'Polo', Rich, Craig and I were fishing Jamaica Bay. Craig and Rich headed to a distant shore about a mile away. Rich was in a bright orange kayak, and Craig was in a sand one. I couldn't see either kayak but it was easy to see the flag on the back of Craig's kayak.

Even when there isn't a swell that will obscure seeing your kayak, a flag is great and if I want to be seen, (sometimes I don't!), I use one. One day while fishing Chokoloskee Bay, I overheard a conversation of some people on an approaching boat. They were talking about the flag on my kayak, saying essentially it was a really smart idea and they wished all kayaks had them. As they got near they complimented me on making my kayak so visible. I've been using a flag for years and I encourage everyone to do so.

Sunscreen & Lip Balm: Sometimes you only intend to be on the water a couple of hours but even the best-laid plans can be altered by weather. Should you end up exposed for a long period of time, the sun will catch up to you. The result could be sunburn or a severe burn. These protective items take up little room but can go a long way toward preventing discomfort.

Insect Repellent: You never know and it doesn't take up much room. I was trapped on a jungle island in a severe thunderstorm and without repellent I couldn't have stayed in the shelter of the trees, as the mosquitoes were relentless.

A few members of the "Wolfpack" return from a night fishing excursion at the 2009 Striper Shootout.

Chapter 4
Outfitting a Kayak for Fishing

Outfitting or rigging is what separates a fishing kayak from an ordinary recreational kayak. It's the addition of accessories that greatly enhances its fishability. Most items are easy to rig and will allow you to tailor the kayak to your preferences. You will end up with a fishing vessel customized to your needs. The choice becomes whether you should have someone else rig it or do it yourself. This chapter will take the mystery out of rigging so no matter who rigs the kayak it will help you determine what to do.

We're all individuals with different needs. That's why I'm not in favor of factory angler models. I see them as a marketing person's idea of how a kayak should be set up for fishing. Things are getting better, though. At first most factories' fishing models weren't even set up by people who fish. The marketing folks at the companies thought by adding a couple of rod holders you had a fishing kayak. There's a lot more to it than that. Just go to a tournament or gathering of kayak fishermen and you will see how diverse the choices are. Lately some companies have been bringing in kayak fishing guides and specialists for their feedback and expertise. This is a major step forward and because of this trend and competitiveness we're going to see better and better offerings. Factory models work, but a customized kayak can obviously be much better, being that it can be set up to your needs. My recommendation is to get the basic kayak and either personally outfit it or have someone appropriately qualified do so. We all seem to do things a bit differently, which is why most fishermen prefer to rig a kayak themselves. No two people I know rig their kayaks exactly the same.

I suggest using my examples as a guide. I've put them in this book more so to take the mystery out of rigging than as specific instructions. Some procedures you'll do the same as me and some will be different. For example, installing a rod holder is fairly finite. The kayak model doesn't matter much. The placement will vary. Conversely installing a rudder is much more dependent upon the kayak model.

Tools

There are certain tools you're going to need to do installations on your kayak. In most situations you will have a choice; however for certain applications only one tool will work.

There are two groups of tools - power tools and hand tools. Power tools obviously require a power source. I prefer cordless models, as they're more flexible in where I can use them. Kayaks are big and there will be times when it's easier to take the tool to the kayak rather than the kayak to a power source. However some tools either aren't available cordless or the few times you're going to use them you can't justify the expense.

Hand tools can be used anywhere and while there is a hand tool that will do everything a power tool can do, power makes life easier. So we'll start off by discussing power tools and move into hand tools from there.

Power Tools

Electric Drill: You're going to be making a lot of holes in the kayak. I know there are hand drills because I remember them in my dad's workshop when I was young. However you don't want to be drilling holes with a hand drill. Drills are very inexpensive and can be bought for less than $20. A variable speed, cordless drill is all you need. Drilling in plastic is very easy, so practically any drill will do. If you're also going to drill metal, then a corded drill is a better choice, and these cost even less than cordless versions. For most jobs, though, the cordless drill will be your workhorse.

Drills require bits and there are two types you will need for rigging a kayak - standard bits and self-tappers. The standards are the regular bits that come with most drills. You will use them a lot, however kayak surfaces can be slippery and relatively precise drilling of holes is often important. Being off by 1/8 inch can be significant.

Self-tapping bits have a pointed tip that holds the bit in position in soft materials like plastic and allows for accurate drilling. If you don't have self-tappers you can use a nail to first make a hole that will prevent the regular bit from wandering. I recommend getting a set of self-tappers, though. You can go to a flea market or dollar store and usually find them there. I believe I paid $4 at the flea market for my set.

An accessory for the drill called a hole saw is a good item for cutting holes for flush-mount rod holders. Hole saws come in kits that will offer a variety of sizes. They cut a perfectly round hole and for some things this makes for better installs. Situations where I use a hole saw are for straight flush-mount rod holders, the through hole for fish finder wires, Scotty flush mount bases, to name a few.

Besides drilling or cutting holes, you can use a cordless drill as a screw gun. It's great for tightening down bolts and screws.

Jig Saw: When you need to cut a larger hole, a jig saw is the preferred tool. I've found blade design not to be very important, though I don't like large teeth. Plastic is easy to cut. For cutting holes for hatches the jig saw can't be beat and it does a fine job for angled flush-mount rod holder holes, as they need to be cut oval.

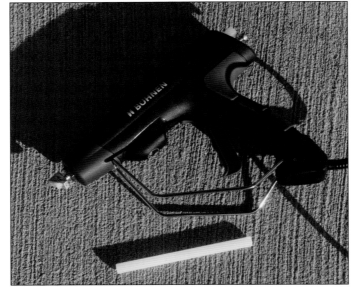

A Welding gun is a useful piece of equipment for kayak work.

Dremel™ Tool: This is one of the best tools for doing a variety of jobs while working on the kayak. As tools go it's not a necessity, however for many advanced applications I consider it so. The Dremel is akin to a hand-held power drill. Its assets are that it is small and easy to handle, has variable speeds up to 35,000 rpm, and has a vast array of attachment bits that allow you to do a myriad of things. The bits I most often use are the rotary saw, sanding/grinding, and cut-off wheel.

Shop Vac: Drilling, cutting and sanding produce excess debris that ends up inside the kayak. You're going to want to remove it and a vacuum does the job. Kayaks often come from the manufacturer with lots of excess material from drilling and cutting inside them, too.

Welding/Glue Gun/Soldering Iron: Whatever you use within this category of tools or call them, they've got a definite place in the shop when working on kayaks. Most jobs won't require their use, but there are special installs and repairs where they're terrific. I prefer a welding gun. It's designed to repair bases on skis and snowboards. It consists of a small iron or tip that has a hole through the middle of it. The gun heats up plastic material (the material is usually available in clear or black) that comes out the tip of the iron when a trigger is pressed.

The gun heats up the material so that it is a thick liquid. When it is pressed against the kayak the iron part of the gun melts the kayak and fuses it with the material coming out of the gun. The tip is approximately 400°F and care must be taken, as it can easily melt a hole in the kayak. The tool can be used for repairing scrapes in the bottom of the yak, filling in holes, and building up material in areas where more material is needed. When drilling or cutting holes in your kayak, it's a good idea to keep the scrap pieces. When making a repair this material can be used so an exact color match is obtained. This would be nice where one would be concerned with cosmetics and would work well for repairing drill holes that were either mis-drilled or are no longer needed.

Heat Gun: There are situations, such as removing dents or repairing cracks, where this tool is useful. I've used a gun to melt a crack and fuse the material in a kayak. For many situations a hair dryer on high will suffice.

Screw Gun or Electric Screwdriver: In the beginning of my outfitting I used a drill with a screwdriver bit, but now I use an electric screwdriver. It's smaller and I find it very handy.

Hand Tools

There is a wide array of hand tools that you will find useful in rigging your kayak. Many are tools you probably already possess. In this section we're not going to cover every tool I use or you might use. I'll keep to the more essential ones. In the section where I show rigging of various accessories and customizations I'll show a specific tool that might only function in that particular capacity.

Screw Drivers: You're going to be using them all the time, most often a Phillips, however a flat blade at times, too. It's good to have both standard and stubby, as there will be places where you're going to need a short driver.

Scissors: These are used to cut items like bungee cord, cord, rope, etc. that are used to rig the kayak.

Pliers: I find I regularly use three - needle nose, heavy pliers with a cutter (used for crimping cable ends for rudders) and vice grips.

Rivet Gun: If you're going to use rivets you can't install them without a gun.

Lighter: This is used for burning the ends of bungee, cord, straps, etc., and leaving a clean edge.

Punch: Used to start a hole so drill bits don't wander. A nail will do.

Wrenches: Used for tightening nuts. The common sizes are 3/8, 7/16, and 1/2 inch.

Magic Marker: I use Sharpies for marking holes for drilling, cutting, etc. A black Sharpie is always by my workbench.

Tape Measure: Used for measuring and marking jobs.

Sanding Block or Sand Paper: This is used for taking excess rough material off of cut areas like hatches. I use sand paper for roughing up areas where I'm going to use an adhesive. Placing fish finder transducer foam is one such application.

Half Moon Rasp: I use it for widening or beveling a hole for angled flush mount rod holders.

Wire Cutter: This is used for cutting stainless steel cable.

Adhesives, Sealants, Gaskets, Etc.: There are a variety of items in this group that I use. Some are more tenacious than others, which means they are more permanent. So if you think that you may wish to remove an item, use an adhesive that isn't so steadfast. The easiest to remove would be silicone. All the others are removable to a degree, with a lot of effort. They include Goop, Lexel, Aquaseal, Epoxy, etc.

There's a new epoxy that Chris from Saltwatersports in Naples, Florida turned me onto. It's called G-Flex and it's made by West End. It's designed to adhere to many dissimilar substances and right on the packing it lists kayaks. It's the only epoxy that lists polyethylene on the package. It's terrific and great for difficult projects or a substitute for welding.

Another substance I use is petroleum jelly. When using nylock nuts it helps to put a bit on the bolt for lubrication. This will prevent any seizing, which sometimes occurs due to the heat generated when using an electric driver. Sheet foam and weather stripping come in handy for making gaskets for hatches and rod holders that don't have them.

Fasteners: Refer to the section below on fasteners for descriptions. Basically you will be using a variety of fasteners to attach/anchor accessories to the kayak. With some applications the fastener you use doesn't matter much, but with others it can be critical. Nuts, bolts and washers are the most stead-fast. If you can get inside the kayak and you're anchoring something that is going to have stress placed on it, like a rod holder, then try to use them. Low stress attachments like paddle keepers don't need it, but I always try to use the most secure fastener I can. I didn't always. I used to use a lot of well nuts even in places where gaining access inside the kayak wasn't difficult. I used them because they were easy, fast and provided a watertight seal. However, over time there were situations where they would break down and need to be replaced. In many of these situations on my personal kayaks, I welded over the holes and moved the placement of the accessory slightly and used nuts, bolts and washers, especially for rod holders.

Fasteners and Other Doodads

Here we have rivets, screws, bolts, well nuts, brass snaps, bungee clips, etc. and all manner of little doodads. Fasteners are the various pieces of hardware that are used on a kayak to attach things. They connect accessories to the kayak and to each other. Without fasteners a kayak wouldn't be nearly as effective a fishing vessel because we need to have items like rod holders, electronics and such attached to the kayak. There are several types of fasteners and each has a purpose. Some are better than others for certain jobs. I'll discuss their merits and specific applications in the rigging section. Here we're just going to get an understanding of them.

Nut, Bolt and Washer: Everyone should be aware of the common nut, bolt and washer. No other fastener is going to hold as well. They're used a lot for installing items on kayaks. I suggest using only marine grade (extra corrosion resistance) stainless steel. The exposure the fastener will have to the elements, especially if the kayak is used in saltwater, is harsh and you don't want to do an install more than once.

It's best to use round heads on bolts, which are referred to as pan heads. You don't want to have sharp corners on the surface of the yak that can catch things, tear clothing or cut skin.

There are two terms used to describe washers - standard and fender. Standard washers are smaller while fenders are huge. If you're mounting something such as a rod holder and have the room for a fender washer, then use them. A fender washer greatly increases the surface holding power and provides the best grip possible. The nuts I recommend are the nylon insert style. By using them there isn't a need for a lock washer and once tightened they don't come loose.

This combination of nut, bolt and washer requires that you have access to both sides of the kayak. If you're putting the accessory on the surface of the kayak you need to get inside to tighten the nut, usually via a hatch. This type of fastener is strongly recommended in any application requiring maximum holding power. Rod holders, especially if used for trolling, are one such example. The strike of a big powerful fish can put a lot of pressure on the system.

There are many places where you will want/need to place an accessory but can't reach inside to fasten the nut. This brings us to the remainder of our attachment type of fasteners. None of them requires interior access. They consist of screws, rivets and well nuts.

Screws: These are the easiest to use. Simply drill a hole and screw the accessory to the kayak. I only use screws for items that don't require a lot of holding power. Accessories like rubber paddle holders, which I use for lip grippers, and flush mount rod holders, are two such examples.

Rivets: These are very common fasteners used by manufacturers to attach items like deck loops, hooks, and the like. They require the use of a special tool called a rivet gun. There are a lot of different rivets but for kayaks only one type should be used. They're called aircraft or cherry rivets and as the name implies they come from the aircraft industry.

A hole the diameter of the rivet is drilled into the kayak and the accessory is riveted with the gun to the kayak. The gun pulls the pin on the rivet and the rivet expands on the inside of the kayak, creating holding power. Rivets work well, are easy to use and inexpensive. Their drawback is that they leak, are difficult to remove, and can fail. The leaking is easily remedied with a dab of sealant. Removing one isn't. It has to be drilled out or cut off. A bit the size of the head of the rivet needs to be used. The size bit is a 3/8 inch for the common rivets used on all the kayaks I've seen. Care needs to be taken when drilling out a rivet. You don't want the bit to slip off the head and damage the kayak or the item you're trying to remove. Once the head is drilled off the rivet it can be

pushed through the kayak and what's left retrieved from the inside.

Well Nuts: These are a rubber insert with a brass thread inside. The rubber has a flange on it and is placed in the hole with the flange resting on the outer surface. As the bolt is tightened the inside expands, grabbing the kayak. Since the entire outside surface of the well nut is rubber it creates a waterproof seal. It has similar holding strength as a rivet but won't leak. Also unlike a rivet, well nuts are easy to remove. Should you have interior access a washer can be used on the inside to give the well nut additional hold. I use well nuts a lot. The downside to well nuts is should it not fulfill the fastening need of the install then you will be left with a rather large hole. The well nut that is most commonly used requires a 3/8-inch diameter hole. That's a big hole if you don't need it.

Deck Loops: Also known as pad eyes and eyelets, are indispensable on kayaks. They're the little U-shaped items you see all over your kayak. It's how manufacturers attach seats, leashes, etc. They come in three different materials. Plastic is the most commonly used. There is also brass and stainless steel. I've never seen a kayak equipped with stainless steel pad eyes by a manufacturer. They're expensive and strictly an aftermarket item. I consider them a nice upgrade but unnecessary for most applications. Plastic works fine but if you're concerned about breakage, (as plastic can break) metal is an option. When using the metal variety, it is a good idea to use a nut, bolt and fender washer set-up for fastening. Since the metal version is unlikely to break, should a severe stress be placed on an item attached to a metal deck loop, a weaker fastener could be ripped from the kayak.

Keeper Hooks: These are used in conjunction with bungee cord to make keepers. They can be used to hold a paddle, hatch or other item to the kayak. I use two types. One is the J-hook and the other I call the deluxe hook. The J is much thinner and I've had them break. I've never broken a deluxe hook.

Bungee End: These are exactly as their name suggests. They attach to a bungee cord and then allow you to attach the bungee to items on the kayak. They come in several styles. There are the hook types and they come either plain (the hook is open) or with a keeper clip. The plain hook is when you don't need or want the hook to stay on the attachment point. Conversely the one with the keeper clip serves the opposite function. Use it when you need to keep it attached. I also like the terminal end type. It allows the bungee to be attached directly to the kayak. They are especially handy for making paddle keepers. I've used them to attach bungee for holding sails and other accessories.

Brass Snaps, Carabineers, etc.: These are used to attached cords, ropes, anchors, drift socks, and other such items to each other. They make connecting items easier. As with deck loops the most common materials are plastic, brass or stainless steel. My pliers, lip gripper and such always have one of these fasteners on the end of their tether. Again it's recommended that you use materials that can handle the abuse the elements dish out.

Accessorizing the Kayak

Many kayaks were designed with pre-molded areas for various accessories. Flush mounts and hatches are the most common examples. This simplifies the placement of some accessories, but doing the installations will vary in difficulty. Some are simple while others are not. A lot depends upon how handy you are and the tools you have available.

Improper rod holder installation is a common beginner mistake. The placement in this picture is well within the paddle stroke.

For example, an easy install would be if you're going to install a flush-mount rod holder in the kayak and the kayak was designed with a specific molded spot for the holder. Make sure it will work for you. Just because the manufacturer has a specific location, it might not be where you need it. If you're really tall you might need them farther back than the company's placement. For add-on hatches it's usually best to go with the pre-molded location. Other accessories require thought.

The most common example is a raised or two-part rod holder in the front of the kayak. Many first-timers will install rod holders on the sides and often place them within reach of their paddle stroke. Everything looks great until they get on the water and find that their paddle keeps hitting the holder. That's a common boo-boo and is a reason I generally don't recommend placing two-part holders on the sides (except with pedal drives). I prefer flush-mounts in this position but not all kayaks will accommodate them.

Before you start cutting or drilling holes, put some thought into what you want to do with the kayak. It's best if you use the kayak a few times to get an idea of how you might wish to set it up. If you have access to the Internet, use it to look at the various web sites to see how others rigged the same models. Ask questions on the forums. Some sites even have forums dedicated to installations and customizing of kayaks for fishing. If there is a kayak-fishing club in your area, get involved. If not then try to get together with people in your area who regularly fish from kayaks and go fishing with them. If a picture is worth a thousand words, seeing a rigged kayak is worth many times that.

If you have a fishing seat then there isn't even a need for any rod holders initially, as you can use the ones in the seat. Another option is using a milk crate in the tank well of the kayak and attaching either rod holders or tubes of PVC, either can be attached by cable ties. Don't be in a hurry, because some of these modifications are semi-permanent.

Performing installations on a kayak isn't rocket science. Most are easy. I've included some in this chapter to serve as examples, sharing proven techniques from the hundreds of kayaks we rigged in my store over the years.

Rod Holders

These come in basically two types as we discussed earlier. Flush mounts, which become a permanent part of the kayak, or add-on removable types. Probably no other accessory sees so much difference in what type and where placed than the rod holder.

Rod holders have two functions on the kayak - to store the rod and to troll. Some fishermen prefer trolling a rod from the front while others prefer having the rod behind the seat. Different holders perform better for certain tasks than others on different places on the kayak. (Refer to the section of this book about rod holders for more info.)

Flush Mount Rod Holders: Let's cover flush mounts first as they require a bigger commitment. You have to make a substantial sized hole in the kayak in order to install them. If you put the hole in the wrong place it's difficult to fix. The shaft of the holder extends into the kayak. It's a hollow tube in which the rod will be placed. They extend nine inches and you need to ascertain if there is sufficient depth to accommodate the shaft. You can trim the shaft if needed, but you don't want to take off too much. Anything less than 7.5 inches isn't going to function very well.

You're also going to need to have enough surface area on the kayak to mount the other part of the flush mount, which is called the flange. It is how the rod holder is attached to the kayak. The mounting area varies within brands. The smallest I've found comes from Cobra Kayaks and the next smallest is made by TH Marine. Either is a great choice where space is tight. You're going to need to choose a flat surface, too, as the mounting area of the holder is flat. Some kayak surfaces may have a slight curve to them. You can still mount a holder there. Obviously a smaller flanged holder will work better. There are other options. You can use a heat gun and soften the flange and when cooled after tightening it will conform to the hull. You can also make/use a gasket or use an adhesive to fill the gap.

There are two types of flush mounts. They come in straight and angled versions. The straight is used much less. The shaft is perpendicular to the flange. They're great for using up front on the sides and are really nice for trolling. Some kayaks have nice flat surfaces here that are beveled (Cobra Navigator and Tourer, and models from Malibu Kayaks) at the proper angle and make this install easy. Most others have a slight curve to them, as it's more aesthetically pleasing. Since these kayaks are designed for gen-

(above) Tools used for installing flush mounts include a cutting tool, marker and drill. **(left)** Angled flush mount rod holder, gasket and screws.

eral recreation, marketers are concerned with looks. Your options in this application are to either build up the area or make a gasket; more on that later.

Installing an Angled Flush Mount Rod Holder

Step 1: You need to choose an area where you're going to want the rod holder. Angled holders are usually used behind the seat on either side of the kayak. Don't put them too close to the seat or you'll find them difficult to use and your elbows might hit the rod while paddling. The placement isn't nearly as critical as with the straight flush up front, though. Some kayaks even have places designed for placing the holder.

Step 2: After you've determined where you're going to install the holder, you need to mark the area to cut with a marker. If the holder has a gasket, use it and trace the inside to mark the hole. If there isn't a gasket, make a cutting line around the diameter of the shaft of the holder where you'll want to install it. It's important to determine the angle at which you're going to want the rod. For trolling, most anglers prefer to flare the rod to the side so you must determine the direction. That's because the hole required for a flush mount isn't round; it's oblong. If you're using the holder for storage you might prefer the rod to be straight back in line with the kayak as it will be less likely to snag trees or any other overhead obstacles. This is only important if you're going to fish places

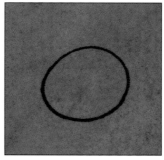

Step 2 - Mark hole for cutting

where these conditions exist. Small rivers and mangrove-lined areas are such places.

Step 3: A variety of power tools can be used to cut this hole. Should you decide to use an electric drill with a hole saw you're going to need to use a half-moon rasp to make the hole oblong. I've found it best to bevel the edge as I use the rasp. This allows the hole to be smaller, as the bevel will match up with the angled shaft of the rod holder. The bevel on the rear part of the hole will be from the top down whereas the one up front will be just the opposite - from the bottom up. My preferred tool for making the hole is the Dremel with the cutting bit. The bit will make its

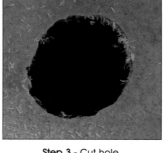

Step 3 - Cut hole.

own pilot hole and then cut along the outside of the line you've marked. Be careful not to let the hole deviate from the marked line too much, but it isn't nearly as critical as with the straight flush. The reason is that the flange of the angled holders is fairly large, which gives you quite a bit of leeway. Jigsaws do a great job, too.

Step 4: Place the holder in the hole and mark the holes where the screws will be. Depending upon the holder there will be three or four holes.

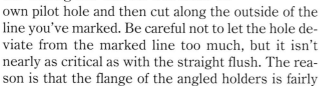

Steps 5 through 8 - Attaching the rod holder.

Step 5: Many of the angled holders come with caps that fit over the bottom, or are already sealed. I rec-

ommend using permanent sealant when you put the cap on; otherwise some have been known to come off. To reinstall the cap in many cases would necessitate removing the rod holder. Why do a job twice when once is all that is needed? If you used a gasket it isn't a very big deal, however if a sealant was used on the flange then it's a lot of work that could have been avoided. Refer to Step 5 of the straight flush installation for sealants and capping shafts that don't have caps included.

Step 6: Use a small drill bit in the neighborhood of 1/16-inch to drill pilot holes that you marked in step 4 or you can simply drive the screws in without making holes. I usually do the latter.

Step 7: Place the sealant on the underside of the rod holder base and place the rod holder in the hole. If the holder has a gasket, sealant isn't required. If it comes with a gasket, great, if not, and you prefer not to use sealant, make a gasket out of foam. Sheets of foam can be purchased at craft stores for loose change.

Step 8: Use 14 x 1-inch screws and tighten them down. As mentioned above, I prefer screws for mounting flush mounts; however you can use any fastener.

Step 9: If you applied sealant, use a paper towel or rag to wipe off the excess sealant that oozed out from under the base when you tightened the screws.

There will be situations where you might want to install a flush mount and the kayak isn't flat at the place where you wish or need it to go. This is common when mounting up front as most kayaks don't have a perfect surface for this application. A gap will exist that needs to be filled with either sealant or a gasket. Using foam to make a gasket isn't hard and it will fill the gap nicely. Sealants are a lot messier.

Installing a Straight Flush Mount Rod Holder

From an installation perspective, installing a straight flush mount rod holder is very similar to installing an angled flush mount except straights usually don't have gaskets.

Step 1: Choose an area where you're going to want the rod holder. If you're putting it up front on one of the sides of the kayak, make certain that it isn't too close to you or else you'll end up hitting the rod with the paddle shaft. This is important and if it's your first time outfitting a kayak you may wish to paddle a few times to determine where it should be. The placement needs to be within a certain zone that is relatively small. As mentioned earlier, if it's too close you'll hit the rod with the paddle, thereby reducing your stroke and affecting performance. If it's placed too far you won't be able to reach it while comfortably seated in the kayak seat. You'll need to move forward and that will put you in a less stable position.

Step 2: Place the bottom of the shaft where you'd like the rod holder to be and trace around it with a marker. This will be your cutting line.

Step 3: A variety of power tools can be used to cut this hole; an electric drill with a hole saw, a jigsaw, or a Dremel tool. The easiest is an electric drill with a hole saw. The size saw is two inches and it makes a perfect hole. You can also use a jigsaw. If you're going to use a saw drill a pilot hole first. A bit 3/8-inch or larger is best. Once the hole is drilled use the saw and cut along the drawn line. The Dremel cutting bit is my least favorite tool for this task, as the bit can have a tendency to wander a little and the narrow flange of the straight flush doesn't allow much room for mistakes.

Step 4: Place the holder in the hole and mark the two holes where the screws will be.

Step 5: The holder is hollow and you're going to need to seal the bottom; otherwise water can and will get into the hull of the kayak. You can use any of the permanent sealants (Goop, Lexel, Aquaseal, etc.) alone or my preferred method is to use a bottle cap (38 mm). It's the cap that's most common on gallon juice bottles, many vitamin and other such bottles. They are an extremely tight fit in the straight holder. Use some type of object to push the cap as deep into the holder as possible starting from the top. At the bottom of the holder is a cross member that will prevent you from pushing the cap completely through. My experience is that I don't quite make it to the bottom with the caps. After pushing the cap down use a sealant to make it watertight.

Step 6: Use a small drill bit in the neighborhood of 1/16-inch to drill the two holes that you marked in step 4.

Step 7: Place sealant on the underside of the rod holder base and place it in the hole.

Step 8: Use flat-faced number 10 screws (3/4-inch length or more) and screw down the holder. I prefer screws; however you can use any fastener. The fastener is used to keep the holder put while the sealant dries. It's the sealant that provides the holding power.

Step 9: With a paper towel or rag wipe off the excess sealant that oozed out from under the base when you tightened the screws.

Removable Rod Holders and Electronics Mounts

Removable rod holders are extremely versatile and can be mounted practically anywhere on the kayak. They are available from many manufacturers. I'm most familiar with Scotty and RAM as they are the units I've used; however mounting any of the others is essentially the same. The bases come in two basic styles: raised and flush mount. The flush mounts require a center hole be made similar to a straight flush mount except the hole is considerably smaller. Mounting one is still relatively easy but isn't as simple as the other bases.

The best fastener to use is a nut, bolt and fender washer. This requires internal access and gives a superb installation that will only fail if the kayak breaks.

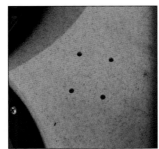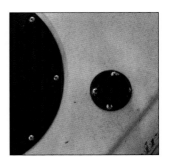

Installing a RAM base using bolts, nuts and washers.

If you have the access it's the best way to do the install. When drilling a hole for bolts, I prefer to make the hole slightly smaller than the bolt diameter. When I screw the bolt into the hole it taps the plastic. I can achieve a watertight seal without sealant. If the hole is larger than the bolt, a dab of sealant will do the trick.

Well nuts are my second choice for installs. I use them a lot, as there are many places where you're not going to have access to the interior of the kayak. Even with places where I do have access, well nuts work great. They create a watertight seal and are good to use for most applications. The well nuts I use are 10/32 and require a 3/8-inch drill bit. The designation is based upon the diameter (10) and the thread type (32) of the bolt that's required by the well nut to tighten. You need to drill a 3/8-inch hole (25/64" is the perfect size, but the 3/8-inch works fine) to install a 10/32 well nut. Make certain of your location before making such a large hole. It's best to tap the hole or make one using a small drill bit. If you have a self-tapping 3/8-inch bit, then use it.

Mounting the Rod or Accessory Mount Bases

It really doesn't matter which base you're mounting, as the process is essentially the same. You need to determine where you want the item to be and then mark it. Determine the fastener you're going to use and make the appropriate hole.

Mounting a Base Using Bolts, Nuts and Washers

Step 1: Place the base where you wish to install it and mark the holes. I use a felt-tipped pen or marker whenever possible. Some bases are deep and the pen won't reach through. In these cases I use a small drill

bit and drill pilot holes. RAM's have a lot of holes in the base. I like to use the ones that form a square but you can use any you wish.

Step 2: Drill a hole with a small drill bit. If you marked the holes using a drill bit then this step has already been done.

Step 3: Now enlarge the hole by using a bit just slightly smaller than the diameter of the fastener.

Step 4: Place the base over the holes and put the bolts in them.

Step 5: Place the washer and nut on the inside and hold it with a wrench while you tighten the bolt with a screw gun or screwdriver.

Mounting with Well Nuts

Step 1: Place the base where you wish to install it and mark the holes. I use a felt-tipped pen or marker whenever possible. Some bases are deep and the pen won't reach through. In these cases I use a small drill bit and drill pilot holes. RAMs have a lot of holes in the base. I like to use the ones that form a square but you can use any you wish.

Step 2: Drill a hole with a small drill bit. If you marked the holes using a drill bit then this step has already been done.

Step 3: Now enlarge the hole by using a 3/8-inch (or 25/64-inch) drill bit.

Step 4: Insert the well nuts into the holes.

Step 5: Place the base on top and put the bolts into

the holes.

Step 6: Put downward pressure on the base so it presses on the well nut flange. You don't need a lot of pressure and the reason you're doing this is so the well nut doesn't get pushed into the kayak. The flange of the well nut is rubber and can be pushed through the hull. On a flat surface with a RAM base its unlikely but with other applications and mounts on not perfectly flat surfaces this isn't the case.

Step 7: Now take a screwdriver or screw gun and tighten the bolt. It's best to begin slowly without much downward pressure on the bolt. This also helps prevent pushing the well nut through the hull. As the well nut tightens it will expand, grabbing the inside of the kayak. You will feel this happening and can then apply more downward pressure to complete the tightening process. Do so for all four bolts.

Step 7a: If you have interior access you can increase the holding power of the well nut by using washers. Use washers with an inside diameter of 3/8-inches; both regular and fender washers work. I only use stainless steel when doing this. The way it works is you put the washer over the well nut on the inside before tightening the bolt. When the well nut expands it grabs the washer. I used this method frequently on kayaks where I wanted to put a mount on a center rib near a front hatch. Some kayak brands are thin in this area and the reinforcement of the washers makes it much more rigid.

Round Mount in a Rectangular Hole

Some companies have areas on the kayak designed for specific rod holders. The Tarpon series of kayaks from Wilderness Systems has two such recesses on the center rib and the Ocean Kayak Prowler 13 has one. These rectangular areas are specific to Scotty-style holders. Wilderness Systems mostly likely did so because they sell Scotty products through their accessory company. Ocean Kayak most likely did so because of the success of the Tarpons and copied Wilderness Systems.

I like Scotty rod holders and use them a lot. However I don't like these pre-determined spots. This is shortsighted, as it dictates what you should mount and where you should mount it. I have found RAM's to be more versatile in this location. Unfortunately the round RAM base doesn't fit flush in the rectangular recess. RAM in response has since added mounts with rectangular bases. They come in 1.5x3 inches, 2x3 inches and 2x4 inches. It makes for a very clean install, though the bases are expensive.

However, long before the RAM rectangular bases I came up with a way to overcome this obstacle of putting a round base over a smaller square area. It requires that you shim the base to fill the gap that will be created when the base is installed. Lots of items can be used for shimming. I use small plastic bushings or stacked SS washers. Why shim when bases are now available? It can save you $20 to $25, that's why!

Installing a RAM Ball Using Shims and Well Nuts

Step 1: Place the RAM ball over the rectangular area on the kayak. Place the ball so the rear (rear is towards the stern) holes will be on the raised area in the back. Mark these two holes with a marker.

Step 2: Drill these two holes with a 7/32-inch self-tapping drill bit.

Step 3: Place bolts in the two rear holes of the RAM ball and put them in the holes you drilled in the kayak. You're doing this so you can mark the other two holes.

Step 4: Now use the same 7/32-inch drill bit and using the RAM ball base as a guide drill the two forward holes.

Step 5: Now enlarge all four holes by using a 3/8-inch drill bit.

Step 6: Insert the well nuts into the holes.

Step 7: Place the RAM ball on top and put the bolts into the rear holes and put the shims between the RAM base and the well nuts of the forward holes. The forward holes are going to require a longer than standard bolt. We use 1-1/2-inch #10/32 bolts.

Step 8: Put downward pressure on the base so it presses on the well nut flange. You don't need a lot of pressure and the reason you're doing this is so the well nut doesn't get pushed into the kayak. The flange of the well nut is rubber and can be pushed through the hull. On a flat surface with a RAM base it's unlikely but with other applications and mounts on surfaces not perfectly flat, this isn't the case.

Step 9: Place a washer over the well nut and press the washer against the kayak hull. I use two fender and two regular washers. I do so as I can't fit four fender washers without overlapping them on each other and that would reduce the holding strength and defeat the reason for the reinforcement. Now take a screwdriver or screw gun and tighten the bolt. It's best to begin slowly without much downward pressure on the bolt. This also helps prevent pushing the well nut through the hull. As the well nut tightens it will expand grabbing the washer. You will feel this happening and can then apply more downward pressure to complete the tightening process. Do so for all four bolts. I have found that the washers aren't necessary in the Tarpons as the material is thick here, however the Ocean Kayaks are much thinner and the washers create a very solid area.

Fish Finders

No other installation garners so many questions as fish finders. People are confused about their installation more than any other kayak fishing accessory. Fish finders aren't difficult. They consist of a few separate installations that work as a whole. At the minimum you need to mount the transducer, power source and the brain. I suggest treating each separately.

There is the actual fish finder unit that has the screen and controls. I call this the brain. Depending upon whether or not you have a portable unit you will either have the batteries inside the main unit or in a separate area. Most people mount a unit that requires a separate battery source. The reason is the portable units tend to be less sophisticated and the battery compartment is huge (except for Vexilar). The last part of the fish finder is the transducer. The transducer is the part that sends the signal through the water and receives it back. It transfers the signal to the brain where it's interpreted into what you see on the screen.

Mounting the brain of the unit is probably the easiest and least confusing part of the installation. It's similar to mounting a two-part rod holder. The only difference is a through hole of some sort is required for the transducer and power wires. This is still easy. The culprit for the confusion is the transducer; more about that later.

Portables

Mounting a portable unit is by far the easiest way to add a fish finder to your kayak. The batteries are contained within the unit, which is usually of substantial size. You really don't install a portable - you bring it along. You'll want to secure it to the kayak, just in case. This can be as simple as strapping the fish finder somewhere in the cockpit. If there is a center rib it's a perfect spot. Some fishermen like to put them on units or design their own to hold the fish finder. Some are mounted to hatches. There are several aftermarket mounts to which the unit can be attached. Portable fish finders come with a suction cup mount for the transducer. This can be attached to the kayak and no drilling or interior mounting is necessary. The fish finder is easily removed and placed in other kayaks, boats, what have you.

Permanent

Most kayak fishermen - myself included - prefer permanent units. There are a number of reasons but the two most important ones are that you have a much wider selection to choose from and you can put the power source somewhere else. The ability of putting the power in another location is probably the more important reason why permanent units are much more popular than portables. The cases for the portables are huge and take up a lot of room in the kayak's cockpit. Most kayaks don't have a lot of room and this waste of space and the bulkiness of the portable are undesirable in most applications. You can make a permanent install portable or semi-portable and take advantage of moving the unit between vessels. Let's break down the installation of a fish finder into each component part.

Mounting the Brain

A lot depends upon the unit and the kayak in which you're going to put it. Some units have a base or bracket and the brain detaches easily. If the kayak has a center rib you might wish to consider this. Keep in mind it will protrude from the kayak. Depending upon how you transport your kayak this might be important, so take this into account before drilling holes. The easiest way to install the brain is on a removable mount. This way you can disconnect the transducer/power cord and remove the mount with the unit. All that will be left on the kayak is a small base.

There are a few different types of mounts. Some, like the Scotty, provide a base to put the unit on and allow for its removal. These are easy to use and are nice for kayaks like Tarpons that already have a dedicated space for the holder. There isn't any adjustment to the unit when it's on the base. Units that utilize a bracket work best with mounts like this. My preferred mount is the RAM. They have universal units and then model-specific base plates. If a fish finder uses a bracket then the universal is the way to go; if it doesn't then either can be used, but the specific mount won't require any cutting or drilling of the unit.

What I like most about the RAM's is they are more versatile than other units. They allow the brain to be placed in a myriad of positions. You can move it either towards you or away, left or right. The other units are fixed, so wherever you put them is where they're going to stay. For fish finder base installs I most often use well nuts, as they are great for this task. You can use nuts, bolts and washers but I never use screws. Even though it is highly unlikely that the screws would pull out, there isn't any reason to take a chance. Installation of the base isn't any different than mounting a detachable rod holder, so please refer to that section for mounting.

Transducer Mounting

The transducer mounting is where I see the most confusion. That's because the instructions that come with the unit are for a boat, and kayak installations are totally different.

Before placing the transducer let's consider how it functions. It shoots a signal through the water that bounces off some object in the water or the bottom itself. The return signal is received and the info is sent to the brain and interpreted. Most kayaks are made from plastic and the signal will shoot through plastic just like water. So rather than mount the transducer on the bottom or stern of the kayak as you would with a boat, you can put it inside the hull. That's right; we're going to put the transducer inside the kayak.

There are a lot of reasons to do so but the most important reason for having the transducer inside is it prevents it from getting damaged. If placed on the outside it will also create drag that will slow you down. Besides that, it will pick up weeds that are a nuisance, as they block the signal.

So we're going to put it inside the kayak and the only thing we have to make sure of is that there isn't any air between transducer and hull. If there is any air you will get an error signal. To avoid this we need a medium that will conduct the signal. Water is one such medium as are sealants, greases and such. Vaseline works very well and is my favorite solution. If the transducer is small and flat (Vexilar) then the install can be as simple as smearing some Vaseline on it, pushing it onto the bottom of the kayak and securing it with duct tape. I tested this method and the tape lasted all season.

Most transducers however aren't flat and a bit more is required. I've found making a vessel to hold and protect the transducer works great. The vessel can be as simple as foam, a piece of PVC or something similar. I prefer a piece of foam for my vessel. It's cheap and very easy to use. Whatever you use you need to determine where in the kayak you want to place the transducer. The location from a functional standpoint isn't important but you may want to choose a spot that's out of the way so it doesn't interfere with storage of other items. If you're using your front hatch to store a cart and the fit is tight, then don't put it there.

Using Foam as a Transducer Vessel

Step 1: Cut a piece of foam that is wider and longer than the transducer.

Step 2: Make a tracing of the outside of the transducer onto the foam with a marker.

Step 3: With a utility knife cut the inside of the tracing out. It's important that this be a very tight fit so err on the side of making the hole too small rather than too large. You can always make it bigger but you can't make it smaller. Check the hole by placing the transducer in it from the top. Place the transducer in the hole and make sure that it's a very snug fit. (The hole is correct when the transducer will stay in an upright position and it takes effort to change its angle.) On the side that will be placed against the hull of the kayak, widen the edge so there isn't any possible interference with the transducer. For the remainder of this discussion, this side of the foam will be referred to as the bottom.

This series of photographs illustrates how to set up a foam pocket for installing a fish finder transducer inside the hull of a kayak. The author has found this to be the best approach by far.

Step 4: Rough up the inside of the hull of the kayak where you plan on mounting the foam.

Step 5: Put sealant/adhesive on the bottom of the foam.

Step 6: Place the foam in the designated area of the kayak and allow it to cure. This will depend upon the cure time of the sealant/adhesive used. I like to put a weight on the foam and let it sit there overnight. It's important the foam be fully glued down so Vaseline won't ooze out the sides.

Step 7: After the sealant has had sufficient time to fully cure (see sealant manufacturer's instructions) fill the bottom of the hole with Vaseline and place the transducer in the hole. Push the transducer down.

The transducer cable needs to be connected to the brain. You can bring it out through a hatch or make a dedicated hole. Should you decide to bring it out via a hatch then you're going to have excess cable (depending upon where you mount the unit) in the cockpit of the kayak. I prefer a dedicated hole that's usually placed adjacent to the brain. The best location depends upon the kayak but it's usually between the bow and the unit. There is a plug on the end of the transducer cable that connects to the brain. This is the male connector that connects to the female

connector on the brain. The diameter of the male connector will determine the size hole you'll need. It varies quite a bit depending upon the manufacturer. Some are less than 3/8-inch while I've seen ones that are close to an inch. Make a hole large enough to pass the connection through. For smaller holes a large drill bit will suffice but some need to be larger. I use a grinding bit on a Dremel or a hole saw for large diameters.

You're going to have to fill in this area, as the diameter of the cable is significantly less than the hole. There are lots of ways to make a seal around the cable. Sealant is one way of doing it, as long as you use a sealant that remains flexible, like silicone or Lexel. I use another method (below) that's cleaner and makes removing the transducer easy. I have a number of kayaks and this system allows me to move the fish finder from one unit to another. Here's how:

Step 1: Get a rubber stopper from a hardware store. The size you need depends upon the male end of the transducer cable. Make sure the stopper is significantly larger than the diameter of the cable.

Step 2: Use a large drill bit (3/8-inch or so) and drill a hole where you wish to have the cable enter the cockpit of the kayak. On some units this will actually be inside the base of the unit (Eagle & Lowrance). It's a good idea to have it close to the base to reduce the amount of cable that will be exposed to being caught by the brain.

Step 3: If necessary enlarge the hole so the stopper fits snuggly.

Step 4: Stoppers are available in a few configurations. One, two or no holes. Most cables are going to have two wires and if you can get a two-hole it's the easiest way to proceed. If not you need to drill a hole in the stopper for the cable to pass through. You'll find it easiest if you put it in a vice or hold it with a vice grip. Use a self-tapping drill bit. The size isn't critical. ¼-inch works fine. Drill the hole through the length of the stopper. Depending upon the diameter of the cable you will probably need to enlarge the hole. Use a larger bit and drill it out again.

Step 5: Take a knife or scissors and cut one side of the stopper along the entire length of the hole. Thread the female end of the cable through the hole in the kayak.

Step 6: Place the stopper over the cable.

Step 7: Feed enough cable through the hole and the stopper so that when the stopper is placed in the hole in the kayak the cable can reach the fish finder brain. Allow a bit extra to give you some play.

Step 8: Push the stopper into the hole in the kayak and connect the male and female connectors.

Setting Up a Power Source

You've got to power the fish finder and a battery is the way. Chipmunks running on a treadmill just won't do. Batteries come in lots of configurations. I use two rechargeable types; small batteries like 'AA' or larger motorcycle type readily available in gel cell or lead acid. If you're going to use the battery for running other accessories like lights, live wells and such, then the larger battery is definitely what you need to use.

You can get one as large as you like but most people are using between four and seven amps. A four will run a basic fish finder for several trips. They're great but heavy, adding a few to several pounds to the kayak and due to their mass they require more of a commitment in securing. Most tend to put them in a small, dry bag, Tupperware or lexan box and leave it on the floor of the kayak.

'AA' batteries are small and many of the items you use on the kayak such as flashlights, portable GPS and radios (FRS & VHF) require them. Having everything use the same batteries is convenient. With an eight- or 10-bank charger you can keep everything on one battery type. I've found that I can run a fish finder on eight AA batteries for a day on a full charge. You can buy the parts at Radio Shack. You'll need an eight-tray battery holder and a 9-volt connector. You can put the batteries in any watertight container - a Tupperware container, cell phone

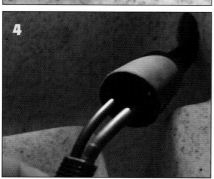

Connecting the brain to the transducer in a semi-portable manner offers several advantages, including the ability to easily move a fish finder unit from one kayak to another. To do this, drill a hole in the kayak where you want the cable to run, preferably near where the unit will be placed. Take a rubber stopper and cut it open through two holes, but not completely through. Put the stopper on the cables and push it into the hole.

bag, Otter box, to name a few, all work well. Whichever battery set-up you plan on going with, the installation is essentially the same. You need to connect the power cord of the fish finder brain to the battery.

The fish finder comes with a fuse. When I installed fish finders in my business I used the fuse, however in discussions with the tech people at Eagle/Lowrance I learned it wasn't necessary. I find the fuse is the first thing to corrode and cause my fish finder not to work. I haven't used a fuse in years. It's your choice.

Connect the appropriate wires (red to red and black to black). You can twist them together and secure with electrical tape, use shrink tubing or solder them. All work fine. If you're using the gel cel or lead acid type battery, put female connectors or alligator clips on the ends of the wires where they connect to the battery. For the AA use the 9-volt hookup. Put the battery(ies) in your container and secure it somewhere in the kayak where it won't get in the way and you're done.

Since the power is going to be inside the kayak and the fish finder is mounted outside, the wiring needs to be run. Some people run the power cord through a hatch but I prefer a dedicated hole. The sequence I've laid out in the pictures is how I do the install. You can do it the same way or use it as a general guide.

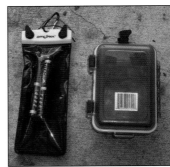

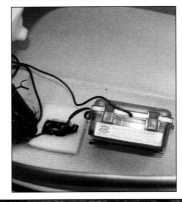

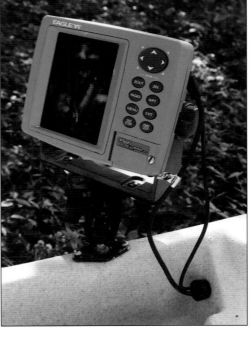

(top two) The author uses either 8 AA batteries or a gel cell battery for powering his kayaks' electronics. The AA batteries are stored in a cell phone dry bag, and the gel cell in a waterproof plastic box. (middle) A finished install, viewed from inside the kayak. (bottom) An installed fish finder unit with cable.

Paddle Keeper System

Many fishing kayaks have incorporated a bungee paddle keeper system into the kayak, however if you have an older model or one that doesn't have a paddle keeper system, they're one of the easiest and most useful accessories to install. The parts are simple. You need a section of bungee cord - somewhere around 11 inches. The length needs to be long enough to reach from the two points where it's attached to the kayak. The next part is a clip. Last you're going to need some fasteners to attach it to the kayak. If you have interior access nuts, bolts and washers are great, but if you can't get inside it's a low load attachment and any type of fastener is going to work.

Most factory bungee systems are on both sides of the kayak. You only have one paddle and for this purpose you only need one holder, however besides holding a paddle they can hold a variety of items and I use both all the time. I like to keep my stakeout pole in one, connected to my anchor trolley. I can unhook it and plant the stake, securing the yak very quickly.

I have found the best place to install the keeper is in the vicinity of the side handle. If your kayak doesn't have a handle, install the holder somewhere around the midpoint of the thigh when you're sitting in the kayak. It isn't critical where you put it but you don't want it where it becomes difficult to operate from your normal seating position.

You're going to make a triangle. The two attachment points for the bungee should be on the same plane. That means equidistant from either the water line or some other reference point. The hook will form the third point of the triangle. I prefer the hook to be on the top of the triangle but it doesn't have to be. Just make sure all attachment points are well above the waterline when the kayak has its maximum load. This shouldn't be an issue with most kayaks but it's still important to make sure. There are neat fasteners called bungee ends and they work great in a keeper system.

Hatches

Hatches are easy to install, especially if your kayak has a dedicated area for hatch placement. There are two different hatches you will be installing and it depends upon the kayak. The most common will be the plastic type. The other will be a gaspachi.

Installing a Plastic Hatch

Step 1: If the hatch came with a template then trace around the outside of it using a marker. If not use the hatch ring for the tracing.

Step 2: Drill a hole somewhere inside the marked circle.

Step 3: Use either a jigsaw or a bit on a rotary tool to cut out along the marked circle. If you used a template cut along the line. If you used the hatch ring you will need to cut on the outside of the line.

Step 4: Place the ring of the hatch in the hole and make sure it fits without binding. If it binds widen the hole. This can be done with the tools you used for cutting. If you use a rotary tool a grinding or sanding bit is a better choice, as it's much easier to control. You can also use a circular rasp file or other sanding tool.

Step 5: If the hatch came with a gasket place it between the ring and the kayak. If there isn't any gasket you can make one by using vinyl foam weather seal. I like the 3/4-inch wide by 3/8-inch thick self-stick. I place it on the inside part of the ring. The foam is straight and with a round hatch you'll need to place triangle cuts in the foam so it will conform to the circle. I much prefer foam but you can also use a sealant, and while I used to use sealant all the time I rarely do so now. Gaskets are cleaner and easier.

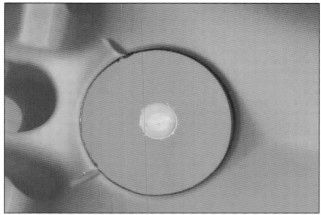

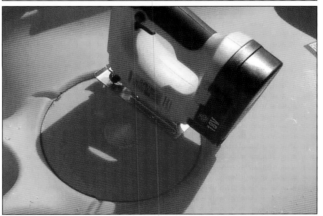

Step 6: With the hatch ring in place drill through all the holes in the ring. After I drill each hole I like to place a bolt through the hole so the ring doesn't shift. The bolt I'm using determines the size drill bit I use. Usually the bolt is a number 10 and the bit I use is approximately 3/16-inch but this isn't rocket science. The hole can be larger or smaller without any adverse affect. I prefer a smaller hole because the bolt will actually cut the plastic and create a thread, tapping the hole.

Step 7: After all the holes have been drilled and bolts inserted, put washers and nuts on the inside and tighten. That's it!

All plastic hatch installations are going to be similar to this install. For square, rectangular or 'A' hatches just use the same methods. The only thing that's going to be different is the size and shape of the hole you cut out.

Installing a Gaspachi Hatch

Step 1: If the hatch came with a template then trace around the outside of it using a marker. If there isn't a template just trace a line inside the outer edge. You want it to be approximately ¼-inch from the edge.

Step 2: Drill a hole somewhere inside the marked circle.

Step 3: Use either a jigsaw or a bit on a rotary tool.

Step 4: Sand down the rough edge that was produced by the cutting. You can use sandpaper on a sanding block, a circular file or a grinding or sanding bit on a rotary tool.

Step 5: Drill a hole for the attachment of the hatch tether if there is one.

Step 6: Snap the hatch over the hole.

Rudders

Installing a rudder in a kayak is usually easy to do by yourself. I use the word usually because there are variables involved - the kayak model and your abilities. The easiest rudder installs are in kayaks that are already set up for a rudder and require minimal drilling or cutting. These are kayaks that provide easy access via hatches - kayaks like the Tarpons and Malibus. Putting a rudder in one of these kayaks is simple. They have easy access and only require holes to be drilled for running the rudder cables and for attaching the foot controls. Even the least handy should be able to do one.

The next group is more difficult and while not hard, requires more thought and ability. Oftentimes there isn't easy access via hatches. Cable tubing needs an access point. When we were doing installs in kayaks like OK Prowlers, we found holes cut for flush mount rod holders behind the seat gave us sufficient access to snake the tubing. The tubing tends to coil inside the kayak, so you need to use a "straightener". If you have a snake, great, if not, use two pieces of heavy, solid copper wire. You want the diameter of the wire to snuggly fit inside the tubing you're going to use. This way once it is jammed inside the tubing it will stay attached while the tubing is snaked through the holes you drill in the kayak. One piece of copper wire gets used as the snake. Put a hook on the second piece and use it to grab the tubing when it becomes accessible at the flush mount hole. Now guide it the rest of the way to where it can be inserted through the forward holes then remove the wire.

Some rudder installs are very difficult. They're usually in a kayak that isn't designed for a rudder or the design falls short. The first group is obvious, as there aren't any frogeyes (a term used to describe the tube exit protrusions in the rear of the kayak) and there isn't a dedicated slide area in the cockpit. When Dave and Scott designed the original Heritage Redfish 14 they knew customers were going to want rudders. The owner didn't want to offer it with a rudder. While the owner was away for a week, the guys snuck in frogeyes and slide paths into the mold in his absence. The owner wasn't happy but it would have cost money to remove these attributes, so they were left in the production kayak. The stern, however, wasn't set up for a rudder bracket. We used the rear drain plug to gain access to through-bolt a tarpon bracket. We used bug glue (a sticky glue made for attaching bugs to hooks without injuring them) to get the nuts on the bolts inside the kayak and made a tool to tighten them.

Many rudder installs are going to have a lot of similarities. They consist of installing separate systems that work together. These include the actual rudder blade on a cam with its up/down cord mechanism, the steering control cables, sheaths and terminal hardware on each end, and the foot slides or pedals in the cockpit of the kayak.

The following example is the way we originally installed an aftermarket Feathercraft rudder on an Ocean Kayak Prowler 15 at KFS. The kayaks have changed and along with it the way one will do installations, however this will give you a good idea on how to install a rudder. Besides the rudder from Feathercraft we used Werner slides in the cockpit. I procured parts from various suppliers in different industries. The tubing came from a plastics manufacturer and the cables and hardware from either aircraft supply manufacturers and/or marine hardware parts suppliers.

Before we used holes for rear flush mounts for access we used the center hatch. So the first step is to cut the hole for the hatch (refer to previous install in this section on installing a plastic hatch). After cutting the hole giving interior access, do the rudder installation. Once you have finished the rudder complete the hatch. The photos used to illustrate the installation are of a Prowler 15. Others will be similar.

Installing the rudder

Step 1: In the Prowler 15 and all early Ocean Kayaks there wasn't a rudder bracket. The through hole for the rudder pin was molded into the kayak. (Now they use a rudder bracket.) The hole usually required reaming (drilling slightly larger) with a drill bit. Inside the through-hole is a sleeve. Sometimes it would come out with the bit. In this case I'd put it in a vice and ream it. Then I'd use a mallet to put it back in the through hole. If the kayak comes with pre-threaded inserts for a rudder bracket then attach the bracket.

Step 2: On the bottom of the rudder pin there will either be a hole for a keeper pin or threads for a nut. Use them to secure the rudder.

Step 3: The up/down cord of the rudder needs to be attached somewhere via a deckline/bungee-rigging clip which is a small plastic guide the cord will pass through. While the cord can be run up either side of the kayak, it seems to be universal (at least every kayak I've seen) that it's run up the starboard side. I found for the smoothest action one guide for each

(top) Reaming the rudder hole to accept a Feathercraft rudder shaft. **(bottom)** A typical rudder system includes the rudder mechanism, slides and foot pegs, tubing, hardware and cable.

cord worked best.

Step 4: At the end of the cord there's a bungee. Use a deck line/bungee-rigging clip and attach it with some tension on the cord.

Installing the tubing

Step 1: On the rear of the kayak locate the frog eyes and with a ¼-inch drill bit make a hole in each of them. In this install I'm using ¼-inch tubing so my hole is ¼-inch. You don't have to use ¼-inch. Wilderness System rudder kits come with 1/8-inch. Use whatever drill bit matches the tubing diameter.

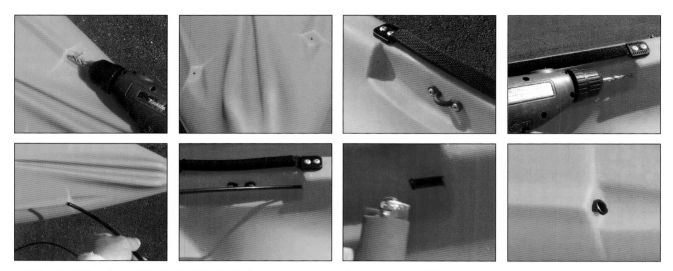

Installing the tubing **(from left to right):** drill holes in the rear frog eyes and mark holes for drilling in the front slide area, and drill these, as well. Feed the tubing through the kayak, and pull it out the slide area. Melt the end of the tubing to create a flange that prevents slippage.

Step 2: In the cockpit there is an area where the cables will come out. Drill the same size hole there.

Step 3: Take the tubing and cut it at an angle so it will go through the hole more easily. Start at the rear hole and push the tubing into the kayak. A fishing rod with a treble hook on the end works well to grab the tubing, as it tends to coil up and might not make it far enough where you can reach it by hand. You can also use the snake method described above. When you can grab it do so and pull some through the hatch opening.

Step 4: Now take the end of the tubing and reach inside the hatch area and push the tubing through the hole you made in step two and pull it so several inches protrude out.

Step 5: Cut the tubing on one end so that there is no longer a point.

Step 6: Take a lighter and melt the end. It will form a flange that will prevent it from being pulled back through the hole. Let it cool.

Step 7: Once cool, cut the other end (at the rear of the kayak) and melt a flange there, too. Be careful not to cut it too short, as it might pull back into the kayak.

Step 8: Repeat steps 3 to 7 on the other side.

Running the cables

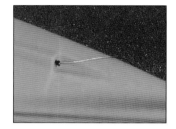

Step 1: Simply slide the cable through the tubing.

Step 2: On the cockpit end form a loop with a crimp.

Step 3: Repeat steps 1 and 2 on the other side.

Attaching the slides and connecting the front part of the cables

The slides consist of three parts: the sleeve, the insert and the foot peg. Place the sleeve in the area of the kayak designed for it and mark the holes.

Step 1: Drill out the holes using a ¼-inch drill bit.

Step 2: Put the insert in the sleeve. One end is threaded. This has to be towards the kayak's stern.

Step 3: Attach the sleeve. The front can be accessed through the front hatch and the rear via the center hatch hole.

Step 4: Use a ¼-inch bolt and put it through the loop you made earlier in the cable then tighten it into the threaded area of the insert.

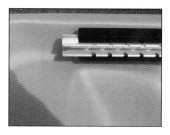

Left to right, attaching the rudder slides and attaching the cables to the slides.

Step 5: Put the foot peg on the insert.

Step 6: Repeat all of the above for the other side of the kayak.

Connecting the rear part of the cables

Step 1: Make sure the front part of the inserts is about two inches or slightly less from the point where they can't go any farther forward.

Step 2: With the rudder in the neutral position (straight) put the rear part of the cable (the part at the back of the kayak that you haven't attached yet)

through the stainless steel fork end. Attach the fork end to the rudder using a clevis pin and secure it with a cotter pin.

Step 3: Slide the copper stop over the end of the cable and check up front to make sure nothing has shifted. After confirming your positioning crimp the copper stop and then trim off the excess cable.

Step 4: Repeat steps 1 to 3 on other side.

Step 5: Make sure the rudder operates properly by pushing the foot pegs forward each way. Once everything checks out, finish installing the center hatch.

End parts, **(clockwise from top left)** include fork end, clevis pin, double cable crimp, single cable crimp, and cotter pin.

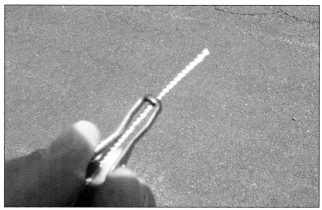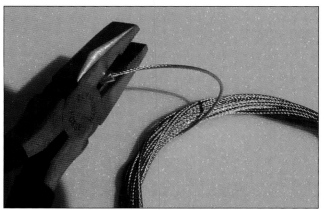

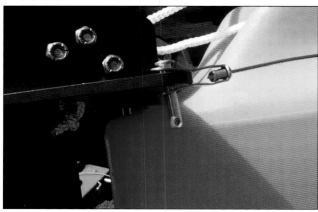

The author's hatch pulley system is essentially a clothesline inside the kayak.

Hatch Pulley System

I came up with this when I got my first center-hatch kayak. Items placed in the center hatch would sometimes wander and weren't where I could reach them when needed. The scupper holes of a SOT kayak provide posts for setting up what is essentially an internal clothesline. All you are doing is putting a continuous cord around either two or four scupper posts.

I like to add plastic clips from a fish stringer. I tie them into the cord. This way I can clip items onto the pulley and toggle them away from the opening. My first center hatch kayak had a bucket for storing gear and if I left accessories directly under the opening they would interfere with the bucket. So once you put an item on the pulley you need to move it out of the way if you have a center bucket.

Chapter 5
Tackle and Techniques

It is my assumption and experience that most people who purchase a kayak for the purpose of fishing are already fishermen. Following this premise, I'm not going to teach you how to fish and use tackle. There are lots of terrific sources where you can learn more about sport fishing. I'm going to concentrate on tackle and techniques that are specific to kayak fishing. I'll break tackle down into two types - spin/conventional and fly. With respect to techniques, we'll discuss trolling, drifting, and anchoring, as well as using stakeout poles and wade fishing. We'll conclude by touching on lures, flies and baits for kayak fishing.

Tackle

Spinning and Conventional Gear

When fishing from a kayak, you should use rods and reels similar to what you would use for boat fishing in the same area, especially while you are acclimating yourself to the sport. There isn't any reason for an angler who already owns gear to run out and buy new tackle simply because it will now be used from a kayak, unless that gear is highly specialized and thus impractical for use on a kayak.

For example, with surf fishing or offshore gear, neither is going to transfer over well for most kayak fishing; but there are exceptions. I've taken surf gear along when using the kayak to access a remote surf fishing spot. Also, offshore gear is sometimes used when tackling large species like grouper, sharks and the like. If you've got high-end gear (expensive) it might not be wise, especially at first, to risk loss, breakage or soaking. After you've gained experience you will have a better idea if you need additional tackle. However, if you do have gear that will work, use it. As a fisherman entering the sport there are plenty of things you're going to need that you most likely don't have. That's the place to put your money.

If you don't have appropriate tackle and need to acquire some, most of the tackle used from a kayak tends to be a bit lighter than what's used for the same size fish from either shore or a boat. It doesn't need to be as heavy for most situations because the kayak becomes part of the drag system when fighting a fish. The fish takes you for a ride, dragging you along. In whaling days this was coined a "Nantucket Sleigh Ride".

Another aspect of using lighter gear is in the offerings you will be presenting to the fish and where you will be doing it. A kayak can fish many places accessible by boat and shore but some of the best places to fish are those environments neither can effectively reach or fish properly. The shallows are such an area, especially if they can't be reached from shore. These areas are usually too shallow for boats to approach or if they can they will spook fish. The ability of a kayak to move effortlessly and stealthily through water only a few inches deep makes it a great tool. These places have some fantastic fishing and the fish are not accustomed to pursuit.

Often these spots are in estuaries and much of the forage base will be smaller. If you choose spin or conventional gear it's going to take light tackle to present small offerings effectively. In shallow water you may need to fish with unweighted or lightly-weighted soft plastics, and these are not easy to cast. Most often spin gear is chosen, as it handles casting light lures the best.

You might think tackle is tackle; however there are differences specific to the kayak even though we're using essentially the same gear. Variables involved with kayak fishing place different demands on tackle and approach. Sometimes the tackle you need to use is going to be dictated by where you're fishing. Other times the determining factor will be the kayak from which you fish. At times it doesn't matter much.

One factor that comes into play is the length of the kayak. The longer kayaks many favor for saltwater fishing sometimes present challenges to conventional length rods. These kayaks have long bows, and a short rod, especially one less than 7 feet, can present clearance problems with some species of fish when they get near the yak in shallow water. When a fish lunges under the kayak and there isn't much depth, a shorter rod simply won't allow the rod to clear the bow without striking it.

There is the potential of damaging or even breaking the rod. Big bluefish are notorious for this, as they tend to wait until they see you to begin fighting. I've found a rod over 7 feet works best for a long kayak under such circumstances. A 7- to 8-foot rod is long enough to clear the bow but not so long as to become unwieldy.

An added bonus to fishing a longer rod is greater casting distance. Kayaks aren't the fastest craft on the water and when fishing for schooling fish that can show up almost anywhere, the extra length results in more distance and a better chance of putting your offering in front of fish. A longer rod when combined with braided line works great. If I'm out fishing and schooling fish are a definite possibility, I'll sometimes take a 9-foot rod with me and keep it rigged with a lure that I can cast far, some type of metal lure, jig or streamlined plug.

When fishing tight places in fresh, salt or in between, or sight fishing, accuracy becomes much more important than casting distance. Sight fishing requires extremely accurate casts. Often the window within which you must present an offering is very small. It depends upon the species and the circumstances. If it's tight you've got a relatively small target area where you need to place your offering. Missing will either result in not getting a strike or worse, you will spook the fish and have to find another target. Many species are ambush predators and

This 16-pound northern pike was caught using a 2500-sized reel, 20-pound braid, and a light action rod.

you need to place your offering in a finite area. Missing most often will result in either not being in the strike zone or snagging. Snagging trees and other obstacles is a pain. Retrieving your lure out of the brush can be difficult, especially if there is current. Even without current or wind, there are spiders, snakes, wasps and other critters in the brush. I prefer not getting that close and personal with the wildlife. Also you will scare any fish that might have been there when you have to retrieve your lure. The species of fish really doesn't matter. In freshwater it can be bass, pike, trout, etc., and in the salt it can be stripers, snook, redfish, grouper and all manner of fish. Getting the lure where it needs to be is often much more important than the actual lure.

Snook are notorious for hanging out under mangrove overhangs. You need to present your lure as far under as you can. Distance is rarely going to be an issue; accuracy is. Shorter rods cast more accurately. Before heading down to the Everglades for the 2007-08 seasons I picked up a 4-foot, 9-inch Ugly Stik® for snook fishing in the backcountry. I kept coming across nice-sized snook in the places I couldn't cast a standard length rod. It opened up new areas I previously couldn't fish. Sight fishing snook in creeks is very exciting, as I would stalk the fish, make a cast, watch the take and then try to keep them out of the mangrove roots.

There were situations where even this short rod was too long. I tried an ice fishing rod. Unfortunately it lacks backbone and isn't designed to cast. I'm either going to take one of the 4-foot, 9-inch rods and cut it down to three feet and give it a shot or build one from a blank. While on the subject of Ugly Stiks, some places a kayak can access wreak havoc on rods. Small rivers and creeks are often choked with vegetation. When using a SOT, other than putting the rod inside it's going to be vulnerable to the brush while paddling. I've broken a few rods when they caught a branch and the force of the current snapped them before I could react. Also, once hooked, many species head right back into the brush. The rod is extremely vulnerable when bashed around trees and other obstacles. When fishing such places I like to use an Ugly Stik, as they stand up well to abuse.

Companies are making kayak-fishing-specific rods. Lamiglas has a complete line of rods specifically for fishing from the kayak. I haven't tried one, as they are one-piece designs. I know that a single piece rod performs better but they don't work with the way I do things. I travel too much and long one-piece rods are very vulnerable to breaking. If a rod is broken it doesn't do me any good when I get to my destination. I'm a big fan of multi-piece rods.

A few years back the folks at Tsunami asked me if there was anything kayak-specific that we needed. I said I'd really like some longer multi-piece rods that would make travel and storage easier, as there wasn't anything like this available. The rods would be great for traveling surf anglers, too. They built a couple of rods, both conventional and spin, to fill the niche. The rods are fairly stout and are part of my heavy arsenal. Since they have surf-length handles, I find cutting the handle back a bit makes them better for using in the kayak. Temple Fork Outfitters has a very extensive line of three- and four-piece rods in both spin and conventional. They are the mainstays of my present arsenal.

Even gear that is used in each area varies. The determining factor is what you're pursuing. For example, in the Northeast we generally use a spinning rod in the 7-foot range, rated for 3/8 to 1 ounce lures coupled with a 3000-sized reel loaded with 20- to 30-pound braid and a 20- to 30-pound leader. This is standard gear for casting lures to striped bass, bluefish and weakfish. However, for Tube-n-Worm fishing, 50- to 80-pound braid on rods rated much heavier and either spin or conventional outfits are the norm. The spin reels jump up to the 4000 size. In May, the big bluefish hit the harbors in the New York Metro area. I joined some buddies in Staten Island during 2007 and Danny commented that my tackle seemed a bit light. I hadn't wrestled big bluefish in a while and figured my standard gear, a medium action spin rod rated for 3/8 to 1-ounce lures and 30-pound braid would be fine. Bluefish, while not huge fish, are notorious for being tough on gear. I ended up breaking two rods that day. I returned a couple of days later with more substantial gear.

In the South the standard gear used in the Northeast would be on the heavy side. Lighter rated rods and lighter braids are more widely used. It makes sense, as smaller lures are the norm. On the flats lightly or non-weighted plastics predominate whereas in the Northeast bigger lures do. In the Southeast I use 20-pound braid and I know guys who use 10. Mono, when used, often is less than 10-pound test. A 2000 spin reel is standard. The first redfish I ever caught was at Cedar Key, Florida. I thought it was a great fight of several minutes. My host, Ken Daubert, commented that it seemed to not fight well as it didn't take very long. I told him I thought it did well. I was using 20-pound braid. Ken commented I broke the poor fish's spirit. Ken was using 6-pound mono.

As we move west towards Texas we see more

The author needed every bit of the length of his 7-foot, 6-inch rod while fighting this fish.

conventional gear in the mix. There are a lot of fresh-water bass fishermen around and it's what they're familiar with. On the West Coast the fish tend to run larger. Yellowtail and white sea bass get to substantial sizes. Conventional gear is standard equipment. Also live bait is used often and conventional gear fishes it better. A standard outfit for Southern California fishing would be used for TnW in the northeast.

As with all things you've got to use common sense. If you're going to fish where a wide array of species and sizes are available, you might wish to go with heavier gear. In some environments the size of the fish has quite a range. Florida is a great example of this. You may be angling for redfish, trout and snook and then a 100-plus pound tarpon, or perhaps a shark, inhales your offering. Having a bit of muscle is beneficial.

The beauty of fishing from a kayak is you can set it up to easily bring a few outfits with you. That way if you run into a situation or see some big fish you will be prepared. When I went to the Dry Tortugas I wish I had packed something heavier. I had heard there were some very large fish there but I was most interested in middleweights and prepared myself for them. What I encountered were small fish and very large fish. There wasn't much in between. The goliath grouper averaged over 200 pounds and the tarpon were huge. The sharks were even bigger, as they ate the tarpon. I was severely under gunned.

By far, your best resource is going to be the kayak fishermen in the region you plan on fishing. Find out what tackle they're using and follow suit.

Fishing Line

Line is an important component when setting up an outfit. For many applications I prefer braids. For the purposes of this book, braid will be used to refer to both braided lines and other non-stretch lines. If you think about it, a kayak is a moving object. Even when sitting still a kayak moves easily when fighting fish as small as a couple of pounds. If you're using monofilament, its inherent stretch combined with how easily a kayak moves creates a situation where it's difficult to get a good hook set. Getting a good hook set becomes especially difficult when one is angling for species with tough mouths.

Several years ago I took my buddy Ken kayak fishing for his first time. It was in Raritan Bay, New Jersey and the species we expected to catch were

striped bass. Ken asked for a lure suggestion and I recommended a school bus Bomber. While paddling out to some structure Ken hooked into a nice bass around 30 inches. He fought the fish for several minutes and I got into position to take a photo of him landing his quarry, as I enjoy documenting someone's first kayak-caught fish. As Ken went to grab the fish it got off.

It turns out Ken assumed the fish was well hooked from striking his trolled Bomber. Ken is an engineer by training, and when we discussed the physics involved he understood. A bomber is a large lure and the treble hooks have big barbs. The stretch of his mono and the movement of the kayak all conspired to making it difficult to set the hook on the troll. Ken switched to braid and has been using it most of the time. The lack of stretch in braided line allows for better hook sets.

If you plan on using braid you need to get a rod and reel that are braid-friendly. Not all tackle accommodates braid. Some older tackle just can't handle it. If the guides on the rod aren't compatible the braid will wear a groove through them. If the reel won't work with braided line it won't be wound properly to facilitate efficient casting and tangles will occur. This can be extremely frustrating as you spend a lot of time untangling knots.

Generally for a spin reel to be braid-friendly it needs some type of line winding system designed specifically to lay down line evenly. If the reel doesn't have such a system it still might be compatible with braid, however you most likely need to use 30-pound or heavier. I've got a few old Daiwa 2600's. The reels are tanks. They can take anything and I've caught a lot of fish with them. Unfortunately they don't like braid so they don't get used much anymore.

There are lots of reasonably priced reels that accommodate braid. You should be able to set up a freshwater outfit for under $100. If you're setting one up for saltwater you've got two choices. You can go with a freshwater reel and rinse it after each use. Even with regular rinsing you're going to have to break it down periodically and lube it. The other choice is to get a saltwater reel, which needs less maintenance and costs more. Expect to pay $100 to $200 or more for this outfit. Having a properly set up outfit makes fishing from the kayak not only more productive but more fun. All conventional reels handle braids well.

There are situations where braided line is not the

preferred choice. Tossing ultra light lures is challenging with braid. Light lures simply don't have enough resistance to provide sufficient tension on the line when retrieving. If there isn't adequate resistance the loose line will cause problems. When fishing micro lures, and by micro lures I'm referring to ultra light spin fishing, you're going to find monofilament to be the best choice. Also as you go heavier the differences tend to blur between braid and mono. When using line in excess of 30 pounds it isn't nearly as important.

Sometimes with big, strong fish some stretch might help. I have found when slugging it out with large bluefish that monofilament's forgiveness is beneficial. Now the determining factor might come down to line capacity. Braids are much thinner in diameter allowing for the use of smaller reels. I have a small offshore reel that holds all the 30-pound braid I need. If I were to spool the reel with 30-pound mono it wouldn't be enough and I'd have to opt for a considerably larger and heavier reel. You'll find braid on the majority of my outfits, but I know lots of very good fishermen who won't use it, or at least prefer mono in many situations.

The pound test line to use will depend on what you're doing. I tend to use 20- and 30-pound braid the most. If casting distance is important I've found 20-pound braid to be a good general choice. If fishing offshore, where there aren't any obstacles for a species like false albacore, I might go lighter as it will increase my distance. Even though braids are thin, the difference between 20 and 30 is substantial. On a trip my buddy Bill had the same rod and reel combo as me but he had 30 and I had 20. Casts with my outfit were 50% farther than Bill's with everything else being the same, including the lure.

The heavier the line the shorter the casting distance but there are situations where the distance isn't going to matter much. Fishing in a tight area where large fish are the quarry isn't going to require long casts but will necessitate muscle. The professional bass circuit is a great example. The participants are catching relatively small fish and using some stout tackle and line because they need to quickly get fish out of heavy cover or away from obstacles. Snook in the backcountry are a great example of this. If you give them a chance they will break you off in the mangroves. While 50-pound line on a short rod might not cast 30 feet, it will winch some good-sized fish out that would otherwise break off.

If distance is the primary need, such as fishing for false albacore or tuna, where it's open water and schools move fast, going lighter along with a longer rod could double the casting distance over your standard outfit. When using a trolling technique like TnW around heavy cover, casting ability is irrelevant, however the ability to stop a big striped bass from getting into the rocks is critical. The lightest line I'd consider is 50 and the two outfits I use for this fishing both have 65 on them. My leader is 80-pound fluorocarbon.

It's generally recommended to set the drag lighter with braids due to the minimal stretch. When fishing from shore or a boat I find this is fine but from a kayak I tighten up because of how easily the kayak moves. I want to get a solid hook set. The fish will drag the kayak, which provides some cushioning for the line.

Leaders

You're rarely going to find me fishing without a leader on my line. With braids it's often important, the exception being fishing heavy weed cover for freshwater bass. Mono or fluorocarbon leaders get hung up in the vegetation and the fish use this leverage to get off. Braid tied directly to the lure slices through the weeds easily. For all other situations I use a leader.

Leader material is either going to be monofilament, fluorocarbon or wire. Wire is used for toothy species that will slice through the others. It comes in a few styles: wire that needs to be crimped and wire that can be tied or twisted. I prefer the latter but it depends upon the application. Sometimes heavy mono or flouro can be used and it will give good results and more hook-ups. When fishing live bait from a kayak where I anticipate sharks but I'm not pursuing them, I prefer not to have wire so any sharks I hook will either slice the line or if hooked in the corner of the mouth I can cut the leader quickly.

I rarely use mono for my leaders. I prefer fluorocarbon even though it costs substantially more. Fluorocarbon has a refractive index similar to water so it's much harder to see. Also it has more abrasion resistance. The stuff is tough. I go as light as 6-pound and as heavy as 80. For freshwater bass I prefer 30, as pickerel are often available and the heavier line gives me a better chance against their teeth. For most of my saltwater I use 20 to 30 but it depends where I'm fishing. In the Everglades I prefer 40 to 50, as the water is murky and there are lots of obstacles. There are oyster bars out in the bays and the backcountry is full of mangroves.

When Sally and Jim from Texas fished with me I had them switch to 50 pound, as we were going to fish the oyster bars. Sally landed a 38.5-inch snook, her first ever and a real trophy for the west coast of Florida. Afterwards I had Jim check the leader. It was badly abraded and it was obvious their standard 20 wouldn't have landed the fish. As I move north in Florida I go lighter because the water is clearer. I usually use 20 but I'll go lighter if necessary.

The first TnW rigs I got had 40-pound mono as the connecting line between the rudder and tube. I use 80 now. On a trip to Cuttyhunk, Massachusetts, I landed a nice striper and the leader had caught a rock that peeled a strip approximately half its diameter, a foot long. 40-pound mono would likely have severed.

If you're using a leader you've got to connect it to the line. Since I use braid a lot I use a knot that was developed for the task by Alberto Knie, aptly called an Alberto Knot and it's the best one I've used for connecting mono or flouro to braid. One of my neighbors in Chokoloskee turned me onto a trick I use to improve knots. Dave puts a light coating of brush-on superglue on his knots. It's great insurance.

(above) To catch this fly rod snook, the author used his kayak to access an oyster bar in Chokoloskee Bay, FL. (below) Here's Dave fighting a fly-rod striped bass in Jamaica Bay, NY.

Fly Rods

Kayaks and fly-fishing go together like peanut butter and jelly. They're a natural. Kayaks are used both to fish from and for access. There are two significant limitations fly fishermen face; the first being a fly rod doesn't cast very far. Luckily the stealth of the kayak allows anglers to get very close to fish.

I learned this the very first time I used a kayak in saltwater. The bluefish were so thick all I needed to do was dangle a fly on the end of the rod. There wasn't any need to cast and I was concerned the fish might attack my line and ruin it. I've often gotten so close to fish I've had to back the kayak up in order to make a cast, as the waving of the rod spooks them.

The second hindrance is many spots are crowded and fly casting needs a certain amount of room. Using a kayak for access to get away from the crowds solves the problem.

The best place to use a fly rod, and where it becomes a terrific tool, is in the estuaries and shallows. These are the nursery areas where most young baitfish and all manner of things that predators like to eat, can be found. In shallow waters, flies imitate many of the critters better than lures and tend to be more effective. Most lures either float or sink to the bottom. Also they require sufficient mass to cast effectively, which can often spook fish in shallow water. Most living things tend to suspend. Flies suspend easily and they're light, as the line is the means of casting. Flies are the opposite of lures whereby the lighter and smaller the fly the easier it is to cast.

Fishing weeds, like lily pads, is great with a fly rod. You can drop small poppers and flies into open pockets and work the area. When you near the end of the pocket you pick up the line and cast to another one.

The weight of the rod I suggest using is one that is appropriate for the situation. It sounds obvious but not always. If you're fishing back bays and estuaries, use gear that is appropriate for your expected quarry.

Keep in mind sometimes large fish can be found in

very shallow areas. Striped bass can be found almost anywhere within their preferred habitat. At night they will go into water that will barely cover their backs. Snook and big tarpon also can be almost anywhere. So don't under gun, or at least have something more substantial along, just in case. Most fly rods are available in four-piece models, which makes them very easy to store inside the kayak and have along just in case.

In the Northeast the most common size is a 9-weight; however I recommend going up to a 10 if you're going to be fishing where the water gets deeper than a few feet. You need the lifting power, as the kayak will end up in a vertical position to the fish and you're going to have to get the fish up to the surface. It's tough to lift a large striper, blue or albie with the nine. It's easier for you and better for the fish to go a bit heavier, and don't rule out an 11. If you're going to be releasing the fish you don't want to wear it out to the point of exhaustion where it might not revive, or it becomes an easy target for a shark. Sharks are going to get their share in some environments; we don't need to make it easier for them.

The kayak becomes part of the drag system but I'd rather go a bit heavier for most situations since I'm releasing most fish. Also a heavier rod is going to handle wind better, too.

If you're using the kayak to access places to wade fish then it's a good idea to bring a stripping basket or similar aide along. They make casting easier and some environments can ruin lines. I had a client using one of my fly rods in Chokoloskee, Florida ruin a line when he caught it on a clump of oysters. The sharp shells literally severed the line 30 feet from the end, rendering it useless. It would be a real bummer to be into some great fishing and something like that happens. A stripping basket solves the problem.

During a day of kayak fishing you might access a variety of situations that will need different lines. For instance a floating line is considered standard in the Everglades; however my first slot snook taken on a fly rod was done so using an intermediate line and a clouser. I was fishing an oyster bar cut that was five feet deep and had a strong current moving through it. The combo got my fly significantly deeper than my buddy, who was using a floater. You can bring a spare spool along with another line for different situations. This works well when most of the fishing is going to be with one line. When I anticipate I'll be moving between situations that would cause me to change lines a few times, I prefer to bring separate outfits. That way I can switch off to the one most appropriate for the situation.

Techniques

Trolling

I describe trolling as when you drag an offering while the kayak is moving with propulsion. It's one of the easiest methods to use while fishing from a kayak and works extremely well. What's great about trolling is there's very little skill involved. It's something anyone can do. All kayak fishermen should troll whenever traveling between spots they plan on fishing. A kayak always travels at trolling speed and you never know where fish will be. Sometimes trolling turns out to be the best method. After I hook a fish trolling I always make some casts in the area before continuing towards my destination. Many times I won't catch another fish casting, but as soon as I start trolling again, I do.

Trolling works best when using a rod holder unless you're fishing from a pedal drive. I prefer having the rod in front of me but I know plenty of fishermen who keep it behind them. It's a matter of personal preference but I feel there are advantages in having the rod in front. For one, I can watch it to see if I get any hits. Also should I pick up some weed it's much easier to spot. I'd rather reach in front of me than behind when removing the rod. Last, when larger fish hit a front-trolled rod, the kayak will be pulled in the direction of the fish more easily since the pull is past the midpoint of the kayak. This places me in a position where I'm facing the fish as opposed to having it behind me.

You can troll almost anything - lures, flies, live bait, or cut bait. It's your choice. My first choice is usually a lure and I've got several types I use. Which one I choose depends upon the circumstances. Water depths, prey species and the species of fish available are all considerations. If it's open water a plug is a good choice. I'll either use a regular minnow type or a deep diver. If I'm marking fish or bait at a certain depth I'll use a lure that will hit that level. To get deep without using wire or a downrigger I'll use a sinking deep diver like a Rapala Magnum. Swim baits are a great choice and I troll jigs a lot as well. If I'm getting a lot of fish with teeth, I will switch to a metal lure.

I use a pedal drive often, which frees my hands. This allows me to cast while underway. It isn't trolling in a true sense but it adds another dimension of what I can do. It depends upon the environment I'm fishing. If there is structure around me I will cast towards it while pedaling and I can still troll with another outfit.

A really effective technique is to have a soft lure or bait a few feet behind a float. It's a common technique in the south for casting but works even better when trolled. Shrimp or plastics are used in the south. In the northeast a sandworm would be the best choice. If there is weed around or the water is shallow I'll rig it weedless on a worm hook so I don't have to worry about snagging. Otherwise I prefer a circle hook. Live bait is great but isn't always available and isn't very convenient from a kayak. A great choice is the artificial bait category offered by companies like Fish Bites and *Gulp!*. You can also impregnate regular plastics with a scent developed for the purpose. You don't have to use a float, either. Sometimes I find an un-weighted slug-type plastic works extremely well. When rigged with a worm hook Texas it's highly weedless. There have been numerous times when I've taken a break while striper fishing and forgotten I had a Slug-Go out until a fish ran off with it.

Drifting

I describe drifting as when you fish from a moving kayak without propulsion. You let the tide, current or wind do that for you. You have a choice in methods. You can cast or drag an offering. The latter is really easy. The float method works great while drifting. A fly is especially deadly as the materials breathe in the water with very little movement. One of my favorites is to drift live bait on a circle hook. In the northeast a sandworm on a 2/0 circle is incredibly deadly. If I were fishing in the south a live shrimp or baitfish fished the same way would work equally as well.

As you float along you can cast. It's especially nice if you're drifting along structure. You can fire off casts to likely looking spots. Keep your paddle across your lap in case you need to correct your course. Better yet is if the kayak has a rudder. It will free up your hands so you cast because you're steering with your feet. If wind is what you're using to propel the kayak and if you want to go slower, you can employ a drift sock. It will slow the kayak down as much as two-thirds.

Fly-fishing while drifting along is very effective, especially when you need to work a finite area within a cast. You can make the same length cast repeatedly because you have the same length of line available when you shoot your cast. Fly-casting is faster, too. Imagine all the fish are sitting within a couple of feet of the bank. When using spin/conventional gear you have to cast, and if you're an accurate caster you will drop it in the zone most of the time. However if you over shoot the area you might get snagged. When this happens you have to go retrieve the lure. After you make a cast you need to retrieve it all the way back to the kayak. The majority of the time the lure is being retrieved through relatively unproductive water. A fish might follow it or there might be strays, but most of the retrieve won't be in the primary fish zone.

The more time your offering spends in the optimal zone the more hits you're going to have. A fly can be cast more accurately and after it's no longer in the zone you can pick it up and cast again. You end up with many more casts in the optimal zone, which should result in more fish caught.

Anchoring

When fishing from pedal driven kayaks I find in many situations they greatly mitigate the need to anchor. Most kayak anglers are using non-pedal driven yaks and will find anchoring in some variation a useful technique that will help you catch more fish. Anchors and their associated devices is a broad term I'm using to describe apparatus that either hold or slow the kayak down.

Anchors do for kayaks what they do for other vessels - hold them in a position. However, that's not always what an angler fishing from a kayak needs. Kayak fishing is diverse, and anchors and their variations can serve a lot of different functions allowing us to help position our kayaks so we can catch more fish. Kayaks are light so it doesn't take much to hold one or for environmental factors to move them. A lot depends on where you plan on anchoring. Some anglers use a ¼ to ½-gallon plastic bottle filled with sand or gravel. This will work for many situations. I use anchors with kayaks in different ways.

Many beginner kayak fishermen think they're going to spend a lot of time fishing from an anchored kayak. However, fishing while anchored in a kayak isn't something most kayak fishermen do much. This next statement is important. Kayaks are not boats. I have said this throughout this book and it's an important point. There is a lot of room in a boat, which gives you freedom to move about. Even a very small boat has much more room than the largest kayak. A kayak becomes an extension of your body. You move, the kayak moves. If you want to face a particular direction you usually turn the kayak rather than reposition yourself in it. With a boat the tendency is for you to move.

Even the way each vessel anchors is different. The best place to anchor from in a kayak is out the stern. In a boat it's just the opposite. Boats anchor from the bow and you fish from the stern. I used to get a good laugh when I'd see factory kayak angler packages, which included an anchor system. The anchor was usually set up so it deployed from the bow like a boat. Why is this comical? Let's look at the situation.

In a kayak you're pretty much restricted to staying in the seat area. You're going to be most comfortable and stable while facing forward. If the anchor is deployed from the front of the kayak the current, tide or wind will move the kayak below where the anchor has been placed. For the point of discussion let's call the direction the bow is pointing 12 o'clock. It's going to be easiest to cast from 10:00 to 2:00. If you hook a fish at 10:00 and it runs to the right, then the fish is going to cross your anchor line. If there is current then the fish will most often run down current. That's behind you and to fight a fish in such a way is awkward at the least. It would probably make the kayak unstable. In a kayak you're most often going to want to have your anchor line out the stern.

I sometimes fish from an anchored kayak. In some situations it's beneficial. Kayaks drift quickly especially if there is any wind or current. If there are active fish present it is sometimes easier fishing if I stay put. There might be a number of reasons why the fish are in that particular spot. Possibly there is structure holding fish and staying within casting range will make fishing easier and more productive. There might be a great rip that developed and I don't want to be in the rough water of the rip, which is dangerous. By anchoring outside the rip and within casting distance, I can take advantage of the rip while having the kayak in a stable and safe place. Should I decide to use chum to attract fish, the best way to do so is while anchored.

You need to be careful where you decide to anchor. Many beginners want to anchor up in a channel or inlet to fish. I strongly discourage doing this. If there is a lot of current, as exists in most inlets, anchoring could create problems. Should some debris, like a mat of weed, get on your line, enough force could easily be created to pull the kayak under. You need to use caution and discretion when using an anchor while fishing from a kayak. As compared with a boat, anchors aren't used nearly as often as one might think. Having said that, it's a good idea to have one along because when you need an anchor you need it, so bringing one along is prudent. I like to keep one in the kayak attached to some cord. Whenever I beach I put it out so the kayak is still there when I return. Tides, wind and current are funny things, especially tides. You may leave your kayak high and dry and be busy fishing, and return to find your yak has floated away. Don't laugh, because I know guys who had to go fetch their yaks by going for a swim.

On a Trip to Cape Cod in the spring of 2004, I was in a sheltered cove adjacent to a house we had rented, with a friend who was new to kayak fishing. I was showing him how the kayak worked when the guys from the house yelled that Perry's kayak had been blown away. I told my friend to wait in the cove while Mark and I paddled off for some kayak retrieval. We found Perry standing on an island and his kayak was on the opposite bank across the channel. After bringing back his kayak he told us he had pulled it high and dry and assumed that it would be fine. It was very windy and there was a rising tide. The tides are substantially bigger in Cape Cod than in New Jersey, where Perry did most of his fishing. Luckily he was near the house in plain sight of several guys or it could have turned out very different.

I almost always use an anchor attached to a bowline whenever I stop and exit the yak. I use 10-15 feet of line with an anchor attached to the bow. I suggest making this set-up part of your gear when fishing shallow places where you will get out of the kayak to fish. This simple precaution could eliminate the need to go for a swim. Your escaping kayak could be easy to retrieve, an inconvenience, dangerous or impossible to recover. Putting an anchor out solves the potential of your yak getting away. If Perry had been out alone he might have been stranded and his kayak lost. It took two of us to retrieve it and with the strong wind, current and waves it wasn't easy.

An anchor is also invaluable when flats fishing. It allows you to get out and be independent of the kayak. Usually the best flats are either surrounded by deep water or far from shore. The Salty Fly Rodders (a fly fishing club) was having its annual conclave and Jack gave me a call with an invite to join them. He suggested I fish for the day then give a presentation to the club about kayak fishing. He also requested that I bring some tools, as he hadn't outfitted one of his kayaks yet. He was nervous about drilling holes. The club holds its conclave on Long Island's north fork. The wind was blowing when I got there so Jack and I found a sheltered place to fish inside a back bay.

There were some nice flats but the tide was slack so I did some exploring while Jack worked the flat. When the tide started to move, I returned to find Jack had left his kayak on the beach and walked a few hundred yards out on the flats. I saw a flat surrounded by deep water just across the channel from where Jack was fishing. I went over to check it out and hooked up immediately, whereas the flat where Jack was fishing wasn't producing. Jack had to walk back to retrieve his yak so he could join me. The tide was rising and he could no longer take the direct path he had used to get to his present position. He had to make a wide circle to find water shallow enough to cross the area and encountered a couple of dead ends that necessitated retracing his tracks. By the time Jack had walked back to his kayak and paddled over to the flat I was on, I had already landed four fish. I caught one more fish and then the action stopped. Jack didn't catch any fish. If he'd had his kayak with him, his chances would have been better.

Having the kayak anchored nearby would have eliminated Jack's long walk back to shore. You can either anchor the kayak or tie it to your waist. If it's calm, tying the kayak to your waist via a bowline works well. However, if there is any wind the kayak will constantly tug on you. This particular day it was too windy to comfortably wade with a kayak attached to me. I found it a much better choice to anchor the kayak near where I was fishing. If I needed the kayak it was close by.

In places where there is a large tidal differential, like Cape Cod, the water can rise on you faster than you would think. When the tide gets moving on some flats there it can increase one foot every 15 minutes. A spot that was high and dry when you left your kayak sitting there can quickly become engulfed and your kayak will float away. An anchor with 10 to 15 feet of line will eliminate any adventures.

Anchoring the kayak in deep water requires more than a short section of line tied to the kayak. The depth will determine how much line you're going to need. As a general rule the line should be two to three times the water depth. I rarely anchor in deep water. Kayaks aren't very good for this and there are so many things that a kayak is good at that I tend to stick to its strengths. In shallower water I'll anchor. These depths tend to be less than 20 feet. I simply deploy the line and use a trolley system on the kayak to position the anchor where I want it in relation to the kayak, which is almost always off the stern.

There are situations where you wouldn't necessarily have the anchor at the stern. When anchoring in a creek channel I've found being able to change the position of the kayak can be very beneficial. This way I don't have to pull the anchor up. I move the kayak along the trolley and the current will change the orientation of the kayak. This allows me to cast into more spots. I use this technique a lot when I do mother ship trips with *Everglades Kayak Fishing*. Several of their most popular spots are creek channels. The tide will move through the channel and it's hard to fish while the kayak is floating with the current. The preferred technique is to anchor in a strategic spot and then maneuver the kayak so you can cast to all spots within range. When you've worked the area over you then pull up the anchor and go to the next spot.

There are many types of anchors for various conditions. For many applications a brick would suffice. You could also get a small detergent container, milk bottle, etc., and fill it with rock or sand. There are mushroom styles. The one that many of us use is a folding grappling hook. It does the job. In still water an anchor as light as 1.5 pounds will do. In the salt, current or wind I prefer a 3 pounder. Adding chain to an anchor increases its holding power. Adding a few feet of chain to a small anchor will make it act like a larger one.

I use three anchor types: a 1.5 or 3-pound grappling style that fold for storage, a 5-pound bar type and a section of chain. These anchors cover most of the situations I encounter. The grappling style of anchor will burrow into a soft bottom like sand or mud or lodge into bottom structure. Sometimes it will attach itself too well and be difficult to remove. At the opposite end of the attachment point for the anchor line is another place to put a line. This is meant for a second line, which can be attached to a buoy or you can use a floating line. Should the anchor get stuck you can pull in up from the opposite direction to free it.

I like the bar type for slow moving waters like a river. I'll use it to anchor above a fishy looking spot and work the area until I've either caught a bunch of fish or I covered it sufficiently. Then I pick up the anchor and allow the kayak to drift down another 20 to 30 feet. I keep repeating this as long as there is water I want to cover.

Chain is an idea I got from Charles Wright of *Everglades Kayak Fishing*. When deployed from the kayak the chain works like brakes in a vehicle. You can paddle along slowly with it dragging the bottom, but as soon as you stop, the chain holds the kayak in place. It's the best way for stalking fish when sight fishing from a kayak, as you often need to stop immediately upon spotting your quarry. The chain stops the kayak as soon as you stop propelling it. I only use chain for this specific circumstance as the dragging can tear up vegetation. It also causes drag and will slow down the kayak.

Anchors require anchor line so you're going to need to keep it somewhere. Having 50 to 100 feet of anchor line lying around the kayak is a disaster waiting to happen. One simple method I've found is using a rope reel. The reel allows you to store line by winding it up. It's also easy to let the line out. I use Paracord and my preferred color is white. It's easier to see where the line is. The reel is easily stored and will fit inside a 10-inch hatch. Since it's made of plastic there aren't any components to break down from saltwater. In shallow areas, 50 feet of line is more than adequate. You can let the entire line out and clip the rope reel to the end of your external pulley. It's a good idea to have either a clip or loop on the end of the anchor line. This way you can easily attach it to the anchor. If you don't let all the line out from the reel you can use a cleat on the kayak to tie it off.

Another simple way to store the anchor line is to use a large cleat. Attach the line to the cleat and wrap it around. The amount of line is limited by the size of the cleat. For the majority of your needs a 5-inch cleat will do.

Another neat trick some of the guys fishing big rivers of the Pacific Northwest are using is a short rod and a saltwater conventional reel. They put heavy line on it and put it on a very short rod (2 feet or so). It makes a terrific anchor line system in theory. Just put the line through the clip of your trolley and you have all the line you could possibly need for any anchoring contingency. It doesn't take much to

hold a kayak. When snagged it works as an anchor. On the West Coast they use a kelp anchor, which is basically a grappling hook that's used to hook onto kelp. The waters they fish are deep, so instead of anchoring to the bottom they attach themselves to the kelp.

I like to add a buoy to my anchor line, then attach the kayak to the anchor line on a quick release. This allows me to quickly unhook from the anchor to fight a fish. The buoy gives a visual of where the anchor is when it's time to retrieve it. A plastic bottle also works well, especially small, brightly colored detergent bottles. You can also buy brightly colored buoys or floats. I've seen sections of pool noodles used. Anything that floats and can be seen will do.

Another anchoring device is what's called a sea anchor or drift sock. I tend to call them drift socks but both terms are commonly used. What it does is slow down a vessel in wind. It's basically a parachute. Instead of filling with air to slow down an object, it uses water. As the wind pushes the kayak, the sock digs into the water and slows it. I started using one early on while kayak fishing. Back in 2001 several of us got together to fish Long Island Sound. We were fishing along an island, the wind was blowing from the northeast and we wanted to drift parallel to the shore. I had the sock on and everyone else flew by me. When they asked how I could go so slowly and controlled I pointed to the drift sock I had deployed. The next time we fished together everyone had a sock.

In New Jersey, there is a fall migration of fish as they head to their preferred wintering grounds. As striped bass, bluefish and weakfish migrate south past our shores we can experience some excellent kayak fishing. The best days to kayak fish are when the winds are blowing from either the west or northwest. Since the New Jersey coast runs north/south, winds from this direction knock the swell down. The surf will usually only be one to two feet, making for an easy time in the surf zone.

Under such conditions, the wind pushes the bait off the beach and even the longest surf casts can't reach them. It's perfect for the kayak, as the fish tend to be a few hundred yards out. Once beyond the protection of the land, the wind wants to push you towards Europe. In these circumstances I find trolling to be the best technique. I keep my drift sock on my lap attached to an anchor trolley. When I hook a fish, the first thing I do is toss the sock in the water and toggle it back to the stern of the kayak. After I do this I grab the rod from the holder and start fighting the fish. Without the sock I could easily end up a mile or more out to sea by the time the fight is over. With the sock it's usually only a couple of hundred yards. It saves me a lot of energy returning to the zone where the fish are.

Even if there isn't any wind, a sock is very handy. When fighting large fish it will help to wear them down by increasing the resistance without increasing the drag on your reel. This way the kayak becomes even more a part of the fighting mechanics in landing a fish. Billfish, tarpon, sharks, halibut, etc. have been known to tow anglers for miles. When Jim Sammons hooked the first marlin from a kayak, the fish towed him several miles. Ken Daubert told me when he used to fish for big tarpon, getting towed three to four miles was common. Ironically the fish never tow you back from where you launched!

Drift socks take up very little room so there isn't any reason not to have one inside the hull of the kayak. Should you find yourself in a situation where it would be good to have one, it will be there. One misconception I often hear from people is using one in rivers. A sock won't work in a current and it might actually increase your speed over the water. That's because it gives more surface area for the current to grab.

Stakeout Poles

As previously mentioned I was familiar with, but had never used, a stakeout pole until I started fishing in Florida. It's a tremendous tool whenever fishing shallow water. A pole is attached to the kayak by some means and jammed into the bottom, holding the kayak in place. Many anglers simply put it through a scupper hole, which works great. I fish from Hobie Mirages often and they have scuppers in the rear tank well only. When fishing the Adventure I use the dagger board hole, but it's the only model that has such an opening.

I don't find the rear scupper holes of the other models practical to use for staking. There are a few reasons. First there's the obvious; reaching behind and placing the pole in the scupper is a great way to dump the kayak. Second, even if it weren't difficult I usually have gear in the tank well and I wouldn't want to give up the storage space. Last, there are times when I need to place the pole quickly and a twist, reach and plant maneuver is too slow. When

staking the kayak via a scupper hole nothing else is necessary; however, when used on the outside of the kayak I attach it to my anchor trolley. All of my stakeout poles have a line attached to the top. I connect this line to the clip on my anchor trolley and keep the pole in my right side paddle keeper. It's ready to go when needed.

There are some great commercially made poles. I've seen several but the ones I use are homemade. Many of the places I fish have soft bottoms so I don't need a sharp point, as is common on most poles. One thing I've discovered though is most of the commercial poles are too short to work in some of my favorite backcountry areas. The Everglades backcountry is a maze of mangrove lakes and ponds connected by creeks. Most of the inlets or outlets of these bodies hold fish. Often the water is too deep for the standard pole and anchoring is a chore compared to a stakeout pole.

I made my own out of a telescoping aluminum painters pole. Mine is 40 inches at its shortest and six feet fully extended. On the top end I attached some cord in a loop that I hook to the clip on my anchor trolley. The extra length allows me to set up and fish places quickly where other anglers can't. It's very easy to use and fast. This worked well for most situations but occasionally I needed something even longer. So I made one out of aluminum conduit and it's over seven feet.

As mentioned earlier, the Everglades backcountry has lots of small ponds. Many are less than 50 feet long and only a kayak length or two across. They hold some nice snook and are hard to fish. One day, while entering one, I saw a good-looking snook along the shore. It ignored my offering and swam into the mangroves. After losing my visual on that fish, I headed off to a larger nearby lake where the snook were really going off and caught a few dozen.

On my way back I noticed that I was spooking a lot of snook in the creeks. As I approached the pond where I had seen the nice snook, I didn't pedal or paddle at all and stayed very still until I drifted out into the middle. I turned the kayak and fired off a long cast back to where the creeks were (both the inlet and outlet were next to each other). My lure hadn't moved more than a couple of feet when I had a solid hook-up. I quickly grabbed my stakeout pole and jammed it into the soft bottom of the pond. The extra length made all the difference, as I was held tight. I barely prevented the snook from gaining the mangroves and landed a very respectable 26-incher. I entered the outlet creek and in the next pond's inlet I staked out in a position to fish it thoroughly. I usually spook fish my first time through, so I always give it a few casts on my way back. I was rewarded with five feisty snook.

Although I first started using a stakeout pole in Florida for flats fishing, I've found it useful anywhere the water is shallow and soft enough to get a hold. It's a terrific addition to the kayak fishing goodies.

Wading

Some of the great things about a kayak are the freedom and choices it gives you on where to fish. Many shore-accessed locations become crowded in season when the fishing is best. Sometimes they are unfishable or you have to get to them very early to get a spot. If you fly fish you're going to need some space around you to cast. A kayak can provide the means you need to escape. Then there are the places where only a small boat or a kayak can reach - places you might have all to yourself.

I often use a kayak to access places where I can wade. It's similar to wading from shore except the kayak extends my range. A flat is the environment that most often comes to mind when one thinks of wading. Stalking bonefish on shallow sandy flats in the Florida Keys or the Caribbean is what comes to most anglers' minds. Flats are not restricted to the tropics and are not all sandy. Oyster bars provide terrific fishing and wading them is very effective. Oftentimes it's the best way to fish them. Sometimes there is deep water between you and a flat and the kayak is necessary to reach wade-able water. A kayak becomes a terrific tackle locker, too, enabling me to carry a lot more gear. Multiple rods rigged differently, food, clothing, tools and such. It allows me to be much better prepared.

There are a number of reasons to wade. Sometimes it's breezy and controlling the kayak becomes difficult. Often it's stealthier to wade or it affords better vision. When wading flats I sometimes attach the kayak to me via a bowline. That way as I wade my kayak comes with me. It's great when there isn't much current or wind. One of my favorite areas to wade is an extensive oyster bar system. I can fish them very effectively while wading and find a fly rod to be especially effective. The fish can be anywhere and I can effectively probe all the spots. It's easier to fish while standing. Often I would get clients who

Kayaks are often used to access good wading areas. Here's Steve with a nice Cape Cod striped bass.

didn't have a lot of experience in kayaks and as part of my charter I would incorporate wading the oyster bars.

Earlier I mentioned Sally and Jim. The first day we fished the current was moving strongly between the bars and there was a significant wind. Sally hadn't been fishing or kayaking very long so I suggested we head over to a particular bar where we could wade. The spot also put the wind at our back. The channel we could access was one of my favorites. It was a major pass through the bars connecting some flats that ran out to a deep hole. On Sally's third cast she hooked a fish of a lifetime and did a great job fighting and landing a 38.5-inch snook. They are having a replica made.

Sally isn't the only one who has benefited from walking the bars. The first clients I ever had were a teacher from Oregon, Seth, and his buddy. It had been a slow morning as the guys were 90 minutes late and we missed the tide. We had caught a few fish going out one of the minor passes and returning via another. I left them on a series of bars and checked out the open water to see if any ladyfish were working the area. I saw that the guys weren't fishing anymore and when they saw me looking their way they waved me over. Seth had seen a commotion in the distance, waded towards the area and on the first cast hooked and landed a 33-inch snook.

When moving water from current or tide becomes too much, getting out can often make the difference between catching and fishing. Using a kayak to access remote parts of rivers and then wading is a great way to catch game fish that don't see much pressure. These spots would be difficult or impossible to reach wading from an access point. The kayak is used to transport you and your gear to the spot where you then fish as if you had hiked in. If it's a slippery stream I either bring boots with studs and felt or a set of Korkers.

This 33-inch snook was spotted while wading oyster bars in Chokoloskee Bay, FL. Seth fired a long cast and the fish hit immediately.

Wading is a great technique that is part of my kayak fishing repertoire.

Lures and Flies

I'm not going to dwell on this much. I'm sure you've got your favorites, as do I. I'll discuss lures first. There are some lures I've found to be very effective and can be used all over. I try to use single hook lures as much as possible. The fewer hooks I have to deal with while fishing from a kayak the better. I go barbless a lot, too. Try to keep it simple. You will find there are certain lures you're going to use most of the time. I tend to fish only a few and once I learn an area I eventually trim down to the ones I use most frequently. I have a ton of lures, as many fishermen do, but probably 99% of them rarely if ever get used.

There are certain types of lures you should include in your arsenal, again depending upon your regional requirements.

Jigs

Before I started kayak fishing I did use jigs, but not to the degree I do now. They are a mainstay of my arsenal, with so many types available. I have three favorite styles. Heads that require a soft plastic added on the hook, ones with hair or feathers tied on and the swim baits (covered below). The swim baits are incredibly realistic looking and take fish everywhere, however if you've got toothy critters in the mix these jigs get destroyed quickly. It gets expensive so I use the first type for these situations. The tails are cheap and it only takes seconds to replace them.

Jig Spoons

These jigs are more like bars of metal. Some are painted, like the candy bar styles common to southern California. They are heavy and very popular where deeper waters are the norm. In the northeast, painted versions aren't used. Instead they are chrome plated and sometimes they have prism tape on them. The most popular ones there are the Ava and Diamonds. They work and get deep in a hurry. In the smaller sizes they are great when you need to cast far and will take most species.

Spoons

Spoons are great kayak fishing lures. Many are available with solo hooks and most tend to cast far. They cover all levels of the water column. The weed less spoons, first introduced by Johnson, is a mainstay anywhere you find redfish. My friend Terry introduced me to the replaceable, fixed hook spoons like the Pet Spoon. Fish love them, and the hooks can be replaced when they become rusted. Everything seems to attack wobblers like Crocodiles. Then there are the heavy spoons that are between the jig spoons and spoons; offerings like Kastmasters and Hopkins.

Swim Baits

When fishing for non-toothy species I love this class of lures. Storm introduced the first lures of this genre, the Wild-Eye Shad, and now it seems every lure manufacturer offers them. That's because they work. Most are jigs covered with plastic. They're very lifelike and I prefer the single hook versions while fishing from the kayak.

Plastic Baits

Another lure type you won't find me without is plastic bait, my favorite class of lures. This is probably because my formative years as a fisherman were pursuing black bass, and plastics work great for them. The first ones I used were worms and I still use them regularly for black bass. I rig them two ways, either wacky or Texas.

Plastics come in all shapes and sizes. It all depends on what I'm pursuing and where, as to which I prefer. For instance, in the northeast I became familiar with Slug-Go's, which are representative of a group of lures called slugs. They are non-descript but fish sure like them. They look like an eel and very much like a Northeast critter called the sand eel, a favorite prey species of striped bass. So they are a natural for them. Stripers, like all bass, have large mouths and inhaling a Slug-Go is easy. A 2-foot striper doesn't have much trouble with a 9-inch Slug-Go, however many other species don't handle them so well.

Slug-Go is bulky and slimmer tailed slugs are a better choice for many other species. The beauty of this class of lures is they can be rigged weedless and fished anywhere. They are a great lure to troll in shallow or weedy areas. You can use a worm hook, weighted hooks, sinkers and even jig heads with them. I've caught striped bass while sitting on a flat eating lunch when I forgot I had been trolling and hadn't reeled in.

This is a broad group of lures. While Slug-Go's have a tapered tail, others have paddles, flippers, long single or double tendrils, etc. In Florida, Bass Assassins, Exudes, DOA and other brands are common. A client, Jim, introduced me to flats minnows made by TTF and I'm very impressed with them. I probably use paddle tails more than any other group of plastics. I either rig them on a jig or weedless with a worm hook or weighted worm hook. In the winter when the snook are in the backcountry they're keying on small baits.

I use a Lunker City 2.5-inch grub and do quite well. One day my buddy Bob got to a launch before me and had thrown out a cast net. When I pulled up he said he knew why I did so well on my small jigs, as they were approximately the size of the bait he had netted.

When plastics are rigged with a worm, power lock or similar type hook, they are extremely weed less. In places where there is a lot of weed in the water, snags or overhanging brush, they're often the best lures to fish. They rarely snag when overcastting to mangroves and such. The only time I seem to snag is when the line, and not the lure itself, wraps around the branch.

Topwaters

Fishing topwaters is exciting and the stealth of the kayak allows you to get close to fish. The low profile you present enables you to get much closer than you can in a boat. Often fish will come extremely close when following a lure. When fish are very aggressive I'll keep pulling the lure away from them until they are almost at the kayak. Watching a fish blast a lure on top near the kayak is the ultimate.

I'm especially partial to walk-the-dog type of topwaters. They are very stealthy and there's something about that side-to-side motion many fish find irresistible. In the northeast the Rebel Jumpin' Minnow is the hot ticket, whereas in the south the Zara Spook, Mirror Lures and Rapalas dominate. I also like to include a popper or two. Sometimes a commotion is needed to get the fish's attention.

On the flats some anglers will use a topwater to find where the fish are and then follow up with a slug or other offering. Speaking of slugs the Slug-Go, when worked on top, is deadly and is one of my favorites. It walks the dog beautifully.

Plugs

This group of lures is diverse and very effective, especially when trolled. Most models dive on retrieve and then float to the surface. The Rapala minnow was the first offering available and now every plug manufacturer has a multitude of models. Just like topwaters, there tend to be regional favorites. In the northeast in the salt, bombers predominate, but you still see Yozuris, Rebels, Redfins, etc. Mirror lures are rare in the northeast but common throughout the South.

While this is far from a complete list, it covers the basics. Most species of fish that will hit artificials will hit one of the above.

Flies

You don't need a lot of flies in the arsenal, so my advice would be to stick to the basics. For saltwater fishing, you're going to want to have an assortment of clousers in a variety of colors and sizes, some deceivers, crease flies, crab and shrimp imitations, poppers and some sliders. A few different sizes, profiles and colors of each of these general patterns will catch fish practically anywhere you go, and under most conditions; however, it doesn't hurt to get on a regional forum and ask others what works for them in that particular area.

Fishing Bait from a Kayak

I've done most of my fishing using artificials but there are times when bait is better. In some environments and situations it's almost mandatory. It might be the water is incredibly clear and the fish simply get too good a look at the lure.

Then there is the situation where fish will key on a specific bait and ignore everything else. If you've ever fished for trout when they're keying in on a hatch, you know they can become incredibly selective. Trout aren't the only species to do this. Most fish will at times key on a particular food. Sometimes a similarly sized artificial will catch fish but often you either need to be fishing the same exact baitfish or a piece of one.

The other time I like using bait is for big game. That's because I can use a circle hook, which will hook the fish in the corner of the mouth. It's better for the fish and when tangling with large game fish like sharks, billfish, tarpon, goliath grouper and the like, if they break off then you are only out a hook. The fish is much better off with a hook that will rust out than a lure attached to it for a bit. Also these are fish I'm not going to keep and a circle hook is going to do the least harm to them. I find circles especially good for tarpon. Tarpon are incredible leapers and have very hard mouths. They are notorious for throwing the hook and the ratio of hooked and landed fish is wide. A tarpon hooked on a circle hook eliminates the swing weight the tarpon uses to throw it.

The vision many of us have when thinking of fishing bait is a worm on a bobber or cut bait on a sinker type rig fished on the bottom with the rod in a sand spike, etc. These methods don't translate well to kayak fishing. They are much too static. Kayak fishing is an active form of fishing and sitting still in a kayak is boring. You are basically stuck in one sitting position without much ability to move about. The action has to be blistering for me to fish this way. I

It took a 6-inch Mayan Ciclid (lower left in the photo) to fool this 9-pound largemouth in a crystal clear quarry lake in southwest Florida. Four additional bass were taken that day, - all on live bait - for a combined 5-fish weight of 36 pounds.

prefer an active bait fishing approach.

Bait comes in many forms and not all bait makes sense kayak fishing. Many of us started fishing with garden worms. I did as a kid and it was easy to collect them myself. They were easy to store, too. As long as they were kept cool they lasted for days. In saltwater there are sea worms. Handling them is similar to land-based worms. Instead of dirt they come in seaweed. Kept moist and cool they, too, will last several days.

Besides worms there is a variety of live creatures available depending upon the region. Many types of bait can be purchased frozen; just thaw and use. There are now bait alternatives like *Gulp!* and Fishbites. In some circumstances they work well and are very convenient.

Most kayak fishermen when using bait are going to be using live bait-fishes. In some places you can buy bait, especially freshwater where it's common practice, as many bait shops have a variety of baitfish species in a variety of sizes. The availability of saltwater baitfish varies greatly, with some places having them available and many not. I posed this question on the KFS forums and learned how much it varies. Some areas have several bait-fishes available. Sometimes the bait is seasonal.

The most convenient place to buy bait is in southern California, where they have bait docks called receivers where you can paddle up and purchase while sitting in your kayak. The species are usually anchovies and sardines. In the northeast there are killies and they come in a box with seaweed. Eels are also available. Throughout the south shrimp is commonly purchased for bait. Some places you can get crabs.

As mentioned earlier, I find static bait fishing from a kayak boring. I like active fishing with large bait-fishes. This style of fishing is deadly, especially for big fish. You can fish the baits a few ways - live whole, dead whole or chunked. How you do each is going to vary depending upon a range of variables.

I know in the northeast more big striped bass and bluefish succumb to bunker (menhaden) or herring than all other offerings combined. Usually when they are keying on adult bunker it's the only thing that is going to work. I've also experienced this with other species.

However, before you can fish with bait you have to have it with you. If it isn't available for purchase you will have to procure it in other ways. Some species

school tightly and can be cast-netted from shore or a dock. Throwing a net from a kayak will require skills far beyond most of us, though there are anglers who do so. I've never even picked up a cast net let alone thrown one, and most of you probably haven't either. There are two other ways to procure bait - either snagging or catching.

Catching is fishing where you target the baitfish. I first did this as a kid when I would catch small bluegills and live-line them for bass. In the salt my first catches were in San Diego and Baja using a Sabiki rig. The rig consists of several tiny fly-like lures. A weight is put on the bottom and the rig is jigged. Most Sabiki's have five flies. I find this to be too many and too long for kayak use. I cut the rig in half and use it that way. In southern California and Baja we used it to catch mackerel. Sometimes we would catch other species, but mostly macs. In the northeast I've used it for herring and in Florida for a variety of species (pinfish, small jacks, pilchards, etc).

Another way of catching fish is using small lures. Ladyfish are great bait in the south and are very aggressive predators in their own right. They readily attack lures and I've found small jigs to be quite effective.

The first time I fished Key Biscayne the grass flats had a variety of bait-fishes. The hot set-up was a small jig. I kept getting hits on the jig I'd use for ladyfish, trout, snook and reds but I had a lot of trouble hooking jacks and pinfish. My buddy Bob cleaned up on a small jig. Almost any fish can be bait as there is always something bigger around to eat it.

It all depends upon what you're targeting. In the Everglades there are a couple of species of catfish. They are considered pests and are easy to catch. I was told they made good bait and the first time I used one it attracted a big tarpon. Unfortunately the hook didn't bite, but it was exciting having a 150-pound tarpon as high as a basketball rim jumping 40 feet from me. Catfish are also one of my favorite baits for sharks.

Some species of baitfish won't hit flies or lures because they are plankton feeders. The two I'm most familiar with are bunker and mullet. Bunkers always bunch in tight schools and mullet often do as well. To gather them I use a snagging treble, which is a weighted treble hook. You can make your own by putting an egg sinker above a treble. I cast the snag hook beyond the school, let it sink, reel it near the school and then I yank hard on the rod. I find a longer rod works better, as I have more sweep. Both species put up a good fight and snagging is fun. I remember the first time I took my buddy Chris fishing for big blues on Long Island's north shore. We first set out to collect some bait. We only needed a few but Chris is used to catching freshwater bass and trout and had a blast fighting the one- to two-pound bunker. When we returned to the launch he had a couple of dozen bunker in the tank well of his kayak.

How you handle the procured bait will depend on the species and circumstances. If they are easy to catch then procure them as needed. Bunker is a prime example of this - very easy to spot and snag. They bunch very tightly and tend to be on the surface. Even when they aren't on top they bunch up in very compact schools and are easy to spot with a fish finder. Many fishermen after snagging a bunker leave it on the snag hook and fish it then and there. The other option is to have another rod and switch the bunker. I prefer switching because I can then put the bunker on a large circle hook. I usually snag a couple of extra and keep them either in the tank well or the drive area of a Hobie just in case they get scarce. If I bring my bait tank with me then I can put several in it.

Dead or chunked bunker makes great bait. Sometimes it's better than live-lining it. Large striped bass, the most sought-after Northeast game fish, is used to seeing chunks, especially the front part. That's because they share their environment with bluefish. Bluefish are very aggressive feeders and tend to attack their prey from the rear. Often they bite the bunker in half and the front part drifts down through the water column. Heads drifting down are normal forage for large bass. They let the bluefish do the heavy lifting and sit below the feeding blues waiting for gravity to deliver their meal.

The other species I've snagged is mullet, which is not as easy to get as bunker. Often mullet are shallow and don't school as tightly. I do find them occasionally in tight schools in the rivers but they disperse more readily when harassed than bunker.

The first mullet I ever snagged was 14 inches - big bait. It was bigger than I wanted but I was fishing for tarpon that were 4 feet or better. No problem for them. I live-lined it on with an 8/0 circle hook placed in the nostrils. After a while I had a run-off and the fish started heading into the mangroves. I figured it was probably a large snook. It was my only mullet so I slowly reeled to pull the fish away. I didn't feel the fish had swallowed the bait yet and it was confirmed when a 3 foot-plus redfish was mouthing the mullet but hadn't swallowed it yet. I lost the red but the mullet was much mellower now and easier prey.

The tarpon in the pond where I was fishing weren't cooperating so I started working my way down the river back towards my parking spot a couple of miles away. There was a series of docks protecting a small bay and a fisherman I had met at the local tackle shop walked out with a fly rod. On his first cast there was a very loud splash, which he said were four of the biggest snook he had ever seen. He got a terrible tangle in his line so etiquette permitted me to cross through a small gap on the side and access the cove.

As I entered the backwater I saw a tarpon swim by. I cast to it but it ignored my lure and disappeared. I then cast around the cove's mangrove edge trying to raise a snook but didn't get a sniff. As I was nearing the exit to the cove there was an explosion by my mullet, which I was trolling approximately 20 feet behind the kayak. The mullet was still there but a few seconds later the line started peeling off the reel and the circle set. A 40-inch tarpon leapt 6 feet into the air and after three more jumps I had the fish at the side of the yak with the big circle securely set in the corner of the mouth.

Some bait-fishes aren't nearly as easy to procure, so keeping them alive with you in the kayak is important. By far the best way to do this is with a bait tank system (please refer to that section of the book for more information). If you don't have a system, the next best thing is a small cooler, especially if the air is warm. I find sometimes a whole fresh dead bait works well and sometimes better than a live one. Joey met a guy in a boat once who was hammering large striped bass. He told Joey he killed the bunker, which made it much easier for the bass to swallow. I like to carry a small cutting board and knife in case I decide to chunk.

The tackle I prefer depends upon my quarry. I use either a conventional reel or a bait runner spinner. For larger fish (upwards of 50 pounds) I prefer the conventional. In the absence of either I've found a loose drag on a spinner works, too. You can tighten the drag or cup the spool to provide tension for setting the hook. Just be careful, especially when cupping with large fish. Too much tension will break the line.

How I rig again depends on what I'm fishing for. My

favorite is to use live bait on a circle hook. Besides bait-fishes it's a great way to fish worms, shrimp, eels and such. If the fish doesn't have teeth I attach the hook via a snell, backed up with some superglue. I usually use fluorocarbon and tie it directly to my main line. I reinforce the knot with superglue. If it's a toothy critter then I'll use some wire. That's if I want to catch them. In places where there are a lot of big sharks I'll forego the wire and let them bite through the heavy fluorocarbon, unless I'm specifically targeting the sharks, in which case the wire is mandatory. I like big hooks. If it's small bait and I'm fishing where large fish might be encountered, I'll go as big as I can while not killing the bait.

When I fished Baja's East Cape with Jim Sammons, the sardinas we were live-lining were small. Jim suggested a #1 hook but I opted for a 2/0. There wasn't any way I was going to use such a small hook with tuna, dorado and possibly billfish. I ended up hooking a large sailfish and I have little doubt that #1 would never have gotten the fish to the kayak but the 2/0 did. It was also a better hook for all the dorado and tuna we caught.

There are two other ways I'll fish bait. Putting bait out on a float while covering water works well. This way you're not consciously fishing the rig but you're constantly fishing. It simply comes along for the ride. It's a very common technique in the south when using shrimp but it can be used anywhere with almost any bait.

When I want to get the bait deep I place a slip sinker above the leader and use either a barrel or breakaway clip to stop the sinker from reaching the bait. I used this technique while fishing a freshwater quarry lake in the Everglades. I had been catching small bass and Mayan cichlids but I knew there were some larger fish because I had seen them. The water was very clear and I figured catching larger fish was going to require live bait on fluorocarbon leaders. So I set up my bait runner with several feet of 15-pound leader and live-lined small bluegills.

The lake had a healthy population of gar that seemed to like it near the surface. They kept killing the bluegills and it seemed when the gar didn't get them the Mayan's did. The lake had depths to 45 feet and like all quarry lakes it dropped off quickly. I put a sinker in front of the bluegills and Mayans to get them deep fast. It worked great. I only fished the lake a couple of days but on my last day I landed five bass that weighed 5, 6.5, 7, 8 and 9.5 pounds!

One of the deadliest techniques, first introduced to me by Doug M., is using a 2/0 circle hook attached to a fluorocarbon leader tied direct to the main line. A sandworm is placed on the hook and drifted with the current. It works wonderfully, especially for early season stripers. We watched bass on the flats of Cape Cod make a beeline to the worm from hundreds of feet away. The action is usually fast when using this method. In the south, substituting shrimp for the worm works equally as well.

When fishing the 10,000 Islands in Florida I would often live-line a large bait-fish behind the kayak while I cast for snook and reds. I like a conventional for this with a loud clicker so I can hear when a fish picks up the bait. However that doesn't always happen. One day I was drifting the oyster bars casting and my drifting stopped and I started going in the opposite direction until I grounded on an oyster bar. It wasn't until the kayak was stopped that the clicker went off. I hit the lever and got dragged across the bar and then on a sleigh ride. The culprit was a five-foot bull shark.

I've developed a technique for hooking bait-fishes that has resulted in a very high ratio of hook-ups. I started using it with sharks and now I use it whenever live-lining fish. I run the circle hook through the upper lip, then through the back of the fish behind the head and in front of the dorsal fin. I completely pull the hook through and let it dangle. That's if it's a species that hits headfirst. If my target species attacks from the rear I continue down the fish and put it in the rear third of the fish and again pull it completely through.

Even though I like using artificials, when targeting large fish I find myself using bait more often. I like catching big fish and going on sleigh rides. Bait is more favorable for doing this.

Fishing at Night

After you've gained substantial experience fishing from a kayak, you're ready to head out at night. Why fish at night, you ask? Well, often it's better. Many places that seem fishless during daylight come alive after dark. Sometimes it's because there is too much daytime human activity in a busy lake or bay. It could be the water temps are too high for the fishes' comfort while the sun is beating down on them. Some species are simply more active at night. All the basses, wherever they live, prefer the dark.

Freshwater species like walleye, carp and catfish are nocturnal. Some lakes experience a phenomenon where from approximately midnight to 5:00 am. the herring feed on the surface in large schools and the predators concentrate on the bounty. It can be spectacular fishing for fish that rival saltwater sizes. Double-digit hybrids and walleyes on light tackle will give you all the sport you could ever want and you'll have it all to yourself, too. The best time to pursue tide runner weakfish is after the sun goes down. In Florida, snook, tarpon and jacks are much more active as well.

It takes a bit of an adjustment when converting to night kayak fishing. As one looses the ability to see well the other senses will compensate; especially your hearing and to a lesser degree your sense of smell. Often fish will move into areas that are too shallow for them to feel comfortable during the day. It's a good idea to become at ease with your kayak with a lot of daytime kayak fishing first before taking on the dark, especially if those sorties are going to be in the salt. You may wish to go freshwater fishing for your initial nighttime forays, as the smaller water and lack of tides and currents will give you less to deal with and adjust to. If there aren't any freshwater opportunities available, stick to more sheltered and smaller salt waters to learn the sport. Once you've become comfortable with your kayak and gear, adding some night excursions may be just what you need to spice up your kayak fishing.

During summer in the northeast, we do much of our fishing after the sun goes down to capitalize on the more favorable conditions. Even if you don't plan on fishing in the dark, the best fishing often occurs during predawn and sunset. To be out on the water and ready to fish at these times you will need to paddle in one direction in the dark, so you will need to have some night fishing gear anyway.

I highly caution you not to go night kayak fishing alone at first. Hook up with others who would like to go or better yet, are already doing it. Keep it simple at night, especially in the beginning. Try to use single hook barb-less lures and if you're fly fishing, wear clear glasses to protect your eyes. Have specific places where you keep things and always place them there. I would also urge you to fish areas you've fished in the daylight so as to be familiar with the topography. Even though you may know an area, it looks very different at night. At least you won't be blind and can key in on some reference points.

There is additional equipment that is going to be required beyond what you generally carry to fish during the day. Since it's dark you're obviously going to need lights. Boating regulations require having a light at night. A flashlight is all that is required and I suggest at the minimum having a waterproof one along. A light is used not only to see but also to be seen. I fully discuss lights in the Accessories Chapter, so I won't go into detail here. I take a few with me on the water, a colored light that won't affect my night vision and a couple of white ones.

While a light is mandatory, other electronic devices come in handy. It's easy to get disoriented while on the water in the dark, so I feel that either a compass or GPS is important. You'll be amazed at how easily you can mistake where you initiated your fishing. A GPS has already saved me considerable paddling to places from where I thought I had launched. Also a fish finder can be a great aid, especially if the water has some depth to it. Many species are structure-oriented and you may not be able to find these places without navigational/sonar aid.

It's fairly easy to lose track of your kayak-fishing buddies at night. Yelling not only might disturb the fish but also has a very limited range. It's a good idea to bring a radio along and a cell phone. The radios can be FRS or VHF. Radios are nice because everyone in the group can be on the same channel and hear and participate in the conversation. However, so can others. If you're into some great stuff while others happen to be on the water and you don't want them to hear you, cell phones provide the most private means of communicating. After that FRS, which are really walkie-talkies. Having ruined a few radios and not wishing to ruin my cell phone, I keep both in a waterproof, floating case made for the task, which I attach to the kayak. These cases come in very handy, as they allow you to talk while fully protecting their contents. Also keep in mind that cell plans tend to have free nighttime calling.

In some areas bug spray can be invaluable, so it's a good idea to bring it along. Some terrific fishing is available in the estuaries at night and if there isn't a breeze the local inhabitants can be very annoying. Sometimes you just can't fish an area, as the bugs might be horrendous and nothing will work. At other times I have to wear a netted bug shirt because the no-see-ums would make fishing unbearable otherwise.

The best places to fish at night can differ from the

best daylight spots. Many game fish will move into the shallows to feed under the cover of darkness. It's very important you keep noise to a minimum or you could alert them that you're there. A quiet kayak is an asset. Have everything rigged before you hit the area you intend to fish and be as stealthy as you can. You know you're stealthy when you end up spooking some fish, as your kayak gets right next to them. The explosion of a big fish right next to you is amazing. Just make sure when you jump that you land in the kayak and not the water. Be prepared for a hit at any time, as fish will often strike as you're lifting the lure to make another cast. When this happens hang on and let the fish take the line so it can get away from the kayak.

(above) Mark, *a.k.a. Surfacetension*, with a nighttime Jamaica Bay striper. **(left)** This 33-inch bass was way up a river in only 2 feet of water.

There are some specific lures and techniques that work well at night. For stripers the Tube and Worm (TnW) is king. Often I don't use any other method when linesiders are the quarry. Black swimmers are great and it's a good idea to either replace the treble hooks with singles or at least remove the barbs. Single hook jig plastics like Tsunamis and Wild-Eyes are good to have in the arsenal. Big Slug-Go's are great and I rig mine with a big single hook. When fishing flies I prefer black ones that move some water. I highly recommend keeping it simple as to choices. I'm guilty of always carrying too much stuff but I can narrow it down to just a few offerings. In the northeast I've got three favorites, the TnW, a black swimmer or a big Slug-Go. I use a Mustad 34007 in 8/0 that I've ground the barb off and created a conical point for the nine-inch Slug-Go and I go down to a 6/0 for the 7.5. I wrap heavy thread around the hook shank to help hold the Slug-Go better. Recently I've experimented with large circle hooks instead of the Mustad and they work well. You can't go wrong with a black swimmer anywhere and while many fish aren't going to take on a nine-inch Slug-Go, I've found few that won't go for a 4- or 6-inch one.

Spending some time on the water kayak fishing at night can be very productive. Just stay aware of your surroundings and in some environments, be partic-

ularly cognizant of hazards, especially where large predators might be encountered. Creatures like sharks and alligators know the hunting is better in the dark too!

Tube and Worm

A who and what. It is a lure and bait combo that has become the deadliest technique for fishing from a kayak in the northeast. It's called the Tube and Worm (TnW). I first became aware of the rig in June of 2002 when Joey, Doug, Jim and I were in a tackle shop in Cape Cod looking at lures. We came upon the TnW and discussed how it was one of the hottest big striped bass lures in New England. Commercial fisherman used them at night in the bays and hammered fish. We discussed how we should try it off of our kayaks but we didn't take it any further.

Fast-forward six weeks to the first Saturday of August. It was the heart of the dog days of summer. A bunch of us decided to get together and kayak fish western Long Island Sound - Joey's backyard. This particular area produces well in the summer, as there is a lot of deep water and terrific structure. The same crew as above and a few others joined us. One of them was our buddy Joev. He had been using something new and had been slaying fish for a few weeks with it. It was a small, burgundy TnW. The rig consisted of a surgical tube, a leader of approximately two feet, and a plastic rudder. The entire rig was tipped with a live sandworm. Everyone caught fish that day with the majority being schoolies to a few keeper-sized fish. Joev did better than everyone else combined. He had 37 stripers with many fish into the

(above) Joev with a Cuttyhunk, MA bass that hit a TnW. (right) One of the author's early Tube and Worm rigs.

upper teens. I was fishing near him and personally watched him lose two very large fish that were well over 20 pounds. After a while Joey couldn't take it any longer and borrowed the rig. He wasn't able to paddle for a minute without a striper hook-up! That was enough for us. We all had to get one of the rigs.

That day was a real eye opener and I concluded two things: I needed to start using the TnW, and our typical outfits loaded with 20 to 30-pound braid were inadequate for the task, especially when fishing near structure. To do so was a recipe to getting rocked by the larger fish and one could go through a lot of rigs this way. The two big fish Joev lost would probably have been landed on stouter gear. I learned this the hard way a few weeks later. I still hadn't set up a heavy outfit and got rocked by a freight train of a fish off of Montauk, Long Island. I was helpless as I watched line peel from my reel.

So what is a TnW? It's a section of surgical tube that has been rigged in such a fashion that it spins through the water. There are numerous variations but they consist of wire that connects a hook to a barrel and the tube is slid over this with a hook at the end of the tube. The lure spins so it's necessary to either use ball-bearing swivels or my preferred anti-twist device, a plastic rudder. A sandworm (I've only used sandworms) or bloodworm is placed on the hook and the entire contraption is trolled; if there are bass around they smash the you-know-what out of

it. It really is amazing, as the hits are savage. Tubes vary in length from a foot up to a few feet. Boats often utilize them with wire line and can troll some real monsters. I do most of my fishing from a kayak and I can't see a reason to use anything longer than two feet, and the TnWs I build are about a foot. People seem to make a big deal about color. The first rigs we got from Joev were all burgundy red; they worked and still do. I've since used several other colors and they all work. Tide runner weakfish seem to like bubblegum. I've concluded that the TnW is an attraction device that gets the fishes' attention. They smell the worm and wham, fish on.

Stripers have a great sense of smell. I hadn't realized just how good until one trip to Cuttyhunk with Mike Laptew, an underwater videographer known as Fisheye. He does nature filming and has a series of fishing DVD's. He wanted to get some footage on kayak fishing and his inquiries led him to me. I was going on a trip with a few members of my fly fishing club and Mike was friendly with a couple of them. We arranged to meet up at Cuttyhunk at first light at the water's edge. Mike, clad in a wetsuit, with kayak tethered in tow behind him, was going to bird-dog the fish. Our intention was for him to find fish, signal me, and I'd troll near the fish while he shot pictures. The only problem was there weren't any fish. Mike didn't see one. I still trolled a TnW and managed two bass. One was almost 20 pounds and Mike got some good shots. He later commented that I pulled those fish from the ether since there didn't seem to be any fish around. That's the power of the rig.

Since kayaks always travel at trolling speed you can't really go wrong using the rig. Toss it out behind you with at least 30 feet of line and start paddling. The TnW tends to run very shallow. Combined with a kayak's stealth it's a terrific way to cover flats. You can fish it anywhere, but if there is any sort of fish-holding structure around, troll as close as you can. To make them go deeper you can weight the head with a barrel sinker or use a weighted rudder. I usually use one without any weight. A kayak is the best way to present a TnW. Kayaks can access places boats can only dream about. They literally get right on top of or in structure and that's the best place to catch fish. A fish finder is a big help, too, as it will show you depth, structure and fish. If I mark fish down deep I'll slow down and let the rig sink. Get the TnW near bass-holding structure and then hang on.

That brings me to tackle. I prefer spinning to conventional reels for this technique, the reason being I can put the outfit in a rod holder and simply flip the bail and paddle if I need to let more line out. It's just as fast to flip the bail back, too. A conventional requires more effort but if you decide to set up a wire line or lead core outfit to fish deeper, then it becomes necessary.

A reel with a line counter built in would be helpful, too. Letting out a lot of line is sometimes necessary in some places. The water up at Cape Cod is very clear. I found I needed to get the TnW more than 100 feet from the kayak to consistently hook up.

Make sure whatever rod you choose has some muscle. When hooking large stripers near structure you need to have some stopping power or else you're going to have a lot of fish swimming around with tubes in their mouths. Let a big bass get up a head of steam in an area where there is structure and you're never going to see just how big she was. Get at least a 7-foot rod and if you're using a touring or longer kayak I prefer one that is 8 feet. Even for shorter kayaks I

Taurus with a 15-pound, 35-inch weakfish that couldn't resist a bubble gum TnW. The fish was caught in Jamaica Bay, NY in May of 2008.

prefer an 8-foot rod. The longer rod really helps when the fish makes those surges upon its first look at you and the kayak. I like a rod rated at least ¾ to 1 ounce for the low end and up to 3 or 4 ounces.

As to a line choice I don't recommend using mono. The stretch is a big negative especially if you need to put the TnW out any distance at all. Go with braid and a minimum of 50 and you can go as high as 80 pound. I use 65 on my outfits. You want a line with minimal stretch and strong so you can really put the

hammer on a big fish. You have to break their spirit and keep them out of the structure or you're going to lose a lot. Light line doesn't let you do this. I keep my drag fairly tight but I also add pressure with my hand on the spool.

Another important accessory is a small ice chest for storing the worms. It's especially important in the warmer weather, as the worms won't last long if not kept cool. Get a small six-pack sized cooler in either hard or soft design. They're less than $10, readily available and will keep your worms lively, which will produce more fish. My favorite has a Velcro section in the lid. It lets me get a worm without unzipping the top.

I've got a buddy who uses fake worms that he soaks in bunker oil. He also puts a sponge in the tube and soaks it in oil, too. It works. As mentioned earlier, I've only used sandworms but I'm told that bloodworms also work. I like rigs with either barb-less hooks or very small barbs. If it's a large barb I grind it off with a Dremel tool and make a conical point. I get a nice puncture and since there aren't any cutting edges on the point (if there were I use the Dremel to eliminate them) the hole remains small. As long as I keep pressure on the fish I won't lose it. Also, since I release almost every bass I can give slack at the kayak and the fish will often get off by itself without my having to handle it. It's better for me and for the fish.

The conical, barb-less hook is also great when I thread the worm on the hook. This way I do minimal damage to the bait. I try to put the point of the hook through the mouth and thread it about an inch. The head of the worm ends up in the end of the tube. The worm is then left dangling. Most fish tend to inhale the entire worm - even small fish. Often the fish will hit it a couple of times. Since I'm trolling I let the fish hook themselves and by the time I get the rod from the rod holder the fish is taking line against the drag and turning the kayak.

If you look online you will see the rig is used for all kinds of species, including tuna. I've only used it from the kayak and it has produced striped bass, bluefish and fluke. Tiderunner weakfish love it too, but I haven't gotten one yet.

The TnW can also be cast to fishy looking spots. For this type of fishing a TnW that doesn't require a rudder is a better rig. You will need to use some high quality, ball-bearing barrels.

So there you have the highly effective TnW up close and personal. It's your ticket to a sleigh ride on the water.

Sailing

Anyone who has spent time on the water kayak fishing has had to contend with wind. Sometimes wind is beneficial, but usually you're going to have to travel in one direction when it's against you. The stronger the wind the harder you're going to have to work when it's not an ally. You can opt not to fish or go out in calm weather only, but even this isn't always possible. Even the calmest of conditions can change and wind can develop unexpectedly. Often the fishing is better when it's windy so it's a good reason to contend with it. I find species like striped bass, bluefish and false albacore feed much better when it's breezy. Conversely it's less common for me to find blitzing fish in calm conditions. A chop on the water provides cover for the kayak, too, making it harder for fish to detect you.

I never really thought about sailing a kayak my first few years in the sport. Ken Daubert, in his book *Kayak Fishing - The Revolution* had a tip where he suggested bringing an umbrella along for traveling downwind. I did and used it occasionally. Then one day I came across an article on the Internet where two guys used modified kayaks to sail the midriff area of Baja, Mexico's Sea of Cortez. What got my attention was that they covered 60 miles in a weekend. The midriff was my stomping ground when I guided in Baja. It's infamous for wind. The light bulb went on as I realized I could utilize wind to access

An **Adventure Island kayak** enabled Mike of Hawaii's Coastal Kayak Tours to reach, hook and land this nice wahoo.

more places to fish.

The guys in the article used a sail and dagger board system to change their kayaks into sailing vessels. I believe they had Ocean Kayak Scupper Pro TWs, but I'm not certain. The dagger boards strapped onto the sides of the kayak and the sail used an installed mount on the front deck. The last piece of equipment was a set of outriggers to stabilize the kayaks while under sail.

Though I was excited, I filed the thoughts away for the future, being the KFS retail store had just opened and my plate was very full. Additionally, even though I knew I could use sailing in my home waters, I really wanted it for offshore and Baja and I wasn't going to be doing either anytime soon.

To truly sail you need a few accessories. First, of course, you've got to have a sail. A sail consists of a mast and some type of material stretched out from it. The wind is caught by the sail and pushes the kayak in the direction the wind is moving. By using a rudder you can steer off the wind direction somewhat, but mostly you're stuck moving in generally the same direction as the wind.

In order to sail in another direction you're going to need a dagger board. This is a board that protrudes down into the water somewhere in the mid section of the vessel. Many things can perform this function. The third accessory, an outrigger system, isn't necessary, but if you want to keep the adrenaline rush reasonable in kayak sailing it's highly recommended. Even the widest kayaks are narrow and unlike a sailboat, they don't have a lot of weight under the waterline to compensate for the power generated on the kayak by the wind via the sail. It's very easy for the wind to blow a kayak over. To compensate for this outriggers are used. Sailing becomes much more user-friendly with them.

After opening the store we soon became a Hobie dealer. Hobie Cat Company has an entire division devoted to sailing. They designed the Outback, their first kayak fishing model, to accommodate a sail. They did this with a built-in mast tube and a sail specifically designed to work with the kayak. Since it's an integrated accessory it works very well and there isn't any installation required. Like other kayaks, an outrigger system can be added or built (see that section of the book). While not having a dedicated dagger board, the Mirage Drive flippers (called sails by Hobie) when placed in a vertical position, will sort of function as one. They aren't as good as a solid board but they do provide some lateral stability.

I love to tinker and I was doing modifications on various kayaks. I was getting ready to make a dagger board using the Mirage plug (a plastic plug that comes with the kayak to fill the drive area when not in use) as a frame for a board. I was going to plastic weld and bolt a plastic cutting board into the plug, knowing it would work pretty well. About this time one of the folks at Hobie contacted me about a modification I was making to the Outback. Since I had their attention, I made some suggestions. One was for a long, low profile touring style kayak with a built-in dagger board system - something we could really sail without having to modify the kayak.

I don't know if Hobie had it in the works or not but I soon learned that they had a long touring style hull with a built in dagger board due to come out the following summer. Now there wasn't any need for me to build a dagger board, so I waited. The kayak was called the Adventure and it was what I wanted. Hobie upped what is possible and released the Adventure Island in late 2006. This is a true sailing vessel and exceeds what I thought was possible in a kayak design. It has three times the mast area of the standard Hobie sail and a set of nine-foot outriggers to handle all the power this sail generates. The kayak is capable of speeds well into the teens. The sail is adjustable as well. It's easy to control the amount of sail you present to the wind. This is important, as it allows you to control your speed.

To test just how maneuverable the Adventure Island could be with a small amount of sail out, I sailed amongst an area in Chokoloskee Bay in Florida that is loaded with oyster bars. I sailed at low tide and was able to maneuver fairly easily. Another terrific feature is the sail breaks down easily in well under a minute and can be lashed alongside the kayak when you reach an area you'd like to fish. Hobie doesn't consider the Island a fishing vessel but I beg to differ. The Island opens up a whole new world in kayak fishing.

My first forays into kayak sailing were with the standard Adventure. In addition to the factory sail I used all factory accessories - the dagger board, sail rudder and outriggers, which the company calls sidekicks. I was able to cover a decent amount of water, much more easily than I could using only the pedals.

I tried fishing with the sail up but hooking the sail was easier than hooking fish. I recognized it was impractical to fish while the sail was up. Putting the sail up and breaking it down while on the water requires furnishing the kayak with features to facilitate this. Without them it's impossible and with them it takes a couple of minutes.

What you can't do is fish while under sail. Only the Adventure Island allows you to do this and the implications are really cool. Over in Hawaii there is a bunch of guys who use Adventure Islands to troll offshore. They are catching mahi mahi, billfish, tuna, wahoo and the like. While I haven't done it I know I can troll while under way in an Adventure Island. While the fish are making their initial run I can break the sail down, if need be, but I'd probably opt for furling (rolling up) the sail. Then I can fight the fish.

What I have learned from sailing is you're going to get wet, so make sure you're dressed for it. Everything needs to be able to handle getting soaked. The first time I used the Adventure Island in a bay there was a 15 mph wind and a nice chop. Water was constantly streaming over the sides. It was early September and a very warm year so the water was in the 70s. I wore wet suit pants and had a Mysterioso top on.

All of my sailing in a kayak has either been using an umbrella or with a Hobie. There are a lot of systems out there. Robert Hess has a terrific multi-part article that covers the subject better than I could with my limited experience. He has done a great job researching the subject and has experimented with several systems.

There is a group of guys who are using Adventure Islands to kayak fish and camp in the Florida Everglades. They've gone on trips as long as seven days with the participants launching in Flamingo and finishing in Chokoloskee, a distance of 70 miles. I know several Floridians who have an Adventure Island in their future so they can participate in this cutting-edge type of excursion. I see these kayak sailing adventures gaining popularity. Besides the Everglades, the Caribbean is a natural and lots of other places come to mind as well: the northern Great Lakes, Baja, the inside passage of Canada and Alaska for starters. Besides the Great Lakes, any large lake like

Powell, Meade, and a host of others are candidates.

Kayak sailing to access fishing doesn't need to be extreme. My sailing has proven to me that it's a viable mode of transportation on a breezy day for day trips, too. When sailing in Chokoloskee Bay one day, I encountered numerous schools of breaking fish. Unfortunately I was only sailing and hadn't brought any tackle along. What's really exciting is on those breezy days when fast moving schools of marauding game fish are difficult to catch, kayak sailing might solve the problem. Its exciting contemplating shuttle trips along the beach going in the direction of the prevailing wind. Such excursions would drastically increase the number of opportunities one would have. Very cool stuff indeed.

Just as kayak fishing was once a very esoteric sport, that's the position kayak sailing fishing holds now. Fishermen like to catch fish and with the increased range and possibilities sailing a kayak presents, sailing isn't going to remain relatively minor for very long. As more fishermen add a sailing kayak to their fleet and share their experiences with others, more kayak fishermen will add sailing as both a means of accessing fishing and just because it's fun to sail on a breezy day. Lastly, the wind is free and as gas prices continue to rise, sailing offers a substantial increase in range over paddling or pedaling without the expense of a motor-driven craft.

Pedal Drive Fishing

This group of kayaks allows for hands free fishing. This feature makes available to the angler some techniques that can't be accomplished with a paddle kayak. The inherent ability to propel the kayak while leaving the hands free enables me to cast when paddling kayaks can't. When I fish with someone who hasn't seen hands free it kind of surprises them at first. As we cruise along to our intended fishing area I'm firing off casts to likely looking spots or rises. Paddle kayaks are limited to trolling while underway. I troll too and I have the option of having the rod in my hand or in a rod holder. I can do other things while underway like change lures or flies, have something to eat, scan the water with my binoculars, and communicate via cell phone or radio. However while those are nice they don't translate into more fish caught.

Where hands free shines is in two of the most difficult kayak angling situations; dealing with current and wind. Both wreak havoc on paddle kayak fishing.

Having my hands free allows me to effectively fish in both of these difficult conditions.

My first experiences where I recognized the benefits of hands free were chasing schools of blitzing fish such as striped bass, bluefish and false albacore on a windy day. The schools move quickly and we teasingly say the blitzes last just long enough for you to almost get within casting range before the fish take off again. It's very frustrating. A pedal drive lets me cast while still moving the kayak at full speed. I've found this has often made the difference between getting a hookup and casting practice.

Another way I use the pedals is to maintain position. During autumn off the Jersey coast the best days to fish the ocean are when the wind has a westerly direction. It knocks down the waves and makes launching through the surf either possible or much easier. The consequence though is once you are beyond the land shadow you have wind that will continually push you out to sea. In a paddle kayak I find myself much farther from shore then I'd like. It's easy to end up getting blown a couple of miles before I realize what's happened. This requires me to paddle in a ways and the entire process repeats itself. A drift sock helps but it isn't a solution as it only slows down the kayak. In a pedal drive I keep my legs working as if I were going for a walk and can easily stay in the zone I desire. I get to fish the entire time in the fish zone instead of spending the majority of my time paddling back in.

One day while on a trip at the Dry Tortugas the wind was easily blowing 20 plus. We saw several tarpon roll in the harbor so we launched. My companions all had paddle kayaks and couldn't maintain position so they quit fishing and went in to shore. I was able to fish by hovering with my pedals. Unfortunately the tarpon didn't cooperate but I didn't have any trouble fishing.

Current has the same affect in the ocean as wind. Montauk Point is a classic example of this. It sits on the eastern tip of Long Island, NY. All the water from Long Island Sound and Block Island Sound moves past the point. It's a tremendous amount of water and the current reflects this. There's a big rip that sets up and you want to stay out of it while accessing the great fishing near it. When I fish there my legs are constantly pumping just to stay out of the rip.

Wind and current aren't limited to the ocean either. They can occur anywhere. In the Everglades one of my favorite fishing environments is the cuts between the oyster bars. As the tide moves through the bars they create a current similar to that of a river. The water flow can be substantial and in a paddle kayak I can only get off one or two casts before being swept out of the desired area. In some instances I could anchor but in many it's not possible. I position my pedal drive and essentially tread water to hold the kayak in position as I fire off casts and work the area. I have caught a lot of fish this way, more than I would have taken in a kayak without pedals.

Meanwhile my friends with paddle kayaks have to fish other places or hop off on the oyster bars and wade fish because they can't access the spots like I can. Even if you could anchor and fish the cut I often see a fish working outside my casting range. The time it would take to get in position to cast usually takes too long and the opportunity has passed, whereas I can react immediately by pedaling within range even if I still have a cast out. The ability to react quickly when pursuing ambush predators is of tremendous value.

The same holds true for fishing in a river as it does with the oyster bar cuts. I can maintain position as I cast to likely spots and then after doing so I can continue to work my way upstream. When holding position it's a lot like treading water. It's fairly easy to do. Some manipulation of the rudders is necessary but the longer the kayak the less I have to adjust.

When fighting fish I have found the ability to maneuver, especially when battling large fish, is often very beneficial. The first tarpon I ever landed is a good example of this. I hooked it behind a long dock and I constantly positioned the kayak to place myself between the fish and the dock. The water was shallow and the fish wouldn't go under the kayak, and thus never reached the dock. There isn't any way I could have done this in a paddle kayak.

Pedal kayaks paddle well too. So even though the primary mode of propulsion is via pedals it doesn't have to be. On some fishing excursions there are situations where I can't pedal, so I don't. What this class of kayaks does is expand what you're able to do. Their increased versatility allows you to fish more environments and that means more fish at the end of the day.

Lingcod, like this specimen taken by Chris from *Liquid Adventures*, make great targets for properly equipped kayak anglers.

Chapter 6
Fishing Environments

One of the most appealing aspects of kayak fishing is the flexibility afforded by the kayak itself. We can effectively fish many waters that our engine-saddled brethern cannot, either due to shallow depths, lack of a nearby boat launch, or the simple fact that a bigger vessel might just be too clumsy to squeeze into a small, but productive location. In this chapter we'll discuss both freshwater and saltwater kayak fishing environments, and some of the special considerations that accompany each.

Freshwater Environments

Freshwater was the undiscovered country, so to speak, of kayak fishing. That's because the majority of kayak fishing evolution has taken place in saltwater. It's ironic. One would think that freshwater applications would be the most natural fit for kayak fishing. For one thing, it's available to more anglers and in many bodies of water there is less inherent perceived risk. When I meet people unfamiliar with the sport, they are always surprised to learn I spend a lot of time fishing saltwater.

Things are changing, as freshwater is where the growth is happening at a much greater rate than in the salt. For one reason, most people can find good freshwater angling within a reasonable distance from their home. Some of these locales don't see much angling pressure, especially if they're near saltwater. Freshwater has many diverse environments that range from small creeks, ponds, lakes and rivers, up to the Great Lakes, which can best be described as inland seas.

One kayak certainly isn't going to cover all these environments and how one fishes these places is going to vary considerably. The basic piece of equipment, the kayak, is going to vary greatly. A kayak that is appropriate and works best for a small river is not going to be the preferred choice for the Great Lakes. Small waters value maneuverability and that's going to be the most important attribute, whereas the Great Lakes are best treated like fishing the open ocean.

If you are going to fish many different environments and you only wish to own one kayak, then a mid-sized model is what you'll want; something in the 12- to 13-foot range. If you spend the majority of your angling in specific environments, then use a kayak that will handle those conditions best. Rather than try to cover all these environments in one section, I'll break them up. Even though you're going to start with one kayak you may eventually get more. I don't know many fishermen who have only one rod. Most have dozens. Many kayak fishermen end up with more than one kayak and then they have appropriate kayaks for most environments.

Small Waters

Moving Water: In most parts of the country small rivers, creeks and streams are the most underutilized fishing environments available. Many of these places are difficult for most anglers to access and fish effectively. In my native state of New Jersey, rivers are typically only

fished during the put and take trout season in spring. Only the Delaware River sees some fishing the rest of the year. On the remaining rivers, when the hatchery trucks stop stocking trout, the fishermen stop coming. That's when I start fishing.

Many of the best spots are always those places with limited access and because of this hardly anyone fishes them. A small kayak is the best tool for reaching such areas. Sometimes I'll fish from the kayak while underway. Other times I'll want the kayak anchored. Many times the kayak is used as an access vessel to get me to remote areas where I can either fish from shore or wade. Small kayaks from 8 feet up to a maximum of 12 feet are best. The reason some smaller, lighter kayaks are preferred is things can get tight. Having the ability to both maneuver and manhandle them is a big plus. There can be all kinds of hazards that need to be negotiated. I've run into deadfalls that block the entire river, shallow rocky areas, and manmade obstacles like a dam. Sometimes I need to carry the kayak or drag it through brush or lift it over something, so the lighter and smaller it is the better. You just can't predict what will show up. Having a kayak that is easy to handle makes a big difference.

If you're looking at fishing a lot of moving water, then the smaller the kayak the better, provided you don't need to paddle much against a strong current.

If you've got to paddle against a current, then opt for the longer kayaks in this group. Each foot in length you go up is substantial in the efficiency you will experience. However I still wouldn't go longer than 12 feet for these situations. If you do go longer, choose a kayak with a lot of camber so it will be more maneuverable. When entering rough terrain keep it simple. The fish that call such places home generally aren't very particular with respect to what you throw at them. It's much more important to be stealthy. Keep gear at a minimum, which will lighten the load for when you can't paddle.

The species of fish for which you will be angling is going to vary. In most parts of the country it's going to be the basses, trout and pan fishes. In some places there will be members of the esox family - pike, musky and pickerel. There will be regional variations like carp, catfish, walleye and the like that are going to be prevalent as well. In a few places, namely the Great Lakes, steelhead and salmon become part of the mix and often the primary quarry. Accordingly, tackle and techniques are going to vary depending upon the species you're pursuing and the technique you incorporate. In a day's fishing on one of my local rivers here in the Northeast, I might encounter brook, rainbow and brown trout, largemouth and smallmouth bass, pickerel, pike, carp, yellow perch, crappie, rock bass, various sunfishes and catfish. The quantity of fish I catch can be staggering. Catching 50 to 100 fish an outing is often easy. Granted, many of the fish will be small but I catch enough medium sized with shots at large fish to keep it interesting.

As with anything new and undiscovered you might come across some real surprises. Relatively small waters can harbor some trophy fish - smallmouths and trout in excess of 5 pounds, and musky and pike much larger. A river not far from my home regularly produces pike in the 10 to 20-pound category and I know anglers who have caught pike approaching 30 pounds. That's great fishing anywhere and is within an hour of over 10-million people! Carp can be huge with a 30 pounder not at all unusual.

If I'm fishing the smaller rivers I tend to scale down my offerings. The appropriate tackle for catching the majority of fish you will encounter makes it especially exciting when tying into larger fish. A medium-sized smallmouth on ultralight spin tackle or a light fly rod will give quite an account of itself. My favorite lures for this type of fishing I refer to as micro lures. Probably the most versatile lure you can use is a small jig in the 1/16 ounce and smaller sizes. Various types of plastics, hair or feathers are used on the rear. Sometimes I'll combine the small lures with a safety pin blade, which turns the offering into mini spinnerbait. This is deadly for most fish, especially when used in stained or muddy water.

I have found the best fishing is on smaller waters that are difficult, if not impossible, to access with a motor. Basically, the harder the given water is for the masses to access, the better. The nomenclature will vary on these types of waters regionally, but essentially we are talking about moving waters that are generally less than 50 feet across but not so small that you can't negotiate them with a kayak.

Since the water moves you have a couple of choices on how best to tackle the fishing. You can either head downstream with the current or go against it by heading upstream. Your decision will be dependent upon the speed or force of the current. When fishing alone on unfamiliar waters, it's best to work up-stream. By taking this approach you really can't get into trouble. Should the current become too strong or you encounter a waterfall, you're not committed. When you've had enough or begin to tire, and it's time to return to your launch point, the current becomes your ally. When fishing alone this is a very smart way to approach this type of environment.

Most fish will be facing up current and approaching from below is a good way to stealthily stalk them. Due to the low seating position in a kayak it is often difficult to see these fish. Use Polaroid glasses to aid in viewing into the water while staying alert for signs of fish. Sometimes you will see the fish but more often you will see a wake or disturbance, something that tells you it's a good spot to try. Often you'll spook fish and by then it is generally too late to catch them, but you will now know a spot that holds fish. When you get over the area in the kayak you will probably understand why they were there and when you return you will know where they could be holding and how best to approach the spot.

The closest river to my home in New Jersey has a lot of out-of-the-way areas. One stretch, in the next

Jim with a nice Red River blue catfish.

town over, runs by a park. Casting to a pool there I caught a couple of smallmouths in the 2-pound range, so I decided to check out the section of river directly upstream of the park via kayak. There was a lot of casting and not much catching, and then I hit a section where I got a few nice bass. When the fish stopped biting I paddled into the area to check it out. I found a deeper hole with several boulders and weeds. It was the best habitat along this entire section for a bass to live.

I have found large sections of some rivers will be barren. The fish will be concentrated in specific sections, so when you run into fish take your time to really check out the area. Usually in late summer and fall the river level will become quite low. This concentrates the fish into deeper pools and tight to structure. You have to be cognizant of this and use a stealthy approach.

What I've found is whether I'm going up or downstream, the first time I go through an area it will be more of a discovery expedition than a fish catching trip. That's not to say I don't catch fish, however there will be a lot of spots where I'll either spook fish or not understand it until I've passed through the area for a better look. That's alright; the sense of discovery is one of my favorite things about kayak fishing. I make a mental note of what the spot was like and how I would best approach it. Unless I'm doing

a one-way trip via a shuttle, I'll pass through the spot again and can take the opportunity to fish it at that time. A GPS can be used to mark the spot to help me recognize it, as things are going to look different when traveling in the opposite direction.

When paddling upstream and encountering a likely looking area, it's often a good idea to get out of the kayak and wade fish the area if possible. You can cover the area more thoroughly than you could while floating in the current. If the water is shallow stay low. Try to use lures that won't hang up easily so you don't have to retrieve them and spoil the spot. The other technique I'll use is to let the kayak stop against the shore or some structure and work the area.

Something else I've learned is the fish aren't always where you expect them to be. There are obvious spots and then there are spots where you'll be shaking your head as you spook the fish. The only way to somewhat prevent this is to stay aware and work the area by spreading some casts around. Make some casts before walking or paddling into an area.

Some type of anchor can be a valuable accessory for this type of fishing. When heading downstream as soon as I hook a fish I'll either have an anchor or stakeout pole ready. This way I can stop above a spot and fish it more thoroughly. This is especially beneficial if I either know the spot already or it looks too fishy not to fish more expansively. After I've effectively covered the water I can either let out more anchor line or pick up the anchor or pole to drift farther down. Either way I'm able to maintain position while I fish the area. When drifting I have to make quick decisions as to where to toss my offering. Often right after I cast a better spot appears, or a fish shows itself. If not anchored, the current would then sweep me away from where I'd prefer to cast. When anchored you have as much time as needed.

Still Waters: Small, out-of-the-way still waters are a blast. Often these places see little if any fishing pressure, for many reasons. They can be isolated or have too much shoreline cover to effectively fish. Whatever the reason, a kayak is a great way to access them. Again, as with moving waters, the best waters are the ones that are difficult for other fishermen to access. It might be a pond or lake that's deep in the woods with only hike-in access. The shoreline could be heavily overgrown and other than a few openings in the foliage there isn't anywhere to cast. The limited casting makes spin fishing restricted and fly fishing impossible. By utilizing a cart, a kayak can be wheeled in. All that is needed to launch is a small opening allowing you to get to the water. The only other vessels that could do this would be a float tube, small canoe or an inflatable. The kayak is more versatile.

What is especially nice is I can bring toys along. Toys, such as a fish finder and GPS, will allow me to investigate the body of water in detail. It might even be the first time it has had such scrutiny. There might be some really terrific structure to be discovered. Once on the water I have complete access and can put casts where no one or few have previously done so. The fish probably don't see much pressure and I'll have all that inaccessible shoreline to cover. Tossing flies to the shoreline can be especially fun and rewarding. If the weeds are thick, using a fly rod to probe the openings can be the best means of angling.

A buddy of mine had access to a small Boy Scout pond and invited me for an afternoon of fishing. The scouts were only allowed to shore fish, making the majority of the pond un-fished. It took a little while to figure the place out but I ended up with over 60 largemouth bass. My largest was a spawned out female of 5.5 pounds. When my buddy saw her he remarked that she'd be 7 pounds full of eggs. I don't know about 7 but I'd say 6.5 easy! I caught several bass over 3 pounds and the second biggest went 4.5. It was a great way to spend an afternoon.

Large rivers where the water level can fluctuate greatly have what are called Oxbow Lakes. These are lakes where the river flooded and upon receding left a lake. Often they are hard to get at. Some can't be reached from land and have to be accessed from the main river. The isolated ones are going to have some terrific fishing. I haven't been to many but I see them discussed in articles and on the TV fishing shows. They're not common in New Jersey but there is one that I know of near my home. It has big pike and bass in it.

The Regular Stuff: Practically anywhere other vessels can fish, a kayak can, too. The ease of transport and the ability to cover water better than other non-motor-

(left) This 8-pound bass came from a small quarry lake and was one of 5 bass taken by the author that day totalling 36 pounds. **(below)** Tony with a beautiful musky caught less than an hour from New York City.

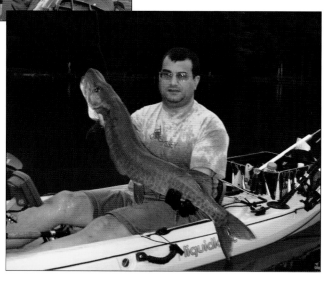

ized vessels give kayaks a lot of places to fish. Granted you're not going to cover large impoundments like a bass boat. However, due to the versatile launch locations you can usually get much closer to where you'd like to fish compared to a boat that is restricted to using a ramp. Practically every larger body of water has environments that larger craft can't effectively fish. Because the body of water is large it has a greater capacity to support more and larger fish. Some of those fish are going to end up in these difficult areas where the kayak has many advantages over other craft.

There will be nooks and crannies, which are difficult if not impossible to fish from a larger vessel. There are going to be shallows that a boat can't fish properly. The low profile and stealth of a kayak allow it to fish skinny water very effectively. I know many bodies of water that have sections where boats can't go. Those are the places to take a kayak. Besides having these places to yourself, you will find some of the best fishing is there.

During one such outing I heard splashes up the inlet creek of the pond I was fishing. As I slowly paddled my way up I saw the source of the noise. On the other side of a group of lily pads a rather large fin was sticking out of the water. The bass was actively chasing something. I was only 20 feet away and fired off a cast. I wanted to be cautious, as the bass would easily spook in such shallow water. It took seven casts until she noticed my plastic worm. When she did it was fantastic, with the fish plowing water, producing a bow wake while rushing the worm from several feet away. A boat would never have given me access to what turned out to be a freshly spawned out 4.5-pound largemouth.

Even the largest bodies of water will have obscure places where you will have an advantage because you're in a kayak. I spent a few days in July 2007 fishing Lake Champlain, which separates New York and Vermont (I recount my trip there in greater detail in the Planning section of the book). It's 110 miles long and connects to the St. Lawrence Seaway just below the outflow of the Great Lakes. Residents have been petitioning for years to have it named as the sixth Great Lake. It isn't as large as the Great Lakes but it's a big body of water by any standard. In fact, after the Great Lakes it's easily one of the largest lakes in the country; a big, imposing body of water.

Before going on the trip I did as much research as I could. I had computer charts and had found a good six-part article about bass fishing the lake. Once I got there I found a book by the same author as the article, which went into greater detail. The area where I was camping, according to the book, saw a lot of pressure; however since many tournaments finished nearby, there was a constant supply of bass that got released in the general area after the weigh-in. Some of these fish, when released, were probably going to head to the nearest habitat that was to their liking. One of the major tributaries emptied into the lake a few minutes from my campsite. It formed an expansive fertile delta with a variety of weeds. There were various lily pads in open areas, reeds and a combination of both types of vegetation. In some of the places the reeds were almost impenetrable and between these sections were corridors. Guess where I found lots of bass? I had a blast fishing for them from the kayak. Besides the bass, I encountered my first bowfins. They were very aggressive and fought great. I also landed a couple of pickerel.

Your choice of kayak can vary greatly. On truly large waters, like the Great Lakes, you should treat them as if you were fishing the ocean. Longer, more seaworthy kayaks are going to be the best if you're venturing out into lakes that are really freshwater, inland seas. When the weather changes and it can do so quickly, you will want both the speed and rough water handling abilities of these craft. The larger the body of water the more I like to equip myself. A GPS and a fish finder help me investigate and zero in to promising water. Again, I treat such large waters as if I were fishing the ocean. I take clothing and food along. Since it's freshwater I don't need to carry a lot of water. Instead I'll bring a filter so that if things dictate that I need more water, I can procure it.

There are so many underutilized freshwater environments where the fish rarely if ever see anglers. Get a kayak and take advantage of this. I've spent many hours of quality time in these places and so can you.

Saltwater

I'm certain fishermen have used kayaks in freshwater for a long time. However the sport became what it is because of saltwater fishing. It seems strange, but the vast majority of the participants got involved to fish saltwater. Florida, Texas and especially southern California are the nurturing grounds where kayak fishing evolved. Most of the pioneering information came from anglers in southern California. Initially surfboards were used and someone got the idea to use a kayak.

The creation of SOT kayaks is when the revolution began. Kayak fishing as a sport owes its existence to saltwater. It is still where the majority of the participants are and the reason I got started. I, like many Northeast fishermen, was frustrated many times when I went surf fishing. Much too often the fish were farther than I could cast. It was like the schools of breaking fish were mocking me because I couldn't reach them. Then I read an article whose author used a kayak to abandon the confines of shore and launch wherever the fish were. The light bulb above my head ignited my journey to becoming a kayak fisherman.

Tides

I grew up inland and because of this all of my early angling was as a freshwater fisherman. Fish are fish and most aspects of fishing in saltwater are very similar to freshwater, however there is one that was totally alien to me - tides.

No book on kayak fishing would be complete without a photo of Lunasea's pet snook taken in the Florida Everglades.

Tides are caused by the gravitational pull of the moon and to a lesser degree the sun. The closer these celestial bodies are to the earth, the more pull they exert upon the water. Rarely are the sun and moon in the same plane, so each pulls differently and this affects the tides. There are times when they are aligned and the pull is the strongest. Conversely the opposite occurs and this is when they are the weakest.

Why is this important? Marine life evolved dealing with this phenomenon with all its intricacies. Fish are tuned into these changes, some of which are subtle. The food chain is affected and as predators, fish act according to available food. Some of the subtle effects may not be apparent to the casual visitor, but fishermen who live within an environment and fish it regularly understand them and fish accordingly. Everyone will notice the effect of a big tide. Not only will the water be higher when in and usually lower

when out, it will be associated with strong currents. Since kayaks are powered by our physical abilities, there will be times when these currents are too powerful to overcome.

One day I wanted to explore an area in the 10,000 Islands adjacent to the Everglades in Florida. It was a full moon and I knew the tide was going to be strong. To get to the bay I wanted to investigate I had to use a pass called Hell's Gate. It got its name because of the strong funneling effect the tide has going through it. I knew the tide would be ripping but I could use this as an ally. If I timed my excursion to use the tide it would propel my kayak. I could do a lot less work. It's akin to going downstream in a river except the strength of the current caused by the tide will vary more. The velocity changes depending on the stage of the tide. Also, unlike a river, the current literally does a 180 and heads in the opposite direction every 6 hours or so.

When I entered Hell's Gate the tide was already moving fervently. On the other side was my destination. The current was so intense I felt as if I was farther north at Disney World on a ride. I was moving at over 4 knots without providing propulsion! In order to steer I had to be going slightly faster than the current so this necessitated that I pedal, too. It was a blast and I got to the next bay quickly at over 5 knots. The big tide made fishing difficult and I'm glad I brought an anchor along. When the tide turned I rode it to the next bay on the way back to my launch point.

Besides being stronger, larger tides increase in altitude. Since the water is higher it can pull a lot of debris into the water, which can make fishing more difficult or impossible. The stronger force of the current often dislodges weeds. If you have to clean weeds or other stuff off your lure or line on every cast, it's probably not worth fishing in such a location. It will also stir up more debris and reduce visibility. In some places a strong tide will be a detriment to fishing but in others an asset. Again, knowing the intricacies of how it affects the environment is important.

The world's oceans are all connected and function as a large basin. The part of the earth that is nearest the moon causes the pull to actually lift the water. As the water is lifted it is obviously higher. There is a counter effect and those places farthest away will be lower. It's about a 12.5-hour cycle. In most places there are two low and two high tides each day, however there are geographical, regional and other anomalies where this isn't always so. The tidal differential between high and low can vary from less than a foot to 50! It's quite a spread. Also it varies from day to day and even from tide to tide.

Tides are also affected by the size of the body of water, its depth, topography and landmasses. Even in the middle of the ocean, far from land, there is an effect. The more variables the more they will influence the tide. Land and depth are two very important factors and most kayak fishermen are going to be in close proximity of land. Sometimes these influences work together creating a stronger tide, but they can also work against each other producing the opposite effect. It's complicated but luckily there are tide tables for most places on the planet and certainly anywhere we would want to fish. By using the tables we can determine the time for each stage of the tide and the height (high tide) or the deficit (low tide).

Tides are part of the saltwater environment and you have to be cognizant of them. Fish are much attuned to them, often being particular of the tidal stage and only feeding in conditions they favor. The 10,000 Islands is the biggest jigsaw puzzle I've ever experienced in fishing. As its name implies, there are thousands of islands and when combined with the effects of tide, wind and weather, to catch fish consistently you've got to understand how each factor interacts. Alter one of the factors and it can have a profound change on fish and bait behavior.

Most predators ambush their prey and in the Everglades there is almost too much structure that creates opportunities for the game fish. Besides all those islands there are channels, oyster bars, sand bars, etc. Predators look for situations where they have an advantage. Strong currents overpower prey and the more powerful predators will stage in places where the bait is funneled or delivered to them. Unlike a river, which mostly varies because of water volume, tidal currents are affected by many variables and are in constant flux. Sometimes a great situation only lasts for an hour or less but during that period the fishing can be superb.

Different species have adapted to different niches within the environment. There are habitat and situations they prefer. Again, it isn't the focus of this book to teach you how to fish each species, but to show you how to adapt the kayak when targeting your quarry.

There is another aspect to tides. We call it current. You often can't see it but its there. Where there's large water movement you'll get current. The most significant I've experienced is at Montauk, NY. Montauk sits at the eastern end of Long Island and water from Long and Block Island Sounds moves past it. It is hard work fishing there but it's one of the world's great fisheries and a fantastic spot to fish from a kayak.

Wind and Tide

Wind can affect tide, too. If you have a wind and tide opposing each other, the influence of the tide is diminished. Conversely when they work together they can increase. Most extreme is when a hurricane or storm makes landfall at high tide. This is referred to as storm surge because you have wind pushing high water. When this occurs water reaches much farther inland than normal and produces flooding and water damage. Predators know certain circumstances will create an opportunity to feed. Some of these only happen a few times a season and some only once.

There is a series of connected saltwater lakes in the Everglades backcountry that I wanted to fish in the winter. As the waters cool down the fish seek out the warmest water. I studied charts and satellite images to get a feel of what I was heading into. The initial part of the sortie required me to use a creek, which started at the highway and would take me down to the first lake. When I got to the lake the combination of a north wind (the creek ran north/south with the eventual outlet several miles south) and an outgoing tide caused there to be very little water in the lake. I decided to give it a shot but there wasn't enough water to get through. I bogged down in the muck and I couldn't pull the kayak across it. Because of the wind the tide was having a substantially lesser effect on water depth. Even though I had invested a significant amount of effort into this foray, I decided to turn around and explore somewhere else and return when conditions were more favorable. The next time I hit the area I did so on a big rising tide. I had plenty of water and really enjoyed the trip.

While I was heading back to the launch on one of the first days I fished Chokoloskee Bay, I came across an interesting rip along a mangrove edge. It was at the corner of a mangrove island that converged with an oyster bar and a main channel. I forget the wind direction but it was blowing at least 10 mph. It looked very fishy. I made a long cast with a three-inch Storm Wild-Eye and let it sink and roll with the current. It stopped after a few feet. My initial reaction was I had hung up in the oysters but that changed quickly as lined peeled from my reel.

The strong current swept the fish towards me, then it surged in the direction of the mangroves and I put as much pressure on the line as I could. The fish ran into the channel, and I still hadn't any idea what it was. It was a great fight and several minutes later I got my first glimpse. It was a keeper snook, my first. A couple of more runs and I managed to get the lip gripper on it. I admired the fish, took a couple of pictures, and released it. I caught a couple more from the spot and then the rip subsided along with the action. This spot was right across from where I subsequently launched the kayak several days each week for two months. The rip never set up again and even though I always fished it I never caught a fish there again.

As I spent more time fishing the 10,000 Islands I became more familiar with my backyard and I began to recognize situations. Often one of these situations would hold only a fish or two. It was much more similar to the freshwater fishing I had grown up with instead of the majority of the saltwater kayak fishing I do in the Northeast for bluefish and striped bass. I would come to a spot and think this looks like a good spot for trout and often I'd catch a mess of them. Or I would say there must be snook or reds here, and sometimes there were.

Inside

When venturing into the salt on your initial forays, I recommend doing so in protected waters. I refer to this as fishing inside. To me, inside are waters that don't have to be accessed via the surf or inlet and aren't open oceans or seas. In some parts of the country inside fishing is very limited due to topogra-phy. Plate tectonics are the reason. Without going into a lengthy description, the North American continent is moving westward. On the east and gulf coasts as the land mass slides westward it has been leaving debris for millions of year. This debris is the continental shelf. It's quite extensive, reaching many miles out to sea.

The slope is quite gradual, too. In many places even though you're dozens of miles from land, the depth is less than 100 feet. What have been left from this sliding are barrier beaches, islands, bays and all sorts of protected waters. Conversely on the West Coast, to reach the same depths you may only have to go 100 yards.

Because the environments are so different, fish behavior has evolved very differently. The abundant habitat of the shallow bays and estuaries of the east and gulf coasts is a food factory. Conversely the West Coast is very limited in this type of habitat and the food factory is different.

Southern California is a great example of this. San Diego, which is a hotbed of activity, has San Diego Harbor and Mission Bay. The entire West Coast of the continental United States has less protected, shallow water fishing than the smallest state in the country, Rhode Island. The species are much more limited in the bays of the West Coast. For example, getting back to San Diego, the species most sought for kayak fishing are yellowtail, white sea bass, halibut, mako and thresher sharks. Inside you're going to find some bass, small halibut and the occasional bonefish. It would be a real fluke of nature to catch the others inside. Both the Atlantic and Gulf Coasts have many species that occupy both environments. In the Northeast striped bass, bluefish, weakfish and fluke are common inside and it isn't restricted to juvenile fish either.

The most sought-after species, the striped bass, is anadromous. This means they spawn in freshwater and live in saltwater. The five Pacific salmon species, which comprise the most well known anadromous fish, only return to freshwater to spawn and die. Striped bass range throughout both environments. You can find large stripers hundreds of miles from saltwater and find immature juveniles in the salt. Many a trout fisherman has had a big bass take his trout in the upper Delaware River.

The first time I ran into stripers in the Delaware I was fishing for smallmouth bass where the Pequest River entered the Big D. It was one of the hottest

(above) The author caught this tarpon in the extreme upper reaches of a canal. (left) A nice striped bass taken near New York City. That's the tower at JFK Airport in the background. (bottom) Joey with a J-Bay striper.

days in a decade and I was sitting in the water while catching bass to stay cool. Then I saw a very large fin sticking out of the water. As I stood up it slid back in. I played this game for a while. The cool waters of the Pequest had attracted several striped bass in the 20-pound class. Interestingly enough a few anglers came down in the late afternoon with five-gallon buckets in which they had 12-inch trout they had purchased at the nearby hatchery. These fishermen told me they regularly fished for stripers by live-lining the trout here.

Striped bass being anadromous range very deep within a watershed. Oftentimes they will go up to where they meet an impediment that prevents them from going farther. Because they're at home in fresh-

water they've been stocked and are doing very well in many inland waters throughout the country. The farther south you fish along the eastern seaboard, the fewer large stripers you will find inshore. This is because the water temps are too warm for them.

As you head south other species fill these niches somewhat. Redfish, southern weakfish (trout) and flounder (fluke) are the inshore equivalents to some extent. I say 'extent', because unlike the striped bass they aren't anadromous, so they can't tolerate fresh-water but can be found in brackish. As we get to Florida and south Texas, snook and to a lesser degree tarpon, occupy this niche. Deep in the back-country of Florida you might catch redfish, tarpon, snook and largemouth bass all in the same area.

The more you can narrow down an environment the better when fishing from a kayak. Inshore waters naturally do this. The fishing there is more akin to freshwater. When I fish the backcountry of the Everglades it is very much like fishing for largemouth bass. If it weren't for the water being salty and the tides it would be the same. Instead of largemouth of a few pounds I'm casting to snook. The tighter the fishing gets the better it is for a kayak, within reason.

I've found snook sitting in mangrove-canopied creeks between backcountry lakes where it was virtually impossible to cast. However, I could stealthily approach close enough to poke them with my rod. Many neophyte kayak anglers think like boaters. I remember a post several years ago made by a new kayak owner who couldn't wait to anchor up in a busy inlet and fish. I responded by pointing out the hazards (besides the wakes from boats, the current when combined with debris on the anchor line could exert sufficient force to pull the kayak under) of such an action and asked why he wanted to be a boat. I suggested he use his new fishing tool, the kayak, in situations where he had all the advantages over boats.

Not far from the inlet there were sedge islands, flats and channels that encompassed terrific fishing the boats couldn't access. I can't blame him for thinking the way he did though. Until you've used a kayak as a fishing tool for a bit it's hard to understand. As previously mentioned, I became a kayak fisherman because I was a frustrated surf fisherman. The ironic part is many eastern surf fishermen, myself included, purchased kayaks to fish the ocean. We did so because we were tired of watching blitzing fish we couldn't reach from shore.

Heading out beyond the waves is often productive but other than in the autumn I rarely venture there, having discovered the bountiful fishing available in back bays and estuaries. The kayak is a great tool for fishing there. There are a lot of fishermen in this country. No matter how you count them it's a staggering number. If there is good fishing at a particular spot and it's accessible, there will be others there, too. It doesn't matter if you're land-based or in a boat. If either fishermen group can access and fish a spot that holds fish, they will.

The best places to fish are those that are either difficult or impossible to access via foot or boat. These are the spots you want to fish. I love fishing them. I feel like the cat that ate the canary when doing so. Not only can the fishing be excellent but the escape factor ranks high too. By this I mean fishing places full of life where it's you, your companions and nature only. It doesn't have to be in the middle of wilderness, either. There are lots of locations very near civilization with great fishing, where you still feel isolated and have them to yourself.

Inshore waters encompass a lot of different environments and are where many of us made our first forays into the salt. It's where I started and the type of setting I recommend. By eliminating surf you dismiss a difficult aspect of saltwater fishing. The season before I got a kayak I regularly fished the Atlantic surf of New Jersey's northern beaches. I kept hearing there was great fishing inside and one day I stopped at a tackle shop and asked what this referred to. Inside was Raritan Bay, New Jersey. Turns out the bay was full of peanut bunker and they had been there since August. There were tens of thousands of hungry striped bass taking advantage of this bounty.

I started fishing off the bay's beaches and I did have some excellent outings despite being shore-bound. However, just like the ocean beaches, the blitzing fish spent a lot of time beyond my reach. Anglers in small boats and even canoes were having 50-plus fish days. The following summer on my very first kayak excursion into the bay I caught somewhere between 50 and 100 bluefish. The highest total caught from shore that day was three!

For a few years I had heard reports about the great fishing in Jamaica Bay, New York. The bay is in Brooklyn and Queens - two of the boroughs of New York City. The eastern border of the bay includes JFK International airport. One of my customers, Polo, purchased a kayak from me to fish the bay. He called me from on the water his first time out, gushing with enthusiasm over how much fun he was having. Polo is a minister, and I'll never forget his next comment. It was low tide and the flats only contained a foot of water. Interspersed in the flats were channels, which were a couple of feet deeper. The striped bass were in the channels and Polo was wading in the shallow water sneaking up on the fish and sight-casting to them. Here he was in the middle of the bay, wading and catching fish. He said he felt like Jesus, walking on water.

I made arrangements to fish the bay with Polo a few days later. We launched and fished near the airport. As I released a nice striper I heard a deafening roar. As I looked toward the noise I watched the Concorde supersonic jet take off. Here we were in what is terrific fishing, in the shadow of one of the largest cities in the world; hardly a place where one would expect good fishing let alone a world-class sport fishery. What makes it especially impressive is that a good deal of it contains water that is not accessible by boat because it is too shallow - perfect for kayak fishing.

When we looked for a locale to host a kayak-fishing tournament, it was the obvious choice. The second year of the event ESPN2 came down and filmed the tournament. They were shocked at the fantastic fishing. On camera they had an angler catch and land a 12-pound weakfish, lots of bluefish and bass to 28 inches, all with the Manhattan skyline as a backdrop. The crew commented that oftentimes they have to manufacture a show, due to the lack of footage. Jamaica Bay was just the opposite. They had too much.

Anytime you fish the bay, jets will be landing from and taking off for all corners of the globe. I often wonder how many of the passengers are fishermen flying off to an angling experience they just flew over. I've had 40-plus fish days and some of the largest weakfish in the world come from here - fish in the upper teens. It won't surprise me if a new world record is caught there in the next couple of years, and from a kayak.

Inside waters vary greatly from open bays, estuaries, rivers, flats and the like. Open bays are going to be most similar to the open ocean, but on a smaller scale. The fishing is similar. The inner parts of the bays and estuaries are my favorite places to fish. These spots are the nurseries where many forms of prey are either reared or call home. The more inaccessible the less likely someone else will be fishing there. Often reaching them from shore is impossible. It might be because of the distance but most often either the terrain to the spot is impenetrable or access is denied because you would have to cross private property. Boats can't reach them, as there are usually stretches where it is too shallow for them to cross or they simply can't access with sufficient stealth not to be discovered by the fish. Kayaks can operate in a few inches of water and the bottom structure means nothing to a kayak, as it floats. I have found huge fish in water that barely covers their backs in places where you would not expect them.

I remember Art, who I met through my fly club, commenting he was getting tired of fishing the inside of Sandy Hook, New Jersey and was looking for a change. Sandy Hook is a several-mile-long peninsula that separates Raritan Bay from the Atlantic Ocean. He asked me to recommend an area to hit and how to access it. I suggested to Art that he fish a specific spot inside the bay fed by a creek-drained brackish pond system. Art found terrific fishing for striped bass that approached 40 inches. He had it all to himself but when boats passed to the outside he kept his rod low when he had a fish on. If the boats discovered the school and raced in, they probably would have spooked the fish in the shallow water. Sometimes you have to disguise what you're doing when catching fish.

My buddy 'Joev' was telling me about some terrific fishing he discovered in a river in New England. I scheduled a weekend to join him. Our first outing was going to be at night. We unloaded the kayaks and as we were carrying them down the trail to the river a gent was heading out with a rod in hand. I asked how the fishing was and he said he hadn't caught anything. He did say he could periodically hear fish break water out of casting range. He figured they were small bass. I just grinned, as I had seen pictures from Joe, and small bass were probably not what were making the splashes. We launched the kayaks from the very spot the gent must have been fishing and on my first cast I hooked and landed a striped bass just under 40 inches!

A flat just downstream was full of bass. I couldn't drift or paddle without constantly spooking fish in the 2 to 5-foot water. We caught our share, too - fish up to Joev's 43-incher. In the same area, a bit upstream, Dougie landed a 50-incher! The next day Jim got spooled while fishing a live eel.

The river looked more like we should have been angling for trout or smallmouth bass, rather than big striped bass. At one particular spot, just below an impenetrable rock rifle, Joe cast his TnW. It looked like a perfect spot to drop a small dry fly awaiting a bass or trout to sip it from the surface. The TnW looked so unwieldy and out of place. Joe hadn't turned his handle more than a few revolutions when a 32-inch striper intercepted it. I learned a valuable lesson of just how far up and shallow game fish would go.

The above scenario is not some rare occurrence. This happens all over. The river highlighted above has roads on either side of it. Thousands of people drive by this spot on a daily basis. The eastern seaboard is loaded with such places as I'm certain are the estuaries of the Gulf States. The discovery is half the fun for me. Joe put in his time to discover such spots and you will need to as well. It is well worth the effort. I've found snook and tarpon in very interesting places. Catching very large fish from small intimate places is incredible.

One of the great things about fishing inside is you don't have to contend with the surf. Another kayak nemesis, wind, is often negated too. However, the third major factor of saltwater fishing, tides, actually becomes very important. Understanding tides is important both as to how the fish and bait are going to behave, and your planning regarding access to and exit from the area. Let's take the second aspect first.

The farther you go into an environment, provided there isn't a feeder river or creek, the shallower the water is going to be. Some places may go dry. This is the fishes' home; the last thing they want is to become trapped. Just as we know our homes and neighborhoods, so do fish. They know where the side roads are, the highways, the snack bar, the grocery store, their bedrooms, everything. Tide and water temperature are the two most important dynamics of their lives.

(above) The piece of water way upstream in New England that the author and friends found to be full of stripers. (left) Joev with a nice one.

Practically all fish, with very few exceptions, are cold-blooded. Water temperature determines their metabolism. All species have specific optimal ranges of water temperature they seek. At optimal ranges their metabolisms will be high and they are going to need to eat. As fishermen we want to find feeding fish. Besides the height of the water, tide affects the temperature too and can vary by several degrees.

Another environment where kayaks often have a distinct advantage is a flat. What is a flat? For our purposes they are shallow areas in saltwater. I know it's a vague description. Generally flats are anywhere from dry at low tide to several feet deep at the top of the tide. In some places shallow enough where you can wade. Flats are most often associated with the Florida Keys and the Caribbean, chasing bonefish and permit; however they aren't limited to the tropics. They exist all over the fishing world. You've got a few ways in which to fish them - while seated in the kayak, standing in the kayak or wading. All are effective and I let the circumstances and my equipment dictate which method I use.

Each spring ravenous bluefish invade certain sections of Raritan Bay, New Jersey. They are hungry and very aggressive. Before I had a kayak I would wade fish from shore. Usually I got fish but Raritan

Bay is very shallow and gradually gets deeper as you move away from shore. When the tide is low you feel as if you can wade out forever and will sometimes end up a half mile from shore. There is practically no structure to hold fish. Sometimes they are within casting range but can just as easily be far enough out where it's too deep to wade. The kayak is perfect for this fishing. Sometimes I'll wade and when the fish move off I can hop in the yak and stay with them.

The first time I sight-fished flats was on my initial trip to Cape Cod, Massachusetts. The first day Doug, Joey and I fished the world renowned Monomoy Flats. However it wasn't until a couple of days later that I got hooked. The efficiency unit we had rented had access to Town Cove. Our buddy Steve, whose in-laws live on the cape, was up for a few weeks and upon learning about our access suggested we hit the cove and the adjacent Nauset Marshes. I was the first to launch and after I crossed the channel there was a flat that I started to paddle across. The water was a couple of feet deep and I couldn't believe my eyes, as a few dozen striped bass scattered from my incursion into their pasture. We stealthily approached all the remaining flats and I've been hooked on this type of fishing ever since. We were wading then, but since that trip we incorporated standing on the kayaks into our repertoire.

I have found sight fishing while standing in a kayak is best done with a tandem. That's because most of the time you're going to be stalking the fish. The front person is the fisherman and he stands. The person in the back has the job of providing propulsion and steering. Both need to communicate as only one can stand and with the greater altitude the front occupant is going to see much more than the one sitting in the rear. When fish are sighted a cast is thrown. Usually casts need to be precise. Flats fish are often feeding on prey they find on the bottom and presentation of your offering must mimic their intended prey.

The first time I tandem kayak-fished was in the Turks and Caicos Islands of the Caribbean. Our quarry was bonefish, a species I had read much about but for which I had never fished. Scott and I were in a Malibu 2. We rounded a point we named Barracuda Point, because while exploring the day before we found a four-foot cuda lurking there. There was a chop to the water but the lee of the land produced a calm, almost mirror-flat surface extending 30 to 40 feet from shore. We hadn't been in this quiet water long when I spotted a bonefish cruising in front of us. I cast my jig in front of the fish and it took my offering immediately. The fight was on. This was my very first bonefish, a 4.5 pounder. What a terrific experience. As the tide dropped we waded the flats and caught several more fish.

Inside waters can get really tight. Mangrove country is such an environment. Mangroves form dense forests and will close in creeks. The creeks are the roadways that connect the lakes and ponds of the backcountry. Both the lakes and creeks will hold fish. For the most part the lakes don't present any angling problems but the creeks are extremely challenging.

You might consider them more trouble than they're worth but I've found some of the biggest fish hang in the creeks. It takes short rods, heavy line, planning and luck to land some of these bruisers.

The author moved from the bay to the ocean to find this nice striper.

Open Ocean

This is where most people in southern California started kayak fishing and the majority of my early research was this type of angling. It's all about fishing beyond the surf. Unlike my native Northeast where we experience blitzes of large schools of game fish in protected waters, the majority of fishing in California is beyond casting range. The fish don't crash the beaches, so other than surf perch and halibut there isn't much opportunity for land-bound anglers. There is some bay fishing but it's limited. In order to experience the best fishing you're going to need to fish the ocean. This requires launching from the beach and heading out through the breakers. I call it gorilla fishing because it takes some fortitude to launch a kayak in the surf and fish the open waters of an ocean. It's not hard to launch and paddle past the waves but it isn't simple either. Many people find it intimidating and won't do it. There is technique that needs to be learned, especially when returning. Southern California has a strong surfing tradition and many folks grew up dealing with the surf, so it isn't a big deal there. It's a way of life.

Nate is up front with Dave providing propulsion as they stalk snook and jacks in the Everglades backcountry.

However, it restricts the number of people who will join the sport because it is a bit more difficult. It's much easier to launch in a bay or sheltered area and never deal with the open ocean. The entire eastern seaboard and Gulf have great fishing beyond the breakers, however those same species are available in the protected inshore waters.

Once beyond the waves each region has different species and methods for fishing. The regional message boards and local articles are top sources for information about what works best. In some areas live bait is much more important to fishing success than in others. I spent a few years fishing San Diego and Baja from a boat in the mid-1980s. Almost 20 years later I fished Baja via a kayak for the first time on a trip with *La Jolla Kayak Fishing*. What was true from a boat was still true from a kayak. Live bait was the ticket to consistently catch fish and we used the same techniques. The water is incredibly clear, making it hard to fool fish with artificials. Bait worked much better. Lures still caught fish but it often took chumming with live baitfish to create a feeding frenzy. In southern California a live bait system is a common accessory in kayak fishing. It's rare to see them on most kayaks in the east

In many places in the ocean you're going to have to contend with boats. It's important to acknowledge this. I've often fished among the fleet. They've generally treated me great but you have to recognize that you're hard to see being so low to the water. Some anglers find it unnerving to be in the midst of this fishing armada. Boats will vary from 20 to over 100 feet. In some places it becomes very competitive with breaking fish. Some boat operators consider kayaks a nuisance and treat participants with distain. If there are breaking fish and I'm between the boat and the fish to which the boaters have made a direct line, I may decide to get out of the way even though I have as much right to be there as any other vessel provided I'm adequately set up and I show the respect that I in turn want. I tend to avoid such places and fish where there are few boats, but sometimes fishing with the fleet is the way to go.

There are also places where you rarely see boats. One of the great things about kayaks is they can be launched in areas that are far from boat access. Anywhere there is a shoreline without harbors the boats will have too far to travel to reach the spot. I love this type of fishing and recommend seeking out these locations. The strength of a kayak is it can be launched virtually anywhere, far from boat access points. Often you are the only one fishing such places and the fishing can be spectacular.

We were way back in Town Cove, Cape Cod waiting for the tide to change when Mark got a call on his cell phone from Jim. He was scouting the beaches and from up on a bluff had spotted a large school of feeding striped bass a few miles north of us. Mark yelled to me that Jim had found fish. A quick call confirmed the spot. I called out to the group to come over so I could explain what we just learned and how we should take advantage of this information. We decided to head in to our launch then proceed to the ocean. If things held up it would be some spectacular fishing. I had experienced this type of fishing the first time I ventured up to Cape Cod and it was some of the best fishing I've ever participated in.

By the time we paddled back to the launch, loaded the kayaks on the trailer and got to the beach, at least 90 minutes had elapsed. A quick scan of the binoculars showed the fish about ¾ mile southeast from the parking lot, so we rolled the kayaks down the bluff and launched.

The group consisted of Mark, Terry, a pair of Rich's and me. This was only Rich G's third time in a kayak and his first sortie through the surf. I spent a few minutes helping him through the process. By the time I got my own kayak together and caught up to the crew they were just hanging around. I asked why they weren't fishing and Mark said they didn't know where the fish were. I pointed a quarter mile to the south where I could see the noticeable difference in the water surface. As we approached Mark yelled he thought they looked like bluefish, probably because in New Jersey, where Mark fished most of the time, it almost always was. I knew better and fired off a cast.

They were stripers and they were big. We fished until dusk and didn't land a fish less than 32 inches. The average exceeded a yard with the largest ones well over 40. The crystal clear water made it especially exciting. I used topwaters and teased the fish to the kayak. I did my best to keep the lure away from the fish until it was right near the kayak. The result from most casts would be several fish crashing the lure as I led them in.

At the kayak one of two things usually occurred. Sometimes the fish would see me and spook. Imagine several bass, from 15 to 40 pounds, all trying to get out of Dodge! More than once bass hit the kayak.

Most of the time one of the fish would get the lure and the fight would be on. When I hooked up there might be as many as 100 fish around the kayak. By the time it was landed the school was usually a quarter mile away. I would fight the fish, release it and then head up tide until I encountered the school again. Practically every first cast resulted in a hook-up and the scenario repeated.

After one particularly long fight I couldn't see the school. I assumed they were still heading up tide and paddled in that direction. Then I spotted scales in the water and followed the glittering silver trail to the pot of gold. That was my last shot at the school, as twilight was coming and I needed to head back. I've encountered this circumstance several times and it's one of my angling favorites. Not only is the fishing great, but because of the distance from boat launch points we didn't have any boats to contend with. The nearest place where a boat could come from was an inlet to the south or a harbor on the other side of the peninsula, over 30 miles away. There is too much good fishing near where the boats leave from for them to make the run where we were.

Wherever boat access is limited or nonexistent you will find great fishing. From the beginning when I started kayak fishing I've wanted to take a kayak on an extended trip to Baja, Mexico. I spent a few years there in the mid 1980s long before I discovered kayaks as a fishing tool. An extended trip to Baja is tops on my lists. Baja looks like kayak fishing heaven. There are a few mother-ship operations and I enjoyed a trip I took with La Jolla Kayak Fishing in 2004. However, that is a tiny part of what this amazing place has to offer. There are close to 2,000 miles of shoreline and less than a couple of dozen-launch ramps. The Pacific coast of Baja has very limited access and the kayak fishing opportunities are infinite, provided you can launch a kayak through the surf.

Surf Launches

That takes us to our next topic - getting through the surf. Even though launching and fishing beyond the surf is more difficult, doing so presents tremendous angling opportunities. In some places like southern California you're not going to have much angling opportunity if you don't. There are thousands of miles of territory that are available with spectacular fishing. As I mentioned earlier, surf launches aren't difficult. There is technique involved and once

learned you can regularly fish the open ocean. The best way to learn is to either hire a guide or go with someone who has experience. I've helped a lot of anglers get started. It's important to be prepared and have lots of respect for the power of nature. There is a tremendous amount of energy in the surf. Preparation is the key.

When I started fishing from a kayak there weren't many folks doing likewise in the Northeast, so when it came time to learn I was on my own. I waited until the water was warm so I could eliminate the need for anything more than shorts. Less to contend with should something go wrong. I left the rods and tackle in the car and played in the waves. I picked a day when the surf was moderate. There were people on the beach so if something went really awry I hoped someone would notice. I tried surfing once and after the board hit me on the head I had enough, and because of this I have a lot of respect for what could happen. Nowadays there are folks to connect with. Every summer another group of newbies meets up on various online forums and plans a day or two of practice. It's a great way to learn.

I ran a trip up to Cape Cod one September. The water was warm, which kept the fish in the ocean. They were spending their time in the lobster pot zone, which is approximately ½ to ¾ of a mile off the beach. Much too far to surf cast, so to catch fish on this trip you had to be in the ocean.

I was the only person in the group who had previously launched through the surf. I remember my buddy Mark standing waist deep in the wash. When I got near him I asked what was up. He said he didn't know about launching. I could see he was intimidated. No wonder, the waves were beating him up as his kayak bucked like a wild animal. He was in the wrong place. I told him there were two places to be, either up on the sand or out beyond the breakers. In the wash he was at the mercy of the waves and the eventual outcome wasn't going to be pretty. We dragged the kayak back up the beach and discussed how to approach the launch.

We started talking about the three zones within a beach launch area. There's the dry land, the wash/breaker zone, and the water beyond the breakers. The land is where you do your preparation. The wash/breaker zone is where all the turbulence is. You want to spend as little time as possible in the mayhem, given that this is where all the turmoil and power are. If things go awry, this is where it will most likely occur. It will happen quickly, too, so while on the sand make sure everything is ready.

Try to expose as little gear as possible. Whatever you can store inside the kayak, do so. What is exposed, attach to something. If an item can't handle getting dunked, put it in a waterproof enclosure. Prepare for the worst and expect the best.

Now that everything is ready, it's time to get into the part of the wash that is closest to the land. How far in you wade with your kayak depends on what's happening. I usually walk out until I'm no more than knee to thigh deep. This puts me in a reasonably stable position.

Now it's time to watch the waves. Waves come in sets, which consist of several waves in a grouping. In between the sets there are often lulls. It's preferable, especially in the beginning, to launch in a lull. Only by observing the surf for a bit will you recognize one. When a lull starts you want to immediately hop into your kayak and propel it like mad.

I use the word propel because you either have to paddle or pedal. If you're going to paddle, have the paddle in your hand when you hop in, and get going immediately. If you're going to pedal, have pedals in the ready position and pump out the power. Either way, the sooner you can get beyond the breakers the better.

If it's a good lull there might not be any breaking waves, however you can't count on it. A wave may start to break and the natural tendency is to brace and stop paddling/pedaling. That's the worst thing you can do. You want your momentum to punch through the wave. It can be intimidating but its proper technique. Even if the wave breaks over your head you will still punch through and end up beyond the breakers. However, if you stop propelling the kayak, your lack of momentum may result in your being pushed backwards. Nothing good will come of this. You may dump and there is a definite possibility of flipping. Your goal should be to get to the third zone beyond the breakers as quickly as possible.

Once there you can pull out your gear and prepare to fish. It only takes a few minutes. Once you gain experience you will know when a launch might be eventful and you can adjust your approach.

You've got to pay attention when in the wash or breaker zone. Waves vary greatly and rogues are possible. A rogue is generally a wave out of the norm. They are possible anywhere but it's especially crucial to be aware of them when in the zone. On a trip to Cuttyhunk Island, Massachusetts, upon landing after an afternoon on the water we found Bill sitting against some driftwood with his kayak. We assumed he had a problem with the kayak but the kayak was fine. He was injured. Turns out while in the wash/breaker zone he went to tighten a strap, taking his eyes off the waves, and one smashed the kayak into his leg. When he returned home he found out it was broken. Bill had made many launches off that beach without incident; however it only takes one time to have an accident.

The only time you are truly safe is when you're well up on the shore. You've always got to keep an eye out to sea even while in the safe zone beyond the surf. That's because a rogue or large set can create problems. Should one come bearing down on you it's important to be aware of it in order to react. The best remedy when a rogue is bearing down on you is to turn the bow so it points into the wave. The next best is to be pointing away. You're most vulnerable when you're broadside. Paralleling the beach is common in many places as one trolls and because of this most waves will come at you broadside. Always pay attention to what's going on around you. When fishing the ocean I'm constantly looking seaward to make sure nothing bad is coming.

After a day of fishing it's time for the most difficult part of the surf experience - landing. Not only is it harder when the waves are behind you but the size can change in a few to several hours. It can be intimidating if they increase a couple of feet. I remember one of my first trips into the Atlantic off of the Jersey coast. It was November and cold. There were pods of breaking fish all over but it was very windy and they were moving quickly. After a couple of hours chasing and not catching, I decided it was time to come in. As I approached shore the surf looked bigger. The swell had increased a couple of feet and it looked menacing. I had little choice and luckily after a very exciting ride I was back on shore. Should something go wrong when landing, you and your kayak, while possibly not still together, should end up on the beach. However, there are circumstances when this isn't necessarily true.

One day I was at Monmouth Beach Club, a favorite launch spot for kayak fishermen in northern New Jersey, when some folks told me earlier that day someone had lost a kayak. They had dumped and swam to get their paddle first, and then went for the kayak. There was a strong west wind, which is

common in New Jersey in fall. The shoreline of the state runs north south, so a west wind blows from the land out to sea. When the person tried to get to his kayak the wind blew it faster than he could swim.

Kayaks that fish well aren't great in the surf. Some models are better than others. There are kayaks designed for surfing waves but what makes a kayak good for kayak surfing doesn't translate well for most fishing. Surf kayaks are short and wide, and they have a fin to help control the kayak in the waves. Waves are faster than a kayak and when they catch up to you while breaking it can get dicey. I have never dumped a kayak heading out but I have a handful of times while coming in.

When a breaking wave catches a kayak the ten-

Anatomy of a surf landing. Here's Danny landing on a beach in Montauk. **(1)** Danny watches the waves, waiting for a quiet set. **(2)** He's made a commitment and starts paddling. **(3)** Riding the wave, paddling as hard as he can. **(4)** Once in shallow surf, he jumps out of the kayak. **(5)** He grabs the front handle and runs up the beach.

dency is to turn it sideways. Should this happen the likelihood of dumping increases, as you're now broadside to the wave. The remedy is to do as much as you can to prevent this. I'm getting ahead of myself a bit, though. Before returning through the surf you need to prepare for it because if things go wrong you can lose gear and break things. Secure everything that is vulnerable. Put the rods below deck or at the very least have them parallel to the kayak and strapped down. Keep in mind if you do dump there is a strong likelihood of sand being ground into things. This really wreaks havoc on reels, unless waterproof and unfortunately very few models are. Also keep in mind the potential for the kayak to be tossed and rolled exists and things can break off and be lost. There is the possibility of having a rod break and lose a reel. I like to remove my very vulnerable electronics.

On the same trip to Cuttyhunk where Bill broke his leg launching, 'Joev' had a bad landing. Again, something he had done many times before. He was landing at dusk and misjudged our preferred landing area. He got turned in the surf and then his kayak hit a rock. (Cuttyhunk is loaded with rocks in the surf.) When the kayak hit the rock he was ejected as the kayak flipped. The waves smashed the kayak in the rocky surf and destroyed his fish finder. Even though most fish finders we use for kayak fishing are waterproof, they are not shatterproof.

I've only dumped a handful of times but have ruined a few things because of it. The first time I dumped was in a spot where there had been some beach replenishment on this section of Jersey shore, which made the waves especially sharp. As my buddy Chris and I landed the surf flipped our kayaks. I had a camera in a zip lock bag and it got ruined. On another landing I broke a rod. Those are my two mishaps. Whatever you can't put in a hatch and doesn't float, you need to secure. While landing up in Rhode Island one day, Terry flipped his kayak. He had several rods standing straight up and a bunch of unsecured gear. One of them was the mirage drive of his kayak. I usually prefer landing on a sandy beach with the drive in. It gives me more control. I thought Terry would follow my lead but he didn't. As we collected his gear I noticed his drive wasn't there and asked about it. The search was on but we never found it. We tried snagging trebles and even returned during low tide, to no avail. The tally was one broken fly rod, a ruined GPS and the drive, totaling several hundred dollars. Ouch!

After securing your gear it's again a good idea to sit in the third zone a bit and watch the waves to determine how the sets are running. Unless you're a thrill jockey it's best to again select a calm period and propel the kayak like mad until you can jump out. Usually this will be when you're in a foot or two of water. I like to have a floating bow rope on the kayak and have it readily accessible when I jump out of the kayak. I grab it and run up the beach dragging the

kayak. It all depends on how the landing zone is. Sometimes it's violent and other times benign. However, no matter how gentle there is always a chance of a rogue, so don't dawdle. Get to the dry area ASAP, as nothing bad can happen there.

I've heard that some guys are coming in backwards. I've never done so. It does allow one to see the waves and react to them. It's easier to control the kayak and keep it perpendicular to the waves. Also the bow handles breakers better then the stern. I understand its being done in southern California. A search on the regional forums would help you with more information if interested in the particulars.

Big Water: The open ocean and bays are big water. There is a lot of territory to cover and kayaks don't cover a lot of ground quickly. What kayaks do well is allow you to cover an area thoroughly. In Chokoloskee Bay, there are lots of oyster bars, which at low tide are easy to see but at high water they disappear. However, they are still there. There is one particular part of the bay that has a ton of bars. I've discovered that it fishes very well at high water and one day I fished it with a buddy in a boat. Boats generally only fish the outside and don't venture into the middle of this labyrinth. However, due to all the time I spent there in a kayak I knew it intimately and because of this I maneuvered without any issues. This resulted in some nice jacks and reds. It's best to break down areas into smaller, more easily fished parts. Have a game plan. In the Northeast we pursue many species that let you know their whereabouts. Fish that blitz usually have birds that follow them. If you see birds diving on bait and there are splashes below, then you've got a blitz. Check recent reports. If you know fish have been in a particular area then start there. One day Ken was down at Raritan Bay, NJ. He found some large bluefish off of an area of the bay by Port Monmouth. The fish had been in the bay for at least a week and since conditions hadn't changed we expected them to be in the vicinity, so we planned a trip. I got to the area about 45 minutes before Ken and did some reconnaissance. I checked to the West first, where I spotted some bird

The open ocean is where you'll find billfish. Here, Adrian fights a Baja sailfish. Photo from a video by Jim Sammons.

activity. I hit a couple of spots farther east and then called Ken to let him know the place that looked the most promising. We launched and got into fish quickly.

Mother-Ship Fishing: This is using a boat to transport kayaks to fish areas you wouldn't be able to reach otherwise. The beauty of this style of fishing is it adds another dimension to kayak fishing. Besides being transported to places too far to access otherwise, you have a boat along with its ability to bring more stuff. A mother-ship can be any boat used to get a kayak somewhere else, as simple as a kayak transported on a skiff up to a long ranger heading off to exotic locales far from port.

Many private boaters take kayaks along and there are a few operations around the continent. I discuss them in greater detail in the Exotic Chapter. In Baja, *La Jolla Kayak Fishing* offers trips out of Rancho Leonero Resort and Hotel Punta Colorado. Captain Charles Wright offers trips in the Everglades. Captain Mark Brassett runs an operation in bayou country. Besides a means of transport the boat carries live bait, extra gear, food, etc.

Regional Variations

Throughout these pages I have made the assumption folks reading this book are fishermen. The focus of this book isn't to teach you how to fish but rather adapting and modifying your existing techniques to maximize getting the most from kayak fishing. Granted there are going to be some techniques you haven't used that work well with the kayak and I'll discuss those, too. Each region has species and specific techniques that consistently produce results. That's not to say one can't use a technique in one area that's not widely known or in use in another. For the most part fish are fish. They eat, try not to be eaten and make more fish.

Although I kayak fish many areas I'm not going to attempt describing how each region varies. I do want to give you food for thought. You're the one who is going to be fishing in a specific area. It's up to you to determine the best way to catch fish. You can either do it on your own, or in some areas you can hire a guide or hook up with others. Your best resources are going to be kayak guides and kayak fishermen in the area you plan on fishing. Kayak fishermen are a friendly group and in my experience very willing to help out. The sport has terrific camaraderie. It's the complete antithesis of some other forms of fishing that function like secret societies.

My buddy Bill had to be in central Florida for a few days on a family trip and he managed to clear time to get in a bit of fishing. If you know Bill, he is always trying to squeeze in more time on the water. A couple of weeks before his trip, he asked me if I knew any kayak fishermen in the area. I suggested he post on the Florida forum of KFS and explain what he was looking for. A local, David, answered Bill's inquiry. He hooked him up with a shop that rented fully rigged fishing kayaks - ironically the same model Bill had at the time. David took Bill fishing a couple of days and even returned the kayak, as the shop was closed the day Bill wanted to turn it in. This allowed Bill to fish an extra day. Bill didn't have any way of knowing who rented kayaks, let alone one already equipped for fishing, and didn't know where he would find the redfish, jacks and snook he sought,

Charles and Jason of *Everglades Kayak Fishing* offloading kayaks from the mothership *Yak Attack* for an excursion up Wizard Creek in the Florida Everglades.

but David did.

By far the best resources for information are the regional web sites. Each one is going to contain varied information, but most have articles, maps and launching areas, and those I've listed at the end of this chapter have online forums. There is a wealth of information available. At KFS we put as much information as we could on the site. Forums are a fantastic place to learn in that you can ask questions and arrange to fish with others. If you have a question about a particular subject, they have search mechanisms which allow you to zero in on a target. Kayak fishing clubs are popping up all over, too - a fantastic way to meet others who have been at this a while. They have meetings, seminars and of course fishing days on the water. Many members have more than one kayak and are willing to bring one along for you to use with them for a day on the water.

Another resource is magazine articles. As mentioned, I have been writing monthly for a regional publication, *New Jersey Angler*, for several years and I know *Shallow Water Angler* regularly has articles about kayak fishing. Many guides write regular columns for their local publications. Seek these out. Some national publications run articles, and there may be info on your area.

Because I so enjoy seeing and experiencing new places and things on my own, I haven't utilized guides much in my fishing. I prefer the challenge of using my lifetime of fishing experiences to figure out a species and its environments. I have been fortunate to fish some varied and diverse surroundings - trout on 2-weight fly rods in small brooks, to fishing blue water for 1000-pound-plus marlin with 130-pound gear. My kayak fishing has been diverse too, having fished small hike in rivers and ponds for those same small trout, bass and panfish, to blue water for billfish.

I grew up fishing for largemouth bass. I had often heard that snook fishing is very similar. Sure there are tides to contend with which added another dimension, but it is more similar than different. I found snook related to structure and ambush points. Both species like to spend a lot of time tight to structure. This requires the angler place offerings close to the obstacle.

No matter how large a body of water you're dealing with, the first thing you need to do is break it down into smaller parts. Once broken down you can attack it. When I started fishing Chokoloskee Bay in

Florida, the first things I noticed were the often mentioned oyster bars. Depending upon the stage of the tide, this structure took on different attributes. A tide is moving water and I treat it like a part of a river, the difference being the water height varies throughout the tide and twice a day it changes direction. When the water is low the fish are in the cuts and when high they are on top of the flooded structure.

Many anglers can use the same techniques they are already using and adapt them to the new area and species. Southern California has been a hotbed of kayak fishing activity since the sport began, but west coast fishing is a small part of the kayak-fishing world when one considers population and access. Some important attributes needed in kayaks for that style of fishing aren't needed for most other regions. During a recent discussion with a kayak designer, we were talking about kayak design. He had just designed his most recent kayak for fishing and ignored the needs of west coast anglers. He designed it for the needs of fishermen from Texas to Maine. We talked about how the environments were similar throughout this region when considering saltwater and how the same kayak could handle them. The majority of the fishing is inshore. Surf launches and fishing in the open ocean is done but it's a small part of the actual fishing that takes place, whereas on the west coast just the opposite is true - the majority of the fishing is in the open Pacific.

Obviously things change as one moves from Texas to Maine. The flora and fauna change - redfish and trout, the stalwarts of the south, give way to striped bass and bluefish. Even though a species may have a broad range they have optimal areas within that range where they're more concentrated, and fishing is better. For instance, striped bass can be found as far south as the St. John River in Florida, however they are small fish, rarely exceeding five pounds. It isn't until you get to North Carolina that you're going to find a significant fishery for them where they sometimes winter over. Lately they've been wintering in Virginia. They make it as far as Maine, where they show up for a couple of months when temperatures are the warmest. I've caught bluefish in the Everglades but I wouldn't target them there. Every year some huge redfish are caught in New Jersey, but again these are accidental fish. To consistently fish for them I wouldn't venture farther north than Virginia.

The biggest saltwater change you're going to encounter within regions is the average tidal differential. In New Jersey a big tide is going to be around 6 feet, whereas in Maine it's two to three times that. Even though you might be fishing for the same species, striped bass, your approach is going to have to be different. The amount of moving water when dealing with a large tide is substantial. A kayak is a human-powered craft and you can't fight a tide that big. The larger the tide differential the more it's going to affect kayak fishing.

In a place like Maine where you have so much change, huge expanses are going to be devoid of water at certain stages and then become flooded. Obviously the fish aren't going to be there when there isn't any water. Maine has a bunch of estuarine systems and they vary in size from small to large. When I fish there, I plan to fish one of the smaller ones and ride the rising tide into its inner reaches and then ride the tide back to my starting point. If I do so at night I expect it will produce excellent fishing. If I started at low water and returned at the same stage of the tide that would encompass 12 hours. I'd probably start halfway through the rise and return with the fall.

Even though tides tend to increase as you head north, there are still variations within each region. I won't go into the how's and why's. For instance, the differential in Chokoloskee can be 4 to 6 feet, whereas in Matalacha it's only a couple of feet. Both places are only a couple of hours apart.

As a fisherman you have a storehouse of knowledge accumulated through experience. Fishing Baja's Sea of Cortez is a far cry from my native Northeast but I used things in Baja that I learned and read while living on Long Island. This was long before my kayak fishing days but they are lessons I learned that stay with me as a fisherman. In the mid 1980s I tail gunned for a caravan fishing business in Baja. Part of my responsibilities was as a fishing guide. On one particular trip the owner of the busi-

Useful Websites

These are the sites I've found to be useful for obtaining kayak fishing information:

- Kayakfishingmagazine.net
- Kayakfishingstuff.com
- Kayak4fish.com
- Texaskayakfishing.com
- Kayakfishing.com
- Paddlefishing.com
- Reel-time.com
- Ultimatekayakfishing.com
- Stripersonline.com
- Northwestkayakanglers.com
- Norcalkayakanglers.com
- Canadiankayakanglers.com
- Stripersurf.com
- Noreast.com
- Tightlineskayak.com
- Newenglandkayakfishing.com

I'm *JonS* on the forums, so don't be shy about saying "Hi."

ness had to leave for a few days so I was left in charge. It was a unique business, as we didn't take clients out on our boats. They would fish from their boats and had the option to fish where we did or explore on their own. It's a lot like kayak fishing in that respect.

We fished the area regularly, usually every other week during the season, and as with anywhere there were a bunch of hot spots and then there were places that sometimes produced. Being there so much we had a very good feel for where the fish would be. I hadn't spent a lot of time fishing Baja and the species were different than any I had fished before. On the first day of my solo someone caught a small white sea bass of approximately 8 pounds. The forage species was mackerel. Near the area where the angler caught the fish there was a cove that led to a wide channel between an island and the mainland. I had read an article a couple of years back about striped bass using drop-offs as they lay in wait for weakened and disoriented bunker, which when swept by the tide came too close to the change in the bottom. I had a buddy from Brooklyn and a friend from San Diego with me on the boat. I told the guys we were going to procure some macs and then explained what I wanted them to do. I was going to use the outgoing tide to drift from the shallow cove to the drop-off.

We didn't have a fish-finder so I had them use heavy weights to maintain occasional contact with the bottom. As we passed over the drop they let out more line and the whites immediately inhaled the macs. We caught fish in the 30 to 40-pound range. When the owner heard about our excursion he called it beginners luck, but I knew luck had nothing to do with it; it was fish being fish. Interestingly, white sea bass aren't bass but members of the croaker family. When we find weakfish (also members of the croaker family) in my native Northeast, the best places are drop-offs just like where I caught the whites in Baja. Use your accumulated wealth of past experience when fishing from a kayak.

Chapter 7
Getting to the Water

If you live next to the water where you plan on using your kayak all the time, you can skip this chapter. Go ahead, I won't mind. However, the fact is that most of us, even those of us lucky enough to have water in our own backyards, end up traveling with our kayaks. There are two basic means of transporting them - either on or in the vehicle or towing it behind on a trailer. The former is the most common.

On the Vehicle

The easiest way to transport a kayak is in the bed of a pickup truck. Some folks actually put a kayak or two inside a vehicle. Large vans and full-sized SUV's will accommodate many kayaks that are used for fishing, but the majority of us aren't going to transport this way. Many outdoor-oriented folks have pickups, though, and it's very easy to load a kayak into the bed of the truck and bring it along. One of the advantages of this method is that you don't have to break the kayak down. This saves time and is especially nice when hopping from location to location. With the tailgate down, a full-sized truck with an 8-foot bed can transport most kayaks. Check your local laws, as there is usually a limit as to how far a kayak can stick out behind the vehicle - most often 3 or 4 feet. If your kayak is longer, the issue is easily remedied with a bed extender. These allow you not only to transport a kayak that would otherwise be beyond the legal limit, but also to carry more than one. Put a bright flag on the end of the kayak(s) and you're set.

For the vast majority of us who transport our kayaks on the roof of our vehicles, the simplest method is a set of foam blocks and a pair of straps. A

The easiest way to transport a kayak is in the bed of a pickup truck. A bed extender is often required to make it legal.

lot of folks start off this way but I'm not a fan. It's fine for local, non-highway use but is very limited. Also, to sufficiently tighten the straps enough to secure the kayak, the vehicle's roof tends to deform. The roof usually pops back, but it could result in damage. Besides the block and straps, there are kits where everything is combined into a unit. Both work the same way. The straps go through the doors and then are tightened.

On a trip to the Turks and Caicos we used this method to get a couple of kayaks from our rental house to an area where we found excellent fishing for bonefish. They served the purpose, but on the last day we had to push the roof back into shape.

Many vehicles today come with factory racks. Some of these have crossbars while others have raised rails. The crossbars are easy to adapt for carrying a kayak. Usually they are oblong shaped, great for single kayaks and often you can carry a second by strapping another on top of the first. Should you double up the kayaks, make certain you strap each one individually. That means four straps for two kayaks.

Rack pads, first popularized for transporting surfboards, attach to the cross bars by using Velcro and ties. These pads provide cushioning for the kayak, and I do recommend using them. Either way, it's best

(above) The best way to transport a kayak on the roof of a vehicle is top down. (right) The proper way to lash down a strap to ensure that nothing comes undone while underway.

to flip the kayak over so the top is facing down. This is the best way to transport a kayak and many kayak manufacturers recommend this method. This is the most secure way to strap a kayak to the crossbars. Should you strap it the other way, you're probably going to need to tie the bow and stern down as well, and the kayak will most likely oil-can, which means the kayak crushes due to an outside force. This is caused by strapping but also can occur just leaning against something. In warm weather a kayak will oil-can just sitting on unpadded bars or other hard objects.

Besides rack pads, all the major rack companies make kayak accessories that attach to the crossbars. The major rack companies like Thule and Yakima all have add-ons that will allow the factory crossbars to carry a pair of kayaks. Malone doesn't make racks but they do make accessories that do the same. However, you must check the weight limits of the rack, as many factory racks have very low maximums. For instance, if your rack has an upper limit of 80 pounds and both of your kayaks weigh about 70 pounds, it's probably not a very good idea to transport two on the rack. For short distances without highway travel you may be fine, but if you're going to regularly transport two or more kayaks then you need to consider an aftermarket rack or trailer.

Aftermarket racks have become very common and sophisticated. The carrying capacities of these racks are significant and the diversity of accessories is al-

most overwhelming. If there is something you want to take along there is probably an attachment to suit your needs. There are accessories for attaching skis, bikes, windsurfing boards, snowboards, luggage and more, and a lot of attachments for kayaks. The most common is some form of cradle that can be adjusted to conform to the shape of the bottom of the kayak. The cradle will carry the kayak bottom down, just as it would sit in the water. Malone, Sportrack, Thule and Yakima have such cradles.

Malone also has cradles that are not adjustable but are built in such a way to conform to most kayaks. Cradles are very important for expensive kayaks made from Kevlar or fiberglass and for most of these kayaks it's the only way they should be transported. Most fishing kayaks are plastic and while cradles are nice, they are not required.

Besides cradles, there are attachments called 'J racks' that hold the kayak at an angle to the vehicle. They were originally designed for small whitewater yaks but are commonly used for larger kayaks. Another attachment is called a stacker, intended to go on a rack and rise perpendicular to the bars. The kayaks are then put on the side and each kayak is strapped to the stacker and bars. A stacker will allow you to carry the most kayaks. When used with a set of 78-inch bars, I can carry six kayaks on my rack. Make sure your rack can handle the weight. Mine is on a fiberglass shell and I reinforced it by bolting it to a metal strip on the inside of the shell. I've got ¼-inch stainless steel bolts every foot.

That brings up another thing to consider. Besides a higher weight capacity, many aftermarket racks are available in a variety of bar widths, usually 48, 56, 66 and 78 inches or fairly close. Motor vehicle laws allow the width of the bars to be the width of the mirrors or less. If you measure from the outside of one mirror to the other, that's how wide your bars can be. I like to be as wide as I can because it allows me to transport more kayaks. With a set of 66-inch bars I used to carry up to four kayaks on the roof of my Pathfinder. How wide you go will depend on the vehicle. The lower the height the shorter I recommend. That's because you will either walk into or hit your head on them. With taller vehicles this isn't an issue. Also the wider they are the easier it becomes to load.

Both Thule and Yakima have extender options that can go in the bars. Since they extend well beyond the vehicle I've found I can load a much heavier kayak on my vehicle than I would otherwise be able to do. My Hobie Adventure Island's hull weighs over 100 pounds. When I load a kayak on top of my Toyota Tundra, I press it overhead and place it on the bars. I can do this with kayaks as heavy as a Hobie Outfitter, which is about 80 pounds, but the Island is much too heavy for me. With the extender I only have to lift half the kayak. While the one half is resting on the bar I pick up and place the second on the rack. This way I can bring the Island with me on the roof and not have to use a trailer.

There are aftermarket lift assists. Thule has a unit they call the Hullivator and there are others. They all work similarly providing boosted assist. The Hullivator provides 30 pounds of lift so if your kayak weights 65 pounds, once you get it into the Hullivator cradle you're only going to be lifting 35 pounds.

78-inch bars with five kayaks on it. If it wasn't for the sail and rod tube in the center, this rack would accomodate six kayaks.

Trailers

Trailers are the ultimate in luxury when it comes to transporting kayaks. They make loading and unloading even easier than using a pickup truck bed. The only negative is they double the length of the vehicle so parking becomes more difficult. Most places it doesn't matter but it is something to consider.

I originally got a trailer for business. The most kayaks I could put on the roof of my Pathfinder was five with a set of 66-inch bars and that took some

very creative loading. Early in my business I found it necessary to pick up a load of kayaks, so we had to get a trailer. I settled on one that was designed for six while flat. There was an option for wider bars, which I ordered. With the kayaks turned on their sides I could get 14 on the trailer - six across on the first and second levels and two flat on the top. The wider bars allowed me to carry four more kayaks. With four on the roof I could transport 18 kayaks. Most folks don't have a need to transport nearly this many. We used to organize trips at KFS and I'd bring the trailer along. In places like Cape Cod and Block Island there wasn't an issue leaving the kayaks fully set up and strapped to the trailer. This made it easy to fish multiple locales without setting up and breaking down.

Trailers are a great way to transport kayaks. This model from Malone has straight bars that allow attachment of a variety of accessories, and can carry four kayaks.

When KFS moved to its second store we started carrying small, personal trailers. These models are designed to carry one to as many as four kayaks. They are sport-specific, very light, and can be rolled about by one person. I'm not sure how many companies build them. I'm familiar with four - Malone, Magneta, Trailex, and Rack 'n Roll. Malone is the new kid on the block and they've built a solid unit.

The first three are similar in design. They consist of a frame attached to a long center that hooks up to the hitch. There are two crossbars and each one has an upright. Trailex makes a single canoe/kayak trailer, but for a bit more money I'd go up to the next model, as it will carry two flat or four on their sides. Transporting only one kayak is limiting, and you'll eventually wish you had room for another.

There is room on the multi-kayak models to mount an accessory box that you can put a lock on. This way you could store paddles, PFDs, drives, seats and the like in the trailer, which would further add to the convenience. Should you want to add a storage box, go with a higher capacity unit. For instance, Trailex has a 250 and a 350. They look very similar and are, except that the 350 has an extra 100 pounds of capacity. Four kayaks could weigh as much as 280 pounds without the weight of a box or gear. The Malone is already set up to handle plenty of weight as the construction was originally intended for boats.

The Rack 'n Roll is the Rolls Royce of kayak trailers. It has an aluminum frame and uses motorcycle tires, and instead of leaf springs it uses shocks. It's not marketed solely as a kayak/canoe trailer but rather as a multi-sport. That's because it's designed to handle rack cross bars. It will accommodate either rectangular or round bars (the Malone version has rectangular bars). Several companies sell accessories that will attach to these bars. This allows the trailer to transport all sorts of stuff. People were constantly commenting on mine and asking questions. You can carry two kayaks flat standard. It doesn't come with uprights but by adding a set along with rack pads you can transport four kayaks on their sides. Because of the bars you can carry an unbelievable array of stuff, like a couple of bikes along with a couple of kayaks, windsurfers, surfboards, space case, practically anything as long as it doesn't exceed the weight capacity of the trailer.

It's a great trailer but it isn't cheap; it will set you back two grand. The others sell for half that. You won't have all the versatility of the Rack 'n Roll, but

that extra grand buys lots of equipment.

Another great feature of the Rack 'n Roll is that each section is removable, allowing for easy break down and storage. Both wheels and the tongue can be removed, and there is a set of small wheels on it so when the mainframe is upright it can be rolled into a garage or shed. When I headed down to the Everglades I had my travel trailer on the back of my truck but I also wanted my Rack 'n Roll, so I broke it down into pieces and brought it along.

Just before going to press with this book, Malone unveiled a breakdown kit that can be used with any of their trailers. This should proved to be very useful for kayak anglers.

My first trailer was a Magneta and it served me well; but it was steel and it rusted. If you're going to use the trailer for saltwater, then get either galvanized (good) or aluminum (better) construction. If the trailer is steel then hose it down after each saltwater use. Keep the bearings lubed and otherwise they require minimal care. Another great thing about a trailer is it gives you a place to store your kayak.

If you don't want to buy one, or already own a trailer for other uses, it can be adapted. I know a lot of folks who have converted boat or utility trailers for kayak transport. Charles at *Everglades Kayak Fishing* has a fleet of kayaks he uses in his business. He has a few boat trailers he modified for kayaks by adding two racks to them. My buddy Rich added a couple of sets of Malone 'J Racks' to a small boat trailer he had and it works great for transporting his yaks. Another option is to get an inexpensive utility trailer, such as the ones offered by Harbor Freight. They too can be adapted to transport kayaks.

Other than the additional cost, the other negative to kayak trailers is the additional vehicle length. The Rack 'n Roll is 14 feet and the Trailex is between 18 and 20 feet. You've got to be mindful of this while on the road and parking. I've been to places where I couldn't park my rig and I've taken the trailer off the hitch and put it in another parking spot.

As previously mentioned, I've got a Hobie Adventure Island and while I can load it on my roof, I preferred to use a trailer. One day the 'Spermaceti Wolf Pack' (a group of North Jersey kayak fishermen) was getting together to fish Sandy Hook. They are a great group of friends and past customers. On the day of the get together the winds were predicted to be brisk - a perfect day to sail the Island. In addition to its hull, the Island has large outriggers and a sail, and unlike the kayak I regularly used, I didn't keep this all on the roof of my Tundra as standard practice; I kept it on the trailer. That way, all I had to do was hook up the trailer when I wanted to use the kayak.

When I got to the parking lot the wind was blowing even harder than expected. There wasn't anywhere to park the truck and trailer as a unit, so I took the Rack 'n Roll off. Another great feature of trailers is they are very easy to roll, functioning like large carts. The launch we were using is across the street and then it's about 100 feet to the water. Rather than take each part of the Adventure Island to the water in pieces, I decided to roll the trailer to the water, unload the contents, and then park it in an empty spot.

When detaching a trailer it's a good idea to have a hitch lock. This way the trailer can't be hooked up to another vehicle and taken. As an even better precaution I like a Kryptonite cable with a padlock threaded through the wheels. This way the trailer can't be moved by anyone. Since I was going over sand I found it necessary to lower the air pressure in the tires to create more flotation. I always carry an inflation device in the truck. The tires didn't dig in and since it was a slight upgrade back to the road it made a big difference.

Whether or not a trailer makes sense, only you can determine. If you're unsure ask folks who have them. You can do so on the forums. Also consider a used one. While not very common they do come up for sale now and then. Should you have one and decide it isn't a viable item, you can sell if for what you paid and have very little out-of-pocket expense. For me, a trailer isn't an absolute must, but it definitely makes transportation easier, as I have outlined for you in this section. The convenience is my favorite feature. I set up the kayak before hitting the road. Upon arrival I unload, add a few accessories and am ready for a great day of fishing. Also, as I get older, I appreciate not having to put the kayak on the roof all the time. Lastly, I fish saltwater a lot and it's corrosive. By using a trailer I don't have my kayak dripping saltwater onto my vehicle. It's easier to hose off the kayak and trailer than wash my truck.

(above) Two carts most often used by the author. Both connect via the scupper holes of the kayak. The big tires are for sand or where flotation is required. The all-terrain pneumatic tires cover everything else. **(left)** This universal-style cart is also popular, and fits most kayaks.

Carts

Cart is a term we use to describe wheels that are attached to the kayak so it can be rolled. Depending upon where you fish a cart will either serve no purpose or be invaluable. I use carts often and I have several. Many places I fish aren't necessarily right next to where I park. Some of the best spots are far from parking. There are a few ways of getting your kayak to the water - carry it, drag it, or use a cart. You can either make your own or buy one that has been designed for the purpose. There are many very good carts available and unless you enjoy the challenge of building your own, buy one.

If you decide to build your own there are many web sites with plans and discussions on how to accomplish this. Visit the sites that cater to kayaks and kayak fishing. You will also find sources for wheels and the other items you need. On the sites' forums you'll be able to discuss your ideas, post and see pictures, and find out what works and also what hasn't worked. I know most people who have built a PVC cart have learned about how to break a PVC cart. Benefit from others who have already made the mistakes.

The wheels are the most important attribute of the cart and there are several different types, ranging in width from skinny 1-inch plastic to 10-inch wide pneumatics. They come in diameters as small as 6 inches up to bicycle wheels.

The other important variable is how the cart attaches to the kayak and there are a few ways. The most common are those that strap the cart to the kayak. A strap-on cart will fit most kayaks. Sometimes you have to incorporate foam to attain a snug fit. There are carts that enclose the bow of the yak; these are the least common. The last type utilizes the scupper holes of a SOT kayak. The latter is easier to use because all you need to do is slip the posts of the cart into the scupper holes. Strapping a kayak to a cart is more secure and there won't be any movement between the cart and kayak as there will be with the scupper hole method. If all you need to do is move the kayak from the parking lot to a ramp then practically any cart will do. The type of wheels and the means of attachment to the kayak won't matter much. The more complex your needs the more important your cart choice is going to be. Some carts won't function in some situations or do such a poor job as to be next to useless.

The strap type is my choice for more difficult terrain. Wheels vary from very narrow to extremely wide and the type of wheel you're going to need depends upon the terrain over which you're going to transport the kayak. I use two different carts on a regular basis. My primary cart is an all-terrain cart and as its name suggests is good for all terrain. It uses 3- to 4-inch wide pneumatic tires that are 11 inches in diameter. I prefer strap-on designs because they hold the kayak more securely, so if the terrain gets rough the kayak and cart work as a unit. Also they position the wheels farther out, making it more stable. This is especially important when wheeling the kayak down any sort of trail. The rougher the trail gets the more you will appreciate this. Scupper hole carts are very secure but the fit isn't exact, resulting in play. The most fragile part of most SOTs is the scupper hole. If they are going to develop a leak this is where it happens the most because there is a seam inside the hole where the two halves of the kayak are joined during manufacturing. Having the post of a cart banging the seam continuously could weaken it and lead to leaking. For beaches and parking lots I like this style but for trails I use the strap models.

One day Craig and I ventured out to fish a river. Access required we wheel the kayaks a couple of hundred yards on an overgrown road reclaimed by Mother Nature. I had a wide cart while Craig's was narrow. Craig ended up dumping his cart three times while mine didn't come close. The distance between the wheels on the cart I was using was twice that of Craig's. Also the cart I was using positioned the kayak lower than his. This created a much more stable scenario. When taking a kayak down a trail, the more stability the better.

When putting the kayak on the cart you will want to strap it at a point that creates a slight amount of tongue weight. Tongue weight for those unfamiliar with the term is the weight on the end of a trailer. In this case the trailer is the kayak and so it's the amount of downward weight that's felt when you hold the front handle of the kayak. What you want is a little bit of weight pushing down but not so it's heavy. You'll know when it's right and it is far from an exact thing. It'll simply feel comfortable.

This way the kayak will balance and pull easier. The balance point to achieve this will vary depending upon how you have the kayak accessorized and loaded. Generally this point will be somewhere near the seat. If you have a lot of gear in the tank well or bow hatch this will change the ideal positioning. I fish freshwater a lot and I like to explore places off the beaten track. Some lakes and rivers are a significant distance from where I park. This can vary from 100 yards up to a mile. I use an all-terrain cart to reach these more remote waters and wouldn't be able to fish them without the aid of the cart.

The other style of cart I use is a big wheel. I like the Wheeleez™ big wheel the most. It has large pneumatic tires and is unparalleled for traversing sand. When sand gets deep and soft, most wheels lose the ability to float the kayak over the terrain. They dig in and the wheels stop spinning. When this occurs you would be better off dragging the kayak without the cart, as the smooth bottom of the kayak drags easier than a kayak with a cart attached.

The first time I fished Cape Cod this point was brought home to me and since then I've always had a Wheeleez cart. Four of us were on the trip - myself, Joey, Doug and Jim. A sand dune stood between our parking spot and the water. The all-terrain cart couldn't handle the deep sand and it took two of us to get each kayak to the launch site. Doug and Jim each had carts they had made using the Wheeleez wheels and the difference was amazing. They easily rolled to the water. Nothing I've used works better than the Wheeleez, but they are expensive. I consider them well worth it but some people don't want to spend the money. I've seen some innovative stuff used to get sufficient flotation. Some use an all-terrain tire and put buckets over them to increase the surface area. It does the job, but if you're going to be doing a lot of sand launches I highly recommend biting the bullet and buying a big wheel cart.

Another feature that can be important in a cart is the ability to break down easily. This will allow you to take the cart with you. Why would you want to do this? Imagine you're going to take off from a beach and its 100 yards from your parking spot. You wheel your kayak to the water, leave it there, take the cart back to your vehicle, and then walk back to the water. That's a lot of walking, especially if you have waders on. If the cart breaks down for storage you can put it in a hatch and forget it until you return.

This way you save a lot of walking but it could come in handy too. You may for whatever reason land somewhere else and if you don't have the cart you're stuck. Besides halving the amount of walking you'll do, there may be places where you don't want to leave your kayak and gear sitting on a beach unattended. Unfortunately we live in a world where one's personal property isn't always respected and gear may disappear while you're hiking to or from your vehicle. Some carts also function as a loading aide. The cart can be strapped in place upside down and used to roll a kayak onto the roof of the vehicle. Here a narrower cart is going to work best.

Carts are great and will expand your fishing opportunities, allowing you to transport your kayak to areas not easily or feasibly accessible without one. I think you'll agree once you add a cart to your essential kayak gear, it will open up more fishing terrain and increase the overall satisfaction level of your kayak fishing experience.

Proper planning is an essential element in many kayak fishing excursions. Here, a ferry service is used to transport kayaks to a remote destination.

Chapter 8
Let's Go Fishing!

I've devoted lots of space in this book to the more technical aspects of kayak fishing, and for good reason. But, if you're reading this your ultimate goal is to catch more fish, and to do it from a kayak. So let's get to the heart of the matter - catching fish! We'll first discuss trip planning, which is a very important aspect of kayak fishing. We'll then talk about fighting, landing and handling fish from a kayak, as well as fishing with children, kayak fishing etiquette and avoiding hazards.

Trip Planning

If you're heading down to a local pond, there isn't much thought or planning needed to have a fun day on the water. Get your gear together, determine what to wear, what tackle to bring, etc. However, the more diverse the excursion the more forethought is required to have a successful outing.

I am adventurous by nature and love exploring. When I lived in Reno, Nevada I would wander all over the western states, camping and fishing with my float tube. Most of the time I did so alone (still do as a kayak fisherman), as most folks didn't have the kind of time to roam around that I did. Adventuring into unknown habitats varies tremendously and proper planning could mean the difference between a great time and something much less so. Along the way I've made my share of mistakes and have learned from them.

Whether you're going fishing for a day or longer, trip planning is important for any kayak fishing excursion. If you're going fishing with others there is a good chance one or more of the group is familiar with where you're heading. That's the easy way. Just pick their brains. If you're alone, then it's up to you. Gather as much information as you can. The Internet has a lot available; use search engines to find articles and books. Regional forums are a tremendous resource. Don't restrict your search to kayak fishing, either. Check general fishing forums and depending on the trip, there's other information you'll need. Use whatever aids you can. Charts, maps, satellite images and mapping programs all have a place.

If the trip is going to be more than one day you've got to stay somewhere. Are you going to camp or stay in lodging? Are you flying to your destination? If you're flying then you're going to need to arrange for kayaks and the like. The longer and more intricate the trip the more things you need to do in advance.

For some years I've wanted to take an extended trip to Baja and another to Alaska. During my time in Baja in the mid 1980s as a tail gunner for a fishing caravan, it was my job to help the rigs safely reach our remote beach camps. I gained lots of invaluable experience, as I saw a lifetime worth of screw-ups in my three years. I've only been back once since then, in 2004, on a trip with Jim Sammons and *La Jolla Kayak Fishing*. Other than coordinating my flight, choosing and packing tackle, there was very little required of me. Unfortunately Baja has become less desirable from a safety perspective and I'm going to have to alter the way I travel there, which will necessitate traveling with others rather than going alone. It's not that I'm a loner; its just most people don't have the time freedom I enjoy. I would prefer to go to Baja for a couple of months and possibly much longer, but due to the limitations of having to hook up with others I recognize this would be very challenging.

For example, if I were to plan an extended, more primitive trip to Baja, a great deal of planning would be required. For starters I'd get a bunch of satellite shots of the roads into the area I'd like to travel. I

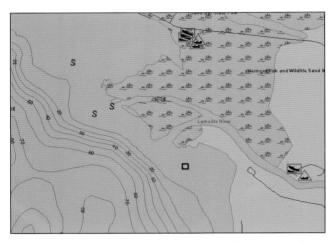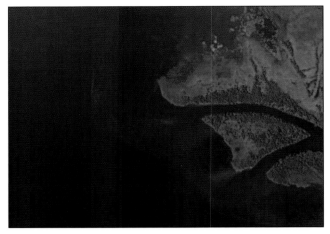

(left) Chart of a river inlet on Lake Champlain. (right) Satellite view of the same area.

already have a topo map book of the entire peninsula, which I'd bring. For when I'd be on the water I'd get the Navionics chip for Baja for my GPS. In addition, I'd have to carry a lot of supplies as well as coordinate the trip with my travel partners. Regarding Alaska, I joined several friends on a two-week trip to the 'Great Land' in July of 2008 (more on this later). I'd like to go there for an extended trip, possibly for an entire summer, but due to time and distance it will have to be properly planned.

On a trip to Vermont in July of 2007 to visit family, I took a couple of days to fish Lake Champlain. I planned on targeting smallies. On the Internet I located an excellent and extensive six-part article by Dale Brown on fishing the lake. Even better, I found his book, *Bass Fishing 101 - Lake Champlain* which I hadn't known existed, in a general store where I stopped to get a sandwich. The author goes into a lot of detail and covered every bass-producing spot he knew. It's a good aid, as Champlain's a big, 110-mile long lake bordering Vermont and New York. Dale suggested breaking Champlain down into a series of smaller lakes and fishing those areas as such. It's still a really big chunk of territory when broken down.

Another great tool I have is 'Fugawi Fishing Lakes USA' DVD, loaded into my laptop. It has in-depth charts and information covering the most popular lakes in the country. There is a wealth of information about the lakes, topography, angling, and species, including prey.

When I was up at Lake Champlain, the weather was really hot so I knew the smallies would be deep. One of the negatives of kayak fishing is that you don't have a motor and the ability to roam all over.

This necessitates good planning, as it can make the difference between a good fishing trip or just exercise. My strategy was to look for offshore humps and shoals and try both the shallow and adjacent deep water. I tried an extensive shoal system adjacent to deep water out in the middle of one of the northern sections of the lake. I managed some small fish but not what I wanted. I went back to camp, did more research and came up with a plan.

My next foray was only minutes from camp. It was a large bay where one of the major rivers, the Lamoille, entered the lake. There were depths to 70 feet, flats with weeds and reeds, and the river delta - a lot of diversity. My plan was to get on the water in the late afternoon and look for the smallies deep. If that didn't pan out I could head shallow as the light got lower and target largemouths.

When I launched, tons of gulls were working offshore a little over a mile away. With the high surface temps, I knew it could only be smallies. I wanted to investigate but I knew by the time I got there the action would be over. Sure enough, the action died when I was less than a third of a mile away. I checked it out anyway, and nothing was happening. I then headed to a sharp spot on the chart where the weedy flat transitioned to deep water. I worked the area and still found nothing, so I headed up the south branch of the river and came out the north entrance. I caught a bunch of panfish.

Before heading back in I hit the weeds and reeds. There were lily pads, too, and I chucked a Slug-Go into the first group of pads and immediately there was a big whoosh and a 3-pound, very fat largemouth. I got a few more as light was fading and the

The author with what turned out to be a typical Lake Champlain largemouth. Planning is a key element in any successful expedition into new territory.

mosquitoes got thick. I don't like fishing weeds in unfamiliar territory at night so I called it quits and planned to return at first light. The next morning I landed about 10 bass, all in the 3- to 4-pound class. I was chucking a weedless Slug-Go into the pads and twitching it on the top. It was a blast. I was landing about one out of every four hits. By 7:30 a.m. the action was over so I went back to camp and took a nap.

The next foray was to the extreme northern part of the Vermont side of the lake where, according to Dale, the lake is loaded with northern pike. It's the northern-most river delta where the Missiquoi River enters. Besides the book and my maps I enlisted another one of my favorite planning tools - satellite maps. I wanted to see the lay of the land on the end of the peninsula to see if I could save a couple of miles of pedaling (I was in my Hobie). It looked promising so I headed up and found an RV park where I was able to launch for $3. Pike aren't a hot weather fish but I did hook a few and brought an 8 pounder to the yak. It was mostly an exploratory trip to gather intel for a future late September visit when the fishing is supposed to be on fire. I drove around the area getting a feel for the layout and noted other launch sites. As usually happens when I explore, I found a couple that weren't listed on any maps. One was very close to a point that Dale says is the best in the lake come fall. I don't know if many of you know this, but Lake Champlain was voted the top bass lake in the country by both the Bassmasters and the FLW tour pros. That's high praise. I look forward to fishing it when the smallies are easier to locate.

The next morning was going to be my last, as afternoon thunderstorms were being forecasted. Being on a large open lake in boomers isn't a good way to go yak fishing. Besides, it was Friday and the section of the lake I was fishing becomes a zoo over the weekend. I launched at 5:30 a.m. and got a few small fish in the more open, outside pads. Then I put a cast into the pads by the really thick reeds and hooked an immediate 3 pounder. The next cast pulled another fish and the third was a bruiser I lost in the weeds. I'll never know how big some of these fish were but next time I fish there I'll have heavier tackle. I'd also like to try it with a heavy fly rod. It would be awesome. The deeper I got into this jungle the better the fishing. I lost count of how many fish I hooked - I landed about a dozen.

I also landed a pickerel and a couple of bowfins. The bows were a lot of fun, as they're very aggressive and fight well. They have a mouth like catfish and teeth a lot like bluefish - nasty critters with a round, prehistoric looking tail. Unlike bass, which have huge mouths and can easily inhale a 6-inch Slug-Go, it took several tries for the bows to get the Slug-Go into their mouths and for me to get a hook-up. They were persistent, though. The two I landed took at least six casts. The first was about 3 pounds and the second was more than twice that size. I love catching new species and the bows were a complete surprise. I realized that several of the fish that missed my Slug-Go were bows. Next time I'm up there I'll target the bows with 4-inch Slug-Gos.

As I pointed out earlier, how you plan an excursion depends upon the destination and duration. You need to determine what fishing and kayaking gear you're going to need. Your expected quarry will determine the fishing tackle, but sometimes your target species may not cooperate. They are fish and don't always want your offerings. If, like me, you'd like to catch something, rather than nothing, it's a good idea to bring appropriate gear for other indigenous and usually reliable species. It could make the difference between having fun catching fish and getting skunked.

For example, when I hit the fresh in New Jersey and my quarry are bass, if I bring smaller stuff along I can connect with panfish as well. When I go pike fishing it's often hit or miss. If I scale things down I'll have lots of action and the pike will hit the same lures.

When I fish the salt in New Jersey, I have to travel about an hour each way. I also have rush hour traffic to contend with so I need to plan around it. This usually means I've got to avoid it in one direction. This creates a time commitment of several hours. I want to be prepared because whatever I find is what I'll have to contend with. There are several species - striped bass, bluefish, weakfish, fluke and false albacore. If I'm chasing striped bass I may encounter bluefish instead. If the blues dominate the action I'm going to want to use a wire leader, otherwise I'll be donating a bunch of lures. False albacore can show up and they are line-shy, necessitating the use of long fluorocarbon leaders and smaller lures. If I happen upon a school of large menhaden I'm going to need a snagging treble and gear appropriate for fishing a 2-pound live bait. Sometimes chunking menhaden is better than using it whole. I'm going to need a knife, and a small cutting board makes the task much easier.

You want to have appropriate clothing for the weather conditions. Again the more commitment involved the better prepared you need to be. If I'm going to be out all day things can, and often do, change. Most kayaks have a lot of internal space and it doesn't hurt to have a dry bag with additional garments.

I fished the Jersey shore one day in mid-October. Usually by mid- to late September we switch over to our dry wear, either waders and dry tops or a dry suit. However, it was an unusually warm fall and the water was still in the upper 60's with air temps in the upper 70's. Too warm for dry wear but shorts and a t-shirt were only appropriate during the middle of the day.

I started off with wetsuit shorts with flats pants over them for sun protection and a short-sleeved Mysterioso top. After a couple of hours on the water, nature was calling and I wanted a break. Whenever possible I try to get out of the kayak at least one or more times. I headed in to shore and landed on the beach.

There was an abrupt edge causing a splash and I got wet. The Mysterioso acts like a thin wetsuit and will insulate when wet, but I prefer being dry. The wind had picked up and I was getting a bit chilled. By the time I pedaled back to where I had launched it would be near sunset, so things were going to cool off. I had packed a dry bag with both a long sleeve and long john's Mysterioso, and a semi-dry shell. I took the wet flat pants off and put the dry Mysterioso top and johns on. It was just the ticket for the remainder of my excursion.

Research

If you're going to fish somewhere you've never been before it's a good idea to do some research. If there are maps or charts available I recommend using them. A waterproof version is best so you can take it along without it getting ruined. Every time I left the marina in Chokoloskee, Florida, I had a waterproof chart with me. Just across the bay from me were the 10,000 Islands. I didn't count them all but that's a lot of terrain. Even though I have a very good sense of direction, it wouldn't be very hard to get lost.

Another tool I use regularly is satellite maps, which are fantastic and free. I like flashearth.com the most. There are several to choose from there. Once

you select a format, zero in on the area you wish to see. I use the print screen function on my computer and then I utilize Microsoft Paint in the Windows accessories. After I print them they're carried with me in a zip lock bag. I can't tell you how many hours I've spent exploring places this way.

Several years back I sold four kayaks to Andrew who had a house in the Turks and Caicos Islands, an island chain just east of the Bahamas. I didn't even know where they were when Andrew contacted me. Long story short, we ended up using his rental property, which I have briefly mentioned throughout the book. Someone had to unwrap and set up the kayaks. It was a tough job but Joey, Scott, Terry and I were up to the challenge.

Before leaving on the trip I familiarized myself with the island. One area in particular stood out and as our plane landed we drooled over the terrain. It took a bit of exploring to find our way there but I had recalled a dirt road to the area. We found the road and were rewarded with the best fishing of our trip. If it weren't for the satellite view I don't know if we would have ever found it.

A GPS is invaluable, especially if it has mapping. The better units accept pre-programmed charts. However, like anything electronic you shouldn't solely rely upon it. There are enough ways that it might not function. Even when it's functioning properly there will be circumstances that prevent you from knowing where you are. In the Everglades many of the rivers and creeks that connect the lakes and ponds of the backcountry have canopies that completely cover the water. They are natural tunnels. I affectionately call them 'Dark Territory' because often you can't get a GPS signal. When you leave a tunnel and come into open territory you end up with a straight line from the last point the unit got a signal. You can't rely upon that GPS track. Having a chart for back up and knowing the topography from a satellite is going to aid in navigating.

In January 2008 I took a trip into the Everglades backcountry. I started on Highway 41 and entered a canal that led to Halfway Creek. I wanted to explore the backcountry between it and the upper Barron River. I had heard rumors of a crossover. Shortly into the trip my GPS decided to stop recognizing my chart chip. I ended up with a blank screen with a GPS track on it. I had an excellent chart of the area so I used it in combination with the track. I was fairly certain of where I was but not positive until I hit an area that left a track resembling a double omega. I now knew exactly where I was as it was such a distinctive feature. I accomplished my goal of connecting the two watersheds. Since I was closer to Everglades City than my commencement, I continued on in the Everglades. I went to Chuck's house and caught a ride back to my truck.

The more isolated the trip the better you need to prepare. When I go off alone in the Everglades back-country I might not see another human being for days. I'm on my own and civilization and help aren't something I can depend on. I find it's better to be prepared and not need something than want it and not have it along. Ever since my experience at Cedar Key (see clothing section of book) I carry a set of Mysterioso and a breathable, waterproof top and pants. I keep them in a dry bag along with a space blanket. I've mentioned many of these points in other areas of the book, which illustrates their importance.

Next on my list are food and water. Always bring water along unless you're fishing the fresh. Then you can bring a filter and procure what you need. Otherwise bring an appropriate amount of water for the excursion. Again the more remote and isolated the trip the more you should carry. Once in the kayak even a gallon of water doesn't affect its performance and there is usually plenty of extra space inside. Besides water I like to bring food along. I do so in two forms. Food I plan on eating and food for "just in case". When I go out for a day of fishing I take a small soft cooler along. In my dry bag I like to bring some type of powdered shake I can mix with water to make a meal replacement drink. I'll also include some nutrition bars.

When heading out for a kayak fishing excursion, whether a day or an extended trip, it pays to plan. Recognize the limitations of range and plan accordingly to maximize your chances to get into fish. Depending upon the excursion it can make the difference between catching and not. Man is rarely going to win the battle with nature. With planning you have a much greater chance to have a safe, enjoyable time on the water.

Fighting, Landing and Handling Fish

The second most asked question by prospective fishermen looking at entering the sport (stability is the first) is how do you handle large fish from a kayak. In the Northeast I was usually asked what I do when I hook a large striped bass. I'd laugh, as a striper is a fairly benign critter from a kayak. They don't present any real problems. Sure, a large striper might drag you somewhere you'd rather not go, like a rip, but otherwise the fish doesn't possess any weapons or antics that cause concern. In the Northeast large bluefish are a much more difficult adversary. They have teeth that can easily injure and remove fingers if handled improperly. Also they jump, often right by the kayak and can land either in it with you or on you.

As an angler you should have an understanding of the species you're pursuing and it's a good idea to become familiar with whatever else is available. If you're pursuing fish in your local waters you're already familiar with them so you know what to expect. If you're going to be fishing for new species then do some research first.

Most species don't present any issues, but some do and you can get injured. The most commonly caught sport species in the world are the freshwater basses. They have a great landing handle, their mouths. Just grab the lower lip and it immobilizes them. The striper also being a bass can be handled the same way. However, there are very few species where this is the case.

In the Everglades the only species I catch that I can lip is the snook. It's the only species that doesn't have teeth but unlike the basses snook don't calm down when lipped. Also, holding a snook by its lip and having its weight pull down on it can seriously injure the fish. So unless you're keeping them please don't do this.

All the other species in the Everglades require different handling. Some you can grab behind the head, which I don't recommend for fish you wish to release, as you can damage the gills. Getting back to snook, they have a set of gill plates that are like razors, and can easily slice you to the bone. So, grabbing commonly caught species with teeth like ladyfish, jacks, trout, and grouper needs to be done with care.

There is a species of catfish that is quite common. It has long fins and is called a sail cat because they look like sails. The fins have poison in them and should you get stuck you're in for a lot of pain and possible infection. There is also another catfish called the hardhead and it too has poison in the fins. I once got nicked by one and my finger swelled up

(Clockwise, from top left) **#1**. The author fighting a striper in J-Bay. **#2**. Getting the lip gripper ready. **#3**. Handling the fish on the gripper. **#4**. The fish ready for release!

and hurt for a couple of hours despite the fact that it barely got me. I've heard fishermen have had to go to the hospital when they've been stabbed. This is important information to be aware of before handling these fish. If you fish with bait, *Gulp!*, or even on the bottom with lures, you're going to catch them.

I grew up catching freshwater basses, panfish, trout and pickerel. Pickerel were the only species that presented any problems at all. They had sharp teeth that I needed to avoid. The others were easy to handle, especially the basses. The first saltwater species I pursued were bluefish and the opposite was true. Small ones could draw blood if given the chance and medium to large ones were capable of altering my anatomy. So understanding how to handle your quarry is a good idea. When in doubt use a lip gripper or some other device. That way you don't have to touch the fish.

Before you land a fish, however, you need to fight it. Generally, the larger the fish the greater the potential for unforeseen consequences. Again, each species is different, and even within a species the size of the fish, your tackle selection, and the existing conditions makes a big difference.

Fighting a fish in open water without any obstacles around is much easier than dealing with the same species in tight quarters. Some fish run for open water even when hooked near obstructions, while others head straight for the toughest cover they can find.

Snook in the open, while a great fight, only present the problem of slicing your leader with their gills. When hooked near structure, especially mangroves, they present quite a challenge, as they will run straight for them. Once in the jungle they are tough to get out and will either tangle your line and get off or break it. I've hooked a bunch of large snook in the backcountry but haven't landed any of them because of this. The largest I've managed to land in the backcountry thus far is only 27 inches, while I've hooked fish approaching 40 inches.

The first thing you're going to notice that's different about fighting a fish from a kayak is how easily they move the kayak. Even a 2-pound bass can drag you. Larger fish can sometimes pull you quickly in direct proportion to their size. I use the word sometimes because some fish race off and burn line while others are all power. I remember hooking a 20-pound striper in Long Island Sound one day and before I knew it I was several dozen yards from where we started. The kayak flew for that short initial burst. As the bass pulled me out into the open sound, Scott was in my way; luckily our lines didn't tangle as my kayak collided with his.

Even a small fish will tow the kayak and the largest fish will actually pull you at speeds faster than you can paddle. Jim Sammons is the first person I know to have hooked a marlin from a kayak, and reports are his buddies had trouble keeping up with him! Species like billfish, tarpon, large jacks, tuna and sharks are going to take you for quite a ride. That's one of the things making kayak fishing so exciting, as there is nothing else in fishing that is comparable. The sensation of going on a ride with a fish on the end of your line is unique and separates kayak fishing from other forms of angling. If you've ever read Hemmingway's "Old Man and the Sea" or seen the screen version, that's what it can be like.

When larger fish are hooked they often take you for what we call a sleigh ride. The fastest I've been towed has been by large tarpon. While on a trip to the Dry Tortugas I live-lined a porgy and as soon as I dropped it in the line started flying off the reel. I closed the bail and next thing I knew the drag was screaming and I was flying up the harbor. The next day I ran into the owner of a sailboat and he asked if I was the guy getting towed out the harbor the previous evening. He was coming in and saw me ripping across the water.

The power of a large fish is amazing. My first kayak trip to Baja was with Jim Sammons on a mother-ship trip. On our first day we were catching some skipjack tuna and our captain, Alonzo, wanted to see if he could raise some dorado or tuna so he started chumming with live sardinas. Bill and Terry were also on the trip and they were away from the boat chasing breaking fish. I parked my kayak within 15 feet of the port stern of the boat. I knew if any fish were going to come for the chum, it was going to be very close to the boat.

The low angle of view from a kayak doesn't give you a good view into the water but I saw a large shape in the slick. I thought it was a large dorado, but really couldn't tell and I yelled to the guys about my sighting. I hadn't completed the sentence when the clicker on my reel went off. I was using a medium/heavy 7-foot two-piece Tsunami standup rod. On it I had an Avet SX lever drag spooled with 65-pound braid. Thirty feet of 30-pound fluorocarbon leader were direct tied to the braid. I reached behind me and moved the lever on the drag to set the hook. Immediately my kayak spun around and I was racing

off faster than I could paddle. It was wild as I was flying across the water.

Turns out at the hook set the sailfish went nuts greyhounding and leaping but I didn't see it as this occurred behind me. I did see the next foray, though, and it was incredible. Only problem was it was much too close to the kayak for comfort. I didn't need a sailfish with a sharp pointy weapon jamming me. Large marlins have been known to ram boats. People have been speared. A couple of times I let off on the drag, as I felt the fish and I were too close and it was still too green and dangerous to have so near the kayak.

Although you're going to be seated in the kayak facing forward (unless fishing side saddle with your feet overboard) the fish isn't necessarily going to run in the direction you're facing. It can run behind you and can zig and zag. When a fish pulls the kayak the normal situation is the kayak will follow the fish. The fish runs east and the kayak gets pulled east. However this isn't always going to happen. That's because there are a variety of circumstances like the wind and current, the hull design, and whether or not you have a rudder.

A popular and effective technique from the kayak is trolling. When you hook a fish on the troll it's going to be behind you. The fish runs and will pull the kayak around. If I have a rudder I turn to the side of the hit and I end up facing the fish. The drag created by the kayak as the fish pulls it through the water becomes part of your fighting tackle. The kayak acts as an additional drag mechanism especially if the kayak is sideways to the fish. In open water this is a great technique.

There are times when you need to follow the fish. It depends and I can't really explain it to you. You'll know when you're there. As I mentioned earlier some fish will head for structure and I've found when some species are forced to drag the kayak sideways they will swim away from the resistance. You can add resistance for the entire fight either through positioning or by using a drift sock. The sock will add a lot of drag and is a great idea for large fish like tarpon and billfish. My favorite way to employ a sock is to have it attached to my anchor trolley. When I'm angling for large fish I'll keep a sock connected so it can be easily deployed. When a substantial fish is hooked I'll toss it in the water and toggle it to the stern while the fish makes its initial run.

Attributes of how your kayak is set up and items

you brought along can affect the fight. Many anglers, myselft included, bring more than one rod so you may have additional rods to deal with. I usually recommend those new to the sport only take one, so there is less to contend with. When you have additional tackle sticking up in a holder while fighting a fish, raise the rod high enough so the line will clear the rods.

Some species of fish are going to drag you into the brush. Those additional rods can easily tangle and I've broken a couple, too. In these situations it is best to keep the extra rods lying flat. Both rudder and pedal-operated kayaks have objects that protrude below the surface. Fish can tangle your line in them and get off. I have lost a few fish when the line got wrapped around one or the other, however I like fighting fish using both and there have been situations when I was able to use them to maneuver and this resulted in a landed fish. It's great to be able to move the kayak while fighting fish, especially as they charge into obstacles where you don't want to be like mangroves, boat moorings, docks and the like. When fighting fish from my Hobie in shallow water, the fish can get the line caught in the drive mechanism. To avoid this I quickly pull the drive to give the line free movement.

A kayak that isn't equipped with a maneuvering device is often at the mercy of a fish as it runs to cover in tight quarters. It's very exciting fishing but you're going to lose a bunch of them. Snook are notorious for running into the mangroves. Trying to maneuver the kayak with one hand on the paddle while fighting a feisty Snook and keeping it out of the hazards is quite challenging, especially when there is also a current to contend with. On a mother-ship trip to Wizard Creek in the Everglades I hooked a 26-inch Snook while fishing from a drifting 12-foot redfish without a rudder. I had my hands full and it was quite a fight and effort to keep it out of the mangroves and land it. My largest Snook, a 36-inch fish was much easier to land as I fought the fish in Rabbit Key Pass, which is very open.

When large fish aren't shallow or decide to go deep, the power can be incredible. It's one thing when fishing from a boat and a fish surges. It's quite another while in a kayak. When a large fish surges it can pull a kayak right over if not compensated for. When I use spin gear I like to have the drag tight enough to get a good hook set, but I'll sometimes loosen the drag a bit when in a situation where there aren't obsta-

The author had his hands full with this 26-inch snook in the mangroves and current in Wizard Creek, Everglades.

cles, just to handle the surges. If it's a spin reel I cup the spool with my hand to provide additional drag when needed. On conventional reels I can also apply pressure on the spool and for large fish I prefer a lever drag. The lever makes it easy to quickly change the drag setting. When Allen ('Polepole' on the Northwest forums) and friends fought huge salmon sharks in Alaska they said you had to be ready to reduce the drag quickly on the fish. They were using lever drag reels that allowed for immediate adjustment, without which they felt the powerful surges from the fish would have pulled them over. Any large, powerful fish has this potential.

As with all fishing the fight is going to depend upon the size of the fish in direct relation to the tackle. Practically any fish can peel drag off a reel during the fight if the gear is light enough. I'm not a fan of going super light because I release most of the fish I catch and I don't want to wear them out to the point where recovery is difficult. Generally I'll use moderate tackle for the situation. Besides not exhausting the fish I've learned to expect the unexpected. You just never know what's going to happen. A fish substantially larger than you're anticipating can take your offering.

In freshwater I've hooked and lost some big fish I couldn't keep out of the weeds. Everyone has heard stories of an angler fishing for bass or trout and a 4-foot musky hits the lure. I don't want to have a rod that makes 15-inch trout or snook sporting, because I'll have practically no chance should a real trophy

The author being towed by an estimated 150-200 pound bull shark near Chokoloskee Pass in Florida.

hit. You can be fishing for snook, and while a 3-foot snook is quite a fight, a 100-plus-pound tarpon, shark, jewfish or big jack could take your offering.

One day my buddy, Bob, and I arranged to try for some tarpon in the Gulf out at the convergence of Chokoloskee and Sandfly Passes in Florida. Bait is important for reliable hook-ups so we were fishing Sabiki rigs. Rather than put a weight on the bottom I used a three-inch Tsunami Swim Shad. That way I could cover my bases and maybe get a ladyfish or small jack to use as bait.

I got a 5-inch Atlantic Bumper and put it on my heavy conventional setup to live-line. I figured I'd make some more casts for bait and see if I could fill up the bait tank system I had brought along. On the next cast I had a hook-up but it wasn't any baitfish. The fish went on a run and took 75 yards of line immediately, towing me to deeper water. Initially I thought it was a redfish but after 15 minutes I ruled it out. Perhaps it was a cobia, and the longer the fight went on the narrower the choices became. Whatever it was, I could tell it was large.

The headshakes were big. It had to be a tarpon, goliath grouper, shark or ray. While the outfit wasn't the set-up I'd prefer to be fighting a fish like this, it wasn't a joke either. I was using the heaviest TFO 7-foot, 6-inch spinning rod. This rod had landed marlin in the 150-pound class. The reel was a quality spinner loaded with 20-pound braid. Luckily the Sabiki was tied with much heavier line than usual. Also it didn't have the customary anemic clips on each end. Instead it had loops. On the end of my braid I also had a loop onto which I had attached a breakaway clip. I even put the swim shad on using a loop, which I threaded over the body so there weren't any knots that could pull. Still, the Sabiki's line had to be the weak link but it allowed me to put as much pressure as I could on the fish.

Lifting the fish took a ton of effort. I was probably towed about 2 miles but luckily the initial ¾ mile was heading in the direction I wanted to go. Then we zigzagged the area. I would gain line and the fish would end up under the kayak. The water was murky and I could only see down a couple of feet. Each time I got the fish near the kayak and started to lift it, it would make another run, hugging the bottom. They weren't fast runs but more like a tractor pulling line reluctantly off the reel.

I cupped the reel and applied as much pressure as I could. Bob at times had trouble keeping up with me and neither of us could believe the fish wasn't tiring. About an hour into the fight my right arm was killing me. I would use my left to lift to spell it. The only other fight I'd ever had like this was when I fought an approximately 1100-pound blue marlin in Baja. That hurt more because it affected my entire body (I was on a boat and in a fighting chair). This fight was wearing out my arms.

At one and a half hours and after the fourteenth run I finally got a look at the fish. Unfortunately it wasn't the huge tarpon I was hoping for. It was an even bigger shark, the very dangerous bull shark. The fish was conservatively 8 feet and maybe 10. Not the type of fish I like encountering from a kayak. At 8 feet in length, it would be well over 200 pounds, and at 10 feet would exceed 400 pounds! It's a fish I'd rather watch on *Mad Fin* than on the end of my line.

I had a lot of energy invested in this fight and I wanted to get it up to the surface again so Bob could take a picture. I got a good look and then it ran again. Twenty minutes later and after its sixteenth run I got another look and then it ran again. The line broke at the end of the Sabiki on run number seventeen. I wanted that picture but part of me was relieved that it was over and I was fine. That was a very large and dangerous animal to deal with in a kayak. Bob and I were amazed that I had hooked it on a swim shad and it stayed hooked for 2 hours. It was definitely the longest fight I'd ever had from a kayak.

It was a great experience fighting that fish. If I had been using the same gear I used for the sailfish the fight would have been considerably shorter. A shorter rod with the same flex and I would have been in trouble. The 7 1/2-foot rod could just barely clear

the bow bent the way it was. Many times when I had the fish close it would change direction. Maybe it could see the kayak or sense it overhead, or it didn't like my trying to lift it. Whatever the reason it would surge at these times and I'd have to clear the bow quickly because if the rod hit the kayak it would likely have broken. When the fish headed in a direction I didn't approve of I'd use the rudder to turn the kayak and apply side pressure. It didn't like towing the yak sideways and would change direction.

Each species has its distinct way of fighting. Often you can tell from the fight what it is. Some fish jump while others don't. Some run for obstacles while others run for open water. Some have mouths that are like concrete while others have soft mouths and require delicate handling. The same advice for fishing from a boat usually applies from the kayak. I don't like to have large fish that jump too close to the kayak. I don't need them in the cockpit with me and this is a real possibility. Bluefish are notorious for not fighting a lot until near the kayak, and then they go nuts. They jump a lot but luckily they tend to telegraph their leaps and you can either avert them or prepare. Species like big dorado, billfish and tarpon are so fast and

This 6-foot bull shark was beaten in less than 30 minutes on medium/heavy conventional gear.

powerful that there is little you can do should they jump and you're in the way. Anglers have been seriously injured and killed by large tarpon in boats. I know many kayak anglers won't fish for them because they're so dangerous, but anglers do catch them from the kayak and do so safely. They recognize the risk and reduce it as much as they can.

While on the subject of jumping, one of the most acrobatic fish is the tarpon. They're known for their leaping and it's why they are hard to keep hooked. There is a common saying in tarpon fishing 'bow to the king'. It means when a tarpon leaps you drop your rod tip so the hook doesn't pull out. I've found due to their power and how easily a kayak moves that this is unnecessary. I just keep constant pressure on them.

After the experience with the bull shark I started targeting them, as they're very common in the 10,000 Islands area from May to December. I spent several days fishing for them and they averaged 6 feet and 150 pounds. They all fought the same; powerful runs that produced great sleigh rides. The water where I was catching them is quite shallow. When I hooked them in Chokoloskee Bay it rarely exceeded 5 feet, so the fish couldn't sound. Still they got as low in the water column as they could and hugged the bottom. Lifting them was hard. Targeting them with heavier gear still produced half-hour fights for a 6-foot fish. It was a lot of fun and I could catch several in a day.

The larger and more powerful the fish the more important it becomes to wear it out before bringing it to the kayak. Some species I don't want to land. When I'm fishing for blues I like when they get off at the latter stages of the fight. I'm thrilled when ladyfish get off, as they're very slimy, have teeth and are difficult to get on a lip gripper as they writhe about. Unless I'm taking the fish home to eat or I want a picture I prefer they get off. That's why I use barbless hooks a lot. Sharks are a blast to fight but I don't really want to handle them at the kayak. My unwillingness to do so is in direct relation to their size.

Once the fight is over and it's time to land the fish you've got several options. I like to set up my kayaks a certain way and land the fish on a particular side. I'm right-handed and am therefore more dexterous with my right hand. I usually use a lip gripper. Working a lip gripper or net is much easier for me with my dominant hand while on this side of the kayak - same with using pliers. I like to reach out rather than

across my body and kayak, so my kayak is set up for landing fish on the starboard side. I keep my paddle and electronics on the port. How I land the fish depends upon the species. If it's a species I can lip (basses or snook) I'll generally do so. Sometimes I'll grab the fish (like sea trout) but I wet my hand before doing it so I don't remove its protective slime. My favorite tool is the lip gripper. I always have one with me in the kayak. It's usually in the starboard rear flush rod holder. I rarely carry a net but when I am fishing for summer flounder (fluke) or sea trout and keeping them I'll land many more with the aid of a net. A net is a great tool when fishing a tournament, as a lost fish at the kayak could be crucial. For larger fish that I plan to keep, a small hand gaff can be invaluable.

If you're inviting some fish home for dinner it's a good idea to prepare beforehand. In freshwater the fish are generally smaller and one can even use a stringer, though in some waters you might attract predators. I've had snapping turtles try to take fish from my stringer. It wasn't a big issue. If you're fishing an environment where alligators are present you could be asking for trouble. I would keep the fish onboard the kayak.

A lot depends on the layout of the yak you're using as to how to store fish. There is a remote possibility the kayak has a built-in fish hold. Over time we're going to see more options in kayaks and fish holds are a feature that will be incorporated into some yaks. A small soft or hard cooler can be taken along. In the Everglades I often brought a soft cooler and kept it in the front hatch of my kayak. It was large enough to handle a keeper red or Snook, or several trout and mangrove snappers. There are also kayak fish bag coolers that are designed to go on the front of the kayak. If the climate is cool you could throw them in the tank well with a wet burlap sack over them. The evaporation provides cooling.

Often immediate bleeding of a fish will improve its gastronome on the table. With some species it makes a big difference. If you're going to bleed fish in many environments you have to be especially careful, as we all know how well sharks can zero in on small amounts of blood in the water. Whenever you're dealing with fish near the kayak, reviving, bleeding or releasing should be done with caution.

A hooked fish sends out signals while struggling, which is akin to ringing the dinner bell for predators. Predators are always looking for an easy meal and

they interpret these signals as such. In freshwater your biggest threat is going to be from alligators, but if it's near salt access then there's the possibility of a shark. That's right, sharks in freshwater and not just any shark but the nastiest of them all, bull sharks. I've never encountered one in the fresh but I see them regularly in brackish water. I've had a few dealings with sharks. All of them in the warmer climes but it can happen almost anywhere. My first shark encounter while kayak fishing was on a trip to Baja. As cited earlier, we were mother-ship fishing and keeping dorado for dinner. I had a dorado on the lip gripper and it was in the water while I paddled over to the boat. I felt something tugging and looked down. There was a 5 to 6-foot hammerhead pulling the fish. I grabbed the gripper and pulled it away. There was a ruckus and I ended up with two thirds of my catch

In Florida sharks are common. I see them all the time working the oyster bars and flats in all but the coldest months, but they are always around. It's the main reason I don't often use live bait, except when tarpon fishing, or targeting the sharks themselves. However when I do use live bait I recognize sharks are likely. I was on a mother-ship trip in the Glades and there were some 30 to 60-pound tarpon around. I got one to hit a plug but that was it. A bit later I ran into some ladyfish and decided to live-line one for tarpon. I hadn't seen any signs of tarpon in a while but figured I'd give it a shot. I lost the first ladyfish to a shark that I didn't see but then it was like ringing the dinner bell. I'd watch, as the sharks would work their way towards my ladyfish. I kept pulling the bait away from them. It became too intense and I gave up trying for the tarpon and resumed snook fishing.

Shallow water fights can present unique challenges. I have experienced problems at times when fighting snook and reds in skinny water. Should the fish head under the kayak in very shallow water you can't plunge the rod under as you would when it's deeper to clear it around the bow or stern because there isn't any water in which to plunge. Anything protruding below the bottom of the kayak presents potential hazards. As previously mentioned, while rudders and pedal drives aid in maneuvering while fighting a fish and can be great assets during battle, they also present obstacles that can tangle your line. I've had to pull the drive a few times because Snook have run the line through it.

While each species exhibits certain tendencies in a fight they are still living creatures and individuals. You just never know. Tarpon are known for being powerful, explosive adversaries. In April 2008 I hooked one that was about 40 inches. As soon as it felt the sting of the hook it leapt 6 feet into the air. I anticipated a strong run, with the fish heading to the adjacent boat dock that separated it from the open bay. The run never came.

My tackle was fairly light for a fish this size. A medium action Ugly Stik with 20-pound braid tied directly to a five-foot, 30-pound fluorocarbon leader. The reel was a 2000 size. The fish towed me around and a couple of times I headed it off before it could go under the dock but the fish never got more than 25 feet from the kayak and spent almost the entire fight within sight. It did jump three more times and they were spectacular, but it was a weird fight. I didn't have any trouble putting the lip gripper on it and removing the circle hook. I felt things were just too easy, as if the fish didn't really know it was hooked.

After the hook came out it went nuts, got off the gripper and was gone. I was using large live bait, a 14-inch mullet, and in retrospect maybe it affected the fish. A big meal slows me down and maybe it did the same to the tarpon. I'll never know.

Fighting fish is why most of us go fishing. It's the best part of the sport and is even more fun from a kayak. While we're more exposed, we're also more in tune with what's going on. Talk about getting closer to nature!

Noise

The amount of noise each kayak model makes can vary significantly. Some models don't make any noise while others announce their presence loudly. Is running quietly important? That depends upon where you fish. If you fish open, deep waters then it usually doesn't matter; conversely if you're going to spend a lot of time fishing shallow flats it could be key. Whenever fish are shallow they are very alert to unknown noises. Often you're going to need stealth to approach within casting range. If you are in a kayak that's making a racket you may never get close enough to reach the fish. The noise a kayak makes is inherent to its design. It's usually in the form of a slap, its common name being 'hull slap' and there is nothing you can do to change it. The first time I heard it was when my brother was using one of my spare kayaks and I thought he was deliberately

making noise. When I turned around I saw he was paddling. Though I had used that same kayak many times, I had never noticed the noise. That's because it's much less noticeable when you're in the kayak. I then realized what people meant by noisy and quiet kayaks. It was a real ear opener. A kayak making that much noise in shallow water would send the fish scurrying for cover. So if you're going to be fishing places where a stealthy approach is necessary, then look for models that are quiet.

The other noise that you can control is that which you make. When I take clients out it always amazes me how noisy some of them are. They are angling for fish in a foot of water or less where you know the fish are wary. Banging paddles, moving tackle boxes, etc. makes a lot of noise and water conducts sound much better than air. Besides recognizing this you can take other steps to be quieter. For one, make careful move-

Vince and Morgan stuffing yellowtails into front hatches off of La Jolla in Southern California.

ments. Two, take less gear, so you have less to mess with. If there is current you're best off approaching fish from down current. I have snuck up on fish and have been close enough to poke them with a fishing rod. That's stealth.

Invitation to Dinner

Human beings have been fishing a very long time. There are many cultures where fish was and still is a major source of protein. Not until very recently has catch and release become common among sport fishermen. If you look at photos from half a century ago you will see huge stringers of fish. The advent of the professional bass fishing circuit and fly-fishing trout fishermen are most responsible for the shift in ideology. Nature's resources were once considered inexhaustible but we now know they are finite and to take more than she can provide will destroy fish populations. Without fish, kayak fishing doesn't offer

much. I'm a big fan of catch and release but I also like eating fresh fish. Assuring that it stays fresh requires some forethought when fishing from a kayak. To keep fish and then have them spoil is a waste.

How to handle fish you're inviting home depends on where you're fishing and the circumstances. Fishing cooler climates with cold water doesn't present much of a problem. The air is usually cold, too. Preserving the eating quality of your fish isn't going to take much. Small- to medium-sized fish aren't too difficult to deal with. Large fish offer more of a challenge. Large is a relative term depending on where you're fishing. In the northeast you're rarely going to have to deal with anything larger than a 30-pound striped bass, whereas in southern California that would be a medium-sized fish. Yellowtails easily get that big and white sea bass are caught more than twice that size.

Your storage choices are either inside the kayak hull or the tank well, depending upon the kayak you're using. When using the inside of the kayak, the entire bottom is in contact with the water and acts as a large ice pack. It's a good way to store a large fish but I personally wouldn't put a lot of small fish in the hull. You can also put large- and medium-sized fish in the tank well. A wetted burlap sack over the fish will keep them cool via evaporation. When fishing most freshwater environs, putting fish on a stringer and keeping them over the side is all that's needed. Occasionally you might get into an argument with a snapping turtle but they're not very hard to deal with. I wouldn't use a stringer in alligator country, as I've told you, as that would be an invitation to a dinner guest you don't want. Fish kept on a stringer should still be alive when you return to the launch. I usually keep an empty cooler in the vehicle to put them in while driving home. If I planned on keeping fish I'll have some ice or blue ice in it. As an option I can pick up some ice at a convenience store.

The challenge with preserving your catch comes when the weather warms up. It doesn't take fish very long to spoil if you don't do something. There are a couple of kayak models with built-in insulated fish holds. These are fiberglass kayaks. If you have one you're set but they are kind of rare. I don't know of any plastic kayaks with built-in holds, probably because it may not be possible to rotomold one.

Many anglers bring a cooler along. A soft cooler is more convenient as it will conform better to the contours of the kayak. When I plan on keeping fish I have one in my front hatch and the bottom is lined with blue ice. I can access the hatch and cooler while on the water. I've also got a hard-sided cooler I can put in the tank well.

Similar to soft coolers are dedicated fish bags. Creative Feathers was the first to offer a dedicated insulated fish bag designed specifically for the kayak fishermen. It's an elongated triangle-shaped bag that's designed to be attached on the bow of a kayak.

New to the scene is the KingFish Koffin. It can be used either on top or inside the kayak via a hatch. Adding cool packs to either of these insulated bags is going to give you hours of protection, which should be enough to preserve your catch.

A little bit of forethought goes a long way in assuring dinner is going to be memorable.

(top) These three redfish were kept in prime condition inside a Creative Feathers Bag. (middle) Sometimes big fish, like this 50-pound Alaskan halibut, need to be lashed to the kayak. (bottom) A game clip is a great way to secure fish.

Etiquette

As kayak fishing grows there are going to be increased numbers of us pursuing the sport and it's going to have an impact. There will be more of us launching and fishing the same places. Before you can kayak fish you need to park and then launch your kayak. I know spots where we once launched that now restrict kayaks. In some places access is already difficult and we don't want to lose more. Kayaks have limitations in range and a few miles can make a big difference in accessing good fishing areas. If there is a trail to the water from the launch, stay on it, as many beach areas are sensitive to being trudged on. Whatever you do, don't litter, and it's a good idea to pick up trash. Also, while on the subject of trash, if I find things floating in the water I'll grab them. It's important to be a good citizen so we're looked upon as assets, not detractors, of the outdoors.

Once on the water be respectful of private property. Don't land in someone's backyard or tie up to a dock, etc. as that can result in a complaint. There have been altercations between boats, jet skis and kayaks. I've been involved in a couple and I wasn't doing anything wrong. Having to yield to non-motorized craft bothers some boaters. When I lived in San Diego and fished on the weekends via a boat, I experienced how annoying this could be. We would leave about 2:00 a.m. to reach the fishing grounds by dawn. Then we would fish several hours and return to the harbor in the late afternoon. When we got near the harbor there would be hundreds of sailboats. They had the right of way and we had to negotiate our way through them when all we wanted was a shower and sleep. We understood this and acted accordingly, but I've experienced bad behavior from boaters and as I look back they were probably annoyed at all the kayaks they had to slow down for and negotiate around. It isn't any excuse, but it happens. For some it's akin to road rage. It is in everyone's best interest to understand the rules of the water and obey them.

The author's cousin, Joshua, with a nice bass. He's in the front of a malibu, sitting in a gator seat.

I was having dinner with several people in the industry and the discussion turned to the growth of kayak fishing. Jimbo related that one of his neighbors, who fishes from a boat, was getting fed up with kayak fishermen. He said his neighbor would anchor and set up a chum slick and catch some fish. Then kayak fishermen would come along and either stake out right next to him or fish in his slick. Some folks believe once on the water they can go anywhere and do what they please. This isn't proper behavior. Be courteous and stay clear or ask permission. Often it will be granted but if it isn't understand and be respectful. The old adage, "Do unto others as you would have them do unto you," certainly applies here.

Use good judgment, common sense, respect and courtesy. Doing so will benefit all of us.

Kayak Fishing with Children

Kids love fishing and you can take them along in the kayak. The first child I took with me was my cousin Joshua, who lives in Vermont. I introduced him to fishing when he was 4 years old. I've gone up to Vermont a few times and taken him out. I think he was seven the first time we went in a kayak. As I type this he's 11 and now he paddles or pedals by himself. On that first trip to Vermont we got into some pretty good bass fishing on the final day. Joshua loves to eat fish so we took one of the bass home with us. I can still see the wheels turning in the head of his sister, Zoe, who was 3 years old at the time and clearly wanted to go along.

During my visit in July 2007 she did. We went to the same pond I took Joshua his first time out, and my brother-in-law, Paul, joined us. Joshua went with Paul in my Hobie Outfitter and Zoe and I took her parents' Malibu Two. Zoe had a push-button spin cast reel. I put on a *Gulp!* earthworm and figured we'd get some pan fish. I cast hers out and grabbed my rod and cast. I looked towards Zoe's bobber and it was gone. I told her to reel in and immediately a

The author's cousin, Zoe, and brother, Peter, get ready to head out in a tandem.

3- foot northern pike jumped. I yelled excitedly and Paul and Joshua caught the second leap. Zoe said it was hard to reel in and I told her that's because the fish was big. She got it to the kayak and as I went to put the lip gripper on the pike the line broke. It was only 6-pound test and it's amazing with the small hook that it stayed on until then. It was exciting, though, and makes for a great story. Zoe landed a bunch of pan fish over the next few days. Both Joshua and Zoe love to fish now.

There are two styles of kayaks I recommend for this type of fishing: either a tandem or a single model with a forward rear-facing jump seat. Tandems are kayaks with seating for two adults. There are also models that have a third option for a seat in the middle; however this doesn't make it a triple. That's because someone can't sit in the middle when either of the other seats is occupied. I highly recommend this type of tandem arrangement because you'll most likely be using the kayak solo at some point and oftentimes a lot. When used alone you need to have a comfortable place to sit. More and more tandems have this central seating and I highly recommend it.

The other style of kayak is the single that offers rear-facing jump seats. The original is the venerable Cobra Fish in Dive, which has been around for years and handles the task well. The Cobra utilizes the same hull as its tandem. The jump seat area is set up to accommodate a back band or seat. This is the type of seating I used the first time I took my cousin out. They are incredibly stable with tons of storage.

The Fish 'n Dive is 12 1/2 feet long and with two hatches weighs in at 70 pounds.

The later introduced kayaks of this genre are from Malibu Kayaks. Malibu Kayaks rethought the jump seat and actually redesigned the front hatch by adding a built-in seat. They call it the Gator Hatch. It is available as an option and comes with a built-in tank well with bungee array. There are even platforms to mount two flush-mount rod holders! It's a great design and can be used with any Malibu models that share the large front hatch. It moves the child farther away from the bow for better handling.

The Malibu X Factor also has a set-up to accommodate a seat in the rear tank well. This seating will easily handle a small adult and with its 500-plus pound capacity it makes a great family kayak. All of the kayaks in this class have tremendous below-deck storage via large hatches. The Cobra, while having tremendous capacity (600 pounds) has the jump seat very far forward. The bigger the child the less I would recommend the Cobra, whereas the Malibu could handle a small adult.

Once the kids approach 10 years of age, they are ready to handle a kayak on their own. I recommend doing so in protected waters. A pond or lake where you can see them at all times is a great way to introduce them to solo. That's what I did with my cousin Joshua. We did a family outing on a small lake in the Vermont Mountains. We were able to swim, fish, and have a picnic lunch. It was a great day and Joshua pedaled all over the lake.

Hazards

For kayak anglers, hazards can take many forms. They can be rips, rapids and currents, animals, boats and more. They can vary from inconvenient to life threatening. Some of these have been touched on elsewhere in the book, but bear repeating. Be humble and recognize your vulnerability, and there are things you can do to limit the chances of having a problem. Be smart and if in doubt, carefully consider the potential consequences. As I've mentioned to you, I seek out adventure and do a lot of my wandering alone. My margin of error is slim because if something bad happens I probably won't have help nearby. I'm on my own. A serious injury or getting bitten by a poisonous snake or spider while many miles from help isn't a good thing to experience, so I don't take unnecessary chances.

While weather is fickle there is some predictability to it. When Joey and I got trapped on an island in serious thunderstorms, such weather had been forecast and we knew there was a possibility of encountering it. If the surf is pounding it's obvious, but sometimes the surf builds as the day goes on, and the same goes for wind. If you're going to be out for several hours, conditions can change significantly.

I remember my first fall when I fished the ocean alone. I believe it was early November and I launched off the north Jersey beaches into the ocean. I was chasing fast moving schools of fish. It was windy and I just couldn't catch them. After a few hours of chasing I was tired, decided I'd had enough, and headed in. When I had launched the wind was out of a westerly direction, which tends to knock down the surf and swells. However, it had shifted and the waves were much larger as I headed to shore. It was an exciting ride in and luckily uneventful.

As I type this it's nice and calm out with a strong chance of thunderstorms this afternoon. If I were to go out fishing I'd stay close in case inclement weather moves in. That way I can get off the water quickly. Modern weather forecasting, while far from perfect, is available and will let you know what is possible - same with surf reports. If wind or surf is predicted to build throughout the day, you will know and can act accordingly. With such information I'd plan a trip encompassing shelter from the wind and I'd make sure not to travel against it when I returned to my commencement point.

In many environments you're going to have to contend with other watercraft. A kayak is a non-motorized vessel and being such has the right of way. However just because you have the right of way during encounters doesn't mean you can blatantly ignore common sense. There are situations where a kayak is required to yield to a boat. When crossing a narrow channel you can't cut in front of a boat, causing them to alter course at the last minute. You have to cross behind.

At the first J-Bay tournament there was a bluefish blitz in the main channel. A couple of dozen anglers were fishing for them. It happened to be one of two major shipping channels in the bay and a huge ship was coming through. None of the kayakers were getting out of the way. The captain blew his horn and still the kayaks stayed in his path. The captain got on his loud speaker and basically said I don't have brakes or power steering and you're in my way. It was comical watching all the kayaks scatter. The kayaks were in the wrong. Generally you want to stay out of channels and inlets or limit, as much as possible, your time in them.

There have been accidental close encounters with craft. This usually happens because the kayak is hard to see. That's why I'm a big fan of using a safety flag, as discussed in the safety section. I'm hard to miss when using one. However there are boaters who aren't paying attention. Even though you may be in the right, getting run over isn't a great way to prove it. Conversely, while rare, it's still unfortunate that there are craft operators who have deliberately gone out of their way to harass kayaks. Most often its people on personal watercraft using kayaks as obstacles for close maneuvers, however there have been incidences with boats as well. I recommend getting the numbers from the craft and as much detail as you can and report it immediately using either a cell or VHF. Provide as much information as you can. A picture can be invaluable.

I wish I had done this the day before the 2008 Paddle-In held at Everglades City. Several of us went on an excursion up the Turner River and Hurdles Creek. The group was comprised of Terry, Terry's daughter Linzy, and her friend also named Lindsay (the girls), Ernie and Hank from the KFS Florida forum, Jim and Sally who were in for the week from Texas and had been my clients the preceding Monday. Hurdles is a serpentine waterway and we heard a boat approaching. We were cutting the corners of the creek to shorten the distance we had to paddle/pedal. We weren't in a tight group. Terry and I were together talking and the girls were about 100 feet in front of us.

Terry and I moved to the side of the creek and the boat passed us. As it was alongside the girls the Captain of the boat yelled that we were on the wrong side of the creek. Calling Hurdles a creek is a misnomer. It's approximately 150 to 200 feet wide at its narrowest. Anyway, the captain of the boat started giving the girls grief and Linzy gave it right back, pointing out as a non-motorized craft they had the right of way. The boater jammed his throttle down and left in a huff. I didn't think much of it at the time.

Terry and I didn't hear much of what was said but Linzy filled us in when we caught up. There were a bunch of things she wished she had said but it all happened so quickly. The entire exchange wasn't even a minute. Before the incident, on our way up the creek we had taken a side trip to a backcountry lake to fish. Ernie was well behind us and had missed the turn. Ernie wanted to see the lake so I volunteered to take him. This side trip easily took 30 minutes and put us behind the group by that much. I expected everyone to be gone from the launch when we got there.

To my surprise as I approached the take-out, Terry, the girls, Jim and Sally were still there. When I landed I learned why. Turns out both Linzy and Terry had flats caused by a tire slash in the sidewall and Jim was changing the second tire. I learned later that one of the tires on my kayak trailer was also slashed. It had to be the guy from the boat and what I think happened was this. It was Terry's birthday and Linzy had attached a balloon to her kayak. We were very visible in the launch area and the two nice-looking girls probably attracted the attention of the men in the launch area at the time. One of them had to be the guy we had the issue with in Hurdles Creek. It's a shame there are idiots like this and if we had gotten his boat make and even better the registration numbers, we could have had some recourse.

Animals are another hazard for which you can plan. When fishing in saltwater I'm always cognizant of sharks. It's their environment and I don't like having altercations with them while in a kayak. The easiest way to avoid them is by not keeping fish on a stringer

(above) Cutting too close to shore and this 7-foot gator might have proven a bit too interesting. **(left)** The author had to fight with a 6-foot hammerhead to earn his dorado dinner.

in the water. I was speaking with a buddy, Jim, the other day as he and a group had just returned from a few days of kayak fishing camping at Mormon Key in the Everglades. One member of the group had caught a nice redfish and put it on the stringer. A while later Jim heard him yelling. When Jim looked there was his buddy being towed backwards by a large bull shark. I would never put a fish on a stringer in Florida, as there are too many sharks. In fact, I don't recommend using a stringer at all in saltwater.

A trip I took to Baja in 2004 provides another example of why not to use a stringer. We were keeping dorado, as they are fantastic eating. After I caught one I'd leave it on my tethered lip gripper and paddle over to the mother-ship where I'd hand the fish to the captain. I had been doing this for two days when I felt a tug on the kayak. I looked down and there was a 5 to 6-foot hammerhead shark on the end of my dorado. I grabbed the gripper and pulled the fish away from the shark. The hammerhead rose up with the fish and it was exciting for several seconds. A third of the dorado was missing.

Deeper in the Everglades I sometimes run into alligators. I leave them alone and them me, but the larger they are the less fear they have. The little ones don't want anything to do with me. This continues as they get to larger sizes. As they approach six feet or more they're not nearly as skittish and the bigger they get the less they move off when I approach. One day in a backcountry lake I heard a huge splash about 100 feet up the shoreline. I had startled an 8-foot gator. I was coasting along and it was

Bill got a double whammy in Baja on our trip. He got stung by both a Portugese Man-O-War and "Montezuma's Revenge".

heading straight out into the middle of the lake. It never changed course allowing me to get 15 feet away. A smaller gator would have never let me get so close. This one kept an eye on me but exhibited no fear. Big gators don't have any natural enemies. Some of them can get huge. There's a 14 foot stuffed one in the Seafood Depot, an Everglades City restaurant and a neighbor in Chokoloskee told me that on his ranch up north, the state came in and killed a 16-footer. I don't want to encounter a 10-footer let alone an animal that big. If the gators are thick I leave the water to them. I don't fish amongst them and again, I would never have a stringer of fish in the water in such habitats.

We've all heard stories of surfers being mistaken for seals and hit by Great Whites. It's also happened to kayakers on rare occasions. I encountered a Great White once when fishing the Atlantic coast of Cape Cod. There was a huge school of stripers about ¾ miles off the beach. Five of us went out and fished for them but our buddy Jim, who originally found the school, wouldn't launch. That's because he had seen the shark in the general vicinity of the blitzing fish. I was the last to get out on the water and I did see the fin about 100 yards away. I headed away from it and told everyone what I had seen and where. Somehow my buddy Terry ended up in the area where the shark was and saw the dorsal fin cutting through the water. He paddled away from it quickly and then slowed and glanced behind him. To his shock there was the dorsal only a couple of kayak lengths behind him and the tip of the tail about 10 feet behind it. Terry paddled for all he was worth and when he stopped it was gone. The water was incredibly clear and I figure the shark was curious; once it got a good look at Terry and saw he wasn't a seal, it lost interest.

In Florida there is the benign manatee. Kayaks are stealthy and you may happen upon a manatee and spook it. They grow to over a half-ton and can easily topple a kayak. You usually see them as they surface for air. At times they've been known to use kayaks to rub their backs and you get no warning this is about to occur. When one comes up under you it's called being manateed. Also if I'm trolling an area and I come across a bunch of them I pull the lure from the water. They're not the brightest creatures and I would hate to snag one.

One day I was fishing a canal and I saw a disturbance along the mangrove-lined shoreline. This canal is loaded with tarpon and I thought it was one. I stopped pedaling and coasted along. Next thing I knew I was being lifted from the water. Turns out it was a manatee. Luckily the water was deep enough for the manatee to leave me. It was exciting though being lifted almost a foot. I looked around and saw the manatee. It wasn't very big, most likely a teenager.

Weird stuff happens in nature. Terry from the tire slashing encounter was out in the Gulf of Mexico fishing for kingfish when she heard a splash in front of her kayak. As she turned a 4 to 5-foot ray was flying at her. She ducked and it hit her in the head and knocked her out of the kayak. Luckily she wasn't knocked out and quickly got back into the kayak as there were a lot of sharks around.

If you're going to wade you're susceptible to stingrays. Remember to shuffle your feet so they know you're coming and can get out of your way. Another stinging animal that can hurt you floats on the water's surface. It's the Portuguese Man-O-War, a type of jellyfish that has stinging tentacles. On a trip to Baja, Bill got stung by one while alongside the mother-ship and besides the pain, he got ill and lost a full day of fishing.

When traveling to foreign countries, be careful what you eat and drink. Places like Mexico have parasites in the water and on foodstuffs that have been washed. I'm sure you've heard of Montezuma's

Revenge, and the result will be at the minimum diarrhea and possibly fever and chills. It can put a real damper on a trip. Even if you get a mild case, needing to use the facilities often doesn't coincide well with sitting in a kayak out on the water.

While on the water you need to pay attention to your surroundings. On a trip to Cape Cod we were fishing the calm side of the peninsula, Cape Cod Bay, and while fishing near an inlet my buddy Chris wasn't paying attention. The tide was moving his kayak backwards and he ended up in an inlet rip and got dumped from the kayak. Current, tide and wind can toss a kayak about. Once wind velocity exceeds a certain speed you're not going to be able to overcome it. There are a lot of criteria. Your physical conditioning and strength, the kayak you're in, whether or not you have a tide or current to contend with and how far you need to go. For short distances I can deal with a 20 mph wind and going against a strong tide, but I don't want to do so for even a mile let alone several.

One day Long Island Sound was glassy calm. A gorgeous summer day that was perfect for being out on the water. I was fishing with my brother, Peter, but I didn't always have him in sight. He came up to me and was soaking wet. I knew he wouldn't have gone for a swim and before I could ask him he told me what had happened. He was landing a fish with a lip gripper. The combination of leaning over and a one-foot boat wake were enough to dump him from the kayak. He hadn't realized there was a wake until after he was in the water. The model kayak he was using didn't have much secondary stability and had an abrupt dump point. All Peter needed to do was pass that point and he was in the water. Boat wakes are a hazard that can happen anytime and can travel long distances and affect you.

When going through tight environments like small rivers, mangrove tunnels and the like, pay attention to your surroundings. In some places you may come across bees and wasps. Running into a nest would be a real bummer and possibly life threatening if you're allergic or if they're killer bees. In the mangroves there are tons of spiders, and while most are just a nuisance, some are dangerous. Snakes are a real possibility in some environments too.

The incoming tide at the entrance to Hell's Half Acre Lake in the Everglades created quite a challenge for Ernie when his rod snagged in an overhanging tree.

Some of the species for which kayak fishermen angle can be dangerous and caution needs to be exercised. Sharks are obvious. They get big, are powerful and there are those teeth. They must be handled with extreme care. Billfish get big enough and leap and cavort. Having a marlin crash into you can be very dangerous. The bills have seriously injured people and in a kayak we are more vulnerable.

When I fought my first kayak billfish, a sailfish about 110 pounds, I was uncomfortable when it was going nuts within 100 feet of me. It could cover the distance to me in seconds and were I to be hit by it I could have been seriously injured. I know many fishermen in boats who won't pursue tarpon, yet there are fishermen who do so in a kayak. People have been killed by tarpon, none in a kayak, but it can happen. Tarpon are incredible leapers, are very strong and they get big - really big. Usually though the big ones are going to tow you a long way. It's the medium-sized ones that stay nearer the kayak that may present more danger.

Kayak fishing is a great sport and while the incidence of things going wrong is relatively low, you have to recognize that you are most certainly vulnerable.

As Craig fought a big 'cuda, the wind blew him directly into these metal pilings. Landing the fish was difficult, but Craig prevailed!

Chapter 9
Kayak Care

Although they're nowhere near as expensive as powerboats, fishing kayaks still represent a signicant investment. It pays to make sure a kayak is cared for properly so that it can be counted on to provide a lifetime of service to its owner. In this chapter we'll discuss security, maintenance, troubleshooting and repair, and we'll devote an entire section to maintaining the Hobie mirage drive pedal mechanism.

Security

Unfortunately many people don't respect other people's property. While kayaks are large and bulky, they can be stolen. I grew up in the New York metro area, and there it would be foolish not to lock things up. However, I do know people who have never locked their kayaks and haven't had any problems. It only takes once and you're out of a lot of coin.

SOT kayaks are very easy to secure. The scupper holes make the perfect place to pass a cable, after which you put the cable through the rack. If you have a factory rack, don't just put the cable through the cross bars because they are easily removed. The rails would be a better choice. If you can't get the cable through the rails, then through the vehicle windows works great if you have enough cable.

In low risk places I use a bicycle cable lock but when I really want to make sure my stuff is secure I use a Kryptonite cable with an American Lock padlock. A thief is going to need to be traveling with some sophisticated tools to remove one of my kayaks. While I haven't used one yet I've seen others using ATV locks and they look great, as they will pass through the smallest scuppers. They are similar to the Kryptonite but they have the lock as part of the cable.

Because kayaks are big and bulky they are hard to steal with people around. However, the gear you attach and put into the kayak is another story. Items such as GPS, fish finders, seats, tackle, cameras, rods and the like are very easily stolen. This stuff is most vulnerable when you're launching, especially if there is some distance between you and the water. If you're fishing with others there are going to be enough eyes to stay on top of things. However, if you're alone and things are out of sight, the potential for theft is very real. I prefer in these circumstances to load the kayak with all my gear and wheel it to the water via a cart. The cart then comes with me. That way when I come back in from fishing I don't have to leave anything out of sight.

Maintenance

Maintaining your kayak isn't very difficult. Many owners don't do anything other than an occasional washing and treatment, while others spend a lot of time cleaning and treating. I tend to be among the former group. When the yak gets dirty or bloody I wash it and occasionally treat hatches and other parts when they need it. Most parts of a kayak can handle the elements with a little help and will stay in very good condition for a long time. There are three adversaries that will age your kayak, ultimately affecting its performance. They are UV (Ultra Violet) radiation from sunlight, oxidation from the oxygen in the air and saltwater corrosion. Let's look at each.

UV will affect plastic and rubber the most. The majority of kayaks used for fishing are made from plastic. Rubber is mainly used as a hatch and handles material. Plastic is incredibly resilient and can take harsh treatment, however like most things, it will age. Given enough time UV will break down the material and eventually make it brittle to the point where it won't function. Although it will take a long

Here's an ATV lock. These are a perfect solution for locking up a kayak.

time (one to a few decades) eventually the kayak will be ruined. Rubber will deteriorate much faster. If left exposed rubber parts can be ruined in a few years. The easiest way to prevent UV damage is to limit exposure. Unless you fish solely at night, which is unrealistic, the kayak is going to be in the sun. However the majority of the time it will be sitting. Reducing sun damage can be as simple as either not storing your kayak in the sun or using a treatment. The treatment I have used is 303. It's a lot like the commonly used automotive product Armor All®. It coats with a layer of protection that neutralizes the harmful UV rays of the sun. However it will make whatever area you treat more slippery. On kayak hulls I usually recommend treating only the bottom and then turning the kayak over so the treated area is exposed to the sun when stored outside. At KFS we treated hatches and seals with 303 before shipping or releasing to customers. It's especially nice when used on gaspachi style hatches. Gaspachi's are usually difficult to put on and off, but once treated with 303 they function easily.

Oxidation and saltwater affect materials similarly on your kayak and because of this I will discuss them together. They mainly affect metal parts but salt buildup will bind hatches. Saltwater can be neutralized via washing with freshwater and allowing it to dry. In many places the kayak isn't going to dry. When things are kept moist there's a much greater tendency for things to corrode. Cool weather and overcast or rainy weather isn't going to facilitate drying. Not every kayak is stored in a dry environment

with a breeze to dry it. Treatments that prevent salt corrosion can be used. I've used Salt-X® and CorrosionX®. I carry CorrosionX with me at all times in my truck.

There is such a wide array of kayak choices out there and different means of putting them together. Most manufacturers are using marine-grade stainless steel hardware but some don't. Also many things we attach to the kayaks weren't necessarily designed for the harsh exposure they're going to get - especially the exposure to saltwater. For such items, washing them in freshwater is all that's needed to keep them in great condition. If there are working metal parts use a lubricant like CorrosionX. Same goes for items that are part of the kayak and start corroding. Sometimes you can replace parts with corrosion-resistant items. I say resistant because even stainless will corrode in time. Aluminum, while it won't rust, tends to oxidize. A white crusty residue will build up. Washing and treatment are the best recourse here.

While kayaks aren't mechanical there are some moving parts associated with some of the add-ons or accessories. Rudders are the most common moving part or system on a kayak. Cables are either stainless steel or braid. Stainless steel cable will corrode but spraying with a treatment occasionally will keep things moving smoothly. Most rudders tend to have two problem areas. The slide tracks in the cockpit and the up/down movement of the rudder blade. The slides tend to get tight with build-up of grime. This grime depends upon where the kayak is being used and the material the slides are made out of.

One common culprit to efficient slide movement is sand. When sand gets in the slides it jams the mechanism and makes it more difficult to operate, sometimes jamming it so badly it won't work. Keeping the area clean with fresh water is the best remedy. Some people use lubricants but while making things more slippery they attract sand and dirt, which defeats what you are trying to accomplish. If your slides freeze up I recommend taking them apart and cleaning thoroughly. Check braid lines for wear. While braid is tough, things do happen. It is much easier to replace a cord that is still in place than to run a new line so if you see wear, replace it.

It doesn't take much to keep a plastic kayak providing service for many years. A little bit of TLC goes a long way and will help make the most of your time on the water.

Troubleshooting

Troubleshooting is much easier than it once was because there is so much information available on the Internet. I deliberately set up forums on KFS for each of the kayak brands we sold so owners of those products could exchange information. Owners discuss problems, their solutions and prevention. Manufacturers read the forums and both responded and used the information to improve products. Very often a potential problem can be averted with a little preventative maintenance or there might be a factory fix. Checking forums is a great way to find out if there is an issue with your kayak.

My friend Terry brought a recently purchased used Hobie Adventure to the 2008 Paddle In. (Ironically while she bought it in Florida, used, it was one that I had sold to a customer in central Florida previously - small world!). It was a first year model and I looked it over. I knew some of the early Adventures and Outback's suffered from the front area of the drive cracking. Hobie redesigned the area in the 2007 models and developed a fix kit to reinforce the area to prevent the failure from occurring. I checked to see if one had been installed. The reinforcement kit consists of a fiberglass brace, epoxy and longer hold-down bolts. Everyone who sent in their warranty card received the kit from Hobie, however many people don't register their kayaks. This was the case with the previous owner of Terry's kayak. Only a small percentage of 2006 Adventures and Outbacks failed. Hobie was great and replaced all the kayaks and should Terry's fail that would be the case; however that would only replace the hull. Most fishing kayaks have had a bunch of accessories added to them and items installed. A replacement hull doesn't include any of these amenities and besides the time there is the labor that would be involved in refitting the kayak. I had the information Terry needed but she could have searched the forums and learned the same.

Sometimes a problem is easily prevented. Large gaspachi hatches, especially those found on early Wilderness System kayaks, are easily lost when transporting at highway speeds. A bungee or strap used to hold it in place while driving will prevent this. My favorite is a hatch bungee system like the one I came up with and started offering as an option on all the tarpons I sold.

The area that sees the most problems in kayaks is the scupper holes. A roto-molded kayak is two halves that are connected along their length, a lot like two halves of a clam. The weakest part is where the halves are joined. Rarely is there a problem along the outside seam. The problem area is going to be where the scuppers join. With the volume we did at KFS, I saw a lot of these. Sometimes the alignment is slightly off. Most often it is small holes and when they are under water for hours a lot of water gets into the kayak. This is a warranty item but at times it becomes a hassle to have a kayak replaced. There are a number of reasons why. As I mentioned above, re-rigging a kayak is time-consuming and if a shop does it, there is the expense. The nearest dealer could be some distance away. If you've got to drive a few hours the cost of gas can really add up. Either way, if the defect is minor why not just fix it? A small hole is easily repaired with G-Flex epoxy. Either you or your dealer could do it. The kayak can probably be declared a blem and you could get some money back. If you go through the dealer it will be documented and still carry the warranty just in case the repair doesn't work or another problem manifests.

There are problems you can prevent. It's very unlikely a kayak set up for fishing won't have installations. When you do an installation on a kayak use the best means available that will have the least propensity for problems later on. If you have interior access to bolt an item, do so. Use marine grade stainless so it will be highly corrosion-resistant. If not, use a well-nut, as they are easily replaced when the rubber breaks down. Use the best materials you can.

Recognize that there is a lot of information out there offering solutions to most situations.

Repairs

Plastic kayaks are pretty tough, but not indestructible. Things break, they get holes in them, fasteners can rust out. Among other issues, manufacturers sometimes use screws where they should have used nuts and bolts, allowing items to be easily removed, sometimes when you don't want them to be. Many repairs can be performed without the need to go to a shop. Replacing parts is easy. Some require simple tools while others need very specific ones. Either way it isn't hard. I'd replace most screws with bolts where possible. Screws can fail and if they do in a critical area while on the water, it could be a problem. If you have interior access it's a simple upgrade.

(above) A welding gun is a great tool for repairing kayaks. The square part is the iron. Notice the hole where the molten plastic comes out. (right) A forklift hole repair on the author's Tarpon 100. The kayak has seen years of use on what most would have considered a ruined kayak.

finger. You can also use Photoflo® or Jet Dry®.

Most epoxies won't adhere well to a kayak. However, Chris from Saltwater Sports, a Naples, Florida kayak dealer introduced me in the fall of 2007 to an epoxy called G Flex®, which claims to adhere to polyethylene and they list kayaks right on the packaging. I've used it, though not extensively, and it does indeed adhere well. They claim it flexes, but since I have not applied it to a flexing area I can't say whether it will hold up to the rigors of a flexing kayak.

The other type of repair method is a weld, where you use melted material and bond it to the plastic of the kayak. There are several different ways to weld and each has its place. For small repairs a soldering iron with a broad tip is all that's needed. The Kayak Welder is a soldering iron with a very broad, flat tip marketed for welding kayaks. The next type of welder comes from the winter sports world of skiing and boarding. It uses heat and a stream of plastic. Like the solder tools, they are best for small repairs. The workhorse tool that I used in my shop is the welding gun. I teasingly say I could build a kayak using one with enough material and time. I've been an avid skier for my entire adult life and I started tuning my skis from the beginning. I purchased my first welder over two decades ago. I had a lot of experience using it both with my own skis and my friends'. The gun is basically a small iron with a hole in it, sort of a glorified glue gun. The iron is about ¾-inch square and the hole in the middle is about 1/8-inch. My original gun had a set temperature of 400 degrees. The one I have now has a variable adjustment from 284 to 428 degrees. I keep it on the highest setting for kayak repairs.

The first time I used it on a kayak was when I got a blem kayak from the Cobra rep. At a demo day someone had rammed a rock creating a hole in the nose. Ron knew I was a skier and asked if I knew how to repair it. I said I figured I'd use my welding gun, with which he agreed. The first thing I discovered is kayaks are much softer than skis. The gun went right through the nose and made the hole

Most kayak fishing models are made of plastic; however it isn't the only material you will find. Some are made of fiberglass or Kevlar. I don't have any experience repairing kayaks made from the latter materials so I'm not going to offer any advice how to repair them.

I'm very familiar with plastic kayaks. Via KFS I saw a lot of kayaks and with volume I saw my share of repairs. The most common repair is a hole. Often it's because a hole was drilled in the wrong place. If the hole is above the water line then there are a couple of methods or materials that can be used. Either use a sealant or epoxy, or weld it. Where the hole is will better determine what's best. If sealing, there are several sealants you can go with. First clean the area with some type of solvent. If you use one that is volatile like lacquer thinner, do so in a well-ventilated area or outside. Once the area is clean and dry, you can put sealant in the hole. I like to use a piece of duct tape on the inside so there is something to hold the sealant in place. Silicone is the least tenacious sealant and would be my last choice for a permanent repair. I prefer Marine Goop, Lexel or 5200. I smooth the surface sealant and make it flush by wetting my larger. Luckily it was still easy to repair.

The way the gun works is the iron melts the ski bottom and then the hot molten plastic extruded from the hole in the iron of the gun fuses with the material you just melted on the ski. When done properly, after cooling, the two materials become one. I use the gun the same way for most kayak repairs. The iron is placed on the area to be welded and once the material starts to liquefy the trigger is pressed on the gun to extrude the melted plastic from the gun's internal reservoir. Once cool I use a Dremel rotary tool with either a grinding tip or a sanding bit to remove excess material. Cooling will take at least several minutes and if a lot of material is used I sometimes wait as long as an hour. When the welded material is the same temperature as the rest of the hull, it's ready. Experience has taught me the speed at which I need to go. Each kayak brand is a bit different. Each color acts differently, too.

The first major repair I did with the gun showed me the true potential of the tool. We had a Tarpon 100 that we rigged and shipped out to a customer. The freight company put a forklift through the bottom. The gouge was five inches long and over an inch wide in places. There was a big flap that was pushed into the kayak. The Tarpon was totaled and we were reimbursed for the hull from the freight company; however that only covered the wholesale cost of the hull and the shipping from the manufacturer to us. We were still out the labor for installing the accessories, wrapping, and the gas costs delivering the kayak to the terminal. I figured I had nothing to lose so why not see if I could fix it. It would be a good experiment.

I knew I wouldn't use a sealant for a repair of this type as it was in the middle of the kayak towards the bottom. Whatever repair I performed was going to have to stand up to banging rocks and logs in the rivers I fished. I figured welding was the only thing to try. I wanted to salvage as much material as I could, so I used a heat gun to soften the flap that was pushed into the kayak by the forklift and pull it back to the exterior of the kayak. I used several sticks of material and less than an hour of total labor resulted in a great repair. I still have the kayak and it has bounced over lots of rocks and logs fishing rivers in northern New Jersey. The repair is very tough and is at least as strong as the rest of the kayak.

Most individuals aren't going to have a forklift hole but a sharp rock hit the wrong way could produce a similar, though smaller gouge. A hunk of metal could produce similar damage. However, punctures of this type are relatively rare. The more common damage is a hole in the bottom of the kayak caused by being dragged by hand or falling off a vehicle or trailer. Smaller holes can either get welded like the Tarpon repair or use G Flex. Vehicle drags tend to be huge and necessitate a patch. The first one I repaired using a patch was brought to me by Dave, who had found a kayak in the trash. It was obvious it had been dragged down the road a while. The hole was approximately five by 10 inches. We saved large cutouts from installing hatches at the shop and I grabbed a piece that matched up best to the kayak. I cut the patch to be slightly smaller than the hole and used the welder to fuse the patch to the hull. Dave still uses the kayak.

The most extensive repair I've done was on an Adventure hull. The kayak was dragged behind a trailer and the ensuing hole was 17 inches by 3.5 inches.

At first, this appeared to be a totaled hull. A few welding sticks, a Dremel™ tool, and a few hours work produced the first patch. A couple of weeks later the hull was tested to confirm the integrity of the patch, then the fin was attached. While not cosmetically perfect, the kayak functions great and the repair is expected to last the lifetime of the kayak.

Something one would ordinarily consider a total. I obtained a new tail section of an Adventure in the same color (for aesthetic reasons). I decided upon a two-part approach to the repair. First I wanted to seal the hole. After that I would add the same piece from another kayak that had been ground off. So I was going to have in essence two separate repairs. I figured the first patch would seal any water out. The second would add the fin so the kayak would function properly. For the patch I made a cardboard cutout of the hole then used the cutout to trace an outline on the patch material. A Dremel with a cutoff wheel was used to cut the patch. I made the patch a bit oversized to allow some wiggle room, figuring it's easier to trim material than add. I laid the patch over the hole and made some lines where material needed to be trimmed. Again I used the cutoff wheel. The patch was a bit warped so I used a hair dryer set on high to soften the plastic. Next I cleaned the hole with lacquer thinner and let it dry. I welded the stern part of the patch to secure it and let it cool.

Once cool I started welding the hull to the patch. I've found it works best if there is a small gap between the two. For some reason fusing the patch directly to the hull doesn't work as well as having the welding material between the two. The technique is like gluing the two sections together using the molten material as the glue.

The fin was attached a couple of weeks later. I cut it to replace the missing fin section and again welded it in place. Subsequent welding and grinding resulted in a fully functional repair that looked OK. It was the best I could do camping out in a marina in the Everglades, which is where I was at the time. I didn't want to haul the kayak back north so I sold it to my buddy Bob and he decided to use G Flex and redo the tail fin repair. He used fiberglass cloth and added color to the epoxy and got a terrific structural and cosmetic result, which is pictured here.

Things break and they can be fixed. Something catastrophic has to happen to a kayak in order for it not to be fixable. It comes down to whether you can perform the repair yourself or need to take it to an expert.

Mirage Drive Maintenance

The mirage drive is the pedal mechanism for Hobie kayaks. Being a mechanical unit, it gets exposed to the elements. It's a tough device but a little TLC goes a long way. Also the unit can get damaged. I've put a lot of hours in mirage drive kayaks, more than most anglers will do in a lifetime. With all this use I've learned a few things. If you own a mirage and use it in shallow environments you're going to do some occasional damage. I had very few issues in the northeast where the only shallow water I saw had a sand bottom. An occasional bent mast (the rod in the rubber fin) is easy to bend back.

In fact, the only significant problem I ever had was a broken sprocket when I crash-landed on a sandbar in the surf at Nauset Inlet at Cape Cod. It was essentially a shallow water encounter. The bar appeared earlier than I anticipated so I didn't fold the fins quickly enough to prevent damage. It was a borderline call whether or not I was going to pull the drive and paddle in.

While on the subject, should you pull the drive, tether it to the kayak. As I mentioned earlier, my buddy Terry made a landing in the surf one day and didn't secure his drive. He dumped and lost it. We searched for quite some time using snagging trebles on our rods and worked the area over. We never found it.

The masts will bend when they hit items. Something has to give. They will still function while bent. However, if a sprocket breaks the drive won't function. It's a good idea to carry a spare sprocket and I highly recommend the mirage repair kit. Besides a sprocket it contains an extra sail, mast, chain and assorted hardware, all in a soft case with lots of room for additional gear. Should you need to change a sprocket while on a trip, you will need a half-inch wrench, the appropriate Allen head tool and pliers to change it out. So bring them along or take the drive plug in case you end up paddling. It makes paddling much more efficient.

In Florida I've had to change several sprockets. There is a lot of shallow water and hitting oyster bars and bottom in the bays is common. The water is very murky and often you can't see more than six inches, so structure like oyster bars will surprise you. In the backcountry the hazards are mangrove roots and cut limbs. When people trim the creeks they just drop the branches because canoes and paddle kayaks don't have any depth issues. Unfortunately that's not the case with a mirage. I love the control the mirage drive gives me in mangrove tunnels but it needs to have sufficient depth. If the tide is out I pull the drive and paddle. On some trips I even leave the drive in the truck if the water level is low.

There is one addition I would make to the mirage repair kit, and that is a rudder pin. While not part of the mirage drive the rudder has a breakaway pin to protect the rudder. While I've never broken one, I've had customers break several. Should you break one, the rudder isn't going to function. Without a rudder the mirage drive is next to useless. Again, carry the drive plug. It doesn't weigh anything and there is plenty of room in the hull.

The drive has a chain that will loosen with use. I remember one customer coming into the shop complaining that his drive was falling apart. The chains were so loose I don't know how the unit even functioned. All I needed to do was tighten up the end nut. Just make sure you keep things snug and it will perform great. Washing the drive down after use is a good idea, especially after saltwater use, and you can periodically spray it with lubricant.

Another potential anomaly is that the Allen screw on the center of the drive can loosen. If it does, the main shaft will come loose and move, and you won't be able to remove the drive from the kayak. When it happened to me it took a minute to determine what was wrong. I had to hammer the shaft back into its normal position in order to remove the drive. I used my lipper tool as the hammer. You can either check it periodically to make sure it's tight or use Loctite.

While not part of the mirage drive, the rudder is an integral part of the system. If you have an issue with the rudder, the drive won't do you very much good, as it will only propel you in a straight line. I remember a trip where my rudder wouldn't work properly on a first year Adventure. I ended up using my paddle as a rudder. I've found the center nut adjustment on the rudder can loosen up and affect the steering, so periodically check the rudder to make sure it's adjusted properly.

Besides the potential of the drive failing, the actual kayak can fail. The drive is held down with cams on either side of the drive well (in 2009 Hobie changed the method of holding the drive in place by going to

Standard mirage drive fins on left and the turbo fins on the right. Notice the protruding rods in the turbos. The standards on this model are tougher, making them my preferred choice for shallow water and potentially hazardous applications.

a click system). I had both of them crack on my first year Revolution. Luckily it occurred the last few days of my seven months in Florida. There isn't any fix for it. It's a warranty replacement. In early Adventures and third generation Outbacks, occasionally the front of the well would fail, resulting in a crack. Hobie redesigned the area and made a fix kit for the earlier models. Refer to the Troubleshooting section for more details.

There can be some issues with mirage drive kayaks but these are very rare. The failures aren't any more common than with other manufacturers' kayaks. The hands-free capability it provides is well worth it.

For those with a sense of adventure, Australia offers some wonderful kayak fishing opportunities.

Chapter 10
Travel and Exotic Kayak Fishing

Most kayak fishing is going to involve some travel in order to get to where one plans on fishing. Getting a kayak to the fishing grounds is covered in the section on transportation. Here, I want to discuss venturing farther away. The dictionary defines *exotic* as, "intriguingly unusual or different, excitingly strange, foreign, not native, experimental in nature". Certainly, for those new to kayak fishing, the sport itself might be considered exotic. For our purposes, it means fishing in places and for species for which one doesn't normally angle. The word *travel* doesn't really need an explanation; whenever one leaves their native waters the species are going to change and by definition this is exotic.

The species I regularly catch in the Northeast are exotic for my kayak angling friends in other locales. When we talk about big weakfish, blues and stripers, they all want a chance to catch them. Travel for me is going places other than my local areas. However exotic kayak fishing can be found in one's backyard too. My first travels as a kayak fisherman were to Cape Cod. We usually went for a few days to as long as two weeks. While the terrain was a bit different, I fished for familiar species I angled for in New Jersey and New York.

I consider my first exotic kayak fishing experience to be a trip Joey and I took to Puerto Rico in January of 2003. We were seeking tarpon and snook, but unfortunately things were off climactically and the fishing was poor. The second trip was to Florida, fishing Cedar Key for redfish. Both trips entailed travel and fishing for species I'd never pursued before.

Most exotic fishing is going to require travel. This can be via vehicle, air or a combination of both. Sometimes a boat ride is required on the final leg. Travel by vehicle is the simplest because you can take everything with you, including kayaks. Load the gear, clear the balances on the credit cards and you're off on an adventure. You can drive to your intended area and get a motel room, or you can bring a tent, camper or motor home, etc. along and stay in more remote places, often with fishing at your feet. There

are a lot of ways to go about it.

Traveling by air is different. Most often you're not going to be bringing a kayak with you unless it's an inflatable (more on this later). You've got a couple of choices - do it on your own or go with an outfitter or guide operation. My first trip with an outfitter was with *La Jolla Kayak Fishing*. Joining me on the trip were Bill and Terry with Adrian joining us two days later. Our guide was Jim Sammons. The trip required us to fly to Baja. Jim met us at San Jose del Cabo airport with the transport vehicle. After driving approximately an hour we were at Hotel Punta Colorado, where we would stay for five days of kayak mothership-fishing in the Sea of Cortez. Meals and kayaks were included so all we needed to bring was our tackle and gear.

The mother ship hauled the kayaks to the fishing. The first day I landed a sailfish we guessed to be a bit over 100 pounds (details in the "Fighting Fish" section). It was my first billfish from a kayak. The next day we got into a few hours of intense action. Alonzo, our mother ship captain, was throwing chum and the dorado and tuna were boiling behind the boat. We had multiple hook-ups with a few hours of fast and furious action. Adrian joined us the next day and he got a sailfish in the 80-pound range. The entire catch is documented on film. Unfortunately Jim didn't have the camera out the first day when I caught my

Action was hot for hours this day in Baja. Here's Terry fighting a dorado as Bill heads to the mother ship to drop one off for dinner. Jim & Alonzo are on the boat.

sailfish but during the course of our trip he filmed some terrific action. We each have a DVD of the trip as a souvenir. Besides the two sailfish, the mother ship enabled us to reach and catch exotic species like tuna and dorado.

These are not species the average shore-bound-launching kayak fisherman usually catches. Getting that first billfish from a kayak is an experience I'll never forget. While available, they're not the expected catch on an East Cape trip. Dorado, yellow fin and skipjack tuna are going to comprise most of the pelagic catch. Closer to shore you should expect a variety of species and if it's late spring to summer there will be roosterfish and they're the species most people want to catch. I've yet to catch a rooster from the kayak and I look forward to it.

The dorado is a great sport fish and a blast from a yak. Unlike tuna, which make a couple of nice runs and sound, dorado go nuts up near the surface. They jump often, and are powerful, majestic creatures. I don't know if there's a more beautiful fish than a lit up dorado. They defy description and pictures don't do them justice. The neon blue is impossible to describe. They're delicious table fare, too. They're easily one of the top kayak fish.

In Southern California dive boats are often arranged by groups to take kayak anglers out to the Channel Islands where the fishing goes up a notch. Southern California also has a long tradition in what is called long-range fishing. Trips can be booked as long as three weeks with a boat full of anglers traveling to distant islands, high spots and reefs off of Central America. One of the boats, *Qualifier 105*, sailing from San Diego, is now offering trips for kayak anglers. It's some of the best fishing in the world and definitely worth checking out. *Qualifier 105* is offering regularly scheduled kayak fishing trips from three to eight days.

The second mother ship trip I made was with *Everglades Kayak Fishing* in November of 2004. I had always wanted to see the Glades and to do so from a kayak while fishing is a terrific way to experience this fascinating natural wonderland. A group consisting of Joey, Terry, Scott, Jack, Steve and me did a multi-day trip. Each day we met our guide, Charles Wright (also the owner) and headed out for a day of fishing to a variety of spots. An hour ride in the boat would transport us to places that would take days to reach on our own. *Everglades Kayak Fishing* offers a variety of trips in Everglades National Park, Florida. Trips vary from single excursions where you return to shore after a six-hour trip, to multi-day camping/kayak fishing. The operation uses a couple of Carolina skiffs to transport up to six kayaks to remote parts of the Everglades where the kayaks are off-loaded. Several spots can be hit in a single day offering anglers the opportunity to catch many species of fish including snook, tarpon, redfish, trout, jacks, grouper, snapper, mackerel, sharks, cobia, permit and such.

Besides skiff mother ship access, they're now offering three-day trips to the Marquesas, which are 30 miles west of Key West, Florida. This is similar to the *Qualifier 105* trips but on a smaller scale. There are a wide variety of flats and reef species available. On the exploratory trip lots of tarpon and permit were caught. It sounds great to me. They have a variety of trips and are expanding what they offer.

In March 2009 I made a trip to Texas and Louisiana and fished both for the first time. I had the opportunity to fish with two mother ship operations. The first was *Cast and Blast* in Arroyo City, Texas. Their fishing grounds are the southern Laguna Madre. Joey and I had fantastic sight fishing for redfish in 6 to 18 inches of water. It was epic! During that morning's fishing we landed over 50 reds averaging 26 inches. The water is very clear and it was more akin to bone fishing the Caribbean than what one would expect in Texas. The mother ship allows access to spots that would be impossible to fish otherwise. The operation has a variety of options and besides redfish, large trout are available as the area is known for big trout.

Another outfitter, *Calmwater Kayaker*, owned and run by Captain Mark Brassett, offers mother ship access in Louisiana's coastal inshore fishing south of New Orleans in the Port Fourchon and Grande Isle area. The waters where Mark guides are considered some of the most productive redfish and trout waters in the world. I had the opportunity to join Mark a couple of days. We caught redfish, black drum and trout. Just offshore there are dozens of oil platforms that attract a wide array of species. We didn't get

The **author** with a *Cast & Blast* redfish in south Laguna Madre, Texas. **(above right)** His first black drum was taken while fishing with *Calmwater Kayakers* in Port Fourchon, Louisiana.

there but Mark tells me bluefish, cobia, jack crevalle, amberjack, snapper, tripletail, redfish, king mackerel, false albacore, sharks and other species are available. That's quite a mix. There are lots of out-of-the-way spots not accessible by boats that are perfect for kayak fishing in the area.

Boats are also being utilized to drop off anglers. *Everglades Kayak Fishing* does this regularly, as do other outfitters in the area. I never did one of these trips in the Everglades but I've spoken to a lot of fishermen who have. They all say it's a special experience and the fishing's great too. On a trip to Alaska in the summer of 2008 we chartered a boat to take six of us with kayaks from Valdez to Montague Island, which was 70 miles out in Prince William Sound. We rented a forest service cabin on the island and fished for halibut, lingcod and rockfish. We also hoped to find salmon, trout and char in the creeks. Five days later the boat would pick us up and return us to Valdez. Basically we rented the boat for a full day each way and had to pay for a charter as the five-plus-hour round trip was essentially the same cost in both time and fuel for the boat as a day's off-shore charter. Our costs were $510 for the round trip per person.

It's a very unique experience doing such a trip. We were essentially on our own for five days. After a ride of almost three hours we had to find the cabin, which was a bit of an adventure in itself. We had a vague description of where it was and nobody had thought to jot down the GPS coordinates. We couldn't see it from the water so Allen and I hopped into kayaks and went searching. We found it at the end of a bay and radioed the boat. The boat used a zodiac to transport our supplies. An hour later we were on a rocky beach with a pile of gear and six kayaks.

The cabin was 30 yards up an incline set at the edge of the tree line. You know you're out there when the outfitter hands you a rifle just in case the bears get too neighborly. The cabin had a rain catch system to collect water as there wasn't a stream nearby. It's recommended that the water either be filtered or boiled, just in case. The cabin was 12 feet by 12 feet and had two sets of bunk beds with a table between them. The lower bunks extended out and doubled as seats. There were two stoves - one burned wood and the other fuel oil. The wood was to provide heat and the oil was for cooking. We had gotten an outfitters kit from Otto, the captain of the

A tasty Alaskan halibut the author invited back to the cabin. The sashimi was fantastic. The group ate great throughout the whole trip!

boat, which included a white fuel two-burner stove. We used this as our primary cooking stove but did use the oil stove as well.

It was mid July and the days were long. We had 19 hours of daylight so there was lots of time to fish. We settled in and then everyone got in kayaks and explored. Joey and I headed up along the main island to check on a couple of creeks and rivers to see if there was salmon or trout. The rest of the crew headed for deep water in the channel between our island and the next one over (Green), which was 4 miles away.

Joey and I found barren water so we headed out to where the rest of the crew was. Everyone had immediate action with rockfish and we kept a mess for supper. Danny lost a big halibut at the kayak so we were encouraged. On the way back we stopped at a shoreline and cleaned the fish. The fish tacos we ate that night were superb.

We caught lots of rockfish, but halibut were scarcer and I caught the only ling. There weren't any salmon in any of the rivers we checked. Alaska was experiencing its coldest summer on record and this had affected the fishing. The previous year Troy and Allen had spent two days at the island to our immediate east and had terrific fishing. They caught 20 to 30 halibut a day in the 15 to 20-pound class along with lingcod to 44 inches and plenty of rockfish. They had pink salmon in the creek right in front of the cabin along with dolly varden. On this trip we caught about 15 halibut between the six of us and two guys didn't land any. They were a lot of fun and I look forward to a future trip anticipating getting into them the way the guys had the previous year.

There aren't many boats that can transport six kayaks, people and gear. When traveling to exotic places like this the limiting factor is usually the availability of kayaks. SOTs are hard to come by in many places. Alaska is no exception as it's a place where long touring SIKs dominate. Valdez has a total of 10 SOTs and I only know of one other place in Alaska that has them. It's called *Liquid Adventures*, based in Seward and they offer guided kayak fishing but not rentals. *Liquid Adventures* has a variety of trips from single and half-day to multi-day camping/fishing excursions.

There's some great terrain around there. Chris, the owner, told Troy and me about a creek a mile or so up the bay. We hiked over the ridge and experienced some terrific fishing for chum and pink salmon. Both Troy and I had never fished for chums and they were

The author and friends make final preparations for their ferry trip to Montague Island - 70 miles from Port of Valdez, Alaska.

high on the list of species we sought. They have a reputation as tough battlers. They confirmed this and willingly took our flies. We had only brought one pair of waders and were trading off. First Troy would catch a couple of fish, and then I would until we were both cold and hungry. The water was excruciatingly cold, especially when in the creek flow. The snowfields and glaciers were only a couple of miles upstream. In order to catch fish you had to wade out a ways at low tide. Troy hooked the first chum and we caught several each. They were a blast on 8-weight fly rods.

Chris was going to check into a water taxi and if one was available the three of us were going to go fish for silver salmon the following day. He couldn't get the taxi and since he was on the water every day he decided he needed a day off. He lent us a couple of Ocean Kayak Prowler 15's and we used them to transport us to back to the creek. We got there at the latter part of the low as it started coming back in. We fished for a couple of hours, caught a bunch of fish, and then did other things because it was difficult fishing at high water. I took lots of pictures, explored, ate and took a nap. Troy fished some and napped, as well.

When the tide dropped we resumed fishing and caught lots of fish. I had one fish take me into the backing three times as deep as 50 yards. On its

Troy with a feisty chum salmon in Resurrection Bay, Alaska.

initial run it jumped and grey hounded with quite an aerial show. We were cold and hungry having been out over 10 hours and decided to head back. The kayaks made the trip much easier and allowed us to carry a lot more stuff.

Places like Alaska have infinite potential for kayak fishing with the limiting factor being a lack of kayaks. Kayak fishing outfitters are pretty rare, too. Besides *Liquid Adventures* in Seward, there's *Ketchikan Kayak Fishing* in Ketchikan owned and operated by Howard McKim. Ketchikan is known as the salmon capital of the world and besides salmon there's a wide array of salt and freshwater species. There's another operation over on Prince of Wales Island by Hoffman Cove.

High on my list of things to do is drive to Alaska for a summer and take a bunch of kayaks with me. This way I'd have the gear I'd need for myself and for others. I would offer trips tailored to the needs of clientele from the lower 48. I discuss this more in Chapter 12.

When one uses a shuttle service it doesn't have to be a mother ship or an outfitter providing the transportation. Other vessels can provide transport to some fantastic places. The Dry Tortugas, 70 miles west of Key West, has a couple of ferries that provide daily service. There's primitive camping allowed on the island where the boats dock. You can take a kayak 15 feet or less and there's a package rate that includes camping gear. You've got to haul in and remove everything. Provided with the camp site are

eco toilets, a space to pitch a tent and a barbecue. Each person is restricted to 65 pounds of gear, excluding water and there's a three night maximum stay.

I had wanted to get there for a number of years and finally arranged a trip May 2008 for three nights. A few guys from the *Tightlines Kayaking* website were going for two nights so I timed my trip to join them, getting there the day before. The ferry ride took approximately 2½ hours. What I found was access to very large fish. Everything big I hooked, except one fish, was within 150 feet of the kayak launch. While it does take some effort to get to the Tortugas, once there everything is very convenient.

This first trip was a learning experience and next time I'll be better prepared. There are things I'd do differently regarding camping gear and food, but they didn't affect my fishing. I made two major mistakes from a fishing perspective. First, I was severely under-gunned in my choice of tackle. I felt like I was on an elephant hunt with a pellet gun. I hooked huge tarpon that I estimated around 150 pounds. Talk about a sleigh ride. The heaviest outfit I had with me was capable of landing them but I didn't hook many due to my next mistake, which was not having brought bait along.

I must have put a hundred casts with an array of lures into and around lots of tarpon. My lures often skipped along their backs. All the fish pretty much ignored artificials. I only hooked three tarpon and as most tarpon anglers know they're one of the most difficult fish to land. The last one I had on for 20 minutes and I thought I was going to land that one but the snell on the hook came out. The goliath grouper I hooked did their name justice and I never had a chance with them. They were in the 250-plus pound class and my heavy outfit was a joke for them. I saw smaller goliaths but the big ones were more common and are the ones I hooked. I don't think they even knew I had hooked them.

There were also some big sharks about. One of the guys hooked a 10-foot hammerhead that inhaled 3 feet of wire and sliced off his main line. I've been told much larger sharks come in to feed on the tarpon in late May and June. I think I'll miss it! At some point I'll get back there with much stouter gear and lots of bait, as bait wasn't readily available once there.

The possibilities are limitless for such excursions. Almost anywhere you can arrange a charter to blue water. It's pricey but there are willing captains.

Usually the species sought is going to be tuna but other species like dorado, billfish and sharks are available too. Just be creative. Each region is going to have its own unique opportunities.

My native New Jersey is a perfect example of this. One wouldn't equate exotic fishing being available within reach of tens of millions of people but it is. Bluefin tuna have made a major comeback in Northeast waters. There are some fish that have reputations as incredibly powerful fish; blue and black marlin, swordfish and bluefin tuna. The only member of this group I've tangled with is blue marlin and the power was humbling.

A few years back my buddy Joel happened upon a school off of Rhode Island while fishing for false albacore. They were small fish in the 15 to 20-pound range and he had a blast. Bluefin rarely come within reach of shore and Joel was very lucky. Cape Cod Bay, in particular, has had a terrific fishery with tuna crashing surface baits. In the winter of 2008/2009 I decided I was going to give it a shot. I picked up appropriate tackle for when the time came. Unfortunately when the reports started coming in the tuna were too big. The fish were well over 100 pounds and closer to 200! That's too much tuna to land from a kayak, at least for a first attempt.

In August of 2009 I got a call from Joey. Danny had arranged a charter with Captain Rich of *MR Charters* out of Neptune, NJ. He and his friend Chris were interested in exploring the potential of getting some kayaks out for bluefins. The fish were running 30 to 70 pounds - a perfect size from the kayak. Fish of this size are big enough to offer quite a challenge but not too big to land. While I have caught much larger fish than these from a kayak the issue becomes leverage and lifting power. Bluefin don't want to come to the surface and you have to power them up. A kayak only offers so much leverage to lift.

The boat was a 29-foot cat and we could only take two kayaks. We figured we could rotate and I'd take

Ferry's can take you to fantastic places. A 2.5-hour ride from of Key West gets you to the Dry Tortugas.

pictures and video. This was a "figure it out trip". None of us knew how it would all work and before taking regular clients out this was a great way to ascertain logistics. All three of us, Joey, Danny and I have a lot of experience catching a wide array of species in varying conditions and circumstances. When we dropped the kayaks in the water, 50 miles from the nearest land, the chatter on the radios was precious. We figured it out and got some bluefin in the 40 to 50-pound range. They're a perfect size from the kayak. They offer a powerful fight that will test your strength and fighting ability.

After we posted on a few forums about the trip, I got lots of interest from anglers wanting to experience this fishery. All along the eastern seaboard this is possible. Besides bluefin, there are yellowfin tuna, marlin, dorado, wahoo, sharks and other species you're not going to catch from shore. I know a mother ship trip to near shore lumps would be a blast angling for false albacore, bonito and skipjack tuna. I've got to work on that one.

Exotic kayak fishing doesn't require a boat to get you into great fishing. There are shore based opportunities and guide operations as well as countless places you can drive to that offer great fishing. Florida is an obvious choice but there's great fishing all over. On the island of Oahu in Hawaii, *Coastal Kayak Tours* has a wide array of shore launched kayak fishing. They have a fleet of paddle and sailing kayaks and offer both inshore and offshore fishing. Inshore one can catch trevalles and lots of species I've never heard of. The same is true offshore. They catch stuff I haven't seen but the stalwarts of the fishery are billfish, tuna, dorado and wahoo.

Down under, in Australia, there are some operations as well. I'm most familiar with *Kimberley Kayak Fishing* because Greg contributes to the *Kayakfishingmagazine.net* guide reports each month. They have some familiar species that go by different names but

Bluefin tuna might just be the toughest fighting fish in the ocean, and catching one from a kayak is a real accomplishment. This one was taken off the New Jersey coast in August, 2009.

they also have fish that are unique to their waters and totally alien to me and anyone outside that part of the world.

Another KFM report contributor is Derrick of *Bite Me Belize Fishing*. He offers an alternative to expensive flats fishing by using stand up Freedom Hawk kayaks in pursuit of bonefish, permit, snook and tarpon.

Joey and I are working with other KFM contributors to help them make their operations viable for travelers. We've been talking with friends with operations in Costa Rica about setting up trips that'll combine both shore and boat accessed fishing for a myriad of species such as snook, roosterfish, pargo, tunas, jacks, dorado and billfish.

Another option is planning trips to resorts or facilities that have kayaks available. A guide might be available or you can find some great fishing on your own. This is a great idea if you have a family and wish to combine some kayak fishing with a family vacation. Many tropical resorts have SOT kayaks. As a guest you're usually free to use them. The first time I took such a trip was when Joey and I went to Puerto Rico to fish for tarpon. We stayed at two places. One was a Bed & Breakfast that had an arsenal of toys included with lodging - over a dozen kayaks, sailboats, windsurfers, snorkel and dive equipment. We just brought our fishing seats and tackle. We spent a few days there and then headed to a motel that had several kayaks. Resort kayaks are unlikely to have rod holders so a fishing seat is invaluable as it'll allow you to bring more than one rod and let you troll.

There are lots of resorts, motels, B&Bs and rental houses available throughout the Caribbean and Central America that have kayaks as part of the amenities. Often the fishing is right in the backyard or nearby. Some research on the Internet will turn them up. The first trip of this nature I took was to the Turks and Caicos, which I discussed earlier in the book. The owner of the rental property, which is a magnificent house on the Caribbean, added four kayaks to enhance the property and make it available as a kayak-fishing rental. We had a great time catching bonefish.

Even though there are properties that have kayaks included there are far more that don't. There's another way to go about this type of fishing. Take a kayak with you. Obviously it isn't easy to take a kayak on a plane. One option is to ship the kayak.

Here's Joey with a Turks & Caicos bonefish. We used kayaks, included with our rental house, to access remote flats.

This is sometimes practical, especially in the United States or Caribbean. Rather than bring it back you could probably sell it. A far more practical solution is to bring one along in the form of an inflatable or folding kayak. Bic makes a kayak that has a hard bottom and the top section inflates. It folds in half for storage and transport and when in this form has wheels on the bottom and a handle up top. It moves about like a large wheeled piece of luggage. Unfortunately by present size restrictions it is going to be considered oversized and that means it'll cost more to take along.

More convenient are fully inflatable kayaks. They pack up smaller and weigh less so they'll be considered luggage. Stearns and Sevylor have been making them for years. New to this group is Hobie. What makes the Hobie unique is it includes the mirage drive, their pedal drive mechanism. Walker Bay Boats has a couple of models and the Airis Angler was designed specifically for the traveling fisherman. It has two built in rod holders. Advanced Elements has the Straightedge. When you can take a kayak with you the possibilities are incredible. Practically anywhere you can fly to you can kayak fish. On my list of things to do is to take one to Christmas Island.

Fuel costs greatly influence the cost of an airline ticket, so prices vary. However bringing gear along has become more expensive. The days of bringing lots of gear along for the price of the ticket are gone. Industry standards for baggage are now just one checked bag per traveler for a coach ticket. The total dimensions are 62 inches and a maximum weight of 50 pounds. Additional bags cost more with the second being $25 and the third often jumping to a whopping $100. Also going over in weight is expensive.

When I returned from my Alaska trip I met a gal who paid $80 for excess weight and that was before she removed a ski helmet from her bag. With the helmet the airline was going to charge her $120! Generally you're allowed one carry-on bag and you can usually carry something else. On my 2008 trip to Alaska I used a duffle as my carry-on on and also brought a 34-inch by 4-inch rod tube. I was able to put quite a bit of gear in the duffle and had 4 rods in the tube.

Kayak fishing is gear intensive but I do recommend simplifying what you bring. You've got to prioritize your equipment when flying. The trip to Alaska was a good learning experience. I had brought some stuff I didn't need and some that was redundant. I brought both a dry suit and waders. Next time I'll forgo the suit and bring waders only. They're a bit more versatile and the neoprene booties are warmer and a better choice for standing in cold water. The zipper had gone on my wading jacket and I hadn't replaced it so I brought a packable raincoat. It wasn't up to the task of the trip, especially the first week where we did a lot of kayak fishing in the rain. I would have much preferred my Kokatat Tempest jacket and either waist high waders or Kokatat's Tempest pants. They would have made a great choice. Waist highs are a more versatile compromise that'll cover all bases very well.

As the sport continues to grow and mature there are going to be more exotic kayak fishing opportunities available. I anticipate more destination locations will come about.

Australia offers some truly "exotic" kayak fishing. This barramundi is a prime example.

Big Game

Some very large fish are being pursued by kayak anglers and while this is a tiny segment of the kayak fishing community it garners a lot of attention both in the kayak fishing world and beyond. Everything is relative when it comes to size. When I speak with people new to kayak fishing in my native Northeast they often ask what I do when I hook a 30-pound striped bass. I always chuckle when asked this. A bass is such a benign fish compared to some of the species being sought and landed. There really aren't any species in the Northeast that are readily accessible that I would consider big game other than at certain times when sharks invade nearshore waters. If one uses a boat for transport then there are species available out at the canyons, but this is expensive, esoteric fishing that very few are going to be able to do. Here I am going to discuss species one can readily access. Many species qualify: billfish, sharks, tarpon, roosterfish, large jacks, halibut and tuna are the most common, but as the sport grows and expands into new environments there are going to be others.

Billfish are probably the most glamorous of the big game species caught from kayaks. I'm fairly sure either Dennis Spike or Jim Sammons was the first sport fisherman to land a billfish from a kayak. Spike's was a sailfish on the East Cape of Baja and Jim's a striped marlin off of San Diego. These days Jim regularly guides patrons in Baja where they catch billfish. While billfish are found in many waters in most places they are far from shore. In Florida sailfish can be reached from shore for a couple of months in the winter. Other than truly exotic species billfish are the least caught of the common big game.

Just before going to press with this book, I discussed this with Jim. He figures that he's assisted at least a dozen or so anglers. So let's say fewer than 20. Spike probably had a few clients and a few have been caught in Hawaii. Figure a few for Florida and you've got a couple dozen to 30 on the high side. That's a fairly small club that I'm proud to be a member of. Other than a lit up dorado there might not be anything more beautiful than a lit billfish and they're

(above) These were the first salmon sharks ever caught from kayaks. Each angler got one and 2 were kept. (left) A still taken from Jim Sammon's video shows Adrian's sailfish.

definitely the most majestic.

While sailfish are available briefly in Florida the big game quarry most Floridians chase is that big silver minnow, the tarpon. While they do range farther north on their summer migration, Florida is really the northernmost state where pursuing them consistently is worthwhile from a kayak. Tarpon are incredibly powerful and dangerous fish. They go nuts when hooked and are often in very shallow water. People in boats have been seriously injured by them. A kayak offers very little protection.

The biggest difference between billfish and tarpon is that billfish are in very deep open water. They are a fish of the great oceans. There are places where they come near shore, like Baja's East Cape, but the water is still very deep. For most of their range they aren't accessible from shore launched kayaks. While they can be reached from shore in Baja, most are being caught from mother ship launched kayaks. That's how I got mine. Tarpon are readily reached from shore. In fact that's how the majority of them are caught. Rarely is it via a mother ship launch

The big game fishes that are the most available are the sharks. Again, Southern California is where I first heard of them being pursued. There's a great fishery for juvenile makos and adult threshers there. Anywhere from the mid Atlantic states south several species of sharks are readily available. It's almost an infestation there are so many in some places. In the Everglades bull sharks are very numerous from May through December. There were days when I could catch as many as I desired, as long as I had some fresh bait. Bulls aren't the only sharks being caught. There are dusky, lemons, hammerhead, spinner, black tip and sand to name a few. Sharks aren't limited to tropical or warm climates either. In July of 2007, Allen, another Allen, Chris and Howard went fishing for salmon sharks in Prince William Sound, Alaska and they each caught one. Salmon sharks are in the same family as makos, porbeagles and great whites. They are massive, impressive fish.

When one ventures to places like Hawaii, or other south pacific island locales, often blue water is very close to shore and just on the other side of the reef. Species like tuna, wahoo, billfish and others become available. Inshore there is giant trevalle, the largest member of the jack family.

In some places the large sea basses grow to huge sizes. Goliath grouper, also called jewfish, can be found weighing hundreds of pounds. As they're protected in U.S. waters, they get monstrous.

Howard McKim, owner of *Ketchikan Kayak Fishing*, landed a halibut exceeding 180 pounds. Halibut are very powerful fish. When caught from boats fish in excess of 70 pounds are routinely shot because they've been known to tear up boats and seriously injure fishermen.

The canyons of the East Coast of the U.S. offer a wide array of big game - blue marlin, bluefin, bigeye and yellowfin tuna, wahoo and pelagic sharks.

What all these giants have in common is that they are incredibly powerful. Some are dangerous be-

(above) Bluewater Jon with a giant trevalle. (below) Howard with his monster halibut.

cause they leap and there's the potential for them to land on you. Then there are the sharks, which don't really need much of an explanation. Everyone knows they have formidable teeth and can be very dangerous in close quarters. What all big game has in common is how strong they are. It's really hard to explain without your having experienced it. When a big fish takes off you're in for quite a ride. All of a sudden you're being towed, and with some species, faster than you can paddle.

My first experience was with a sailfish and it was quite a rush. On the initial run I was flying across the water. The same is true with large tarpon. As line melts from the reel you're covering quite a bit of territory as you go on a sleigh ride. Most sharks don't tend to tow you quite as fast, but what they lack in speed they make up for in strength and endurance.

Big game kayak fishing isn't for most but it sure is fun. With such large fish it's a good idea to go with someone who's got experience. Also exercise some caution because you can get seriously injured or worse. These are big, powerful, dangerous animals that don't know you're doing it for fun. They are fighting for survival so make sure you don't bring them to the kayak before they're worn out. The alternative is to cut the line. That's what's routinely done with the blue marlins. Their stamina is legendary and fights have lasted several hours. I don't believe any have been brought to the kayak so far. When pursuing big game use your head and have fun.

Chapter 11
Tournaments

Tournaments have been around for a long time in sport fishing. The best known are the freshwater bass tournaments. It's hard to miss them on the various sports channels. Within the past decade walleye tournaments have hit the scene as well. In saltwater there are billfish, kingfish, shark and most recently redfish competitions. I'm certain competing has been part of our nature for a long time and if one were to go way back in prehistory you'd find a couple of guys with spears competing on who could get the largest or most fish. Kayak fishing isn't any different. When Joey proposed that we run a tournament I knew it was important for the sport even though I wasn't interested in competing myself. While I like competing in some things, fishing has never been one of them.

In many tournaments fish are kept in a live well and brought back to a weigh-in. Without the development of specialized equipment, this isn't realistic in kayak fishing. A few solutions have been implemented. Some tournaments use weigh boats. The fish are kept in a live well. When you catch a fish you radio and a boat comes and weighs the fish. After weighing, the fish is released. I first learned of this method from Jim Sammons and Vince Console. It's used with bay bass, which are small and can be kept in bait tanks. The same could be done with other species like largemouth bass.

Most tournaments don't use this format. They are either a kill tournament or catch and release. In kill events there is often a fish fry afterwards so there isn't any waste. However some species aren't very good to eat but make great sport. A solution was found early on and many kayak-fishing tournaments use this method. It's a catch/photo/release tournament.

A photo is used in combination with a measurement to determine placing. A flexible ruler is placed on the kayak with the fish on top. A digital photo is taken and the angler records the length on a card. At what would be the weigh-in, the judges download the chip from the camera.

The species angled for varies by region. In fresh-water bass competitions the obvious critter is bass. Most saltwater tournaments are for multiple species. This is called a slam. The tournament Joey and I held, the 'Jamaica Bay Tournament', was for striped bass, bluefish and weakfish. We did the grand prize based on longest fish. It could be any species. There was also a slam, which was the combined length of all three species. Every year a striped bass has taken the grand prize but weakfish are getting bigger each year. In 2008 a weakfish in the 15-pound class took second place.

Farther south the species change over. In South Carolina's BARF (Beaufort Area Redfish Flotilla) they are redfish, trout and flounder. In the Southeast Florida Kayak Slam Series they were snook, redfish and trout. Over in Bayou country it's redfish, trout and flounder.

Each tournament series is different but there are essentially three types: charity, club or fun, and professional events. I've been involved in each type as either an organizer or competitor. Rather than generalize about each type I'll describe how the ones I've been involved with function. We created the Jamaica Bay Kayak Fishing Tournament and Jamboree to promote the sport. It was deliberately set it up so the profits would go to worthy charities. We did so for a few reasons. Since we were a business selling

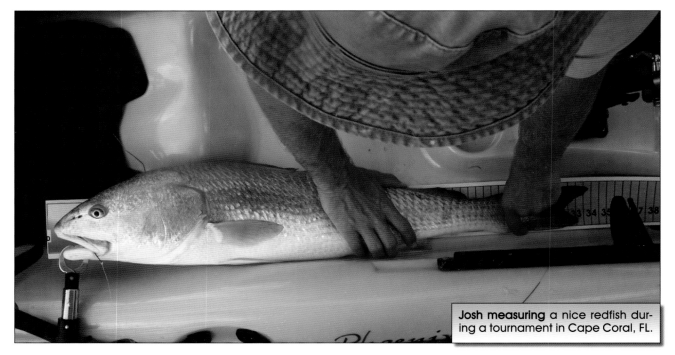

Josh measuring a nice redfish during a tournament in Cape Coral, FL.

kayak fishing gear we wanted to remove our business, as much as possible, from the event. By having the profits going to charities it would make it easier for participants to fork over money.

We had two beneficiaries, Gateway Parks and Casting for Recovery. Gateway provided the use of Floyd Bennett Field, part of its park system, for the tournament. The Jamaica Bay Kayak Fishing Tournament and Jamboree is held in Brooklyn, New York, and it's rare to find anywhere within a major city where one can hold such an event. We chose Jamaica Bay because the fishing is terrific. Anglers travel from all over the country to attend and we wanted to give them the best angling experience we could. We also wanted to promote Floyd Bennett Field and bring attention to what the folks at Gateway were doing to enhance outdoor recreation within the New York metro area. It's a terrific resource in the country's largest city.

The first year it was a single day event. We had a captains' meeting the night before, but most participants didn't attend. Sign-ups started at 6:00 a.m. with the tournament kicking off at 7:00 a.m. and the weigh-in at 2:00 p.m. Grand prize was for the longest fish from the three species: striped bass, bluefish or weakfish. Second and third were also awarded. We also had a slam that consisted of the aggregate length of the largest of each species combined. We only had one place in the slam. Additionally we had a separate fly-fishing division with its own three places, along with eligibility for the grand prize. Anglers competing in that division were required to launch from the main area so we could inspect their kayaks to make sure they didn't have any other rods along. Fly fishermen were eligible for the grand prize, too. Non-fly anglers could launch anywhere in the bay.

After the participants launched we got ready for a demo day where prospective participants of the sport could try out kayaks. We had most of the kayaks KFS carried. The demo ran from 9:00 a.m. until shortly before the competitors came back at 2:00 p.m. We felt prospective fishermen looking at entering the sport would find it both helpful and fascinating seeing all the rigged kayaks and could ask questions of participants. It would be a great learning experience.

Things went well, but we were overwhelmed. We decided to turn the event into a multi-day experience, which better suited the needs of the participants and ourselves. Several of the guys camped out in the parking lot and in ensuing years we had quite a tent city with several dozen anglers camping. After the sale of KFS I joined the guys in the tent city with approximately 70 campers and it was a blast. Most, like me, were there for the camaraderie and the actual tournament wasn't nearly as important.

Prizes were solicited from manufacturers. We gave away several kayaks, and lots of other stuff. That first year we had 52 contestants and by year three it was nearly 200. The first year we used disposable cameras and had to develop film at a One-Hour photo shop. The following year we went to a digital format.

Turning the event into a multi-day worked out great. The demo day was held a different day than the tournament and it made things easier. One of our buddies, Scott, is into competitive barbecue and he got some of the guys to come down and cook dinner after the captains' meeting and breakfast the day of the tournament. This encouraged more people to attend the captains' meeting.

The tournament has evolved to the competition being on Saturday, with a rain/weather date on Sunday. The fourth year it was still on Sunday and it was very windy with small craft warnings. For liability reasons the actual competition had to be cancelled. There was a tournament held in Texas a couple of years back and a storm moved in early and gale force winds created havoc and made it very dangerous. Nobody was lost or seriously injured but a lot of kayaks were either flipped or swamped and fishing was impossible. They were lucky. Having more than one day to work with helps alleviate this.

I love the camaraderie of kayak fishing and that's why I pushed for the Jamaica Bay event to be multiple days. Most of the competitors come to fish and have fun. The competition is secondary. That brings us to the fun competitions amongst friends or club members, where there isn't a fee or it's small to cover food, t-shirts, etc.

On my way to spend the winter in the Everglades (fall 2007) I stopped off at the BARF tournament. The headquarters for the event was Hunting Island State Park, which is southeast of Beaufort, SC. It's a beautiful setting where the Vietnam scenes of the movie Forest Gump were filmed. The entry fee was $20 and with it came a t-shirt and dinner. The captains' meeting was held Friday night and included dinner, which consisted of Frogmore Stew (a regional concoction of shrimp, sausage, potatoes, onions and seasoning). Also there was a huge pot of blue claw crabs. The meal was fantastic with all you could eat and well worth the entry fee.

The competition started at 6:00 the following morning and ran until 6:00 p.m. Most tournaments end earlier in the afternoon so awards can be handled in daylight. Prizes were all donated. Milton Mazariegos won with a 57-inch slam and received a custom made wooden flats kayak. Second prize received a Penn rod and reel combo and third a carbon fiber paddle.

The third type of tournament consists of the professional events. The Pro competitions are gaining in popularity. The entry fees are usually substantial and prize money is given out at the end of the tournament along with some prizes. I was talked into competing in the Naples Kayak Slam by a couple of fellow guides with Everglades Kayak Fishing. I figured it was my backyard and I'd write about it. It was the Southwest division series. There was also a West Central division. Top point earners became eligible for the championship.

I ended up taking third in the initial event and while hoping to just get my money back I received enough in prize money to pay for the next two events. The Kayak Slam Series was run much like other professional fishing tournaments. The organizers have been running a boat tournament for years that's aired on TV in Florida. They are well organized.

The night before was the Captains' meeting. The Naples tournament held theirs in a room at a restaurant. Here, if you hadn't previously registered by mail or on the Internet, fees were collected. Rulers, rules and other gear were handed out. The competition began the following morning at dawn.

Before launching you'd take a picture of your kayak with the ruler laying in it. A colored clip was attached to the ruler and had to be in the first picture. Competitors can fish anywhere but they had to get back to the weigh-in by an appointed time. Eligible species were snook, redfish and trout. Any competitor who missed the time slot was disqualified. Competitors submitted the longest fish of each species. One result per species counted, so if you caught two snook, the longest was taken.

A "slam" was the grand prize with the longest aggregate length winning and getting the most points. A slam superseded two fish. Here's how it worked. Say you had a total of 55 inches for the combination of redfish, snook and trout, and someone else had a total of 56 inches but they only caught a redfish and snook. Because you got all three species (a slam) you placed higher. Even though their total was an inch longer, your slam trumped their total.

Points were awarded based on the length of each fish submitted and there was an invitation to the championship based upon point totals. There was also an award for the longest of each species and the participant received gear donated by sponsors. Additionally, there were youth and women's divisions.

The second leg was held in Cape Coral, Florida, which is almost two hours from where I was living at the time. I stayed with a buddy, Josh, who is a kayak-fishing guide. He had won the first event. We fished Matlacha and Josh placed third catching five reds. While Josh got five reds I didn't catch any and we were fishing the same waters. That's fishing.

The final leg was Ft. Myers, which is right next to Cape Coral, so again I stayed with Josh. He had recently discovered a new area so we headed there. It was behind an island off the main channel. As we approached the entrance there was a boat leaving. They yelled to us that it was awfully shallow and we laughed and said "good". We went through the pass and there was a bay. Josh went left and I fished right. On his third cast Josh got a 27.5-inch red and shortly after he got one slightly smaller. It was frustrating because there were a lot of tailing reds but I wasn't hooking up. The tide was going out and we decided we'd better leave while we could.

On the outside we picked up trout and then headed across the channel to more familiar grounds. Josh went looking for a snook and I hit a flat that holds reds, where I picked up a 27 incher. Josh got a small snook so he now had his slam. Then it was off to the snook spot so I could get one and Josh could upgrade from his 16 incher. Josh lost one that was well over 30 inches right at the yak as the fish gilled his leader. Josh was bummed, as that fish would have put him in great shape. I lost a snook and that was it. The

The hard work paid off for Josh. Here he is with his 1st-place check at Naples' Kayak Slam, 2008.

weather was miserable and we needed to head back.

Since the turnout for the series was light, all competitors were invited to the championship, which was held at Punta Gorda. Again you could fish anywhere you liked; you just had to be at the weigh-in on time. I only managed one trout and skipped the awards, as they were a half-hour north and would have added an hour to my trip home. I was leaving on a trip to the Dry Tortugas the following night and had lots to do. Josh managed a slam.

It was tough fishing. We saw a lot of big, uncooperative redfish. There were a lot of tarpon about, too. I had one circling the kayak while I measured my trout. Josh hooked two - one deliberately and the other blind-casting.

All tournaments have a specified time when you must be back at the weigh-in. Miss the time and it doesn't matter what you caught. At the championships a couple of guys had big slams but they didn't know how to get back to the weigh-in from where they were without taking a much longer route. They arrived late and I believe they had a first and third place total but were disqualified for being late. A tough lesson, but I bet they won't do that again. The money they didn't earn could have bought a nice GPS so they'd always be able to find their way.

If you want to participate in a tournament, best to consult your regional forums to learn about events in your area.

Chapter 12
The Future

Chris at *Saltwater Sports*, a Naples, Florida kayak shop, asked if I'd speak at one of their monthly kayak fishing club meetings. I've done seminars for a number of groups and exhibitions over the years, so I agreed. I love sharing the sport. For groups I like to do a three-part presentation that has been very well received. The first part consists of a slide show. Rather than just showing pictures of anglers holding up fish in a kayak I show what the sport is about - how we use kayaks in a variety of ways to catch fish, not only locally but also around the country. The next part is show and tell. I bring one of my personal kayaks rigged with all the bells and whistles and explain each item, what it is and how it's used. The last part is a question and answer session. Because I didn't have my slides with me, I figured I'd talk and then entertain questions, so I asked Chris what he'd like me to talk about. He asked me to discuss the future of the sport as I saw it.

I missed the beginning of kayak fishing. I joined the sport in its second tier. If kayak fishing were a person, I joined while it was still crawling and missed the birth. At present I think the child is in early grade school. There's a long way until maturity. What's great now is the kayak industry recognizes it. No longer is kayak fishing the orphan child of the kayak world. It's a major force within the industry. After bird-watching, fishing is the largest outdoor activity in this country. That's a huge pool from which to draw.

We're going to see a lot more people fishing from kayaks. Many fishermen who have tried it get hooked. There is something special about catching fish from small vessels. It's a combination of intimacy, being towed, the environments we can access and assorted intangibles. Economics is also helping. Gas prices are going to continue to go up, most likely disproportionately to the cost of living, so it's going to get more and more expensive to operate boats. Gas prices alone aren't going to restrict boat use. We're going to see more areas closed to motor access. In Florida there are areas like the Mosquito Lagoon No Motor Zone, Clam Pass and Ding Darling State Park. There is talk of closing off the Everglades

backcountry to motors. There are areas in the Florida Keys, too. This is the trend that's going to continue and the reasons are twofold: to protect the environment and have places where people can escape civilization.

Another great reason to kayak fish is the great exercise it provides. Kayak fishing isn't practiced as a form of exercise; people do it because it is fun, but the by-product, exercise, is very healthy. It's also non-impact so you're unlikely to strain connective tissue. Imagine your doctor asking if you like to fish. You say, "Yes", and he or she suggests that you get a kayak and go fishing a few times a week.

It's the loading and unloading of kayaks where there is the greatest potential for injury. This is where we'll see the next revolution in kayak fishing. Polyethylene, the plastic used for the majority of kayaks, is a great kayak material, very durable and easily repaired. It's very moldable but it has one drawback in that the kayaks made from it are heavy. There have been composite materials like fiberglass and Kevlar around for years but they don't do well with the abuse kayak fishing places upon them. Hurricane Kayaks introduced Trylon, a different type of plastic a few years back. It's a good material and cuts weight by a third. It isn't rotomolded like poly kayaks. The kayak is formed in two halves that are then caulked together. It's a step in the right direction.

At the 2006 EORA, an industry trade show, Legacy Paddlesports had a prototype 13-foot SIK that weighed in around 30 pounds. We were all excited about what this meant for the future. The future has arrived with the first model, the Native Ultimate Tegris. It's constructed out of a new material called Tegris™, which was created by Milliken. Unlike other light materials such as the composites, Tegris has an impact resistance similar to poly, but has the incredible light weight similar to Kevlar - the best of both worlds. Even better, it's also a very environmentally friendly material that doesn't require all the volatile products in construction as composites, and it's recyclable. The hull weight of the 12-foot Ultimate is only 29 pounds! The seat takes it up to 36 - a quarter of the weight of the total package. The Ultimate 12 is a hybrid but I see light materials being used in SOT construction, too. The manufacturers have to go lighter. Many models used by fishermen are in the 70-pound class and many users are baby boomers who aren't getting any younger or stronger. I'm 54 and while I can wrestle an 80-pound kayak onto the roof of my truck, I'd rather not. At least I can; many kayak fishermen can't and eventually I won't be able to either. If the weight is cut in half I'd be thrilled, as would everyone else.

Here's Shanna carrying the *Tegris..*

We're going to see a big increase in the use of motorized kayaks. Escalating gas prices will create a demand for cost effective vessels that can go farther than human power alone. No matter how many anglers become kayak fishermen there will be plenty who won't because they don't want to put in the physical effort. Purists won't like them but kayak fishermen aren't purists anyway. They got a kayak to catch more fish and if a motorized kayak helps them to do so they're all for it. Even anglers who like the physical benefits a kayak provides may simply want to venture farther than their physical capabilities. That's what attracted me to them. One day in the spring of 2008 I had learned the tarpon were thick in the evenings at Rabbit Key Pass in Florida. It's less than 2 miles from where I would launch in Chokoloskee, but the wind was blowing hard, there were scattered thunderstorms and a strong tide would be against me coming back in. Plus if I hooked up with a big tarpon it was most likely going to head out to the Gulf of Mexico, taking me farther away from port. There were plenty of fish around in excess of 100 pounds and with the outgoing tide and their brute strength I could end up miles from where I started. All these factors were such that I decided to wait for another day. Integrated electric propulsion in a kayak would have solved the problem.

I've also been on excursions where I've been out all day to get to some remote place and could only stay an hour or two, as I had to head back to catch my tide. Some locations require most of my time spent traveling to the fishing location and while I can fish along the way it's not where I'd prefer to do most of my angling. Again a motor would significantly reduce these limitations and greatly increase my range. I see a large market for such craft.

The first commercial offering in the U.S. is a company called Bassyaks. They provide a wide array of electric options. What Bassyaks does is take Minn Kota motors and integrate them by modifying and building parts to make a system that works with many kayaks. You can drop a kayak off and have them do the work, order a kit and install it yourself or go to one of their dealers. They also provide kits for those same kayaks and several other manufacturers' models. They are factory authorized for Nu Canoe. They have an affiliation with dealers or companies and can provide complete installations for Freedom Hawk, Heritage, Ocean Kayak, Old Town and Wilderness Systems. They also have kits and can do installations in Hobie Kayaks. Bassyaks can also customize a system to practically any vessel if you drop it off at their facility in Eastern

Connecticut. In Australia they have had motorized Viking Kayaks for several years. They're now being offered in this country as well.

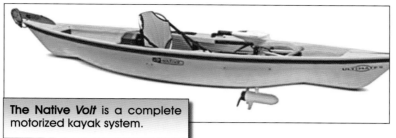
The Native *Volt* is a complete motorized kayak system.

kayak into a regular paddling model.

In July of 2009 I added the first electric kayak to my fleet. I did so for a few reasons. I feel they're going to be important for the sport and since I write about kayak fishing I can't really intelligently discuss them without using them. This is going to take time as there's a huge difference between trying or using a kayak for a day and living with it long term. They increase the range beyond ones physical abilities and they'll allow one to fish in environments that may be difficult or impossible in human powered craft. I want to do more photography and video and an electric gives me greater control over the kayak and allows me to position the kayak much more easily. This will make for better pictures and video.

In the spring of 2009 Legacy introduced four electric models. They were the first American company to do so. They call their electric line the Volt and there are three Natives (12, 14.5 and 16) and a 12-foot Mariner. The Mariner is a SOT. The Volts use a Motor Guide motor that utilizes the multi propel slot in the middle of the kayak. Right on their heels, Johnson Outdoors, the parent company of both Ocean Kayak and Minn Kota, released the Torque in the summer of 2009. It consists of a specially designed Minn Kota motor that drops into an opening in the back tank well of what is essentially a Trident 13 kayak. The center rod pod is replaced with a battery box compartment designed to use a group 24 battery. Both companies' kayaks can be used without the motors as a fully functioning kayak. In the Volt's you simply don't put the motor in the kayak and with the Torque there's a plug with a skeg that turns the

While kayaking is a nice form of exercise I also like mountain biking. Ever since I started kayak fishing I hardly ever bike. I didn't want to wear out my legs biking because it greatly reduces my range when I pedal a kayak. Conversely if I do an upper body workout it affects how much I can paddle. I added a Bassyak.

Here's a fully-rigged electric kayak from Bassyaks.

I chose an Ocean Kayak Trident 13 and had it set up the same as the Torque. That translates into putting a 33-pound-thrust Maximizer motor in the kayak. Just before this book went to press, I also added a Torque to my fleet. These two kayaks are as similar as similar can be, yet they still have differences. While they essentially use the same propulsion and hull, the approach is totally different. The Bassyak has the motor replacing the rudder on the stern of the kayak, whereas the Torque has a fully independent rudder and the motor provides no steering. I'm sure each system will have advantages and disadvantages. Only after living with and using each will I be able to know. Early impressions by many on the Torque are that they love the fact that, when not used with a motor, it is still a fully functioning kayak with a rudder. The Bassyak's motor isn't a great rudder, and it's best left off the kayak when you'll only be paddling. Thus, you won't have a rudder. Another big difference is price. The MSRP for the Torque, while a reasonable $1999, is more than a Bassyak is going to run. If you're handy you can get the system and install it in a used kayak of your choice and save even more.

I've only had my Bassyak a month but I really like it. My head is spinning with all the possibilities. The limiting factor is battery power. While more than my own human capabilities, it's still finite. The Torque is designed for a group 24 battery which translates into an average of 75AH. AH stands for amp hours and without getting technical a battery of this size should give a range of a dozen to 15 miles.

The first significant trip I took with the kayak was up a slow moving river. I didn't know how far I could go so after I had done at least 5 miles I decided to turn around. I ran out of juice at the ramp so I timed it well. From what I've been told battery capacity will increase a bit with use. You'll get a feel for it or friends have told me I could carry a voltmeter. I've gone a different route with my Bassyak. I got two 35AH batteries and when I run out of juice in one I know I've used half my power. The 35AH are relatively small and I can take as many as four along. I'll probably get another because it takes overnight to charge one so if I'm on a trip and fishing every day I can always have fully charged batteries. My other option is to get another charger.

Standard batteries are heavy. My 55AH weighs 38 pounds. Most group 24s are going to be around 60! There is another company that offers a completely new option into the fray. The company is called Torqueedo and they use a state-of-the-art lithium/manganese battery. The entire system is only 15 pounds and that includes the battery. The company uses a Hobie Revolution as their test kayak and claims an 11-mile range at half throttle. That equates to the range I got from my 55AH battery. That's very impressive. The only drawback is cutting edge technology usually has a price tag and that's the case here. The MSRP for the system is $1799 and you still have to add the cost of a kayak. I imagine the majority of the cost is the battery so having a spare is probably financially prohibitive. However I expect this technology will get more cost effective since this is what usually happens. Hopefully in a few to several years we'll be able to purchase large lithium batteries instead of lead acid batteries. They will reduce weight significantly and increase range dramatically. That will revolutionize what's possible. You could launch in Flamingo and camp and fish your way to Everglades City (Everglades, FL.) which at its shortest is 70 miles!

Hobie, always an innovative company, has recognized the electric revolution too. Just before I went to press I learned about their offering. They've jumped in with both feet. It's called the eVolve and uses a Torqueedo system which gives the user two options. The unit can either be used on the rudder to provide propulsion at the stern of the kayak or it can replace the mirage drive amidships. Why both options? Hobie feels you may wish to use a motor as solo propulsion or in combination with the mirage drive. This way you have a choice. The MSRP is $1899. It is expected to be available by the time this book hits bookshelves.

Over the next few months, I plan on spending lots of time living with electric kayaks. I'll be writing about my observations and experiences in articles and on the KFM forums. So, if you're interested in these craft you'll find a lot more information there.

There are still going to be folks who won't use a motor but want to increase their range. The choice is either long, skinny, very efficient kayaks or using another form of power besides human. Sailing is the non-motorized means of accomplishing this, but it's more limited as it does require wind. In many places there is wind but it isn't going to be reliable. Still there are going to be more anglers harnessing the wind to fish from kayaks. Sail systems will be used both for ranging farther and also as a means of trolling. Offshore is the logical application and there are already folks utilizing sailing to catch offshore pelagic species. Mentioned earlier in this book, the Hawaiian guide operation *Coastal Kayak Tours* uses Hobie Adventure Islands to do just that. Kayak sailing combined with camping is going to increase. There will be more dagger board and outriggers systems to use with sails. Right now only one company, Hobie, has a fully integrated sail system. Hobie is a sailing company, after all. However, kayak sailing, while it's going to increase significantly, will likely remain a tiny segment of the kayak fishing world. I do see motorized kayaks becoming very popular. The purists won't like it but kayak fishing isn't a purist's sport. For starters SOTs greatly outnumber SIKs in their use by fishermen and hardcore kayakers don't even consider SOTs kayaks.

Even more distained by kayaking traditionalists are pedal drives. Pedal drives are kayaks that negate the need to paddle as the primary form of propulsion. Hobie introduced the mirage drive in the 1990s and Legacy introduced the Propel in 2008. Having one's hands free to fish while propelling the kayak has a lot of applications in kayak fishing. Legacy's Native Ultimate kayak with a leg-driven propeller is the most recent addition to this arena. The company has taken a different approach than Hobie's mirage and it has some advantages and disadvantages over the Hobie craft. Each is a viable system. The mirage drive has a decade of use and evolution under its belt but only provides forward propulsion while the Native has reverse.

Kayak fishing clubs are springing up around the country. It's a great way to find kayak fishing buddies. If you're new to the sport, are doing your initial research and haven't purchased a kayak yet, many members have more than one kayak and will take a new member along. It's a great way to see what the sport is about before making purchases. You'll get exposed to kayaks, gear and techniques. Members will also run trips. Clubs will most likely have discounts with various businesses. As the sport grows there will be guest experts doing seminars.

Competitions are increasing around the country and the trend is going to continue. Initially most were for charity and still are but the growth is going to be in professional tournaments. The professional bass circuit has been interested in kayak fishing tournaments for a couple of years. I remember when bass fishing tournaments were small. Now they're huge.

Big money, high-profile sponsors and television are all a part of the circuits. Kayak fishing will follow suit.

We're going to see more guide operations surfacing all over which will take a number of forms. Some are simple operations where the guide meets you at a specified location and you go fishing. This is a great way to learn a new area, techniques and the like. Prices vary quite a bit geographically. Kayakjak in Nebraska offers guided trips for less than it costs for a tank of gas. He offers incredible value. However the norm seems to be about $150 for approximately five hours of fishing. Usually each additional person is about $50. At the other end are mother-ship trips. Usually more people are transported and the services provided can vary. Sometimes the guide is along just to provide transportation and it's up to you to find fish. We're going to see more diverse operations become available. I know some outfitters offer multi-day guided camping trips with boat assist. The first one I heard of was offered by Gary Bulla in Baja's Sea of Cortez. He has one week trips camping and fishing islands near La Paz. Now several outfitters offer similar excursions. I know Everglades Kayak Fishing in Florida does as well as Liquid Adventures in Alaska.

While on the subject it's a good idea to interview a guide or operation to see what you're getting. I've spoken with many people who have enlisted a kayak fishing guide and have been disappointed. Most of these people have chartered boats and are used to a guide being a guide. However many kayak fishing guides don't have any previous boat guiding experience and treat it almost like taking some friends fishing. Some clients are looking for more. When I guided I did very little fishing. After all I don't want to be catching the fish. I want my clients to. That's what they're paying for. I stay close and tell them where I expect the fish to be and how best to fish the places where we are. If I wander off it's to check things out and if I find a favorable situation I get the clients. If I discover a particular pattern or lure that's working I share the information. That to me is guiding but it might not be what the guide or operation is offering. It's best to find out beforehand so you can determine if it's a service in which you are interested.

One of the neat things I see coming are kayak fishing destinations. B&B's with kayak fishing included, small resorts in fantastic locations, not just tailored to the romantic weekend getaway for couples, but for anyone who fishes. As the sport continues to grow we're going to see more and more offerings; exotic mother-ship trips, more long-range trips, and operators offering a myriad of excursions.

We're going to see more DVD's. There will be instructional ones like Ken Daubert's series, and fun viewing videos. Kayak fishing is starting to appear on TV more often. Still there isn't much. When ESPN2 Outdoors contacted me a several years ago, they checked with kayak manufacturers to see if they would advertise a show and all declined. However, through my contact at ESPN2 Bassmasters came and filmed the J-Bay Tournament. The footage was aired on one show but then additional footage they couldn't fit was aired periodically throughout the year. Hank Parker did a show using Hobie kayaks. *Dollar Wise Fly* has a couple of kayak fishing episodes that I've seen.

Eventually as the sport gains in popularity there will be a regularly scheduled show just about kayak fishing. Jon Schwartz, aka 'Bluewater Jon', has been chasing big game and in October of 2008 appeared on National Geographic's 'Hooked' series catching striped marlin in Cabo. The most ambitious project to date is from Heliconia Productions. They've done two feature length films on kayak fishing North America starring Jim Sammons. Footage in the first movie includes the East Cape of Baja, Ontario, Alaska, Florida, Chesapeake Bay and Texas. I know Jim spent some time in Panama fishing for the second one. The more exposure kayak fishing gets the more it's going to grow. It's simply too much fun.

At this time the sport has two magazines. They are *Kayak Fisherman*, a quarterly publication of which I'm the East Coast Editor, and the bi-yearly *Kayak Angler*. Both are available at most kayak shops that are involved in kayak fishing. Subscriptions are available for both, too. Contact them directly for more information.

My Future

I get asked often what's next for me. Now that the book is done I'm considering a variety of things. I am a principal in *www.kayakfishingmagazine.net* (KFM) along with its founder, Joe Cambria. I'm excited about the platform it provides. It's an information entity bridging the industry and the participants on a global scale. We don't have any limitations as we're independent of all companies. We've both always been at the forefront of dispensing information and

with KFM we'll be able to accomplish some great things to continue to support the sport we love. KFM is an information liaison between the kayak fishing public and the industry. We've got lots of great things we'll be incorporating into it.

I will continue writing my column in *New Jersey Angler* and articles in *Kayak Fisherman*. I'd also like to expand my writing and contribute to other publications. I have done seminars in the past and I am available and plan on doing more. Beyond that I'm flexible.

If you have some ideas, please don't hesitate to run them by me. I have a lot of my own ideas, too. I have a great idea for a regular TV show about the sport, and I'm sure it would be successful. I also have some ideas on kayak fishing destination bed and breakfast resorts. I'm seriously considering a summer in Alaska and offering guided kayak fishing and outfitting. I expect I will write other books as the sport continues to grow and evolve. I'm available for seminars, lectures and consulting. I certainly expect to spend more time guiding, but I doubt it will ever be a full time occupation unless it entails excursions around the globe.

I've caught a lot of different species of fish from the kayak. At present well over 60, but there are many more I'd like to land, and I look forward to passing the century mark. Also, while I've been fortunate to kayak fish a lot of interesting places I've only scratched the surface of what's available. I will continue to explore new places and expand the sport in my own way.

Conclusion

No matter how "cutting edge" a book like this might be when it is published, it is inevitable that the information contained herein will eventually become dated. As the sport of kayak fishing evolves there will certainly be additional editions of this book published, but the best way for you, the reader, to keep abreast of what's new in the sport is to read about it online at *kayakfishingmagazine.net*. There, you'll find all sorts information about new equipment, techniques and locations that'll keep you on the cutting edge of kayak fishing, no matter how quickly the sport evolves. I'll be a regular contributor there, along with many of the sport's most knowledgeable and respected participants.

I'll see you on the water!